A Personal

During the twentieth c progress that we came to believe that, given enough science and technology, we could control our own fate — if not as individuals, then at least collectively. What the Internet has shown us is that this assumption is false. As you will see in this book, we are influenced by strong forces that are far beyond our control.

The Internet is so complex, so powerful, so important and so new, that no one can truly explain what it is. Nobody knows why we built the Internet or what it really means to us. As a result, our society is awash in an enormous amount of misinformation.

Most of our worries and concerns about the Internet come from misconceptions and from our inability to understand our motivations clearly. It is my job to explain those misconceptions, and to put everything in perspective — to explain what is happening and why.

Have you noticed how much the world has changed since the mid-1990s when the Internet began to spread so widely? Have you also noticed how, in such a short time, the Internet has insinuated itself into every important aspect of our lives?

I do not want you worrying needlessly about things that are not really a problem. For example, regardless of what you might hear, you do not need to worry about computer viruses or about unknown perpetrators breaking into your system — not if you take a few simple precautions (which I will explain in Chapters 10 and 11).

There are far more important things I want you to think about: how the Internet affects your privacy, your security, your money, your relationships, your work, and your family.

In this book, I am going to explain a lot of ideas that other people don't want you to know: Why are companies so mean-spirited when it comes to treating people well? Why is government so ineffective when it comes to standing up to big business? Why do people love to pass on misinformation to their friends? Why do so many "experts" try to scare us?

I am also going to explain ideas that are crucial to using the Net well, but are mostly ignored in our popular culture. Do we have a biological need for privacy? What is money, and why is it important to us? Why do we need relationships, and what happens to them when we start using the Internet?

The Internet is a lot more than a global computer network. It is a permanent part of our everyday life and, if you and I are to use it well, we must first understand ourselves and our culture.

For this reason, I am going to talk about much more than technology and computers. I am going to discuss psychology, history, philosophy, science, money and relationships. Although these may seem like unrelated topics, I promise you that, by the time you finish reading this book, it will all come together.

I hope by now you understand that this is not a normal computer book, not by a long shot. Indeed, it is my hope that you will find this book to be unlike anything you have ever read.

If you buy this book, I will make you several promises:

- I promise to explain everything you need to know to use the Internet in a way that makes you and your family safe and comfortable.
- I promise to show you the best strategies for protecting yourself against the strong forces that control so much of our society.

And finally,

- I promise that, as long as you are reading this book, you will never be bored.

I want you to read this book for two reasons. First, it is interesting and useful. Second, by the time you finish, you will understand the world a lot better than you do now.

I promise.

HARLEY HAHN

www.harley.com

HARLEY HAHN'S

INTERNET
*IN*SECURITY

ISBN 0-13-033448-0

90000

9 780130 334480

Library of Congress Cataloging-in-Publication Data

A CIP catalog record for this book can be obtained
from the Library of Congress.

© 2002 by Harley Hahn
Published by Prentice Hall PTR
Prentice-Hall, Inc.
Upper Saddle River, New Jersey 07458

Prentice Hall books are widely used by corporations and government agencies
for training, marketing, and resale.

The publisher offers discounts on this book when ordered in bulk quantities.
For more information, contact Corporate Sales Department
Phone: 800-382-3419; FAX: 201-236-7141;
E-mail: corpsales@prenhall.com
Or write: Prentice Hall PTR, Corporate Sales Dept.,
One Lake Street, Upper Saddle River, NJ 07458.

Printed in the United States of America

10 9 8 7 6 5 4 3 2 1

ISBN 0-13-033448-0

Pearson Education LTD.
Pearson Education Australia PTY, Limited
Pearson Education Singapore, Pte. Ltd.
Pearson Education North Asia Ltd.
Pearson Education Canada, Ltd.
Pearson Educación de Mexico, S.A. de C.V.
Pearson Education—Japan
Pearson Education Malaysia, Pte. Ltd.

HARLEY HAHN'S

INTERNET *IN*SECURITY

Why Your Privacy, Security, and Safety are at risk and what you can do about it

PH
PTR

Prentice Hall PTR
One Lake Street
Upper Saddle River, NJ 07458
www.phptr.com

To Suzanne,
For patience, kindness, wisdom and understanding.

Coming of Age

"You just want material", she said. "I'll never see you again."

It worried her. She was a writer, as I was, and she knew the writer's mind. And maybe she was right.

We were sitting at a booth in Cantor's, a 24-hour deli in the Fairfax district of Los Angeles. The hour was late — after 4 AM — and Diana and I had been eating large bowls of chicken soup. I had told her I was just starting to work on a new book (this one). Every now and then I would stop and take notes, writing down something she said. (When I am working on a book, everything — and everybody — is fair game.)

I was thinking mightily about the Internet: about privacy, security and safety. I realized that, although the book would have to get into technical details, I would have to do a lot more than document procedures. I would have to hunt down, learn to understand, and then come to terms with the bewilderment all of us feel about modern life. Yes, Man can be the most rational of creatures, but he can also be childish, arbitrary and scared of dark places.

So what scared Diana? Certainly not what scares many of us. I had met her earlier that night at the Hollywood Bowl, and she was completely comfortable with talking to me, driving around the city and sitting up all night with a stranger.

I thought of how brave and sensible Diana was, but I also saw that she had real fears. She was afraid of having her feelings hurt. She was afraid of not being special. She was afraid that someone might invade her privacy, stir up her emotions, and leave her feeling violated.

Now I was getting somewhere. I realized that what drives and motivates us — on and off the Internet — has a lot more to do with human nature than technology.

I could never understand why so many people are content to flounder around, using a global network they can't comprehend and a computer system they will never master. Don't these people feel a sense of bewilderment? Doesn't it bother them that they have so little understanding of how anything works? And yet, it is these exact people who, more often than not, feel the most safe on the Net. They don't worry. They just send email, chat with their friends, look at Web pages, and enjoy themselves.

Most of the people I know who worry are the ones who know what they are doing. They obsess over possible, but highly unlikely, esoteric privacy violations. They worry that some day, a hacker might sneak up a shared network cable, insinuate his way into their computer, and perform some vague but hideous exorcism on their carefully tuned system.

Unlike their duller, less technical counterparts, the smart people see their computers as extensions of themselves. And, like all people with enough foresight to see danger, they will go to extremes to protect themselves against their enemies, both real and imaginary.

The plain truth is that much of what people fear on the Net is just not real. Never has been and never will be. And yet, there are real concerns we do need to understand. How do we separate the real from the imaginary, the serious from the frivolous, the bothersome from the dangerous?

That is what we will explore in this book, you and I. Along the way, we will investigate human nature, looking for the timeless characteristics that define humanness and how they relate to the Internet.

But where to start? For me, it started with a concert on a Friday evening in the warm Santa Barbara autumn. Suzanne and I had gone to the Santa Barbara Bowl to see Brian Wilson in concert, and that led me, two days later to Los Angeles, to Diana the writer, to a late-night search around the city for the only 24-hour newsstand, so we could buy a copy of a newspaper that had just printed one of Diana's articles, and, finally, to a long conversation at Cantor's, during which Diana and I ate soup, shared, argued, emoted and, as one writer to another, talked and talked and talked.

And that, as you will see, is what led me to start to understand what the Internet was doing to us, how it was affecting our judgment, and how it resonated with our fears and concerns: feelings that originate deep within us, mature in the outside world, and flourish in a new electronic environment very few of us understand.

Until you know someone enough to trust him, you can be anyone you want to be.

— Diana

I had been looking for someone to go with me to the Brian Wilson concert, and finally, I had asked Suzanne. It was Friday night, and we walked quickly up the sloping entrance to the bowl. We were late, and by the time we found our seats, the overture had started. Brian Wilson was the genius behind the Beach Boys, and as we entered, the Santa Barbara Symphony was playing a 17-minute overture, a tapestry of old Beach Boys melodies.

As the overture ended, the orchestra left and Wilson came on with his 10-piece band. The music was exquisite, mostly classic Beach Boys songs, along with Wilson's all-time favorite rock song "Be My Baby". But the highlight — what every Brian Wilson fan had come to see — came after the intermission: Pet Sounds.

Pet Sounds was an album that Wilson had created thirty-four years earlier, in 1966, when he was 24 years old. Tonight, Wilson, his band, and members of the orchestra played and sung the album in its entirely. Within the world of pop music, it's difficult to overvalue the influence of Pet Sounds. It was the first real concept album — the one that inspired Paul McCartney to create Sergeant Pepper's — a work that has been praised over the years by many professional musicians and has been called the best pop album of all time.

Why was Pet Sounds so important? It took me a while to get it.

I must admit that, on that warm Friday autumn night, I wasn't there to hear the most influential pop album of all time. I was there to listen to old Beach Boys songs; to stand and dance and sing "Help Me Rhonda" with several thousand other baby boomers who knew, deep in their hearts, that it was other people, not them, who would one day grow old and die.

On Sunday, I drove by myself to Los Angeles, to the Hollywood Bowl, to hear the concert once again. That is where I met Diana — she and a friend were sitting next to me — and after the concert, I stayed up all night with her, talking and thinking.

Over the next two days, I listened to Pet Sounds, over and over, and finally — I got it. It wasn't only the music, rich and lush with seductive chord changes and California sun-filled harmonies. It was the words, the meaning behind the songs and the album as a whole. Pet Sounds — I finally realized — was a statement about Coming of Age.

The songs describe a young man on the threshold of making the transition beyond adolescence. It is a time of dreams. The young man is about to enter the first stage of adulthood, a time of realism, disappointment, and difficulties. Right now, his biggest problems have to do with love, girls and fun, but soon he will be leaving the Age of Innocence and entering the Age of Responsibility.

I thought about this, and I thought about my own life, and I thought about the Internet, and I realized why all this was so important. The Internet has a massive influence on human affairs, an influence that has expanded and changed significantly in the last few years.

When a technology is new, it is first used by the experimenters: people who have the technical know-how and the motivation to adopt and struggle with a new environment. However, by the time a technology matures, the once formidable system has become easy to use and, hence, accessible to less technical people. Once this happens, the creative floodgates open and we see a flourishing of activity that, in retrospect, we call a Golden Age. Thus, we have the Golden Age of Radio, the Golden Age of Television, the Golden Age of Comic Books, the Golden Age of Science Fiction, and so on.

What characterizes a Golden Age? It is more than creative activity. In a Golden Age, the technology is still rather new, and the people who participate are still innocent. Compare, for example, TV shows of the 60s ("Leave it to Beaver") to shows of the 90s ("Buffy the Vampire Slayer").

Eventually, however, the outside world intrudes upon the new environment. Once this happens, the Golden Age is overtaken by the "real world" and things change drastically. In particular, people find that life is not as simple as it used to be. There are more sharks in the water, and simply participating calls for more caution, knowledge and judgment. People start to get hurt.

The Golden Age of the Internet is over. It ended when the overriding purpose of the Net ceased to be simple creativity and sharing.

True, there is more creativity and sharing on the Net than ever before, but there is also advertising, commerce, pornography, politics, misinformation, broken relationships, and many, many mixed-up malevolent individuals.

The original motivation to create the Internet was as an aid to the academic and research community. Today, the Net has no particular focus. Everyone and anyone can and does use the Net. In fact, it is more common to find people on the Net participating in master/slave bondage-oriented relationships than it is to find astronomers discussing the latest information from the Hubble Telescope.

The Internet is still a wonderful invention — I maintain, the most important invention in the history of mankind — but in recent years, its character has broadened to include everyone and everything. This brings into play all the weaknesses, traps, temptations and evils of humanity.

Moreover, because the Net harnesses so much raw power, it acts as an amplifier, increasing the effect of the good, the bad and the indifferent. As a result, the Internet has become too much for any individual, any group, or any government to handle on its own.

During the Golden Age, it was possible to approach the Net blindly, and trust to the native goodness of other people (and of the Net itself). This is not so anymore, and will never be so again. The Golden Age is gone and, along with it, the short-lived Age of Innocence.

There is more good on the Net than ever before, and its usefulness and importance increases daily, so, yes, you should know how to use the Net and use it well. And you should encourage your children to embrace the Net.

However, you must — we all must — recognize that by allowing the world, with all its imperfections and temptations, to connect to the Net, we have opened a Pandora's Box: one that is more powerful than we understand, and one that is far beyond our capacity to manage. No one, no group, no government can control the Net, or even make sense out of it.

As surely as you are reading this, the Internet is humanity's staircase to the next level of human evolution. However, staircases run both ways and, more than anything we have ever created, the Net demands our respect and our attention. As human beings, we have no choice. The box has been opened and there is no turning back. As individuals, we must develop the values, morals, customs, and strength of character necessary to survive and to thrive.

Perhaps you think you can ignore the Net. Just don't use it, or use it sparingly, you might think, and everything will be okay. That sounds good, but what do you do when you find out your boyfriend is sending long email messages to other women, some of whom are married? What does it mean when you find your kids spending hours talking to people they will never meet in person? How do you know what to think when you hear of mysterious computer viruses that, supposedly, can attack your computer and wipe out your entire collection of recipes or all your genealogy research?

The Internet has passed through the first two stages: the Age of Experimentation and the Age of Innocence. We are now in a state of transition, preparing to enter the Age of Responsibility. Although the Internet has much more to offer than ever before, pitfalls abound, and before much time passes, we are all going to have to change.

You and I are going to be forced to examine who we are, what we want from life, what we have to offer, and how we choose to relate to other people and the world. As we teach ourselves the technical nuances of using our computers and the Net, we are going to have to spend more and more time thinking about values, morals, customs, and strength of character.

That is what you and I are going to do, together, in this book. We are going to examine the most important aspects of using the Net and relate them to our lives and to the security, safety and privacy that is crucial to our well-being. I will show you what is real, what is not real, and how to tell the difference. We will discuss what is important — on and off the Net — and how to stop, look and listen in a way that protects you and your family, while still allowing you to use the Net for all its wonder, beauty and enrichment.

In other words, I am going to show you how to dance with the devil and not be hurt.

I had to prove that I could make it alone
But that's not me,
I wanted to show how independent I'd grown now
But that's not me...

— Brian Wilson & Tony Asher
  ("That's Not Me", from Pet Sounds)

Acknowledgments

What do you think an editor does?

I bet you think an editor is a kindly, wise person — an insightful, knowledgeable professional who cares enormously about the written word. Perhaps you imagine that every writer has an editor to act as a personal advisor, someone who is always available with support, ideas, inspiration and infinite patience.

Until I started to write books professionally, 15 years ago, that's the way I thought it worked. Well, I'm here to tell you that it doesn't work like that at all. There are a lot of people in the publishing industry with the word "editor" in their job title, but they are nothing like the mythical person I described above.

To be sure, there used to be editors like that. Perhaps the most well-known was Maxwell Perkins (1884–1946), one of the most important editors of the twentieth century. Perkins worked at the Charles Scribner's Sons publishing house. During a long and distinguished career, he worked with Ernest Hemingway, F. Scott Fitzgerald, Thomas Wolfe, Marjorie Kinnan Rawlings, James Jones, Ring Lardner and many other talented authors, helping them to develop their talent and ideas. Perkins was a lot more than an advisor; he was an advisor and collaborator, always ready with ideas, suggestions and encouragement.

It is the dream of every serious writer that, one day, he will be able to work with an editor of this stamp. However, modern publishing is driven by budgets, not by artistic value. Virtually everyone in every publishing house I have ever known is horribly overworked. In such an environment, where are you going to find an editor who respects the writer's talent so much that he is willing to spend hours helping to shape a manuscript, one idea at a time? If you had asked me, before I started this book, if I thought I would ever have the chance to work with such an editor, I would have answered, no; people like Maxwell Perkins don't exist anymore.

I was wrong. There is one such person, and his name is Greg Doench, a senior editor at Prentice Hall PTR, the publisher of this book.

Greg helped me in every stage of the writing of this book, from the initial discussions, through the planning, writing, editing, book design and marketing. For more than a year, Greg and I spent many hours talking and working together, often at night and on weekends. No detail was too small; no idea was too trivial for Greg. He was there when I needed him, willingly giving me the time and advice I needed to produce the very best book I could. Truly, if I can see farther than other people, it is because I am standing on the shoulders of a giant.

Next, I want to mention the one person whose contributions to this book were so important that it would be difficult to over-praise her (but let me try anyway), Lydia Hearn, my Chief of Staff.

Lydia is a Professor of English at De Anza College in Cupertino, California. In spite of her heavy schedule as a teacher, Lydia found time to participate in numerous strategic meetings with Greg and me. During one of these meetings, Lydia was instrumental in helping us choose a title for the book. Lydia also copy edited all the chapters, and took infinite pains to format the files exactly, to ensure that everything turned out perfectly (which it did).

So how did this book get started? The idea arose in a conversation I had, well over a year ago, with Greg and Jeff Pepper. Jeff is the head of Prentice Hall PTR (Professional Technical Reference), the company that published this book. Officially, Jeff's title is Publisher, which means that he spends a lot of time in meetings, eating M&Ms, adding up columns of numbers, making marketing projections, and planning new meetings (at which he will eat M&Ms, add up columns of numbers, make marketing projections, and plan even more meetings).

This is the fourth book that Jeff and I have done together, although the first at Prentice Hall. (He used to work for a division of McGraw-Hill.) What I like best about Jeff is that he comes up with an idea, asks me if I'd like to write a book about it, and then leaves me alone to do the book the way I want.

More than anything, this is a book of ideas, and good ideas take a long time to develop. When I first started planning, I spent an evening with two good friends of mine, Hal Kopeikin and Suzanne Delmerico, debating and discussing. By the end of the evening, I was able to use a single piece of paper to conceptualize the ideas that would, eventually, form the nucleus of this book. Take a look at the accompanying figure, where you see a copy of the actual piece of paper. Notice the six main ideas that form the themes of the book: Trust, Comfort, Relationships, Security, Excitement and Responsibility. (You know, if I could raise $50 million dollars, I could run for President on that platform.)

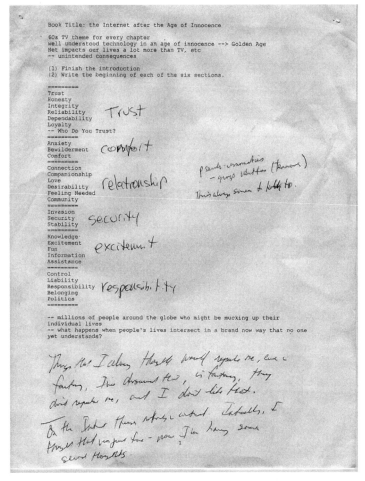

Harley's original notes for this book.

A number of people helped me with gathering material. First, there are two of my long-time researchers: Kelly Murdock-Billy, chief researcher for this book, and Elaine McIntyre, who contributed as an adjunct researcher. (If you want to read a story about Kelly, see the beginning of Chapter 13.)

In addition to the research done by Kelly and Elaine, I learned a lot from various people who were kind enough to talk to me regarding specific topics about which they are particularly knowledgeable. These people and the topics we discussed are: Alex Taylor (virus protection), Bruce Slane (privacy), Dave Buckingham (online auctions), Hal Kopeikin (psychology), Joel Macnamara (early macro viruses), Kurt Albershardt (security), Len Babin (security) and Terry Keramaris (online chatting).

Once the chapters were written, I sent them to another group of people, my technical reviewers. Their job is to read each chapter, look for mistakes (always hard to find in one of my books) and make comments. These reviewers, to whom I am indebted for their time and expertise, are Alex Taylor, Eugene Katunin, Len Babin, Michael Schuster, and Tammy Cravit.

If you look through the book, you will see a number of pictures, one per chapter, used to illustrate various interesting ideas. These pictures were selected by Elizabeth Mjelde, a Professor of Art History at De Anza College (the same school at which Lydia teaches). Elizabeth put in a lot of time looking for the best possible picture for each chapter.

After the entire book is written, an index must be created. Now, I believe that the index is a particularly important part of a book. For that reason, I wanted the very best indexer I know, and I requested her specifically: Cheryl Lenser. During the production of one of my earlier books, Cheryl and I developed an indexing style called Jackson Double-Post Indexing (her maiden name was Jackson), and that is what we used for the index in this book.

Of course, writing a book is only part of the job. Books must be designed, printed, marketed and so on. This work was done by various people at Prentice Hall.

First, I thank the artist, Tom Post, who was able to take an idea created by Greg Doench and me, and turn it into the marvelous picture you see on the front cover. The over cover design was created carefully by Talar Boorujy under the supervision of Jerry Votta.

The design of the inside of the book also requires a great deal of expertise. The typefaces, the spacing, the appearance of the various elements — all of these elements must be carefully handled. This work was done by Gail Cocker-Bogusz, who worked with Greg and me to make the book attractive and fun to read. This is an especially difficult job, which Gail did competently with a cooperative spirit (always a good thing to have when you are dealing with a picky author).

The creation of the pages of the book — a terribly time-consuming job — was done by several people, Nick Radhuber, Kathleen Caren, and Patti Guerrieri, who also supervised the production process. The proofreading was done by Barbara Danziger, Faye Gemmellaro, Jeanette Salib and Mildred Schulte; and the manufacturing was supervised by Alexis Heydt-Long. Special thanks go to Lisa Iarkowski, the Production Manager, who did an excellent job, ensuring that this book was produced in record time.

Four other Prentice Hall people deserve a special mention: Debby vanDijk, who handled the marketing; Rob Norton, who organized the publicity; Greg's assistant Brandt Kenna who handled the paperwork and administrative details; and Eileen Clark, an acquisitions editor, who found me a bit of crucial information, just when I needed it, on the last day I was working on this book.

At a completely different company, I'd like to thank the people who work at the IBM PC Company Product Reviews Lab for hardware support: Sid Baker (the manager), James Lumpkin, Loring Montague, Michael Redd and Robert Armbruster.

Finally, I'd like to thank Suzanne Delmerico for patience, kindness, wisdom and understanding, qualities which are so important, and which I greatly appreciate.

List of Chapters

List of Illustrations

Contents

Chapter 3
Staying One Step Ahead 49

Chapter 4
Taking Control 79

Chapter 8

Our Need to Communicate: Email, Chatting and Privacy 189

Chapter 9
The Mystery of Viruses: Revealed 249

Chapter 10
Protecting Your Stuff:
Viruses and Common Sense 277

Chapter 11

Protecting Your Stuff:
Configuring Your System 303

Chapter 12

Understanding Money (Really!) 329

Chapter 13

Protecting Your Money:
Shopping and Selling Without Fear 381

Chapter 14
Protecting Your Family:
Sex, Relationships and Children 433

Appendix 469

Index 475

1

Toward A Grand Unified Theory

I want you to think the Net as a large, mysterious growing organism that is more powerful and important than we can even imagine.

Toward A Grand Unified Theory

- The Roots of the Internet
- The Internet is Now "The Net"
- Is Big Brother Really Watching?
- Carnivore is an Omnivore
- What the FBI Assistant Director Has to Say
- When Internet Law Enforcement Runs Amok
- What Superintendent Babin Has to Say
- How the Internet Works: TCP/IP
- Moving the Data: Routers, ISPs, NSPs and NAPs
- Who Runs the Internet?
- The Nature of the Net
- Is It Realistic to Have an Expectation of Privacy?

The Roots of the Internet

The INTERNET is a large, global system that allows us to connect computer networks. The roots of the Internet stretch back to 1968. In that year, the U.S. Department of Defense funded a project to connect computers over a long distance, in order for researchers to be able to use computers at remote locations. At the time, the funding came from a program called ARPA (Advanced Research Projects Agency), so the first experimental network was called the ARPANET, and it was the Arpanet that evolved into the Internet.

On November 21, 1969, the first two computers were connected: one at UCLA in Los Angeles, the other at Stanford Research Institute in Menlo Park, California. On December 5, 1969, the Arpanet was officially established by connecting these two computers to two other computers, one at U.C. Santa Barbara, the other at the University of Utah. (So, if you would like to celebrate the birthday of the Internet, you can do so on December 5.)

During the 1970s and 1980s, the Arpanet was expanded to include many other universities, research companies and government offices (including the military). Eventually, non-research institutions were allowed to join and the name was changed to the Internet.

In the early 1980s, PCs (personal computers) became available and, within a few years, the technology to connect them into networks was developed. Throughout the 1980s and 1990s, more and more networks of PCs were created, and eventually, those networks were connected to the Internet.

In the olden days (before 1995), a company that wanted to connect LANs from distant offices would have had to arrange their own connections. This would require leasing special telecommunication lines, and involve a lot of expense, equipment, technical expertise and administration. Now, all the company has to do is create their own local networks and connect them to the Internet.

The Internet is Now "The Net"

At first, the Internet was seen primarily as a way to connect networks around the world into one large super-network. (The original motivation for the Internet, as I mentioned, was to allow researchers to use remote computers.) However, since the mid-1990s, hundreds of millions of people have been connecting their personal computers to the Internet, and an amazing thing has happened: we have found that when a huge number of people and computers are connected into one large network, something is created that is much more powerful — and much more wonderful — than anyone ever anticipated.

To understand why, we must stop looking at the Internet as a very large network. Instead, we must view it as a complex system in which hundreds of millions of computers and people have the potential to interact, and where a massive amount of information is available for free.

The power of networks comes from being able to connect two or more LANs to form a larger network. Once you do, all the computers and all the people on all the networks can talk to each other. In other words, they can communicate and share information.

Think of the Internet as a large organism, made up of many different cells, the cells being the computers and the people who use those computers. Now, let's compare a biological organism, for example, you, to the Internet.

There are more than 75,000,000,000,000 (75 trillion) cells in your body, and they are so complex that even biologists don't understand much of what happens inside them. The Internet consists of, perhaps, hundreds of millions of cells (about 1/300,000th the number of cells in your body). There are two basic types of Internet cells: computers and people. Compared to biological cells, Internet cells operate in a relatively simple way (from the point of view of the Internet). Thus, we can expect the Internet, considered as a single large organism, to be a lot simpler than your body — and it is.

However, this doesn't mean we really understand the Internet. After all, we are biological organisms and we have studied ourselves for many years.

Before we move on, I want to introduce two important terms. For some years, it has been common to refer to the Internet as THE NET, and in this book, I will use the two terms as synonyms. When we refer to services that are available on the Net, we often describe them as being ONLINE. For example, in Chapter 13, we are going to talk about online auctions.

I like the idea of "the Net" because it makes me think of something large and mysterious, and that's how I want you to think of it: as a large, mysterious growing organism that is more powerful and important than we can even imagine.

Is Big Brother Really Watching?

Have you read George Orwell's novel *1984*? It is the tale of a society in which people are controlled and spied upon by an all-powerful, totalitarian government.

In the book, the leader of the government is referred to as Big Brother, and described as being "infallible and all-powerful". Throughout the city, there are many posters with a picture of Big Brother and the caption "Big Brother is Watching You". This is to remind the citizenry that, no matter where they go, no matter what they do, the government is watching.

The image is a compelling one, and since 1949, when Orwell's book was published, the idea of Big Brother watching us has been a metaphor for a society in which privacy has vanished. So to ask the question, "Is Big Brother really watching?" is to ask whether or not we are being spied upon by an outside agency such as a government organization or a company, or even by various malevolent people. The question is especially important in that today's technology is advanced enough to make such spying feasible and silent.

So, when we use the Internet, is Big Brother really watching? The answer is mixed. We certainly don't have a society, like the one in *1984*, in which we are spied upon continuously. However, there is a lot more going on than most people realize, and even many casual Internet users are aware that a great many companies with Web sites are in the business of gathering information about the people who visit those sites. There is no doubt that privacy is an important issue to many of us and, there is also no doubt that many government organizations and companies are ready and willing to invade our privacy to forward their own ends.

So what keeps them from doing so? Not the technology, which is already up to the job. (I'll give you a few examples in a moment.) What keeps the government and corporations out of our electronic lives is the sense that we want privacy and that any organization that steps too far is going to face public outrage.

Carnivore is an Omnivore

Law enforcement agencies around the world have been, for some time, grappling with the problem of how to deal with criminals who use the Internet to communicate. In the United States, the FBI (Federal Bureau of Investigation) has developed a tool named Carnivore that is used to spy on people. Carnivore is a box that can be attached to a computer through which electronic communications are passing. Typically, the FBI would attach a Carnivore box to an ISP's computer in order to monitor that ISP's customers. (Your ISP — Internet Service Provider — is the company that connects your computer to the Internet. The largest ISP in the world is AOL, but there are many, many others, ranging from very large companies to small, privately run businesses.)

The FBI developed Carnivore for themselves, because the commercially available Internet monitoring devices (called "sniffers") were not good enough. Carnivore was created for one reason and one reason only: to provide the FBI with an easy way to monitor Internet communications. Although Carnivore is mostly aimed at monitoring email, the device can track everything, including how people use the Web and what they say in a chat room or discussion forum.

If you are concerned at the thought of someone — even an authorized government agent — having the capability of legally monitoring Internet communications, you are in good company. In the United States, free speech is guaranteed by the Constitution, and the right to privacy, although not mandated by the Constitution, is a generally accepted fact of life supported by a long history of case law and legal precedent.

To me, the chief concern is the possibility of abuse in the name of government. The FBI addresses such concerns in two ways. First, spin. After Carnivore began to generate a huge amount of controversy, the FBI rechristened the device. Starting in February 2001, the FBI began to refer to Carnivore by the more benign sounding name of DCS1000 ("Digital Collection System").

Second, in the tradition of all law enforcement authorities who must explain to civilians why the means justify the ends, the FBI trots out the age-old story of good vs. evil. We, the good guys, (the FBI says) are in a never-ending battle against the bad guys (the criminals). The bad guys don't follow the rules and for the good of society, you must not restrict us if you want us to be effective fighting evil on your behalf. The bad guys are very, very evil and dishonest, and are doing their best to steal, cheat and corrupt society. We, on the other hand, are here to protect you. You can trust us.

What the FBI Assistant Director Has to Say

July 24, 2000, FBI Assistant Director Donald M. Kerr testified before Congress about Carnivore. Kerr begins by describing the threat:

"Criminals use computers to send child pornography to each other using anonymous, encrypted communications; hackers break into financial service companies' systems and steal customer home addresses and credit card information; criminals use the Internet's inexpensive and easy communications to commit large-scale fraud on victims all over the world; and terrorist bombers plan their strikes using the Internet."

Certainly there is some kernel of truth in these statements, but still, they are highly exaggerated. Read, for example, the following statement from later testimony given by Mr. Kerr. In answer to the question "Why does the FBI need a system like Carnivore?" he asserts.

"By now, it has become common knowledge that terrorists, spies, hackers, and dangerous criminals are increasingly using computers and computer networks, including the Internet, to carry out their heinous acts. In response to their serious threats to our Nation, to the safety of the American people, to the security of our communications infrastructure, and to the important commercial and private potentialities of a safe, secure, and vibrant Internet, the FBI has responded by concentrating its efforts, including its technological efforts and resources, to fight a broad array of Cyber-crimes."

Let's take another look at that first sentence:

"...it has become common knowledge that terrorists, spies, hackers, and dangerous criminals are increasingly using computers and computer networks, including the Internet, to carry out their heinous acts..."

Is it just my imagination or does this sound like a sheriff in the Old West, explaining why he is getting together a posse to go after a gang of incorrigible bank robbers?

If you are the type of person who worries about well-meaning government agencies running amok, you might be starting to become concerned. I am. In my experience with law enforcement officers, I have found that they always mean well. However, they are often ignorant of basic facts (I'll tell you a story about that later), and they have a particularly slanted view of humanity. To many officials, the checks and balances we use to protect our freedoms simply get in the way of effective law enforcement.

Should we worry about Carnivore? The FBI says no. According to Donald Kerr (again testifying before Congress), "There are a number of reasons why the public should have confidence in the FBI's lawful use of Carnivore." These reasons can be summarized as follows.

First, Congress has created legal protection for electronic communication, and the FBI (and presumably other government agencies) must follow the rules. Second, all electronic surveillance requires some type of court order. In order to get such an order, the FBI has to meet specific criteria. Third, the laws are such that the FBI can only use Carnivore to gather "hard evidence". They cannot "snoop".

What happens when the FBI manages to get such a court order allowing them to spy on a particular user? They serve it on the user's ISP and, with the help of the ISP's technical staff, install Carnivore.

All of this takes time and requires the FBI to jump through various legal and procedural hoops. However, as Kerr points out: "Of course, there are 'emergency' provisions whereby surveillance is permitted to proceed immediately, when high-level Department of Justice authorization is obtained, so long as a court order is filed within 48 hours."

When Internet Law Enforcement Runs Amok

The FBI is not the only government organization in the world that covertly monitors Internet communications. In fact, when it comes to monitoring people and organizations, the United States National Security Agency (NSA) makes the FBI look like amateurs. I have talked about Carnivore in detail to show you that the government has developed, and uses, sophisticated devices that allow them to eavesdrop on everything we do on the Net without our knowing it. And when we ask "How are we protected against abuse?" the answer comes back, "You are protected because we have to follow the rules. Moreover, you can trust us."

Tell that to a friend of mine. He has his own domain name — let's call it *something.com* — that he uses for email and a Web site.

One day his house was visited by two U.S. Customs officers. My friend was away from the house at the time so they left a message. Later they called him on the phone. "We want to meet with you," they said, but they refused to say why. "If we come over to your house, will you be there?" My friend was suspicious so he said he would meet them, but only at his lawyer's office. The Customs officers agreed but they weren't happy about it.

A couple of hours later, at the lawyer's office, my friend found out what was happening. Evidently, Customs officers had been monitoring a child pornography discussion group, and a suspect on the other side of the country (a person who had, actually, not even broken a law) had sent a message with a forged address in the form *name@something.com*. In other words, some guy made up a fake email address that used the domain owned by my friend. (As a matter of fact, if you think about it, wouldn't you expect the type of person who deals in child pornography to use a fake email address?)

The Customs officers, not understanding this, looked up the ownership of the domain *something.com*, which happened to be owned by my friend, and found his street address. Since it was on the other side of the country, they contacted Customs officers in that area, and asked them to investigate. These officers, as I have related, dutifully went to my friend's house and, later, met him at his lawyer's office.

Here's the scary thing. My friend had nothing to do with any of this. All that had happened is that someone had posted a message with a fake email address that used my friend's domain. However, the Customs officers, when they went to his house, had a computer expert with them in their car, and they were prepared to come in, hook up their own equipment to my friend's computers, search them thoroughly, and, if they felt justified, confiscate his equipment — all because someone on the other side of the country had posted a fake email address that used my friend's domain.

In this case, the story does have a happy ending. My friend insisted the officers meet him at his lawyer's office, and the lawyer protected my friend. He made sure the officers understood their mistake and, before they left, they apologized for the trouble. In fact, during the conversation, it became clear that the officers understood next to nothing about the Internet.

What scares me is that, even though my friend did nothing wrong, official government agents, who didn't understand what they were doing, were prepared to accuse him of being a child pornographer and violate the privacy of his computer systems (not to mention ruin his reputation in the neighborhood). During this whole experience, the Customs agents were following all the proper rules and procedures, but that didn't help my friend. Fortunately, he had a smart lawyer.

But how many people do you know who can afford to pay a lawyer to protect them when the Feds knock on their door accusing them falsely of a crime that didn't really happen, because they monitored something on the Internet and didn't understand what they were monitoring? Can you?

Don't get me wrong. I'm not saying that no one in the government understands the Net, or that law enforcement officials have poor judgment. To the contrary, some of the most knowledgeable Internet people I know are in law enforcement, and I respect them enormously. They really are the good guys.

However, we do need to realize that, for some time, the government has had the tools and the inclination to monitor what we do on the Net. In non-democratic countries, monitoring Internet communications is the norm. Although we live in a democratic country, we must recognize how dependent we have become upon the Internet. We need to be aware of how the government has mastered the art of eavesdropping on the Net, and we need to hold the government accountable for its actions. Moreover, this is not an issue that is ever going to go away. When it comes to the Net, the price of freedom will always be eternal vigilance. We must insist that every government department that snoops on our communications be required to tell us what they are doing — without the double-talk and without the scare stories — and be accountable to the public.

What Superintendent Babin Has to Say

The Internet has grown enormously in just a few years, and the technology has created significant problems for law enforcement officers. To understand some of these problems and put them in perspective, I talked to Len Babin, a Senior Superintendent in the RCMP. The RCMP (Royal Canadian Mounted Police) is Canada's national police force, in many ways similar to the American FBI. Superintendent Babin is a high-ranking officer who is a long-time expert in crime, computers and the Internet. In the following statement, Babin explains some of the problems modern law officers face.

"The Internet is not defined geopolitically — it is supra-national. To a modern policeman, the criminal element now consists of more than just local criminals. Potentially, one might have to worry about criminals anywhere in the world. This is a brand new situation for law enforcement agencies. Never before have they had to understand and interpret distant actions in order to stay on top of crime in their local jurisdiction.

"Courts and legal systems are limited in their powers and, even now, the Internet is pushing the boundaries. Countries are making agreements about how existing laws are to be applied to Internet activities and, eventually, you may see such cooperation pushed to the level of a world court.

"It is important to remember that police officers are the agents of society. They are not autonomous, nor are they there by their own volition. Society defines everything police can do, right down to what they wear when they go to work.

"Society has made laws to protect personal communications, but there are also laws to make it possible for officers to eavesdrop on these communications when necessary.

"A police officer is called upon to be the expert witness of the state. As such, the world of law enforcement is full of laws, rules and procedures designed to help a police officer succeed in court. An officer using electronic surveillance to collect legal evidence is bound by the same rules that apply to any type of evidence collection. In other words, whether an officer is investigating a murder or a traffic violation, the standards he or she must follow are the same.

"For example, in Canada, a court order will allow me to monitor communications, but only for those people that I have specifically identified in court. If I am monitoring a phone conversation, I am only allowed to listen when I recognize the voices of those specific people. If I hear other people talking, I must hang up.

"In terms of legal authority, the growth of the Internet has changed nothing. The law still gives police officers the authority to intercept certain communications. However, on the Internet, it is much more difficult to identify the originator of a communication. Internet technology, especially when used with encryption, threatens to take away the capability of police to carry out their legally authorized mandate to monitor certain private communications.

"As a result, police are starting to feel that power slip away, which may be why, in some cases, they may seem to be zealots. However, we do have a responsibility to keep up with the technology. For example, if there were a large terrorist act tomorrow, and it came out that the terrorists were using encrypted Internet communications that the FBI were unable to monitor, the FBI would undoubtedly be subject to criticism.

"I think you'll see the day when there will be pressure even on local police to monitor such communications. However, the question of how much to monitor is crucial. If you cast a very wide net, everyone loses some freedom, and we would end up living in a zoo where, potentially, everyone could be controlled and spied upon.

"When it comes to breaking the law, a wide net would catch almost everyone in one way or another. However, it is necessary to catch the more blatant, serious criminals; so where do you draw the line?

"Who should decide? Usually, it's the legislators. However, when technology changes so quickly, the line moves quickly without the public or the legislators understanding what has happened.

"Police have always lived in the world of damned-if-you-do and damned-if-you-don't, and this is just another example. But you must realize that police officers are trying to do their job — the job they were hired to do."

How the Internet Works: TCP/IP

The Internet is vast beyond human comprehension and is very, very complicated. What is amazing is that, as large and complex as the Net may be, no one actually runs it. No person, no government, no organization, no one — if you can believe it — is in charge.

How can this be? Before I explain, I want to take a few minutes to discuss how the Internet works. By the time we are finished, you'll understand how such a large network can run automatically without having anyone in charge. The details are fascinating, and to explain them I'll have to get a bit technical. (But this is fun technical stuff, so don't worry.)

To start, let's talk about how information gets passed from one place to another on the Net.

Information, often referred to as DATA, is constantly being transported all over the Internet. Behind the scenes, data is passed from one computer to another until it reaches its final destination. For example, when you send an email message to a friend, your message is passed from your computer, to another computer, to another computer, and so on, until it reaches your friend's computer.

Of course, for this system to work, all the computers on the Internet must follow the same standards of data transmission. They do so by using a system called TCP/IP. (The name stands for "Transmission Control Protocol / Internet Protocol". When you talk about TCP/IP, pronounce it as five separate letters — "T C P I P" — without the slash. If you want to sound cool, say the letters quickly.)

The reason the Internet works is that all the computers on the Net — including your computer — use TCP/IP to communicate. More precisely, each computer on the Net runs a program that allows it to send and receive data using TCP/IP. Thus, in one sense, we can say that the Internet is simply a huge collection of computers, all of which exchange data according to the TCP/IP system. (Actually, from a technical viewpoint, this is a perfectly adequate definition of the Internet.)

Informally, we often speak about computers as if they were alive (which, of course, they aren't). For example, as I mentioned earlier, when computers exchange data, we say that they talk to one another. So, we might say that TCP/IP is the system that allows computers on the Internet to talk to one another.

The details of TCP/IP, as you might imagine, are hideously technical. However, the fundamental idea is easy to understand.

Let's say a chunk of data (such as an email message, or the text of a Web page, or a picture) has to be sent from one computer to another. The first computer breaks up the data into pieces, each of which is placed into a small package called a PACKET. Along with a portion of the data, each packet also contains the address of the destination computer and a sequence number. The packets are sent onto the Internet, where they are passed from one computer to another. At each point, the computer that receives a packet looks at the destination address and passes the packet to another computer that is one step closer to the destination. The packets all travel separately, and they may not even take the same route, but, eventually, they all reach the destination.

At that point, a program on the destination computer extracts the contents of each packet and, using the sequence numbers, reassembles the pieces into a copy of the original data. Thus, you can think of your email message (or Web page text or picture) as being broken into pieces, sent out over the Net, and reassembled at the destination. What is amazing is that the Internet is so fast that the whole thing often takes place in seconds, even when the packets have to travel a long distance.

Moving the Data: Routers, ISPs, NSPs and NAPs

From the very beginning (1968), the Internet was designed to grow indefinitely without requiring any type of central administration. The idea was to construct a system in which a great many small parts (computers) would, by their very nature, form a large entity (a network) as soon as they were connected. To make such a network grow, all you would need to do is add more computers. Moreover, if you removed one or more computers, it wouldn't affect the integrity of the network as a whole. The network would just get smaller.

Every computer on the Internet (including your computer) uses TCP/IP to send and receive data. The beauty of TCP/IP is that, because it uses small packets with a standard size and format, the overall communication system can be designed efficiently. So, although the Internet itself is very complicated, the underlying communication system is conceptually simple. Each computer on the Net does its part simply by running a program that knows how to look at, interpret and transport small, standardized data packets.

However, there is more. There are a great many specialized computers, called ROUTERS, whose primary purpose is just to send and receive data packets. It is the routers that provide the communication links that hold the Net together.

There are millions of routers on the Net, many of which are connected to more than one communication line. This means that if a line happens to go down, there is almost always an alternate route. As I explained earlier, TCP/IP is designed so that it doesn't really matter how packets get from point A to point B. When a communication line or a specific router goes down (which happens from time to time), the other routers simply send their data packets by an alternate route until the problem is fixed.

You might ask, where are the routers located? They are all over the place: in telephone central offices, in computer rooms, in specialized switching facilities, and so on. (In fact, I have one in my basement.)

As we discussed earlier, access to the Internet is provided by ISPs (Internet Service Providers). To use the Net, you arrange for service from an ISP. Once you connect your computer to the ISP, you are on the Net.

Similarly, an organization with a network also connects to the Net via an ISP. In this case, the network administrator arranges for a connection between the network and the ISP. Once this connection is established, every computer on the network is also on the Net.

So, as you can see, the Internet has many, many communication lines all over the world. For the system to work, there must be a way for the various ISPs to connect to one another. To do so, they use the services of what are called NSPs (Network Service Providers). The NSPs, which are large telecommunication companies, maintain a system of high-capacity communication lines called the BACKBONE of the Internet. Along the backbone, there are special points at which ISPs can connect. These points, which act as communication hubs, are called NAPs (Network Access Points).

Thus, to use the Net, you connect your computer to an ISP, which uses a NAP to connect to the Internet backbone. In the United States, there are several tens of NAPs. If one of the NAPs were to go down temporarily, it would cause a lot of inconvenience but, because there so many of them, the outage would not be fatal to the Net.

Who Runs the Internet?

By now, you can understand that the Internet, as a whole, is completely automated. As long as enough computers are running and enough communication lines are intact, everything works without human intervention, and when a computer or a communication line does go down, the Internet works around it until a human being can make the necessary repairs.

With such a system, all that is necessary is for each organization and each person to take care of their particular part of the Net. For example, every organization (companies, universities, and so on) must take care of their own networks, and arrange for their

"I know it seems strange to realize that we have created something so complex and powerful that we can't control it, but that's okay. We just need to get used to the idea."

own connection to the Net. Each person must do the same him- or herself. You, for example, are responsible for making sure that your computer and your Internet connection are up and running.

The secret of the Internet's success is that it is completely decentralized. Indeed, by its very nature, the way it was designed, the Internet must be decentralized to work properly. In fact, if the Internet had been designed to require a central authority, the network would have collapsed under its own weight a long time ago.

Thus, there is no need for a central authority.

Think of the cells in your body. Although they are specialized and some may be more important than others, you can safely remove any particular cell — or, in some cases, many cells — without hurting the body as a whole. Moreover, at any time, various parts of your body can grow simply by creating new cells.

Because the Internet does not require a central authority to run the system, it can grow without bound in such a way that no one is in charge. And if no one is in charge, who will police the system? Who will set standards of behavior, and who will enforce the rules?

The short answer is, nobody. Nobody is in charge. Nobody is in control.

You are on your own, but don't let that bother you. No one controls the weather or the rotation of the planets around the Sun or most of the plants and animals in the world, but the world and the universe get along just fine.

I know it seems strange to realize that, as human beings, we have created (and we maintain) something that is so complex and so powerful that we can't control it, but that's okay. We just need to get used to the idea.

The Nature of the Net

By its very nature, the Internet is beyond the control of human beings. However, that doesn't stop various organizations and people from trying to exert control. There are a number of motivations for wanting such control, the most common of which is money.

One of the best-known examples is AOL, the largest ISP in the United States. (At one time, the company was named America Online, but now it is just plain AOL.)

As you know, the basic role of an ISP is to allow you to connect your computer to the Internet. AOL, however, goes a lot further. They use their own software (which they give away for free) to create a special environment for their customers. The AOL environment is especially easy to use for beginners. It allows AOL customers to send and receive email, to talk to one another, to look at Web sites, and to access a large number of proprietary services.

So what's the problem? There are several, and to appreciate them, you need to understand an important aspect of human nature.

Human beings are adept at forming hierarchical systems in which responsibility is centralized and someone is clearly in charge. Indeed, being able to form such systems is one of the most important reasons for our success as a species. Creating well-defined hierarchies allows us to organize ourselves into groups of any size and to accomplish much more than if we had to work alone.

Because we are built this way, we tend to measure the value of an organization by its size. For example, we value a large, international conglomerate a lot more than a small, local business. One reason, of course, is that a large, international conglomerate can make a lot more money than a small, local business. Another reason is that the people running a large, international conglomerate have a great deal of power and, generally speaking, human beings admire such people.

In the business world, it is common — some people might even say natural — for the people who run companies to want those companies to grow as large as possible. Large companies mean more customers, more money and more power.

The Internet, however, is designed as a distributed system that works best when it is decentralized. Any Internet company (and AOL is not the only one) that tries to centralize and grow too large, finds that it runs into unexpected problems. Outside the Net, larger companies can enjoy a great deal of efficiency because of the economies of scale. On the Net, the opposite is true. Every Internet communication requires a one-to-one connection between two computers, and the more connections you have, the more you create bottlenecks.

Up to a point, it is possible to alleviate the bottlenecks by spending money on more computers, more routers, more communication lines, and more employees. Such actions, however, work against the basic nature of the Net. Internet companies that become too large find out that, the more they centralize and grow, the less efficient they become. On the Net, having too many customers makes it harder to earn money, because you quickly reach the point where each new customer adds proportionally more to the overhead than he or she can contribute in potential revenue.

Once an Internet company gets too large, it starts to collapse from its own weight, and the business model (the plan for making money) that the company used when it started soon becomes inadequate. What follows is an intense pressure to generate profits. This force gives rise to a determined effort on the part of the company to squeeze out as much money as possible, as quickly as possible, in any way they can. Many such companies go out of business. Others manage to stay alive, but only by changing the basic nature of their business.

Now, back to AOL. AOL started as an ISP that offered extra services to their customers. At the time, they made their money by charging a monthly fee. However, within a few years, AOL became a victim of its own success. They acquired so many customers that the monthly fees were not nearly enough to cover the increased overhead. For this reason, they changed themselves from an ISP to a marketing company. That is why, if you use AOL, you will find yourself looking at so many advertisements.

Now you can understand why it is crucial that AOL require its customers to use proprietary software to access the Internet. Having control of the software enables AOL to control what their customers look at as they use the Net, and that is the only way they can use every opportunity to sell, sell, sell.

Actually, the basic nature of the Net makes such a course inevitable. Any Internet company that grows large enough is going to encounter enormous overhead. When that happens, the choice is either (1) die, or (2) look for ways to sell as much as possible to their customer base.

For that reason, AOL's primary business is no longer Internet access. AOL is actually a marketing company that uses Internet access and special services to attract a customer base. (If you are an AOL user, I am sure you know exactly what I mean.)

However, AOL is not alone; Microsoft is also in the game. Some years ago, Microsoft started their own ISP business, MSN (Microsoft Network). At first, MSN users used standard Internet software, with a few extra Microsoft programs, to access the Net. Then Microsoft decided to compete head-to-head with AOL. To do so, they created MSN Explorer, a proprietary program that, like the AOL software, does its best to create an all-encompassing environment for their Internet customers.

Eventually, all such efforts are doomed to failure, because they work against the basic nature of the Net. On the Internet, trying to become prosperous by becoming large is like rolling a heavy rock uphill. You can do it for awhile — maybe even a long while if you have enough money — but eventually, the nature of the rock will have its way.

Does this mean I am saying that AOL's and Microsoft's ISP efforts are going to fail eventually? Yes, I am. (You just wait and see if I am not right.) The Internet works best with sharing, collaborating and one-to-one communication, all of which are decentralized activities. However, in order to make a large amount of money on the Internet, a company must create a large centralized, hierarchical organization, and that is just not the way the Net works.

The business of the Internet is not business.

The reason I want you to understand this principle is because it extends far past the possibilities of commercial enterprise. From time to time, we hear people call for government control over the Internet, to protect us from bad things such as crime, child pornography, propaganda, and so on. However, because the Net is a distributed system, it cannot ever be run by anyone. No person, no government, no police force — no organization is ever going to be able to control or censor the Net.

You must accept the fact that no authority is ever going to be able to arrange things so that you and your loved ones can be perfectly comfortable all of the time. AOL and Microsoft try to do that, but only at the expense of creating a basically unsound system, in which using the Internet turns into an irritating marketing experience.

For better or for worse, no one is in charge of the Net, and no one ever will be in charge. This means that — as a society and as individuals — it is up to us to develop the maturity, the values and the judgment to use the Net wisely and productively. No one is going to do it for us.

And that is one reason why the Net is going to change us a lot more than we expect.

Is It Realistic to Have an Expectation of Privacy?

With everything we have discussed so far, it is natural to wonder whether or not we can expect to have privacy when we use the Internet. The answer is yes and no. It depends very much on what we mean by "privacy".

I think you'll agree that when you go out in public, you have less privacy than when you stay home. For example, say that you and your spouse decide to watch a movie tonight. You can either stay home and watch the movie on television, or you can go out to a theater.

If you stay home, you have privacy. If you talk during the movie, only one person (whom you know well) will hear you. If you go to a theater, and you talk during the movie, it is likely that people whom you do not know will overhear you.

Similarly, when you leave your house and give up your privacy, you also expose yourself to potential problems. Somebody might hurt you or rob you. You might have an accident in your car or while walking on the street. You might run into someone unpleasant and have a bad experience.

These situations are so common that it almost seems superfluous to even discuss them. We all recognize that going out in public affects our expectations of privacy and safety, and we act accordingly. Thus, when you are in a theater watching a movie, you are more careful discussing personal matters than when you stay home and watch the same movie on television. Similarly, whenever you leave your house, you take simple precautions to ensure your comfort and safety. You avoid unsafe areas, you lock your car, you look both ways before you cross the street, and so on.

When you first start using the Internet, you need to adjust to a brand new environment. What you may not realize is that your period of adjustment will last a lot longer than you think. It may take several years before you really understand the nuances of the Net. (Indeed, some people never figure it out.)

One of the most confusing ideas is that of privacy. In the outside world, you know when you are in public: you are outside your home, there are people around you, and so on. On the Internet, it's totally different. As soon as you connect to the Net, you are in public.

Of course, you are not in public the same way as when you leave your house but, nonetheless, you are in a situation in which you (and your computer) can be affected by forces beyond your control, often without your knowledge.

As you read this book, you will learn more about the real nature of the Internet experience. As you do, you will develop a better understanding of how much privacy you can expect. I will explain which issues are important, and how you can best think about them.

Some people think that if they use the Net sparingly (or not at all), their privacy is assured. Such is not the case. The Net has a lot more information than anyone realizes, and even if you don't use the Net, other people may be able to use it to find out about you. For example, if you have a listed phone number, your name, address and number are on the Net. If you have done anything even remotely newsworthy, there is probably information about you on the Net. For example, I know someone who runs marathons. Information about him is on the Net, because the results of such competitions are often posted on a Web site.

I have a friend whose grandmother likes to use the Internet to find information about the various houses in which she has lived. She lives in Ohio, and in the course of her investigations, she discovered that Ohio makes a great deal of real estate information available for free on the Net. She found out that, without leaving her home or talking to anyone, she can find out how much her neighbors paid for their houses, what they pay in taxes, who owns the property, who used to own the property, and so on.

Such information is, of course, already public. If it weren't, the government wouldn't have released it. However, once the information is on the Net, it becomes easy to access. You don't have to go to a government office and hunt for what you want.

Right now, there is a huge amount of public information that is effectively private, simply because it is too much trouble to access. Once it is put on the Net, everything changes, and that information becomes accessible to anyone in the world.

So, how much privacy can you expect to have? Technically, it is possible for someone to eavesdrop on your Internet activities. Realistically, no one is watching what you do on the Net any more than anyone is listening to your phone calls. If you haven't done anything egregious that has drawn the attention of the police, no one on the Net really cares what you are doing. On the other hand, you can't stop the Net from collecting information about you. There is probably information about you on the Net right now, and there will be a lot more in the future.

Clearly, how our society thinks about privacy is going to have to change. We are going to redefine what we mean by privacy and how much we have a right to expect. We will also have to make some collective decisions as to what type of information should be available on the Net.

It will take years for these new attitudes to evolve. In the meantime, the Internet is going to affect your life in ways that nobody anticipates. We do, indeed, live in interesting times.

2

Is Your Business Their Business?

Using the Net at work requires you to develop a particular set of habits to protect yourself and your privacy.

Is Your Business Their Business?

It's Different at Work

We all have expectations regarding our privacy. For example, when we are alone at home, we instinctively feel that we can more or less do what we want and no one else will know. When we are in public, however, we know that we do not have the same degree of privacy, and we act accordingly.

Once we start using the Internet, our environment changes and so must our expectations. Whenever we connect to the Net, we expose our computers (and ourselves) to the influence of forces beyond our control, often without our knowledge. It is my assertion — and one of the themes of this book — that, with the integration of the Internet into our everyday lives, our understanding of privacy will have to change. Collectively and individually, we are going to have to struggle with these new external forces and revise our attitudes, especially with respect to our expectations of privacy.

In Chapter 1, we discussed the importance of the Internet, and how our individual interaction with it transforms what looks like a solitary activity into a public experience. In this chapter, we will explore the Internet and the workplace. You will see that — when it comes to using computers and the Internet — the experience of using the Net at work is fundamentally different from using the Net at home. As such, the work environment requires you to develop a particular set of habits to protect yourself and your privacy.

Before we discuss these ideas in detail, I would like to take a few moments to consider the workplace itself — in particular, its nature and the unique demands it makes upon us. Even if you do not work at an office, please read this chapter, because I am going to discuss some important ideas that apply to everyone.

The Rules Rule

If you work for a company or for the government, you know that there are rules — sometimes many rules — that you must follow.

In a large organization, there will likely be a sizable Policies and Procedures manual. There is no doubt that some of these guidelines are useful and help people carry out their jobs. A large number of the policies, however, are only there to protect and further the interests of the company.

For example, many businesses have policies regarding sexual harassment. In some sense, these policies help protect the employees. However, to a large extent, the rules are written by company lawyers to protect the company from lawsuits. I have a friend who works for a large publishing company. According to a rule at his company, if someone from outside the company were to send him an email message that, for some reason, his female assistant read and found to be offensive, he would be held responsible.

If you work in an industry that is particularly subject to regulation, you will find that many of the pages in your Policies and Procedures manual will be devoted to keeping your company from running afoul of the government. This is especially true if your company works in an area where there are environmental or safety concerns, or if your company does business with the government directly. However, all large companies must worry about the government. In the U.S., for example, there is a federal agency named OSHA (Occupational Safety and Health Administration) that regulates many aspects of the workplace. In large companies, it is not uncommon to find many workplace rules based on OSHA requirements.

This is not to say that company rules are bad. Many such rules are necessary. What is important for you to understand is that the company or organization you work for has a life of its own, and insofar as it can, it will protect itself at the expense of any particular individual (including you). Although you may think that the workplace rules are there to protect individuals and to encourage the principles of safety, equality and opportunity, they are enforced primarily to safeguard the interests of the company. One very big consideration is avoiding lawsuits and government sanctions, and towards such ends, many companies are prone to making their employees follow otherwise silly rules.

You would think that, with all the rules, the one area that would be heavily regulated would be personal privacy. To some extent, it is. For example, your company would not make public the information in your personnel file. However, when it comes to computers and the Internet, you have no privacy rights, and therein lies a real paradox.

Why You Are on Your Own

While you are at work, you take it for granted that there will be a significant lack of privacy. However, in our culture, human beings have an undeniable need for privacy and, in a semipublic arena such as a workplace, the psychological needs of the individual are usually balanced against the needs of the company. For example, if you work in an office, you are probably left alone to arrange your own desk drawers and (within reason) decorate your office. Companies know that, by their very nature, they necessarily impose upon your privacy, so they do make an effort to be sensitive to your most important needs. For instance, even the most company-oriented manager would think twice before installing security cameras in the employee bathrooms, or dictating what you may or may not do on your lunch hour.

Imagine a large circle drawn around the building in which you work. Every morning, as soon as you enter that circle, your privacy is limited, and you understand that. Now imagine the circle shrinking. Eventually, it is small enough that it contains only your office or cubicle. As the circle gets smaller and smaller, you expect more and more privacy. This is a psychological need we all share.

The smallest possible imaginary circle would be one that encompasses your inner self, that is, your mind and your thinking. If your company were to attempt to penetrate your very thought processes, you would consider it a gross invasion of your privacy, no matter how virtuous the rationalization. That is why, for example, if your manager asks for a report on your last month's work you would, no doubt, comply cheerfully, but if he or she were to ask you to take a lie detector test, you would almost certainly be offended. Indeed, you would probably refuse to take such a test (and as one of my readers, you have every right to do so).

Since the most personal part of your work is your thinking process — the very ideas and thoughts that exist in your head from minute to minute as you work — you would be most upset if someone found a way to monitor your thoughts. Is it possible for your employer to invade your head in this manner? Literally, no, but, practically speaking, yes it is possible. It can be done by monitoring what you do on your computer and how you use the Internet.

Most people assume that no one is ever going to care about how they use their computers as long as they get their work done. Similarly, they also believe that — unless there are specific rules regarding the Internet — they can do whatever they want, whenever they want, as long as they stay clear of obviously inappropriate behavior (such as looking at pornography, or sending harassing email).

We make these assumptions unwittingly, because we misunderstand the nature of using a computer within an organization. Computers are powerful tools that interact with our minds. Whenever we use such mind-oriented tools, we instinctively perceive the experience as being highly personal and intimate, and we assume that our employer will respect our right to have such activities remain private.

Most of the time, of course, this is the case. In most companies, no one looks over your shoulder as you type and click your mouse, and no one checks your computer at night looking for contraband. However, your company (or department or organization) has a life of its own, and its long-term interests are not the same as yours. If the company feels its interests are threatened, it will not hesitate to invade your most private activities, including spying on you while you use your computer and the Internet, or having experts examine your computer and its files looking for damaging information. Indeed, some companies use monitoring software that can record each keystroke you make and every Web site you visit. (We'll talk more about such software later in the chapter.)

We generally don't realize that, as we use a computer, we make many small decisions and choose strategies that, later, can allow an expert to find out a great deal about our thinking processes. For example, from time to time we are all called upon to organize the files and the folders (directories) on our computer. It is my experience that if you let me examine someone's computer, I can tell you a lot about the person by looking at how they choose to organize their files, what names they used, and so on. You would be shocked what a skillful expert can find out about you by looking at your email (including messages you thought were deleted), your browser history, the many hidden files that your programs create without your knowledge, and so on. Let's hope you never have to find out.

However, just in case, I'll show you, in the next few chapters, how to protect yourself and how to ensure your life at work is filled with as few such surprises as possible. When it comes to using your computer and the Internet at work, don't hold your breath waiting for anyone to look out for your interests and your rights to privacy. You are on your own. Your computer is owned by your employer, and they own everything on it, including the love notes your fiancee emailed to you (which you thought you erased) and the records kept by your browser that indicate how many Web sites you visited to do your Christmas shopping on company time.

What Not to Do at Work

At home, you have control over your computer, your programs, and (if you have one) your network. At work, everything is owned by your employer: the computer, the software, the network, and all the data (including your email messages). As a general rule, anything you do on company time using company resources is the property of the company. This means that, whenever you use your office computer for anything, your activities fall under the rules set by your company.

Many companies have policies to cover computer and Internet usage, but even if your company doesn't, it is wise to protect yourself from potential trouble. The easiest way to do this is to follow two guidelines:

1. **Never use your computer for personal activities.**
2. **Make a habit of regularly deleting all transient data from your computer.**

Let's take these guidelines one at a time. To start, I am suggesting that you should never, ever use your office computer for personal matters. I know this sounds extreme. After all, we all do some personal things at work. For example, many people make personal phone calls; even if your company is strict about such calls, it would probably be okay to use a company phone on your lunch hour.

Some companies keep a record of the numbers you call, how long you talk, and even (if the calls are recorded) what you talk about. If your company tracks you in this way, it would be foolish to use your office phone for personal calls. For one thing, you might inadvertently say something that could be misinterpreted in an unfavorable light. Moreover, if you and the company were ever in adversarial positions — for instance, if you were leaving your job under less than pleasant circumstances — you can bet that it wouldn't be difficult for an enterprising lawyer to go through your conversations and dig up something incriminating.

Of course, in most companies, this is unlikely to happen because no one records what you talk about each time you use your phone. However, this is not the case with your computer. Whether you realize it or not — and most people don't — a lot of what you do on your computer leaves traces, and it is impossible to erase them all without wiping out your entire system and reinstalling all your software.

Some companies use special spy programs that monitor your Internet activities and make a permanent record of everything you do on the Net, including every Web site you visit and what you do when you get there. However, even if your company doesn't use such a program, don't assume you are safe. Your friendly operating system (Windows), your Web browser

(Internet Explorer or Netscape), and many of your programs store lots of information about your activities.

In Chapters 3 and 4, I'll go over the ways in which your computer records your activities and what you can do to wipe out such records. However, I have to tell you, it is impossible to find everything and, even if you could, it would be an enormous bother to have to clean your computer regularly. Believe me, the best thing is to refrain from using your computer for personal activities at work. This will eliminate virtually all potential problems.

Does this mean I am saying that you shouldn't check your AOL or Hotmail account for email, even during your lunch hour? Yes, exactly. Wait till you get home.

Have you ever heard the saying, "If you never lie, you'll never have to remember what you said"? Let me tell you a similar bit of wisdom. If you never use your office computer for personal pursuits, you'll never have to remember what you did (and you'll never have to worry about erasing the evidence).

"Some companies use special spy programs that monitor your Internet activities and make a permanent record of everything you do on the Net."

The Weak Links in the Chain of Privacy

You may not realize it, but much of what you do at work on your computer is accessible to other people. With respect to using the Internet, we'll talk about the details in Chapters 3 and 4, and at that time, I'll show you what you can do to protect your privacy. I'll also explain some of the basic ideas along with the technical terminology. Right now, however, let's consider, in general terms, what would happen if someone were to check out your computer when you were not around.

For example, what if you were at lunch for an hour, and a coworker wandered in and started playing with your computer? Suppose you went away for a week or two on a vacation or a business trip, and someone used your office during that time? In less pleasant circumstances, what if, for some reason, your company were looking for evidence to use against you, and they started by scrutinizing your PC?

Let's pretend that you are away from your office and an investigator has access to your computer. He wants to find out as much as he can about you and what you have been doing. Let me show you what he might do.

To start, he turns on your computer and watches what happens. Do you have any chatting or email programs that start automatically, such as AOL Instant Messenger or Microsoft's MSN Messenger Service? If so, you may be logged in automatically each time your computer starts. In this case, the first thing the investigator does is check all your personal email. At the same time, he looks at the list of people you talk to (your Buddy List or Contact List). He may even chat with them, under your name, to find out more information. When he does, they will think they are talking to you.

The investigator then starts the email program you use for your work. He begins by reading your messages, not only your incoming mail, but all the messages you have ever sent, as well as the ones you think you have deleted. At this point, it will be obvious to him if you have been using the company system for personal email. (As I will show you in Chapter 4, many of the messages you think you have deleted may still be on your system.)

Moving on, the investigator opens your Web browser, Internet Explorer or Netscape. A wealth of information is now available. (In Chapters 3 and 4, I'll show you what steps to take to protect your privacy.)

The first thing he sees is your home page, the Web page that loads automatically each time your browser starts. (We'll talk about your home page in Chapter 3.) You can set your home page to be whatever you want but, remember, that is the first thing anyone will see when he starts your browser.

Next, the investigator looks at your browser history. This shows him the names of all the Web pages you have visited in the recent past. He can find out if you have been checking personal email, buying and selling at online auctions, looking at sports scores, checking your stock portfolio, reading the news, and so on. In particular, he checks to see if you have been visiting any forbidden Web sites, including anything even remotely connected with sex. Perhaps more important, if you have posted your resume at a job search Web site, the investigator will find out.

He then looks at your list of Favorites (Internet Explorer) or Bookmarks (Netscape). These are Web addresses you have saved. You would be surprised how many people save questionable Web addresses on their work computers, but nothing will surprise the investigator. He has seen it all.

After spending a few hours tracking down your Web activities, the investigator turns his attention to the rest of your system. Using a program called Windows Explorer, he starts looking at your files and folders (see Chapter 3).

First, he examines all the files in your cache, a storage area used by your browser. By doing so, he can see everything you have looked at, *including the pictures*. If you have ever looked at a questionable picture, there is a good chance there will be a copy of it in your cache.

The investigator then starts rooting around your system, looking for anything interesting. He looks at all your files and your folders checking out, not only the contents and how everything is organized, but all the names. (Although you might not realize it, it is possible to tell a lot about a person by looking at the names he or she chooses for files).

Another way the investigator examines your files is to use the Windows Find facility (Start | Find). That is, he displays the Start Menu by clicking on the Start button, and then clicks on Find. He searches for files with a particular name as well as files that contain specific words or phrases. He then looks on your Documents list (Start | Documents), to see what documents you have been using.

He then looks at all the programs you have installed, and all the data files they have created. He finds your programs in three ways. First, he looks at the Add/Remove Programs facility (Start | Settings | Control Panel | Add/Remove Programs). Next, he looks at which programs are in your Start menu (Start | Programs). Finally, he uses Windows Explorer to look at the folders on your hard disk, especially the **Program Files** folder. This is the place where most programs install themselves.

True story: I once knew someone who had been using AOL on a work computer to participate in chats and email with a group of people who favored certain, shall we say, "unusual" sexual and social practices. She thought she cleaned up her computer when she left. What she didn't know is that AOL had obligingly left a list of all her companions in a file in a special AOL folder. It was there for anyone who knew where to look for it.

By this point, the investigator has a good grasp of your habits, your interests and your activities. If he is astute, and he has the time and inclination, there is a lot more that he can find in your computer by using technical tools that I won't go into here (such as the registry editor, see Chapter 4). For now, the investigator contents himself with one last inquiry. He looks at each icon (small picture) on your desktop, checking when it was created, and what it does. If it represents a program, he runs it to see what you have been doing. If it represents a Web page, he checks out the page to see what you have been looking at.

It's Worse Than You Think

In the last section, I told the story of what an investigator might do if he were investigating you by examining your computer where you work. I assumed that all this happened when you were away from your office for some reason. But, actually, in most companies, that's not even necessary. If your computer is on a network, the network administrator can access all your files and, in principle, he or she can find out a lot of what you are doing without going anywhere near your computer.

If you have any files on a file server (a special computer that provides data storage to users on the network, see Chapter 3), it is easy for the administrator to look at them. This is certainly the case with all of your incoming and outgoing email messages, which are stored centrally on a computer called a mail server (see Chapter 4).

If you have ever had any questionable files, don't think you are safe just because you deleted them. One of the responsibilities of your network administrator is to ensure the safekeeping of all the data on the network, and toward this end, he or she will make sure that a copy of all the data on the network, called a BACKUP, is made regularly. Typically, this process will be automated and will be done every day, often in the middle of the night. (We call this BACKING UP the data.)

The backups will be stored on a medium, such as tapes or CDs, that can be removed and stored in a safe area. If you have ever had the experience of accidentally deleting an important file and having the network administrator restore it for you, you will know how valuable backups can be. However, they can work against you too. It is possible to restore, say, the contents of the mail server from two years ago and, in the process, recover all the mail messages that you thought were deleted a long time ago.

Don't get me wrong. I'm not saying here that your network administrator is going to spend his time idly looking through your files, or your mail, seeking entertainment or diversion. Network administrators have too much to do as it is, to bother with snooping for fun. The important point is that anyone with authority can arrange to have access to your files and your email, whenever they want. If you think I am being overcautious, I am not. I was recently talking to a friend who works for a well-known company, who was told by the president of the company, that he (the president) routinely looked at various people's email.

Before you get too outraged at such behavior, let me remind you that, when you work in a company, what you do on company time and with company resources belongs to the company. It may be uncomfortable to think about it, but the easiest way to stay out of trouble is to assume you are being monitored, and to act accordingly.

Never forget that you are just an employee and that your interests will not always coincide with the interests of the company. In February 2000, a great many people were being laid off by Internet-related companies. A writer who, at the time, was covering the San Francisco Bay Area for an English newspaper wrote that "lay-offs are announced with 15 minutes' notice and bewildered employees are escorted to the door by security guards. Frequently, employees' computers are seized and their hard drives scoured for evidence of any indiscretion that could justify a firing without severance privileges."

Even Paranoids Have Real Enemies

Earlier in the chapter, I described how someone with access to your computer could find out a lot about you. However, such a person can do more than merely investigate your activities. He can cause you a lot of trouble if he is so inclined, especially if you work in an environment in which there are strict policies about how the Internet may and may not be used.

The main reason you are so vulnerable to such troublemakers is that whenever someone does something on your computer without your knowledge, it looks as if you did it. For example, I mentioned earlier that, if you use a chat facility from your work computer, it might be possible for someone to access it when you are away. If so, the person can start talking to other people under your name. I have seen this happen and, believe me, it doesn't take long for a creative troublemaker to ruin your reputation.

The same holds for email, both work-related and personal. If an intruder wanted to cause mischief, he or she could easily use your email program to send a rude email message to your boss, with a copy to the president of the company, as well as all the people in your work group. Of course, it would look as if you had sent the message.

Similarly, something like this could happen if you use a Web-based email service like AOL or Hotmail (see Chapter 4), and you are logged in automatically whenever your computer starts. In this case, a troublemaker could send messages to everyone in your address book.

In addition, an intruder could use your browser to visit forbidden Web sites. Later, if anyone checked your computer, it would look as if you had looked at the sites. For example, someone who wanted to get you in trouble could, in just a few moments, visit a number of pornographic Web sites and save their addresses in your Favorites/Bookmarks list. At the same time, your browser would faithfully be keeping a record of all the Web addresses, as well as copies of all the pictures (see Chapter 3).

Protecting Yourself

It is my contention that, even if you never do anything wrong, you still need to take steps to protect yourself. How you use your computer and the Internet, and how your company perceives that you use them can become very important when you least expect it. This is especially true if you have a job in which you work with sensitive information, if you are, for example, a lawyer or a financial officer or a human resources worker. Similarly, it is prudent to be careful if you are in a highly competitive industry and you are expected to keep your work away from prying eyes. In such cases, there are legitimate business reasons — aside from any native paranoia you may enjoy — for being extra scrupulous with your computer and your data.

In general, people have an innate need for privacy. When you were a kid, for instance, you probably hid stuff under your bed. (If you have forgotten how important it was to have such privacy, go look under your kid's bed right now.) As adults, we maintain this same need. For example, if you knew that friends were coming by your home for a visit, you wouldn't leave personal papers on the coffee table in the living room.

Consider this example from work. Say that you work in an office or cubicle and you have your own filing cabinet. From time to time, you use the filing cabinet to store some of your personal papers. One day, as you are preparing to go on vacation, you find out that there is a chance that someone else may use your office when you are gone. In such a case, wouldn't you take a moment to remove all the personal material from the filing cabinet?

Now, let's say you knew someone might be using your computer while you were gone. What steps could you take to safeguard your personal information? Cleaning out your filing cabinet is straightforward and easy, but cleaning out your computer is more problematic. Unlike a filing cabinet, it's hard to clean out your computer selectively, because you don't really know what's there. Believe me, once you have been using a PC with Windows for awhile, there will be all kinds of personal information on your computer and there is no way to be sure that you have found it all.

The best advice I can give you is to do two things. First, never use your computer at work for personal activities. Be careful of what you do and what you say with your computer, especially on the Net. Don't assume that you can use the Web or send email anonymously. If your company has a good enough reason to find out what you have been doing, they will. For example, most ISPs and email providers will give out information about your "secret" user names if they get a court order. Some of them will even give out the information with nothing more than a request from a company lawyer. Closer to home, did you know that all Microsoft Word documents have a unique, hidden identifier? If a controversial Word document is circulating around the company, it is possible to find out who created it.

In other words, don't try to beat the system. Be prudent and follow the rules. Save your personal computer and Internet activities for home.

My second piece of advice is to guard against becoming complacent. Learn how to clean out your computer as well as possible, and do it regularly.

With respect to your filing cabinet, it's probably all right to use it to store a few personal files, because it is easy enough to remove them whenever you want. No one is going to come in the middle of the night, photocopy all the papers in your cabinet and store them in a vault. If, however, you store personal data on your computer, it will be backed up automatically, and the backup will be kept indefinitely. There may even be multiple copies in different places. (A good network administrator will keep several sets of backups offsite, in case the building burns down.)

How would you feel about your filing cabinet if you knew that it would remember each time you opened and closed it, and what you put in, took out, and looked at? Your computer can, and does, keep such information with respect to many of your activities, such as using the Web. When you use a filing cabinet, it's easy to see what's inside. With a computer, it's not possible to keep track of everything on your disk, so it is easy to become complacent.

How much information does your computer keep as you work and as you use the Net? The answer to this question is complex and we will deal with it at length in Chapters 3 and 4. At the time, I'll show you what you can do to protect yourself and, in Chapter 4, I'll give you a checklist that you can follow every day to clean out your computer.

Software That Snoops

So far, we have talked about the ways in which you might inadvertently leave tracks on your computer regarding your Internet activities. However, some companies are proactive: they use software that monitors and records everything their employees do on the Net. Is this a gross invasion of privacy, or is it simply prudent behavior on the part of the company? A lot depends on your attitude towards such spying.

Most of us leave the house to go to work, and when we do, we fully expect to spend our working hours in public. Even if we have our own offices, we don't have the same expectation of privacy that we do in our own homes. For example, most companies have a wealth of corporate policies, covering a variety of activities: dress codes, sick days, vacations, customer interactions, complaint procedures, and so on. Moreover, the physical layout of the work environment — especially the ubiquitous cubicles — will often enforce a lack of privacy for all but the most senior employees. In many companies, control extends even further, to monitoring people's movements (for "security"), their time on the phone (for "efficiency"), and how long they take to resolve a problem or inquiry (for "customer service").

Although companies are quick to justify heavy-handed surveillance, such environments clash with basic human nature and sometimes workers rebel. For example, in August 2000, workers at Verizon went on strike. There were a number of reasons, but chief among them was the lack of privacy and dignity. The workers' performance was controlled to the point of intense discomfort and pressure. As one Verizon employee explained, "You're constantly monitored and if you don't say or do certain things on every phone call, you're subject to discipline." A union press release observed: "Employees talk of breaking down and crying at work, of seeing therapists and taking anti-depressants for stress. They describe rigid rules that strip them of their dignity. They commonly refer to their work sites as 'modern-day sweatshops' or 'kindergarten', because of the childish way they're treated."

Could this happen at your company? Before you say no, consider that many companies already use software that monitors and records all Internet activity. Although such software may not put you under the same pressure as the Verizon workers, you might find yourself working with a similar loss of basic privacy. Moreover, the Verizon workers in question spent their time dealing with the public. In some sense, it was justifiable for management to listen in on the conversations. Does this principle apply to regular office workers with an Internet connection?

Maybe yes and maybe no. To find out more, I interviewed Kevin Blakeman, the President of the U.S. division of Surf Control, a company that sells Internet monitoring software. Surf Control has a number of products, one of which, Super Scout, is used by companies to monitor Internet usage.

Surf Control is a powerful program. It can monitor every type of Internet activity, including Web access and email (although Blakeman claims that the program doesn't look at the content of email). Surf Control can block access to specific sites or, alternatively, allow access only to a list of approved sites. Moreover, the program enables managers to watch what people are doing in real time. This means your boss, or someone in the human resources department, can snoop on anything you do over the Net, as you are working. If you do happen to break a rule, even inadvertently, denying it won't help, because Surf Control can record everything you do, down to the exact keystroke and mouse click.

Let's not be one-sided. The goal of most companies is not to catch people breaking the rules. Rather, the hope is that, once employees know they are being monitored, they will stop breaking the rules voluntarily. For instance, if you know that everything you do on the Net is being recorded and your manager could spy on you any time he or she wanted, how likely are you to spend two hours on an online auctions site, looking for that hard-to-find album of Julie Andrews Christmas songs?

What bothers me more than the actual spying — and it is spying — is the lack of thought that goes into the ethical and practical consequences of such systems. Is it right to create software that allows companies to spy on their employees? When I asked Blakeman, I found out that, although he was eager to talk about the features of his product, he quickly became defensive when I inquired about ethical considerations.

According to Blakeman, the software is set up by the network administrator, according to rules and policies dictated by the human resources department, so his company has no responsibility with regard to how the product is used. I asked him directly, what about the people who create such products? Is there ever any discussion of ethics within your company? "No," he replied, "we only talk about content."

I noticed, however, that Blakeman was also quick to use loaded words, such as "dangerous", when he described the types of activity that Super Scout is designed to stop. Let's be real here. Internet monitoring programs are *not* our last bulwark between purity and the dangers that lurk on the Net. The real purpose of these programs is to scare people so they are more apt to keep their minds on their work.

Even more common is that many companies routinely monitor incoming and outgoing email. For example, my editor at Prentice-Hall, the publisher of this book, once sent email to a reviewer. It happened that, in the message, were the words "offshore accounts". The message was sent without a problem, but the reply was caught by an automated anti-spam program running on the Prentice-Hall mail server. (Spam is unsolicited email.)

Since the reply contained the words "offshore accounts", the program judged the message to be spam. Instead of allowing the message to pass through, the anti-spam program sent my editor a note informing him that the offending message had been placed in "quarantine".

Interestingly enough, the note gave no indication of how to get the message — which was not spam — out of quarantine. Perhaps even more interesting, was that, as a test, I sent my editor a message consisting of the words "Make money fast", and it passed through the sieve without a bit of trouble.

Does any of this remind you of George Orwell's novel *1984*? Orwell described ubiquitous devices, called telescreens, which allowed the totalitarian government to spy on its citizens at work, at home and in the streets. "Big Brother is watching you" was the slogan of the day.

Although today's corporate monitoring is not as extreme as *1984*, constant spying does create an uncomfortable environment. When people must always act as if their activities are being monitored, it creates an ongoing, low-grade anxiety. In some companies, this is already part of the corporate culture, so adding a new form of Internet-related observation may not seem like such a big deal. Still, we should wonder about the long-term effects on morale and productivity, and how such an environment affects our minute-to-minute comfort as we work. Clearly, companies cannot and will not police themselves, which raises the specter of government intervention.

Considering all of this, I couldn't help but wonder what the president of Surf Control, the company that makes the spy programs, really thinks about such products.

"Tell me," I asked Kevin Blakeman, "do you guys use Super Scout to monitor the people at your company?"

His reply was quick, so quick that I know he didn't pause to consider what he was saying.

"Of course not," was his answer.

3

Staying One Step Ahead

*A knowledgeable person with access
to your computer can easily figure
out what you have been doing.*

Staying One Step Ahead

Some Web Terminology

You may not know it, but each time you use the Web, your browser builds trails of information documenting your activities. A knowledgeable person with access to your computer can easily follow those trails and figure out what you have been doing. (I have had to perform such investigations myself on occasion.) In a moment, I will explain how this works, and then I'll show you how to protect your privacy. However, before we can do that, we need to discuss a few important technical terms.

No doubt you have seen many Web addresses in the form:

`http://`something-or-other

For example, the address of my Web site is:

`http://www.harley.com/`

The technical name for this type of Web address is a URL, which stands for "Uniform Resource Locator". (You pronounce the name as three separate letters: "U-R-L".) As the name implies, the purpose of a URL is to provide a uniform way to locate an Internet resource.

Most of the time, we use URLs to specify the addresses of Web pages. The URL above, for example, specifies the address of my Web site. However, URLs were designed to be a general specification that could be used to indicate any type of Internet resource. For instance, the following URL specifies the email address of the President of the United States:

`mailto:president@whitehouse.gov`

Compare the two URLs:

`http://www.harley.com/`
`mailto:president@whitehouse.gov`

The first one refers to a Web page, the second one to an email address. As you can see, the first part of a URL tells you what type of resource the URL refers to. This designation is called the SCHEME. In our examples, the scheme of the first URL is `http` (which indicates a Web page); the scheme of the second URL is `mailto` (which indicates an email address). There are other schemes as well, but you won't see them much, so let's not worry about them.

Within a URL, the scheme is always followed by a colon (:) and, in some cases, two slashes (//). The two slashes are a technical designation to indicate that the resource resides on a specific computer. Web pages always exist on a specific computer, so Web addresses always contain the two slashes. Email addresses, on the other hand, do not represent resources that exist on a specific computer, so they do not have the two slashes. Although the technical distinction may seem irrelevant to you, it is important to your browser when it is called upon to interpret a particular URL, so the two slashes are important.

In case you are wondering what **http** means, here is the explanation.

Web pages can contain text (characters, numbers and punctuation), pictures, sounds, video, and so on. In addition, Web pages can contain LINKS. When you click on a link, it takes you to a different resource, usually another Web page.

When text contains links, we call it HYPERTEXT. The name comes from science fiction stories, in which rocket ships can travel very large distances in a short time by jumping through "hyperspace". When you are reading a Web page and you click on a link, it looks as if you are jumping from one Web page to another, hence the name hypertext.

The system used to transport Web data on the Net is called HTTP, which stands for "Hypertext Transport Protocol". For this reason, when a URL refers to a Web page, the URL will have the scheme **http**. (In retrospect, perhaps **web** would have been a better choice.)

Originally, URLs were conceived as a way to refer to various types of Internet resources. However, the Web has become so dominant that virtually all the URLs you will ever use refer to Web pages. Since all of these start with **http://**, your browser lets you leave out this part when you type a Web address.

For example, as far as your browser is concerned, the following two Web addresses both refer to the same resource:

```
http://www.harley.com
www.harley.com
```

Only the first address is a proper URL, but if you type the second one, your browser will change it to the proper format automatically.

In other words, whenever you type an address that does not start with a scheme, your browser will assume it refers to a Web address and insert the `http://` for you.

Before we finish this section, I want to discuss just a few more technical terms. These are words I am sure you have seen, but I want you to appreciate their meanings precisely.

As I mentioned, hypertext is data that contains links to other data and resources. The basic job of your browser is to request a file containing hypertext and then display it on your computer. When such a file is displayed, what you see is called a WEB PAGE. In this sense, the word "page" is just a metaphor that has nothing to do with printed pages. A Web page can be any length, often much longer than a normal printed page.

A collection of related Web pages, maintained by a person or an organization, is called a WEB SITE (sometimes written as one word, WEBSITE). A Web site can contain any number of pages: some large Web sites have hundreds of Web pages, while a few small sites consist of only a single page.

Virtually all Web sites are organized so as to have one special page that acts as the door to the Web site. This page, called the HOME PAGE, is designed to be the first page you see when you visit the site. For example, if you were to give your browser the address of my Web site, you would see the home page that I designed for people visiting the site. A home page, like any Web page, can contain text, pictures, links, sounds, video, and so on. Typically, however, home pages are designed to introduce the Web site and to help people find what they want.

Just so your aren't confused, the term "home page" has another, completely different meaning. When you first start your browser, it displays a particular Web page automatically. This is your personal home page, and you can change it whenever you want.

Your Browser History

As you use the Web, there are several ways in which your browser stores information about your activities. These are:

- History
- Cache
- Auto-Complete information (including passwords)
- Address bar list
- Radio station list

I'll discuss each one of these in turn, and then show you how to safeguard your privacy as much as possible. As you read, please remember one thing. It's true that you can take steps to erase most of the information that your browser accumulates about what you do on the Web. However, no precautions are foolproof. Your best defense against privacy invasion — and the very best way to stay out of trouble at work — is simple: never use your computer for personal activities.

Each time you visit a new Web page, your browser saves the URL for that page in what is called your HISTORY. Internet Explorer, in particular, keeps a long history, detailing your activities over many days.

Internet Explorer was designed to record your history as a favor to you. Whenever you want, you can click on the History button, display the history, and jump to any URL you want. This feature can come in handy, for example, when you want to look at a Web site that you remember visiting last Tuesday. All you need to do is find it in your history.

On the other hand, anyone who has access to your computer can find out all the Web sites you have visited lately, just by looking at your history. Obviously, this could be trouble for you if your boss finds out that you have been looking at questionable Web sites. However, even if you are a paragon of virtue, your history can get you into trouble by accident.

Suppose, for example, you have a few spare moments before a big meeting, and you decide to take a look at the White House Web site in order to read the latest press releases (a noble and admirable pastime). It happens that the URL for the White House Web site is:

`http://www.whitehouse.gov`

However, by accident, you type:

`http://www.whitehouse.com`

To your surprise, you find out this is not the White House. In fact, after looking at some pictures of "interns", you realize that this is a porno site! To retype the correct address and jump to the White House Web site is, for you, the work of a moment. However, it is too late. Your visit to the porno site is already recorded in your history, where anyone can find it.

So to be prudent, you take a look at your history and, much to your surprise, you find a whole series of questionable URLs from two days ago. It must have been from the time when you were on your way to lunch, and that nice young man from the accounting department asked if he could use your computer for a few minutes to check a few numbers.

You start to panic. Before you can say "I was framed", your boss is going to drop in on his way to the meeting. You quickly clear the history (I'll show you how it works in a moment), and you go to a Web page showing stock market reports. No sooner does the page appear on your screen when your boss walks in. He looks at your computer, and nods his head approvingly. As the two of you leave your office and walk down the hall, you breathe a sigh of relief. That was a close call, but all's well that ends well. You are safe.

Or so you think. What you don't know is that the nice young man from accounting used your computer to look at pictures of a beautiful young woman having intimate relations with a platypus, and, right now, as you are walking down the hall feeling as confident as a politician with the check in his pocket, a copy of each of those pictures is sitting on your hard disk, accessible to anyone who knows where to look for them.

Where the Pictures Are: Your Cache

You may have noticed that most Web pages contain a number of elements. To be sure, there will be text, but most pages also have pictures (photos or graphics). Sometimes you will even hear sounds. All of these elements exist in separate files. When your browser contacts the Web site, it asks for whatever is necessary to display a particular page. The Web site sends the appropriate files to your browser, which then puts them together to create the actual Web page.

What happens if you want to view the same page at a later time? Well, your browser could ask the Web site to resend all the files again. However, this would be wasteful. Instead, your browser saves the files on your hard disk in a temporary storage area. Later, if you want to look at the same page again, it is a simple task for your browser to retrieve the files from its storage area and, once again, create the Web page. Moreover, this time, it all happens a lot faster, because the files are already on your computer and don't have to be downloaded (copied) from the Net.

The temporary storage area used by your browser is called a CACHE. Actually, the word "cache" is a general term, referring to a special, easy-to-access storage area used to hold data. Lots of programs use caches, as do various hardware components, such as processors and disk controllers. The idea is to use the cache to hold data that is likely to be needed in the near future.

Think of it this way. Let's say you work in a library, and you notice that a small number of books are very popular. People ask you for them all the time, so instead of putting them on the shelves, you keep these particular books behind the counter. That way, when someone asks for one of the books, you can hand it to him right away. In this case, you are using the storage space behind the counter as a cache.

Of course, out of all the files for all the pages you have viewed, your browser doesn't know which ones you are going to want to see again — so it keeps them all. That means, that when you revisit a Web page, it appears faster the second time than the first time. It also means that, if someone knows where to look on your hard disk, he or she can see everything you have been looking at, particularly the pictures.

This is only possible if someone knows where your cache is. However, Internet Explorer always keeps its cache in the same place: in a sub-folder residing in the **Windows** folder on your **c:** drive (hard disk). In a fit of creativity, Microsoft chose to give the cache folder the cunning name of **Temporary Internet Files**, so the folder is easy to find.

In other words, anyone with access to your computer can see what you have been doing on the Web simply by looking at the files in the folder named:

C:\Windows\Temporary Internet Files

(If you are using Windows 2000 or Windows NT, the location will be a bit different. See Chapter 4 for the details.)

> *"I know this is confusing. Just think of it this way: if you want to inactivate AutoComplete, you need to turn off two separate switches."*

Don't worry if you don't understand the terminology, or if you wouldn't know a folder from a mangel-wurzel. The point is that, technically speaking, it's an easy thing to do, and that anyone who understands the Windows file system can do it if he or she gets access to your computer. Moreover, such a person would not necessarily have to be in your office. He or she might be able to access your computer from another location on the company network.

So, how do you safeguard your privacy? You empty your cache regularly. When you do this, we say that you FLUSH the cache. (I'll show you how to do it later in the chapter.)

Before we leave this section, I want to go back to a technical term I used a moment ago, when I talked about copying data from the Net. The term is DOWNLOADING.

Downloading refers to copying information from the Internet to your computer. When you copy information from your computer to the Internet, it is called UPLOADING. When you first encounter these terms, it's easy to get them confused, so here is an easy way to remember. Just imagine the Internet floating above you in the sky. Data from the Net comes down, while data going to the Net must go up.

(At this point, if you recall the section in Chapter 1 in which I discussed how the Net is a large, unfathomable entity of enormous importance to human beings, you might want to take a moment and reflect on the similarity between the Internet and God.)

AutoComplete

Have you ever known someone whose mind raced so fast that he didn't have the patience to wait for people to talk at their own speed? For example, you are delivering a report during an important meeting, "...and so I sent the order to the Bumble—", when Mr. Know-it-all completes your sentence for you, "—Yes, yes, yes, the Bumblethorpe Company."

Well, computers are fast, and when it comes to certain types of information, they can certainly be programmed to be know-italls. This is the case with Internet Explorer, which has a feature called AUTOCOMPLETE. Whenever you are called upon to type some information, the browser watches what you are doing and tries to complete it for you.

For example, let's say that last week you visited my Web site, and today, you want to visit it again. You click on the ADDRESS BAR (the empty area to the right of the word **Address**) and you start to type the URL:

www.harley

At this point, the browser guesses what you are doing and completes the address for you:

http://www.harley.com

It also shows you a list of similar URLs that you have visited in the past.

You now have three choices. First, you can press the Enter key. This signals that you want to accept the browser's suggestion. Second, you can select one of the URLs from the list, if that's what you want. Or, if you don't like your browser's suggestion, you can keep typing and override it.

How does AutoComplete work? Whenever you type a URL into the Address Bar, fill out a form, or enter a password, the browser saves the information. Later, when you type something new, the browser can make suggestions based on the data you entered previously.

The AutoComplete feature can be useful, but it does create a privacy problem for you. Anyone who uses your browser will see the same list of choices that you do. In the example I gave above, this means that someone who is typing a URL into the Address Bar will, all of a sudden, be presented with a list of URLs you have typed.

Moreover, Internet Explorer has an interesting shortcut that also presents a privacy problem. If you press the F4 key, the browser will show you the complete list of everything you have typed into the Address Bar. You can then press the Down Arrow or Page-Down keys to scroll through the list. (Note: When you type a URL, AutoComplete looks for possible matches. To do so, it compares what you are typing to all the addresses you have ever typed into the Address Bar, as well as all the URLs of pages you have visited by clicking on links. When you press F4, the browser shows you only those addresses that you yourself typed into the Address Bar.)

Most people don't know about this trick, so if you want to look cool and impress someone, walk up when they have their browser open, press F4, and start looking through the list of addresses. Hint: This is a great way to make friends, when it is your first day on a new job.

AutoComplete also remembers passwords, which poses a particularly important problem. If you use the Web much, you'll end up with a number of favorite sites that require you to enter a user name and password. Internet Explorer will remember such information for you, but it will also expose you to other people being able to log in under your name, if they can access your browser.

As a safety feature, when your browser inserts a password for you, it will not display the actual characters. When you press Enter to submit the information, the real password will be sent. However, on your screen, you will only see asterisks (**********). But, don't feel too safe. If someone can get to your computer when you are not around, he can use AutoComplete to log in to your favorite Web sites under your name, even if he can't see the real password. Moreover, there are free programs that anyone can download that will show a password, even when your browser displays asterisks.

AutoComplete is a feature that permeates the Microsoft way of thinking, and you will find variations all over the place. For example, if you use Microsoft Word or Excel, the program will save a list of your most recently accessed documents and spreadsheets. (Just pull down the File menu.) You will also find AutoComplete-like assistance inside of Windows Explorer (the Windows file manager).

One last example: Within Internet Explorer, there is a built-in toolbar to make it easy to listen to radio stations around the world. (Pull down the View menu, select Toolbars, and then click on Radio.) Within the Radio toolbar, there is a button named Radio Stations. When you click on this button, the browser will show you a list of the last few stations you have accessed. Even if you clear out all URLs, all the form information and all the passwords, Internet Explorer will *not* clear the radio station list.

Controlling Your Browser History

So far, we have discussed three ways by which your browser monitors what you do and records your actions: the history, the cache, and AutoComplete. To safeguard your privacy, you need to be able to turn these services off and on, and clear out the data storage whenever you want. Each of these features works differently, so I'm going to cover them one by one, starting with the history. (Note: The instructions I will give you are for Internet Explorer. The details may vary a bit on your computer, depending on what version of the program you are using.)

To control your history, pull down the Tools menu and select Internet Options. This will open a new window. The various types of options are displayed in separate "pages". To move from one page to another, click the appropriate tab near the top of the window. When you are finished using this window, you can close it by clicking on the OK button.

When you first open the Internet Options window, you will see the General page, and that is the one we want to control the history. Look at the History section, and you will see that you can do two things. First, you can click on the Clear History button. That deletes all the URLs of the Web pages you have viewed. It also deletes all the addresses used by the AutoComplete feature.

Second, you can control the number of days that URLs are kept in the history. To do this, simply change the number. However, you should be aware that setting the number to 0 will *not* keep Internet Explorer from creating a history. Sorry, but Microsoft in their infinite wisdom has decreed that you can't turn off this feature.

When you are finished, click on the OK button to close the Internet Options window.

If you want, there is a way to selectively delete part of your history. Open the history by clicking on the History button. You can now right-click on any item and choose Delete from the pop-up menu.

Internet Explorer keeps your history in the folder:

`C:\Windows\History`

(If you are using Windows 2000 or Windows NT, the location will be a bit different. See Chapter 4 for the details.)

If you know how to use Windows Explorer (which I'll discuss later in the chapter), you can navigate to this directory and clean it out yourself. Although there is no real advantage to doing this — compared to clearing out the history from within Internet Explorer — showing that you know how to use Windows Explorer is a good way to impress someone on a first date.

Controlling AutoComplete

To control the AutoComplete feature, pull down the Tools menu and select Internet Options. This will open a new window. Click on the Content tab near the top of this window. Within the "Personal information" section, click on the AutoComplete button. You will now see another window containing the settings that allow you to control AutoComplete.

There are two things you can do. First, you can specify what type of AutoComplete information your browser should maintain. There are three types of information:

- Web addresses (when you type a URL in the Address bar)
- Forms (when a Web page asks you to specify information)
- User names and passwords

You can turn each of these off and on as you wish. For maximum privacy, turn them all off. If you don't turn them all off, you can maintain your privacy by deleting whatever AutoComplete information has accumulated.

To delete the Web address information, you clear the history, as I described in the previous section.

To delete the information that you have typed into forms, click on the Clear Forms button.

To delete all the passwords you have entered, click on the Clear Passwords button.

When you are finished, click on the OK button to close this window. Then click on the OK button to close the Internet Options window.

Aside from the AutoComplete options I just described, there are two more options in a completely different location. To see these options, you start the same way: pull down the Tools menu and select Internet Options. This time, however, click on the Advanced tab. Within the Settings box, scroll down to the bottom of the Browsing section. You will see two settings related to Auto-Control, which you can turn on or off.

The first setting is "Use inline AutoComplete for Web Addresses". This setting controls whether or not AutoComplete is active when you type a URL into the Address Bar.

You might ask, what is the difference between this off/on switch and the other off/on switch, the one you access via the Content page? The difference is subtle. This switch tells the browser to complete a URL for you as you type it in the Address Bar. The other switch tells the browser not only to complete the URL, but also to show you a list of similar URLs that you have previously typed.

I know this is confusing (and the next time I see Bill Gates, you can be sure I will mention it). Just think of it this way: if you want to inactivate AutoComplete, you need to turn off two separate switches.

The second AutoComplete setting on the Advanced page is "Use inline AutoComplete in Windows Explorer". (We'll talk about Windows Explorer in the next section.) This setting is supposed to allow you to turn on or off the AutoComplete feature when you type the name of one of your folders or files into the Internet Explorer Address Bar. I say "supposed to", because this option doesn't really do much of anything, so you can ignore it.

(Again, this is something I am going to have to mention to Bill Gates.)

Disks and Discs

At this point, I would like to introduce you to an important tool called Windows Explorer, the program that you use to manipulate the files and folders on your computer. However, before we get to the details, I need to cover some background material, starting with disks: the devices that are used to store data on your computer.

Long-term data storage is supplied by various types of DISKS (sometimes referred to as DISCS), the most important of which are floppy disks, hard disks and CDs.

To understand the floppy/hard disk terminology, we have to go back to August 1981, when IBM introduced the first PC. At the time, the only permanent data storage was provided by large (5.25 inches), thin, removable disks. These disks were flexible and, as such, were called FLOPPY DISKS or FLOPPIES. In August 1984, the IBM PC AT computer introduced a new type of floppy disk. The new floppy was smaller, 3.5 inches, could hold more data, and was encased in a hard protective plastic shell. Since then, floppy disk technology has improved, but the basic design hasn't changed much. Today's floppies look pretty much the same as they did in 1984.

The reason that floppy disk technology hasn't changed all that much is because, early on, it was overtaken by a more important technology. In March 1982, IBM announced the PC XT, the first personal computer with a HARD DISK. This was a medium-sized box inside the computer, that provided a large amount of fast, permanent data storage. This device was faster and could hold a lot more data than a floppy disk. Today, all computers have a hard disk; in fact, the hard disk on your computer is where all your programs and data are stored. The name "hard disk" comes from the fact that, inside the device, data is stored on several hard, disc-shaped plates.

Although a modern floppy disk has a hard shell, if you break it open, you will see that, inside, the data is stored on a very thin, round, brown surface that is, indeed, floppy. (If you have never opened a floppy disk, you should do so, just for fun. Find an old floppy that you can afford to throw away, and put a label on it that says "Nuclear Research Data". Then gather a bunch of people around you and say, "Have you ever wondered what is inside of these things?", and rip open the plastic shell. Your friends will be more impressed than you can imagine.)

If you work in a company with a network, there is a good chance that all or part of your disk storage is provided centrally, by a FILE SERVER. A file server is a special computer with a large amount of disk storage, that is made available to the various users on the network. The advantage of file servers — large networks might have several of them — is that they can be set up to be fast and extra reliable. Moreover, because they are maintained centrally, they can be backed up regularly by the network administrator.

The third important type of data storage is provided by CDs. Although all CDs look the same, there are actually five different types that are used with computers.

First, there are regular music CDs, the type that were originally designed for CD players. Modern computers can read such discs and play music from them.

Second, there are CD-ROMs. These are CDs that hold computer data. When you buy a program that comes on a CD, you are getting a CD-ROM. (The name stands for "read-only memory", an old-fashioned term that indicates that the data is permanent and can't be changed.)

The third type of CD is the DVD. This type of CD is used to distribute movies. Originally, the name stood for Digital Video Disc, but for marketing reasons, the DVD industry changed the name to Digital Versatile Disc.

The last two types of CDs are CD-Rs and CD-RWs. (The names stand for "readable" and "rewritable".) Both CD-Rs and CD-RWs are used to create your own CDs. The difference is that CD-Rs are cheaper, but you can only write on them once. Once you put data on them, the data can be deleted, but not changed. You use CD-Rs when you want to create your own music CDs or CD-ROMs.

CD-RWs cost more than CD-Rs, but you can change the data as much as you want. Thus, they provide long-term, removable storage, sort of like super floppy disks. This makes them perfect for storing backups (copies) of important data. You can copy important data to a CD-RW, and then store the disc in a safe place away from the computer.

The device that reads and writes data to a disk is called a DRIVE. Most computers come with a floppy disk drive and a CD drive. Consumer-oriented computers, such as the ones that are sold in stores, come with a CD drive that reads music CDs, CD-ROMs and DVDs. Professional computers, such as the ones used in companies, don't usually have DVD capabilities.

In all computers, it takes a special type of CD drive, called a CD-RW drive, to read and write CD-Rs and CD-RWs. Some computers come with such a drive, although many do not. If your computer doesn't have one, you will have to add the drive yourself. If you are buying a new computer, a CD-RW drive is definitely something you should have, because it will allow you to make your own music CDs and use CD-RWs for backups.

Note: When we talk about floppies and hard disks, we refer to them as disks. This dates back to the early 1980s, when IBM referred to floppy disks as "diskettes". When we talk about CDs, however, we call them discs.

How Data is Measured on a Disk

We measure the storage capacity of a disk in BYTES. Without getting too technical, we can say that 1 byte can hold 1 character of data. Thus, to store the name of my cat, "The Little Nipper", would require 17 bytes. (Each space counts as a single character.) Storing numbers is a bit different, and again I don't want to be too technical. As a general rule, it takes either 2 or 4 bytes to store a number, depending on the size of the number.

Disks can hold millions or billions of bytes, so to make it easy, we use the prefixes from the metric system. The ones we use the most are the abbreviations for thousand, million and billion:

1 KB = 1 kilobyte = 1,000 bytes

1 MB = 1 megabyte = 1,000,000 bytes

1 GB = 1 gigabyte = 1,000,000,000 bytes

In the PC world, typical hard disks come in sizes from 30 GB to 100 GB (30 to 100 billion bytes). To put this in perspective, the very first PC, in 1981, came with floppy disks that could hold 360 KB (360 thousand bytes). In 1982, the very first PC hard disk could store 10 MB (10 million bytes) of data.

The amount of data a CD can hold depends on the type of CD. Music CDs hold 740 MBs of data. DVDs hold a lot more, from 4.4 to 15.9 GB, depending on the type of DVD.

CD-RWs and CD-Rs can hold 650 MB of data. However, before CD-RWs can be used, the discs must be prepared in a certain way (called FORMATTING), which takes up some of the space. A formatted CD-RW can hold 530 MB of data (which is still a lot).

Floppy disks hold 1.44 MB, which hasn't changed for years. Because hard disk and CD technology developed so quickly in the mid-1980s, there wasn't a need to enhance the storage capacity of the standard floppy.

Strange Metric Terminology

In the previous section, I talked about the metric terminology we use to describe the storage capacity of disks. We talked about kilobytes, megabytes and gigabytes. Just for fun, I thought you might be interested in seeing how high the terminology can take us. Here's a complete list:

- 1 Kilobyte = thousand bytes
  1,000 bytes

- 1 Megabyte = million bytes
  1,000,000 bytes
- 1 Gigabyte = billion bytes
  1,000,000,000 bytes
- 1 Terabyte = trillion bytes
  1,000,000,000,000 bytes
- 1 Petabyte = quadrillion bytes
  1,000,000,000,000,000 bytes
- 1 Exabyte = quintillion bytes
  1,000,000,000,000,000,000 bytes
- 1 Zettabyte = sextillion bytes
  1,000,000,000,000,000,000,000 bytes
- 1 Yottabyte = septillion bytes
  1,000,000,000,000,000,000,000,000 bytes

At this point, I bet you are asking, what about the very small numbers? Don't they have metric prefixes? They certainly do. To illustrate them, I'll use time measurements: a thousandth of a second is a millisecond, a millionth of a second in a microsecond, and so on.

- 1 Millisecond = thousandth of a second
  1/1,000 of a second
- 1 Microsecond = millionth of a second
  1/1,000,000 of a second
- 1 Nanosecond = billionth of a second
  1/1,000,000,000 of a second
- 1 Picosecond = trillionth of a second
  1/1,000,000,000,000 of a second
- 1 Femtosecond = quadrillionth of a second
  1/1,000,000,000,000,000 of a second
- 1 Attosecond = quintillionth of a second
  1/1,000,000,000,000,000,000 of a second
- 1 Zeptosecond = sextillionth of a second
  1/1,000,000,000,000,000,000,000 of a second

- 1 Yoctosecond = septillionth of a second
  1/1,000,000,000,000,000,000,000,000 of a second

To understand just how small these numbers really are, consider this. If Bill Gates were to give away a tenth of a penny every femtosecond, he would be completely broke in 99.4 picoseconds.

Files and Folders

Having strayed for a bit, let's get back on track by discussing Windows Explorer, a tool that helps you maintain the contents of your hard disk. Windows Explorer is important because, when you use the Net, many of the actions you need to take to protect your privacy require you to manipulate files and folders, and to do so, you need to use Windows Explorer.

However, before we can talk about Windows Explorer, I'd like to take a moment to go over the basic ideas concerning files and folders.

On any disk, data is organized into FILES, each of which has a name. File names consist of two parts, separated by a . (period) character. The second part, called the EXTENSION, tells us what type of data is contained in the file. For example, here are two typical file names:

```
harley.jpg
happy-birthday.mp3
```

In this case, the extension of the first file is **jpg**, and the extension of the second file is **mp3**.

There are a great many different file extensions, most of which you will never have to worry about. The following table shows the most common file extensions and what they mean. Notice that I have also indicated the pronunciation. This is so that, when you talk to people, they will realize you know what you are talking about. Hint: When you pronounce file names, be aware that the period is pronounced as "dot" (just as with Internet addresses). For example, the file names above would be pronounced "harley dot jay-peg" and "happy birthday dot m-p-3".

Extension	Pronunciation	Meaning
html	"h-t-m-l"	Web page
htm	"h-t-m"	Web page
asp	"a-s-p"	Web page generated in a special way
gif	"giff" or "jiff"	Picture stored in GIF format
jpg	"jay-peg"	Picture stored in JPEG format
txt	"t-x-t" or "text"	Plain text
zip	"zip"	Compressed collection of files
exe	"e-x-e" or "exy"	Executable program
com	"comm"	Executable program
wav	"wave"	Sound/music file
mp3	"m-p-3" or "em-peg"	Music file
doc	"doc"	Microsoft Word document

A hard disk can hold, literally, tens of thousands of files, far too many to keep track of easily. For this reason, files are organized into what are called FOLDERS or DIRECTORIES. For instance, you might store all your mp3 files in a folder named Music.

To help you organize your files and folders, you can create SUB-FOLDERS (also called SUB-DIRECTORIES) within other folders. For example, let's say you have a great many music files, too many to organize within a single folder. You might create several sub-folders called, Big-band, Jazz, Rock and Classical, and place them within the Music folder. You could then put each music file into the appropriate sub-folder.

With the computer systems that preceded Windows (for example, Unix and DOS), people talked about directories and sub-directories. However, when the first version of Windows debuted (November 1983), Microsoft decided to use the name "folders", which they took from the Macintosh. The choice was based on the belief that most people were not very smart, and the idea of folders would be easier to understand than the idea of directories.

Actually, disk folders are nothing at all like the paper folders we use in an office, and the analogy is actually more confusing than helpful. Still, the name stuck, and today, "folder" and "directory" are synonymous. Hint: If you want to sound like a nerd, talk about directories. If you want to sound like a normal person, talk about folders. If you want to sound really cool, switch back and forth depending on whether or not you are talking to a nerd.

The last thing I want to mention is the way in which we write down a file name. Within this system, we specify the name of the disk on which the file resides, followed by the relevant folder and sub-folders, followed by the name of the file, including the extension. This type of specification is called a PATHNAME or a PATH. Here is an example:

`C:\Music\Big-band\in-the-mood.mp3`

To understand this name, you need to know several things. First, within Windows, each disk has its own name. A disk name consists of a single letter followed by a **:** (colon) character. The floppy disk is called **A:**, and the hard disk is **C:**. (In the olden days, when many computers had two floppy disk drives, the name **B:** was reserved for a second floppy.) Your CD will probably be **D:** or **E:**.

Thus, in the address above, we can see that the file resides on the hard disk named **C:**.

After the name of the disk comes a series of folders and sub-folders, leading to the one in which the file resides. To separate the disk name and the various folders, we use **** (backslash) characters. (On a standard U.S. keyboard, the backslash is the character above the Enter key.)

So, now you can understand the pathname above. It tells you that the **C:** disk contains a folder named **Music**; within this folder lies a sub-folder named **Big-band**; and within that folder is the file **in-the-mood.mpg**.

Some people prefer to read pathnames from right to left. In this case, you could say that the file named **in-the-mood.mpg** lies in the **Big-band** folder, which lies in the **Music** folder, which is on the **c:** disk.

When it comes to folder and file names, Windows does not distinguish between UPPER CASE (capital letters) and LOWER CASE (small letters). For example, as far as Windows is concerned, the following three pathnames are equivalent:

```
C:\Documents\Stories\Lydia.doc
C:\DOCUMENTS\STORIES\LYDIA.DOC
c:\documents\stories\lydia.doc
```

If you are at all obsessive, you will want to impose a system of your own for using upper and lower case letters when you create files and folders. On my computer, I use all lower case for file names, and a single upper case letter followed by lower case for folder names. For example, I would write the previous pathname as:

```
C:\Documents\Stories\lydia.doc
```

This works well for me, and you may want to adopt the same convention for yourself.

Windows Explorer

WINDOWS EXPLORER is the name of the program that you use to organize how data is stored on your computer. You can use Windows Explorer to move, copy, rename, delete and create files and folders.

Windows Explorer is built into Windows. To start the program, click on the Start button, select Programs, and then click on Windows Explorer.

You may not be aware of it, but Windows Explorer and Internet Explorer are linked to one another. For instance, you can type a URL into Windows Explorer and it will show you a Web page. Or you can type a folder address into Internet Explorer and it will show you the contents of that folder.

Why is this the case? Because Microsoft made a strategic decision some time ago to integrate Windows with the Internet. Toward this end, they tied together Windows Explorer and Internet Explorer. The idea is that the Windows/Internet Explorer hybrid should allow you to look at whatever information you need — on your hard disk, on your network, or on the Internet — using a simple, consistent interface.

As a result of this forced marriage, both Windows Explorer and Internet Explorer are large, unwieldy, awkward programs that are difficult to learn and particularly unenjoyable to use. (Well-designed programs are fun to use.) I can tell you now that there will be times, as you use Windows Explorer, when you will find yourself performing mindless repetitive actions. There will also be times when you will want to perform a conceptually simple operation, and it will take you a great many mouse clicks or keystrokes. At such times, remember that all smart people dislike Windows Explorer. Put simply, it sucks.

I realize that, unless you have experience with different types of computer systems, you may have trouble appreciating my observations. If you have only used Windows (or a Macintosh, for that matter), you have never really experienced what it is like to use a well-designed computer system, suitable for smart people.

I mention all this because, for better or for worse, Windows Explorer is a crucial program, and you do need to learn how to use it well. Even if you use your computer only to access the Internet, you will find it valuable to be able to look at your files and folders, and to manipulate them as you see fit. Having these skills are crucial if you want to have control over your working environment.

I wish I could show you, in detail, how to use Windows Explorer. Unfortunately, learning how to use the program — especially learning how to use it well — is a problem. The built-in help is confusing and incomplete, and there is no simple way to teach yourself the details.

To help you, I have five general hints. First, if you know someone who is very good at Windows, ask him or her to teach you how to use Windows Explorer, even if you have to use a bribe. (A good bribe would be a copy of one of my books.)

Second, spend some time experimenting with the program. Pull down each menu and examine all the items. Try different things and see what happens. Practice using the short-cut keys and it won't be long until you memorize them. Eventually, you'll figure out how to use the program well. Once you do, teach someone else. (Teaching another person is the best way to really understand the details.)

The next hint is important when you are deleting. To delete one or more files or folders, start by using your mouse to select the items you want to delete. You now have three choices, and they all have the same effect. Either press the Delete key, or pull down the File menu and select Delete, or right-click on the items and select Delete from the pop-up menu.

You might think that when you delete a file it is gone for good, but that is not the case. When you delete a file, it only seems to vanish. It really goes to a special folder with the silly name of RECYCLE BIN. At any time, you can open your Recycle Bin, and examine any of your previously "deleted" files or folders. If you want, you can even restore a file, or folder to its original location. (To do so, select the item, pull down the File menu and select Restore.)

(At this point, you might want to take a moment to relate this system to your own existence. The philosophical implications are profound.)

The Recycle Bin is handy when you have changed your mind about deleting an item and you want it back. If you delete files a lot, you will eventually be glad there is a Recycle Bin to give you a second chance. However, the Recycle Bin is also a threat to your privacy, because anyone with access to your computer can examine any of the files you think you have deleted.

So, how do you get rid of a file or folder permanently? After you delete it from its original location, you must go to the Recycle Bin and delete it again. Be careful, though. Once you delete an item from the Recycle Bin, the item is gone for good and there is no way to get it back. If you want to delete the entire contents of the Recycle Bin, there is an easy way. Open it, and then pull down the File menu and select Empty Recycle Bin.

As you might imagine, it is a bother to have to delete something twice just to get rid of it permanently, so here is a shortcut that very few people know about. First select the files or folders you want to delete, then hold down the Shift key as you perform the deletion. This causes the items to be deleted without being sent to the Recycle Bin.

The fourth Windows Explorer hint has to do with the right-mouse button. Within Windows Explorer — and all Microsoft programs, for that matter — you can perform various actions by clicking the right mouse button. Doing so will bring up a list of actions that are appropriate to the context in which you are working, and you can then select the action you want. If you right-click on a file name, for example, you will get a completely different menu than if you right-click on an empty area of the window. Try it and see for yourself; then experiment.

The last hint applies when you are moving or copying files from one folder or disk to another. In such cases, it is often helpful to start two copies of Windows Explorer. Use one to show you the source folder, and another to show you the destination folder. It is then a simple matter to select one or more files from the source folder and then drag them to the destination folder. (To select a file, click on it. To select several files, hold down the Ctrl key and click on each file in turn.) To drag a selection, hold down either the left or right mouse button and move the mouse.

If you hold down the left mouse button as you drag one or more files, there are two possibilities. If the source and destination folders are on the same disk, Windows Explorer will move the files. If the source and destination folders are on different disks, Windows Explorer will copy the files. (Experiment and you will see what I mean.)

For more control, hold down the right mouse button as you drag a selection. When you are finished dragging, Windows Explorer will give you a choice: you can either move, copy or create a shortcut.

A SHORTCUT is something that points to a file, but is not the actual file. Creating a shortcut allows you to access a file from more than one location. For example, close or minimize all the windows that are currently open on your computer. What you are now looking at, the background, is called your DESKTOP. Notice that your desktop contains some ICONS (small pictures). These are all shortcuts. If you double-click on an icon, Windows will start the program or open the file that is associated with that shortcut.

Windows Explorer Options

My final advice about Windows Explorer has to do with adjusting your working environment. Within the program, it is possible to set certain preferences. Here are instructions for setting these options in a way that is suitable for a smart person. By default, Microsoft sets them so as to be appropriate for a stupid person. (I'm not kidding. They do it on purpose.)

The following instructions might be a bit different on your computer, depending on what version of Windows you are using. However, the general ideas will be the same, and it won't be hard to figure out what to do.

To start, pull down the View menu and select Details.

Then pull down the View menu (on some systems the Tools menu) again and select Folder Options. This will open up a new window, named Folder Options, that will have three pages: General, View and File Types. Start on the General page.

Under Windows Desktop Update, click on Custom. Then click on the Settings button. This will open a new window named "Custom Settings". Select the following options:

- Use Windows classic desktop
- Open each folder in its own window
- (View Web content) Only for folders where I select "as Web Page"
- Double-click to open an item.

Hint: When you get really good at Windows Explorer, try changing this last option to "Single-click".

Click the OK button to close the Window. You will now return to the Folders Options Window.

Click on the View tab to bring up the View page. Under Folder Views, click on "Like Current Folder". The program will ask you to confirm your choice. Click on Yes.

Now look under "Advanced settings", where you will see a number of options that you can turn off and on. You won't be able to see all of them at once, but you can pull down the bar to the right in order to view the bottom part of the list.

Under the "Files and Folders" heading, make sure the following options are turned *on*:

- Display the full path in title bar
- Hidden files: Show all files
- Show file attributes in Detail View

Now make sure the following options are turned *off*:

- Hide file extensions for known file types
- Remember each folder's view settings

Next, under the "Visual Settings" heading, make sure the following options are turned *on*:

- Show window contents while dragging
- Smooth edges of screen fonts

To finish, click on the Close button to close the window.

Flushing the Cache

As I explained earlier in the chapter, the cache is a special folder where your browser keeps a copy of all the files that it has downloaded from the Net on your behalf. This includes all the content of the Web pages you have looked at, including all the pictures. The cache is actually a folder with the name **Temporary Internet**

Files. To maintain your privacy, you need to empty your cache. When you do this, we say you flush the cache.

To flush your cache, pull down the Tools menu and select Internet Options. This will open a new window, and within this window, you will be looking at the General page. To flush your cache, click on the Delete Files button in the Temporary Internet Files section. As soon as you do this, Internet Explorer will delete all the files in your cache.

Although flushing your cache is simple, it is a bother. If you are very concerned about your privacy, you will have to remember to flush the cache every time you finish using your browser. However, there is a way to have this happen automatically.

Pull down the Tools menu and select Internet Options. Now click on the Advanced tab. Within the Settings box, scroll down to the section named Security. Within this section, turn on the option "Empty Temporary Internet Files folder when browser is closed". Then press the OK button to close the window. From now on, every time you close your browser, the contents of your cache will vanish automatically, like the last breath of dew on the petals of a field of daisies as the sun rises in the early morning.

Remember, however, you are not fully protected. You must still empty your browser history, and that can't be done as easily. You will have to do that manually. (See the instructions earlier in the chapter.)

4

Taking Control

If you are worried about a lack of privacy, you must take steps to protect yourself.

Taking Control

Clients and Servers

As you use the Web, visiting one Web site after another, have you ever wondered if there is a way the remote computers can keep track of your activities? The answer is, yes, to a limited extent, they can. They do this by using a facility called cookies. To appreciate how cookies work, however, you need to understand the idea of clients and servers, so let's take a moment to talk about them first.

In Chapter 1, I explained that the Internet is a large, worldwide network, in which data is transported in packets using a system called TCP/IP. This is certainly one way to understand the Net, and, in a technical sense, it is actually a definition of the Internet. From a functional point of view, however, there is a better way to describe the Net: as a system in which all communication takes place between two type of programs, clients and servers.

A SERVER is a program that provides a specific service over the Internet. A CLIENT is a program that requests a service.

Here is a common example. To read email messages, you use a program, called a MAIL CLIENT, that runs on your computer. The most common mail clients are Microsoft Outlook and Outlook Express, Netscape Messenger, and Eudora. (If you use AOL, it works in a different way — using a Web-based mail system — that I will explain later in the chapter.)

When people send you messages, they don't go to your computer directly. Rather, they are stored on a remote computer by a program called a MAIL SERVER. To check your mail, your mail client contacts the mail server and asks if there are any messages waiting for you. If so, the mail server sends the messages to your computer, where your mail client displays them for you.

When you send an email message, the process works in reverse. You use your mail client to compose the message. Once it is finished, your mail client sends the message to the mail server. The mail server then sees that your message is delivered properly (by sending it to the mail server of the person to whom the message is addressed).

Strictly speaking, a server is a program. However, we also use the term to refer to the actual computer on which the server program is running. For example, say that you are taking a tour of a large company. As you visit a room filled with computers, the tour guide points to one of the machines and says, "That is our mail server."

You will notice that the mail client/server system actually uses two types of servers: one to accept incoming mail, and one to send outgoing mail. Indeed, these are actually two different server programs. The one that sends incoming mail to your client program is called a POP SERVER. (The name stands for "Post Office Protocol".) The server that accepts your outgoing mail and delivers it for you is called an SMTP SERVER. (The name stands for "Simple Mail Transfer Protocol".)

If you have ever set up a brand new mail program, you will know that one of the things you have to do is specify the name of the computer that houses your POP server and your SMTP server. In most cases, the POP server and the SMTP server both run on the same computer (which, is often referred to, generically, as the "mail server"). When you use the Internet from home, your mail server is maintained by your ISP. When you use the Internet at work, your mail server is maintained by your company.

Web Clients and Servers

Now that you understand the basic idea of clients and servers, let's talk about what happens when you use the Web.

To use the Web you need a Web client program. Such programs are known as BROWSERS, because, in the olden days, it was thought that people would use their Web clients to browse the Web (as many people do). The most popular browsers are INTERNET EXPLORER (from Microsoft) and NETSCAPE (from AOL).

In order for you to look at a Web page, your browser must contact a Web server and request the data for that particular page. The server then sends the data to your browser, which displays the page for you.

As I mentioned above, the term "server" is used in two ways: to refer to the program that communicates with your browser, and to refer to the computer in which that program runs. Thus, we can say that the Web server (a program) runs on a Web server (the computer).

This, by the way, is a typical example why it can be so hard for normal people to understand the nuances of computers and the Internet. Programmers will often use the same term in two similar, but different, ways. In this case, "server" can refer to either a computer or a program. Although programmers understand, by context, what is meant when the word "server" is used, normal people find it easy to be confused.

Let's consider an example. Here is the URL (address) of my Web site:

`http://www.harley.com`

The second part of the URL, **www.harley.com**, is the name of a computer. This computer — my Web server — runs a Web server program. When you tell your browser that you want to look at my Web site — say, by typing the URL in your Address Bar, or by clicking on a link to the site — your browser sends a message to the computer named **www.harley.com**. When the message arrives, it is processed by the Web server program, which then sends the appropriate data back to your browser.

Web-Based Email

Broadly speaking, there are two ways in which you can use email services. You can use either a separate mail program as a client, or your Web browser as a client.

With both systems, you still need a mail server to send and receive mail on your behalf. The mail server resides on a remote computer and is maintained by your ISP or — when you use mail at work — by your company.

With the first system, you run a mail client on your computer, and the client communicates with the remote mail server on your behalf. (As I mentioned earlier, the most common mail clients are Microsoft Outlook and Outlook Express, Netscape Messenger, and Eudora.)

With a Web-based mail system, you use your browser as a client, and everything you do with your messages — reading, replying, composing, and so on — is presented to you on Web pages. This is the system that is used by the many free, Web-based mail systems. For example, Hotmail, which is owned by Microsoft, works in this way.

From a technical point of view, the biggest difference between a standard client/server mail system and a Web-based mail system lies in where the messages are stored. When you use a regular mail client, your messages are downloaded from the server to your computer. Once the messages are on your computer, it is fast and easy to manipulate them. Moreover, you can keep them as long as you want, and dispose of them as you wish. You also have maximum privacy: as long as no one else has access to your computer.

With a Web-based system, the messages always stay on the remote server, which makes everything slower. Moreover, using Web-based mail is more awkward because browsers are not designed to be mail clients. When you use a separate mail client, you are using a program that was designed specifically to handle mail and, as such, has more sophisticated capabilities than a general-purpose Web browser.

Web-based systems, however, do have an important advantage. Because you don't need a special program, you can check your mail from any computer that has a browser. This is handy if you travel or — as we will see in the next section — if you want to keep your email private from other people.

AOL, by the way, uses both systems. The AOL software (which is distributed free) contains a mail client. This client, which runs on your computer, contacts the AOL mail server on your behalf whenever you want to send and receive mail. In addition, you can also check your AOL mail by using an ordinary browser, as with other Web-based email.

In both cases, the messages stay on the remote AOL server. They are not downloaded to your computer, even when you use the mail client. This is why you can check your AOL mail from any computer that has Internet access, whether or not it has the AOL software installed. It is also the reason why checking your AOL mail is a slow, clunky experience, no matter what system you use.

How Private is Web-Based Email?

When you use a regular mail client, the program runs on your computer, and every time you check your mail, the incoming messages are downloaded to your computer. This means that anyone with access to your computer can use your mail program to read all your messages. Moreover, whenever you send messages, copies are kept on your computer, so someone using your computer can also see all your outgoing messages. For that matter, such a person could even use your program to send email to other people, and it would look as if the mail came from you.

Web-based mail systems do not keep any messages on your computer. Moreover, they require you to log in with a user name and password before you can use the system. This means that no one can look at your mail unless they have your password. For these reasons, many people use a Web-based mail system for privacy.

As you might expect, this is common in the workplace, where people do not want to use their work address for personal mail. When you use your company's email system, all your messages go through the company mail server, which means that the company has access to your communications.

Moreover, there is another consideration. It is common practice for network administrators to back up the data on their computers. This involves copying the data from the hard disks to tapes or CDs, which are kept in long-term storage. If something goes wrong with a hard disk, or if information is lost by accident, it is a simple matter to recover the information from the backup.

This means that, as a matter of course, all the messages on the mail server are backed up regularly. So even after you read and delete your messages, they could be stored indefinitely on a backup tape, where they can be recovered anytime the company chooses to do so. To be sure, no one is going to go to the trouble of restoring old messages without an important reason, but if it happens that you fall out of favor with the company, it wouldn't be hard for them to prove that you were using company resources for personal mail (if, indeed, you were). If you use a Web-based system for personal mail, your company does not have direct access to your messages.

However… don't think you are completely safe. Some companies use monitoring programs, which record everything you do on the Net. If your company has such a program, you can bet it is keeping track of your email as well as your Web activity.

Moreover, it's not as hard as you might think to see what someone has been up to with a Web-based mail account. True, you need a user name and password to access the account, but that won't stop a smart investigator. Here is an example.

I know someone who was hiding his activities (actually, a double life) by using what he thought were private email accounts and a list of fake names. After he left the company, an investigator began to check out the fellow's computer. Using the computer, the investigator typed the address of a well-known, free Web-based email system. The system prompted the investigator to enter a user name and password.

As the investigator started to type a user name, the browser (Internet Explorer) cooperated by using its AutoComplete function to list all the names the employee had ever typed into the form on that particular Web page. In an instant, the investigator knew all the fake names the fellow had been using.

Finding the passwords wasn't that hard. The designers of Web-based systems know that many people forget their passwords, so they always provide ways to get around the problem. A common feature is to allow someone to request that a message be sent to them with their user name and password. The message is sent to the email address the person used when he first set up the account.

(When you set up a Web-based mail account, you must furnish information about yourself, including a valid email address. This process is called REGISTERING. The companies that provide these services know that many people use them for questionable purposes. To protect themselves, the companies do their best to ensure that they have a real name and email address for each account.)

Thus, if an ex-employee specified a company email address when he or she registered the Web-based mail account, it is easy for an investigator to get the user name and password. All he has to do is request the information to be sent to the registered email address.

In this case, it was even easier. Some Web-based services have another way to help you if you forget your password. When you register, you make up a question. Later, if you forget your password, the system will ask you that question. If you answer successfully, you will be automatically logged in. So, all the investigator had to do was tell the system he had forgotten the password. After a few tries, the investigator was able to guess the answer to the question, and was logged in to the account. (And, believe me, it was hot stuff!)

It is common for people to use Web-based mail accounts at work in order to send and receive private email, and as you can see, it's not as private as you might think (or hope). But work isn't the only place you will find people trying to hide their activities. Many people use such email accounts at home, in order to keep secrets from a husband, wife or significant other. (I know of a number of people who do this regularly.) Children also use Web-based email accounts to keep their messages safe from the prying eyes of their parents.

If you use a home computer, anyone in the household can access your programs. In particular, anyone can start your mail program and read all your messages. (More than one relationship has broken up in this way.) However, if you use a Web-based mail system, all the messages are stored remotely, and there is no way for an unsuspecting spouse to accidentally (or purposely) find your secret messages. In fact, many people have completely secret Internet personalities that their spouses know nothing about. This phenomenon is a lot more common than you might think, and it is one of the ways in which the Internet can put a great deal of strain on a relationship. We'll talk about all of this more in Chapter 14.

For now, all I will say is that, if you are doing this, you shouldn't be, and you're not as safe as you think you are (especially if your spouse, girlfriend, boyfriend or parents are smart and persistent).

How Private is Regular Email?

As we discussed above, when you use Web-based email, your browser acts as a mail client, and your messages stay on a remote server that is beyond your control.

Regular email works differently in two important ways. First, your client is a dedicated mail program that runs on your own computer. (The most common mail programs are Microsoft Outlook and Outlook Express, Netscape Messenger, and Eudora.) Such programs are designed specifically for email and, as such, are much better tools for mail handling than are browsers. In particular, mail programs are faster and more powerful.

Second, when you use a mail program, your messages are copied from the server to your computer, and then deleted from the server. This means that you have a lot more control. You can keep your messages indefinitely. It is up to you when to delete them. In the meantime they are not stored on the server, so you have control over your own privacy.

In general, I prefer regular email to Web-based mail, because I like using a real mail program (not a browser), and I like to control how long my messages are saved. However, if other people have access to your computer, there can be a privacy problem because, when you are not around, another person can simply start your mail program and look at all the messages.

If you are worried about a lack of privacy, you must take steps to make sure this doesn't happen. The best policy is to make sure that there are never any messages lying around that you would not want other people to read. Even if you think no one in your house or at work would deliberately spy on you, it could happen by accident.

Let's be honest. Let's say a friend of yours is away and you need to use his computer for a moment (say, to find a place to buy a

Harley Hahn book). What would you do if his mail program was open and you happened to see a message with a provocative subject? ("See you tonight, don't tell anyone" or "Your embezzlement was discovered".)

If you have ever looked through someone else's mail, you will find out pretty quickly that it is almost always a boring experience. On the other hand, it's human nature to want to look at things you are not supposed to see, so let's be realistic. If someone has the chance, eventually, they are going to look at your mail, so if privacy is crucial, you need to be prepared.

Within your mail program, messages are kept in what are called FOLDERS (Microsoft Outlook and Netscape Messenger) or MAILBOXES (Eudora). These are not the same thing as the folders used by Windows to hold files. (A Windows folder contains separate files. A mail folder is actually one large file containing a number of messages.) Moreover, the only way to manipulate mail folders is from within the mail program itself; you can't use Windows Explorer.

All mail programs have a few standard folders, and you can create more if you need them. Here are the names of the standard folders and what they are used for.

Outlook	Messenger	Eudora	
Inbox	Inbox	In	Incoming messages that have not been processed
Drafts	Drafts	Out	Unfinished messages that have not been sent
Outbox	Unsent Messages	Out	Finished messages that have not been sent
Sent Items	Sent	Out	Messages that have been sent
Deleted Items	Trash	Trash	Deleted messages

How these folders are used varies somewhat from one program to another. However, when it comes to privacy, there are two important things you must remember. First, anyone with access to your computer can look at all your mail folders. They can see not only what is waiting in your inbox, but all the mail you have sent or received. At work, you should be aware that it is possible for a network administrator to check your mailboxes over the network, without even being near your computer.

The second important point is that when you delete messages, they are not removed permanently. They are simply moved to your Deleted Items/Trash folder. This means that to remove a file permanently, you must first delete it from its original folder, and then delete it a second time from the Deleted Items folder.

If you are serious about privacy, never forget to empty your Deleted Items folder. If someone is snooping on you, that is the first place they will look.

Sneaky Browser Tricks: Cookies

Now that we have discussed Web clients (browsers) and Web servers, let's return to the question of privacy I raised earlier in the chapter. Is it possible for Web servers to keep track of your activities? If so, this is important, because many Web servers are maintained by companies who do not care about your personal privacy. If a company can track what you do, you are going to have to look out for yourself.

The answer is yes. Web servers can, to a limited degree, keep track of what you do on the Web. They do so by using what are called "cookies".

A COOKIE is data that is placed on your computer by a Web server. The data consists of several lines of text, and is stored in a special folder on your hard disk. Later, that Web server — or in some cases, a different Web server — can retrieve the cookie, examine it, and even leave another one. In most cases, you have no idea that any of this is happening. You visit a Web site, never dreaming that the remote computer is actually putting information on your hard disk.

Why is this necessary? Your browser and the remote Web servers you access are not connected permanently: they simply pass information back and forth as necessary. Each time you click on a link, your browser sends a request for data to a remote Web server. However, each request is independent of any previous communication. Thus, if a Web server needs to keep track of what you are doing, it must leave cookies for itself on your computer. A copy of the cookies is sent back whenever you click on a link pointing to that server.

The idea behind a cookie is to enable Web servers to relate a previous transaction to a later one. Consider this analogy. You drive into a parking lot and are given a ticket on which the time and date are stamped. When you leave, you must show the ticket, which is then used to determine how much you should pay. In this case, the ticket is acting like a cookie.

The name "cookie", as used on the Web, came from an operating system named Unix (a master control program that is much older than Windows). Within Unix, a program can store a special type of data to be read later. Such data is called a "magic cookie". No one knows the exact origin of the term, but clearly, it was chosen to be whimsical.

Cookies on the Web are used for various purposes. The programmers who create Web sites have developed ingenious ways to use cookies to track your movements on the Web, and to remember your preferences and your identity.

All of this, of course, raises questions of privacy. How do you feel about companies being able to track your movements on the Web, even in a limited way? How do you feel about companies accumulating information about you and your purchases in order to sell you things more effectively?

The original justification for cookies was that it would help the consumer (that is, you) in various useful ways. For example, many Web-based stores allow you to accumulate purchases, one at a time, as you browse the Web site. This facility is referred to as an electronic SHOPPING BASKET or SHOPPING CART. Each time you select an item for possible purchase, the Web server saves this information on your computer in the form of a cookie. In other words, your shopping basket is really a set of cookies stored on your own computer. (We'll talk about the details of buying and selling on the Net in Chapter 13.)

Another justification for cookies is that they can make life easier by making it unnecessary for you to enter the same information each time you visit a Web site. For example, some Web sites require you to register in order to use the site. Once you are registered, you can access the Web site whenever you want, as long as you enter a user name and password to identify yourself. (You choose your user name and password when you register.) This process is called LOGGING IN. (Obviously, companies force you to log in so they can keep track of who you are and what you are doing.)

On some Web sites, when you log in, you are given a chance to specify that your user name and password should be saved permanently on your computer. If you accept this choice, the Web server stores a cookie with this information on your computer. That way, you won't have to enter the same information each time you want to visit the site.

These rationalizations for cookies — shopping and remembering personal data — are certainly useful, and they are trotted out each time the business side of the Internet tries to justify its ability to leave cookies on your personal computer without your knowing. However, most cookies are not of that nature.

How do I know this? In order to make my browsing more enjoyable, I use a program that blocks Web advertisements. One of the other functions this program provides is blocking cookies. The program keeps track of the number of cookies it blocks, and I can tell you that in the last month (as I write this), the program has blocked 15,954 cookies from being stored on my computer — and in that time, I have not even bought one item from a Web site!

The cookie system has a built-in privacy safeguard: a cookie can only be stored by a Web server when you visit its Web site, and only that server can ever look at the cookie. However, in practice, the spirit of this safeguard is routinely circumvented. Here is one way in which it works.

As you know most Web pages contain pictures of some type: photos, graphics, and so on. You might think that such a page is stored on a Web server as one large file, which is sent to your computer at the request of your browser. Actually, the text of the page is stored in one file, and all the pictures are stored in separate files. When your browser requests the data for a Web page, all of these files are sent to your computer separately. Your browser then receives the files and puts them together to create an image of the complete page. Thus, looking at a single Web page usually initiates a number of separate file transfers.

A great number of Web sites contain advertisements in the form of pictures. In many cases, these pictures do not actually reside on the main Web server. Instead, they are stored on servers maintained by advertising companies. This means that, each time you look at a page with ads, there is a good chance that the ads themselves are coming from special-purpose advertising servers. And each time one of these servers sends a picture to your browser, it can also leave one or more cookies.

This means that, as you use the Web, you will accumulate many, many cookies from Web servers you had no idea you were contacting: servers that are run primarily to send out ads and track people's movements. These cookies are stored under the name of the ad server. Later, you might visit a completely new Web site that uses ads from the same server. At that time, your browser will automatically send the server copies of all the cookies stored under its name on your computer.

Are you starting to see how advertising and marketing companies can use cookies to trace your activities and remember your personal information? Well, it gets worse.

Imagine that, for some reason, you type your name, email address and phone number into a form at a particular Web site. You do this because you want to get something for free (such as access to an online newspaper) or because you want to buy something. It happens that, unknown to you, the company maintaining the Web site has a data-sharing arrangement with the Acme Marketing Company. Also unknown to you, the Acme Marketing Company maintains a sophisticated system that uses cookies to track your movements among all the sites that display its advertisements. It is now possible for them to relate your name, email address and phone number to your activities on the Web. All of this information is stored in a database which is sold to other companies who want to sell you things. This is one way in which your email address can end up on junk mailers lists. (In Chapter 8, I'll show you the strategies you can use to protect yourself against this kind of marketing abuse.)

Why Are Cookies Used So Much?

The cookie system was first proposed and implemented by the Netscape company in the late 1990s. As I mentioned above, the official justification was (and still is) that cookies are good for consumers. However, it is clear that cookies are being used for all types of things that go way beyond customer convenience. Cookies are a major marketing tool, used by companies to accumulate data by tracking what you do and how you do it.

Some people are offended by cookies just out of general principle. After all, what right do companies (and other organizations) have to track our actions on the Internet? Why should merchants who only care about our money be able to store information about our activities and our preferences? The answer to this question is complex and has as much to do with economics and psychology as it does with technical considerations.

As I explained in Chapter 1, the Internet is based on one-to-one connections. As such, the Net is, most definitely, *not* a broadcast medium. For this reason, it is not possible to use the Net to reach a lot of people, reliably and repeatedly, in a cost-effective manner. Moreover, the economies of scale, which work so well outside the Net, do not work well on the Net itself. On the Net, services grow *less efficient* as they grow larger.

For this reason, businesses that depend upon a large audience do not thrive on the Net unless they are married to a substantial and significant non-Internet enterprise. Even then, it is surprisingly difficult for most companies to make money on the Net.

It is a characteristic of business that — month after month, year after year — a company must generate more and more profit in order to remain healthy. This is not greed: this is a normal part of the system. A business whose profits do not grow regularly will eventually stagnate, and, if the business has stock that is publicly traded, the price of its stock will fall.

Generally speaking, businesses are able to increase their profits in two ways: by selling more goods or services, or by becoming more efficient and raising their profit margin. (The term PROFIT MARGIN refers to the percentage of revenue that a company retains as profit after paying all its expenses.)

All companies, on and off the Net, are under constant pressure to increase their profits. This is especially true for companies with publicly traded stock. However, the business environment on the Net is so competitive that there is not much room for raising prices or lowering costs (both of which would increase the profit margin). Instead, companies really only have one choice: they must sell more and more goods or services, either by attracting more customers or by selling more to their existing customers.

This is why all Internet companies (as well as Internet divisions within other companies) eventually find themselves under great pressure to increase their audience and to sell, sell, sell. Up to a point, it is possible to build up a substantial Internet audience by giving away something valuable for free (usually some type of information). However, making money from this audience is quite a different thing.

This is why Internet companies, no matter how substantial they may look, are constantly worried about money. As such, they do everything they can to squeeze out as much money as possible. This is why, when you visit commercial Web sites, you will find yourself bombarded with a great many advertisements (nearly all of which, by the way, are hopelessly inefficient).

This is also why so many Web sites leave cookies on your computer. Internet companies lust after as much marketing data as they can find, hoping that, in some way, they can use that data to increase their sales. And if an ever-increasing treasury of data doesn't lead to more sales... well, the company can always try to sell it.

An Approach to the Privacy Dilemma

It's important to realize that when a company acts in a way to further its own interests at the expense of your privacy, the company is not necessarily acting immorally. You see, companies — and other organizations, such as universities and governments — are entities in their own right. As such, they have a powerful tendency to protect their existence and further their aims.

So don't waste a moment being bothered by the fact that companies on the Net do not really care about your privacy. Of course they don't. They care about what they need to care about: making money, projecting a particular image, attracting customers, increasing their profit, dominating their particular industry, raising their stock price, and so on.

So let's be realistic. There is no vast conspiracy to ferret out your personal secrets and sell them to the highest bidder just for the sake of being malevolent. Companies act according to their nature, so instead of getting upset or trying to fight the system, see what *you* can do about preserving your privacy. Recognize that it's hard for anyone to make money on the Net, and companies that give you something for free (even if it is information) are going to have to do anything they can to squeeze out every dollar they can. This means, yes, that they will use cookies, and any other trick that might work, to find out information about you, if they think that information might lead to profit.

You will remember that, in Chapter 1, I explained that when you use the Net, you are in public. To be sure, it is not the same as when you leave your house and mix with other people, but you are in public just the same. As you know, being in public requires you to give up a certain amount of privacy and, from time to time, to put up with a certain amount of inconvenience.

So, don't get excited each time you read about a new Internet privacy violation. Rather, accept it as being part of the Net. Just look at the problem carefully, ask yourself how it affects you, and then take whatever steps are necessary to protect yourself.

In general, this is the approach I want you to use when you analyze any Internet problem. To see how it works, let's take a look at the problem of cookies.

What to Do About Cookies

Everyone dislikes being manipulated by big companies, so it's easy to understand why you might resent having your activities and your preferences monitored without your approval. Lots of people feel this way and they especially dislike the way this information is used to target them as potential consumers. I have to admit that I sometimes feel the same way because I am, by my nature, a private person who likes to control his environment. However, let's set our feelings aside and be reasonable.

I am sure you have had the experience of buying groceries at a supermarket with a computerized checkout system. After all your items are scanned, a special device prints customized coupons for you based on what you have bought. For example, if you have bought a particular cereal, you might have received a coupon for 50 cents off a similar cereal from a different company. Obviously, a computer is examining your purchases and using the information to market a product to you directly.

Does this bother you? Frankly, it doesn't bother me. Even though I don't use such coupons, and I just throw them away, I don't really see the system as an invasion of my privacy. After all, the cereal company isn't interested in me as a person; they only want to sell me cereal.

Similarly, when a company uses cookies to try to market to you more effectively is it really that big a deal? The answer is no. It's not all that different from the coupon machine in the supermarket. However, it feels different, for two reasons. First, you access the Net by using your computer. As we discussed in Chapter 2, your computer interacts directly with your mind and, as such, you see it as a highly personal tool. Second, the Net is a much more mysterious place than a supermarket, so it's understandable why you would instinctively dislike the idea of information about you floating around out there, beyond your control.

I have thought about this question carefully over a long period of time — remember, as I told you, I myself am a private person — and I have come to the conclusion that cookies, although philosophically offensive, aren't really that big a deal, and don't really infringe upon our privacy in a meaningful way. From time to time, you may read about some Internet privacy advocate ranting against the hidden menace of cookies. Ignore the diatribe. There are more important things to worry about.

If you really hate the idea of cookies, you can get a cookie blocking program that will let you control which Web sites (if any) are allowed to leave cookies on your computer.

In fact, you can set up your browser to block cookies if you really want to. With Internet Explorer:

1. **Pull down the Tools menu and select Internet Options.**

2. **Click on the Security tab, and then on Custom Level. This will open a new window called Security Settings.**

3. **Within this window, scroll down to the Cookies section, and choose the setting you want. Then Click on OK to close the window.**

(Note: You will see an option related to "per-session cookies". This is for cookies that are meant to be temporary. For example, if you are buying something at an Internet store, the Web site might use temporary cookies to remember the contents of your shopping basket. Such cookies are automatically removed when you stop your browser program, so you can ignore the setting for this option.)

So, as I say, you can block cookies if you want but, for practical purposes, it's really not worth the trouble. (You may remember me mentioning a program I use that blocks cookies. Actually, I use the program to block advertisements. It just happens to block cookies at the same time. I care more about the ads than the cookies.)

So, does my recommendation not to worry about blocking cookies mean that you can ignore them altogether? No, you do need to think about cookies, because in certain situations, they *can* cause a severe privacy problem, but in a completely different way than you might have thought.

Tossing Your Cookies

As I explained earlier, cookies are stored on your computer in a special folder. Anyone with a bit of technical knowledge, who has access to your computer, can easily examine your cookies. Each cookie is identified by the name of its Web site. This means that someone with access to your computer can see the names of many of the Web sites you have visited just by looking at your cookies. Moreover, the person doesn't need to be in front of your machine. If you are on a network, the administrator can look at your cookies remotely, over the network. (Actually, if you really want to be paranoid, you can worry about the fact that the network administrator can look at any of your files any time he wants.)

Thus, if you work in an environment in which you are especially concerned about privacy, it behooves you to delete your cookies regularly. After all, if you have been visiting contraband Web sites, it doesn't do you much good to delete your history and flush your cache, when sitting peacefully on your hard disk are a half dozen cookies under the name **www.barnyardsex.com**. So let's spend some time discussing how to examine and delete your cookies.

With Internet Explorer, your cookies are kept in a folder called:

`C:\Windows\Temporary Internet Files`

"Anyone with a bit of technical knowledge,
who has access to your computer,
can easily examine your cookies."

This is the folder that is also used as your cache (see the discussion in Chapter 3). To examine the contents of this folder, start Windows Explorer — the file management program — and navigate to the folder. (If you are using Windows 2000 or Windows NT, the location of this folder and other similar folders will be a bit different. I'll discuss the details later in the chapter.)

Alternatively, you can get to the folder by following these steps:

1. Pull down the Tools menu and select Internet Options. You should be looking at the General page.

2. In the Temporary Internet Files section, click on the Settings button. This will open a new window.

3. Within this window, click on View files. This will open a copy of Windows Explorer. You will now be looking at the contents of the `Temporary Internet Files` folder.

Each cookie is actually a small file, and they are easy to see. Under a column named Internet Address, each cookie will have the designation **Cookie.** You will also see the name of the Web site that left the cookie.

To see the contents of a cookie, double-click on its name (in the leftmost column). When you do so, you may see a message like:

Running a system command and this item might be unsafe. Do you wish to continue?

Don't worry about it, just click on the Yes button. There is nothing unsafe about looking inside a cookie. When you click on the Yes button, a window will open showing you the contents of the cookie. (Do this a few times and you'll realize there's no point in looking inside cookies.)

To delete a cookie, right-click on the name. A menu will appear. Choose Delete. You will be asked to confirm that you really want to delete the cookie. Click on Yes.

To delete all the cookies at once, press Ctrl-A. This will select all the items in the folder. (Alternatively, pull down the Edit menu and click on Select All.) You can tell that all the items are selected because they will be highlighted. Right-click on one of the names and choose Delete. Again, you will be asked to confirm the deletion.

Once you have done this, it looks like you have deleted all the cookies from your computer. You haven't. Windows keeps another copy of all your cookies in a different folder named:

C:\Windows\Cookies

You will have to display the contents of this folder and delete all the cookies (and sub-folders) it contains. One way to display this folder is to type the full name into the Windows Explorer address bar.

Are you finished yet? Maybe yes, and maybe no. Sometimes Windows stores yet another copy of the cookies in a folder named:

C:\Windows\Local Settings\Temporary Internet Files

If this folder exists on your computer, you will have to clear it out completely, including all the sub-folders.

(Are you starting to see why, in Chapter 3, I suggested that you should learn how to use Windows Explorer well?)

The Balance of Power

It seems as if, when it comes to gathering information, the Internet deck is stacked in favor of the companies and merchants and not the consumers. For example, cookies are often used to invade your privacy (there's no doubt about that), and yet there's not a lot you can do except block them, delete them after the fact, or ignore them. Moreover, you will find that, if you block cookies completely, some Web sites won't work properly (they are purposely designed that way).

Cookies are not the only example of electronic perfidy. Here is one that is even harder to see. Whenever you click on a link, your browser contacts a Web server on your behalf, and every time this happens, your browser cheerfully sends the address of the current Web page to the remote server. This information is called the REFERER FIELD. In other words, each time you click on a link, your browser silently sends the referer field, telling the remote server which page you were reading when you clicked on the link.

This betrayal is more extensive than you realize, because it often happens that the Web page your browser is fetching requires elements from more than one Web server. If so, the referer field is sent to all such servers. For example, many Web pages contain ads that come from special Web servers maintained by Internet advertising companies. When your browser sends out the referer field, all the servers — including those run by the advertising companies — are sent information about what you were looking at when you clicked on the link.

How common is this? Earlier I mentioned that I use an ad blocking program that also blocks cookies. Well, this same program blocks referer fields from being transmitted to "third-party" Web servers, such as those that supply advertisements. In the last month (as I write this) my program has blocked 8,054 such referer fields.

Your browser does not allow you the option of refusing to send such information. So let's say you have just clicked on a link to a Web page that contains advertisements, and your browser has dutifully just sent the referer field to the Web server that is supplying the ads. There is a good chance that the advertising company's Web server has, at one time, stored cookies on your hard disk. (The cookies were put there when you visited other Web pages that contained ads from the same server.) Your browser will quietly send all these cookies along with the referer field. As it happens, one of these cookies is a unique identification number, identifying you to the server (this is common).

But wait, there's more. At one time, you visited a Web page that offered you a free something-or-other, if you would only type your name and email address into a form. It happens that the company offering the free something-or-other has a marketing deal with the same Internet advertising company that has just received the cookies (including your ID number) and the referer field (showing the Web page you were just visiting).

Yet, as bad as the lack of Internet privacy might seem, and as much as people like you and I might cry out for relief, it seems that the browser companies are going out of their way to make it easy for Web servers to find out as much as they can about us. For example, Microsoft has built a system called PROFILE ASSISTANT into their software. The sole purpose of Profile Assistant is to make it as easy as possible for Web sites to extract personal information from your computer. What type of information? Your first name, your last name, your email address, your gender, your job title, your mailing address, your phone number, your business phone number, and your business address. (The information comes from the address book maintained by your Microsoft email program.)

During my research at the Microsoft Web site, I found a technical article written for Web programmers, with the ever-so-coy title: "Collecting Personal Information from Your Users Easily with the Microsoft Profile Assistant and Internet Explorer." Fortunately, Profile Assistant is not used widely, so we don't need to learn the details and conjure up a huge amount of righteous indignation.

However, what we do need to do is take a moment to think about these types of systems — cookies, referer fields, Profile Assistant, and so on — and ask ourselves: Why are they created in the first place?

You Are Not the Customer

Why is it that the people who build browsers work so hard to make life easy for third-party commercial marketers and care so little about our desire for privacy? The answer to this question is important, because it gives us insight into the economic dynamics that control the computer software industry. Understand this, and you'll understand a lot.

Let's start by asking what seems to be a simple question. From the point of view of the browser companies, who are the customers?

At first, you might think the answer is the users. People like you and I are the customers. After all, we are the ones who use the browsers. We are the consumers.

But are we? Businesses don't care so much about consumers as they do about consumers who pay for what they consume. So ask yourself, how much did you pay for your browser?

The answer is nothing. You got your browser for free. It was either pre-installed when you bought your computer, or you downloaded it from the Internet, or someone at work installed it on your computer. Regardless, you paid nothing at all to the browser company for the right to use a powerful, sophisticated program (and you expect free updates).

Perhaps you have heard the old joke about the car salesman who brags that his prices are so low that he sells cars below cost. Someone asks him, if you sell cars for less than you pay for them, how do you make any money? His answer: I make it up on volume.

It is true that Microsoft (which makes Internet Explorer) and AOL (which makes Netscape) are large, successful companies, but not so large or so successful that they can make money by giving away millions of free browsers. Microsoft and AOL must not only create the browsers, they must maintain them. This means developing new versions, fixing bugs (problems), and creating specific editions to run on different systems (Windows, Macintosh, Unix), all of which runs into big bucks.

So where does the money come from? It comes from businesses: from companies that (in Microsoft's case) buy the programming tools and service contracts necessary to create Web sites; or from companies that (in AOL's case) make marketing deals based on the captive audience provided by free browsers.

So who are the real customers? Not you and not me. The real customers are the companies that pay money. So is it any wonder that Microsoft and AOL put the interests of such companies above the interests of the end users?

From time to time, I will make remarks about how Microsoft, AOL, and other Internet companies care more about making money than the needs of the people who use their software. This is certainly true, but let's be realistic. All companies need to make money and, since we don't pay for most Internet software, it only makes sense that software companies are going to listen to the people who do pay.

From a technical point of view, it would be easy for your browser to filter out advertisements, stop referer fields, protect your privacy, and allow you to selectively block cookies.

Now you know why it doesn't.

Cleaning Out Your Computer Every Day

If you live or work in an environment where someone might have access to your computer when you are not around, you may be worried about your privacy. If so, here is a brief checklist of what you can do every day to clean out your computer.

Before we start, I want to point out that these actions are not foolproof. They are useful as far as they go, and they will eliminate the easiest ways that a casual snooper might intrude upon your privacy. However, Windows is designed so that any programs can leave traces in various places, and there is no practical way for you to remove them all: a skillful, determined investigator will always be able to find something.

The only foolproof way to clean your computer completely is to wipe out the contents of the hard disk and reinstall Windows. (Even then, you still have to worry about any existing backups.) For more information on this topic, see the discussion in the next section on how to clean your computer permanently.

You can clean your computer at the end of each day, by following these 7 steps. The exact details on how to perform each action are explained earlier in this chapter and in Chapter 3.

Browser:
1. **Clear your history.**
2. **Flush the cache.**
3. **Delete your cookies.**

Mail Program:
4. **For each folder, delete all the messages you don't want anyone else to see, then...**
5. **Delete everything in your trash folder.**

Windows:
6. **Delete any files or folders you don't want anyone else to see, then...**
7. **Empty your Recycle Bin.**

Bequeathing Your Computer

Having discussed how to clean your computer on a daily basis, let's consider a less common situation, one in which you are called upon to give up your computer to someone else. If this is personal, for example, if you are giving your old computer to your brother-in-law or donating it to a church group, the solution is simple. You must delete everything on your hard disk.

The best way to wipe out your hard disk is to perform what is called a low-level format. Before any disk can be used, it must be prepared in a certain way. This process is called FORMATTING. Every disk must be formatted before it can be used, including hard disks, floppy disks and CDs. With floppy disks, formatting destroys all the data on the disk. With a hard disk, however, this is not the case. If you want to destroy all the data, you must use a special procedure called LOW-LEVEL FORMATTING.

Normally, low-level formatting is only done once, at the factory, before the disk is shipped to the computer manufacturer. Although the procedure is automatic, once it starts, it is a long process that will take hours. Still, it is the only sure way to wipe all the data on your hard disk.

Once you have formatted a disk in this way, you will not be able to use your computer until you have reinstalled Windows. The instructions for low-level formatting and Windows installation differ from one system to another, so I will have to refer you to your computer manual or to the company that made your machine.

In a work situation, giving up your computer to another person presents you with different problems, especially if you are being fired or if there is a conflict between you and the company.

Moreover, as we discussed in Chapter 2, if your computer is on a network, there is a good chance that a backup has been made of your files. If this is the case, cleaning your computer is still a good idea, but you must recognize that if the company wants to get your old files, including your email, they can do so by restoring them from a backup.

Unlike a home situation, your company may have strict policies about what you may or may not delete from your computer. This only makes sense. The last thing a company wants is for a disgruntled employee to delete, say, last year's sales figures or all the personnel records. (This is where backups come in.)

There is a good chance that the person who administers your computers will not allow you to wipe out everything on your hard disk. Indeed, if you are using Windows 2000 or Windows NT in a networked environment, you will probably be limited as to what system facilities (such as formatting) you can even use on your computer.

If you have never used your office computer for personal work, you are in a good position. All you really need to do is clean your computer the way I described in the previous section. However, if you have used your computer for personal work, you need take a few extra steps.

First, uninstall all the programs that you have ever installed for your own use, such as AOL software. The best way to uninstall software is to use the Windows Add/Remove Programs facility. Click on the Start button. Select Settings, then Control Panel, then Add/Remove Programs.

Now look through the list of programs. When you see one you want to uninstall, click on it and then click on the Add/Remove button. Repeat this procedure until you have removed all the programs you have ever installed for your own use. Hint: This can be a slow process because, with some programs, you will have to reboot to complete the uninstall process.

Once you have finished uninstalling your personal programs, use Windows Explorer and go through your hard disk, deleting all your personal files and folders. Be aware that some programs do not completely remove all their files when they are uninstalled, so you may have to clean up after them.

As you examine your disk, be sure to check the following folders, and any sub-folders, to see if they contain personal data that should be removed:

```
C:\Program Files
C:\Windows\All Users\Start Menu
C:\Windows\Application Data\Identities
C:\Windows\Cookies
C:\Windows\Downloaded Program Files
C:\Windows\Favorites
C:\Windows\History
C:\Windows\Local Settings\Temporary Internet Files
C:\Windows\Offline Web Pages
C:\Windows\Start Menu
C:\Windows\Start Menu\Programs
C:\Windows\Temp
C:\Windows\Temporary Internet Files
```

If you are using Windows 2000 or Windows NT, the location of these files will be a bit different. For Windows 2000, look in the following folders:

```
C:\Documents and Settings\All Users\
C:\Documents and Settings\username\
C:\Documents and Settings\username\Local Settings\
```

where *username* is the name you use to log in. For example, if you log in as **harley**, you would look in:

```
C:\Documents and Settings\All Users\
C:\Documents and Settings\harley\
C:\Documents and Settings\harley\Local Settings\
```

For Windows NT, look in:

```
C:\WINNT\Profiles\username\
```

Note: Your Windows 2000 or NT system may be set up to prevent you from accessing these folders.

The Windows Registry

Within your computer is a special collection of technical information known as the Windows REGISTRY. The registry contains data relating to (1) the hardware components in your computer, (2) the programs installed on your computer, and (3) Windows itself. The registry is very important, because Windows and your programs depend on it to store crucial data from one work session to the next. Indeed, without the registry, you couldn't even start Windows, and if you accidentally damage the registry, your entire system can become inoperative.

A large portion of the information in the registry is stored in special files, which you should never, ever touch under any circumstances:

```
C:\Windows\user.dat
C:\Windows\system.dat
```

The rest of the information is related to your hardware components, and is recreated each time you start the computer.

In Windows 2000 and Windows NT, the registry is even more complicated. The actual data is stored in a number of files. Most of them are in the folder:

`C:\WINNT\System32\Config\`

Others are in the folders:

`C:\Documents and Settings\Administrator\`
`C:\Documents and Settings\`*`username`*`\`

Again, these are files that you should never touch directly.

If you are a super-nerd, you can look at the contents of the registry and even make changes by using a program that comes with Windows, called **regedit** ("registry editor"). However, **regedit** is not for beginners. Do not even think about it unless you are sure you know what you are doing. If you make a mistake, it could permanently disable your system.

The reason I am telling you about the registry is that it contains the many different preferences you can set that affect your working environment. For example, when you set options in Windows Explorer, you are actually making changes in the registry. (Of course, Windows Explorer makes the changes for you, so you don't accidentally cause a catastrophe.) Another common use of the registry is to specify which programs should be run automatically each time you start your computer.

There exists a program called TweakUI ("tweak the user interface") that was written by a group of programmers at Microsoft. TweakUI allows you to make many different changes to the registry in a simple, safe manner. In particular, TweakUI lets you set certain options that will help you wipe out certain data automatically to protect your privacy.

I'll explain those options in a second, but first I'll tell you how to install TweakUI on your system. (If you don't understand these instructions, get a friend to help you.)

If you use the original edition of Windows 98 and you have the installation CD, you can find TweakUI on the CD. Insert the CD into your CD drive and look for the file:

`Tools\Reskit\Powertoy\Tweakui.inf`

To install the program, right-click on this file and select Install.

If you don't have this particular CD, you will have to find TweakUI on the Net. (It is available for free.) Before you begin your search, you should know that there are two different versions of TweakUI, one for Windows 95 and one for Windows 98. (The Windows 98 version will also work for Windows ME, Windows NT and Windows 2000.)

To find the version of TweakUI you need, use a search engine to search for one of the following patterns:

```
+tweakui +"windows 98"
+tweakui +"windows 95"
```

You should be able to find the program along with the installation instructions.

Once you have TweakUI up and running, you will notice that it is in the form of a medium-sized window with a number of tabs along the top. Look for the tab named Paranoia and click on it. You will now see a number of different options that you can turn off and on that allow you to clear various types of information automatically each time your computer starts. For example, you can clear your Internet Explorer history.

Turn on the options you want and then click the OK button. Now, each time you restart your computer (or log in, if you share your computer with someone else), Windows will protect your privacy by deleting the information automatically.

One last hint: If you feel like experimenting with TweakUI, be sure to read the help information first. To do so, click on the Tips button on the first page. I know you won't want to, especially because Microsoft help information is usually so useless, but TweakUI is different. You need to know what you are doing. (Moreover, as I mentioned, TweakUI was written by a small group of programmers, and they did an especially good job on both the programming and the help information.)

Programs That Take <u>Your</u> Side

Aside from TweakUI, there are a large variety of other programs that are designed to enhance the privacy and security features of your computer. You can find such programs by searching at a software archive using the keywords `privacy` or `security` or both.

In case you don't know any software archives, you can find a lot of resources in the Software section of my book *Harley Hahn's Internet Yellow Pages*. Or, you can try one of the following Web sites. (Note: Even though the third URL says `win95`, it contains software for all the Windows systems.)

```
http://www.tucows.com
http://www.freewarehome.com/
http://www.zdnet.com/downloads/win95.html
```

Internet Resources: Windows software archives

The programs you will find will offer you many different privacy and security features. Here is a short list to give you an idea of what is available:

- Keep other people from using your computer when you are not around.
- Securely store and manage all your passwords for Web sites that require you to log in.
- Encrypt and decrypt files so no one else can read them without a password.
- Hide and restrict access to specific files and folders.
- Block other people from using certain programs (such as your mail program).
- Overwrite the contents of a file before it is deleted, so that even if someone restores, the data will be gone.
- Control cookies as you use the Web.
- Create a diary or journal that is encrypted, so only you can read it.
- Clean out your browser history and other accumulations of information showing your activities.

5

The Psychology of Privacy

Understanding your needs for privacy has long-term benefits that may be more significant than you realize.

The Psychology of Privacy

Transition and Ignorance

One of the themes of this book is that the internal forces that control our thoughts and our actions are frequently out of sync with reality. All too often, we feel emotions and take action based on ignorance only to find that, looking back from a distance, our actions were wasteful — even, on occasion, to the point of being contrary to our own interests. At the same time, while we are sidetracked, worrying about unimportant issues, we are likely to miss the real problems, the ones that do require our attention and our planning.

In Chapter 1, you may remember, we discussed the basic ideas regarding how data is transported over the Net (in packets, using a distributed system). This knowledge led us to an understanding (in Chapter 4) of why Internet companies become *less* efficient as they grow, and why the Internet is not, and cannot be, an efficient broadcast medium.

In the late 1990s, the Internet began to attract the attention of the business community in a big way. At the time, the people making business decisions didn't understand the nature of the Net. As such, they were led to the false conclusion that it was possible to create impossibly profitable companies whose success could be assured by advertising and selling to an ever-growing audience of Internet-savvy consumers. The collapse of Internet stocks in 2000 demonstrated that such ignorance was not confined to the boardrooms of the world. It was shared in large part by a vast number of investors who created a classic, inevitable boom/bust scenario.

It is true that the creation of the Internet stock bubble and its subsequent implosion had much to do with greed and fear, the mainstay forces that drive the market even in normal times. However, in this particular case, there was another force involved: ignorance. Too many people were being distracted by too many ideas that were just plain wrong.

Such phenomena are common during times of great change, when the salient characteristics of particular issues have not yet penetrated into the culture at large. At such times, when conventional wisdom has yet to catch up to reality, people are apt to make decisions based on their feelings, feelings that are based on fundamental misunderstandings.

There is nothing inherently wrong with this. Whenever we are confronted with a new and important technology, for instance, it takes some time for us to come to terms with how the technology is affecting us. During the time of transition, we tend to run around with half-cocked ideas but, eventually, we figure out what's what, and Reason once again returns to Her throne.

The popularity of the Internet provides us with compelling examples of such activity, for instance, the temporary stock market turbulence. However, the Internet is deeply important to us in many ways, and it is only reasonable to expect that, as the Net creates social change, we are going to find ourselves in the position of having to deal with issues that we do not yet fully understand. One such issue is that of privacy.

Why Talk About Privacy?

The Internet, by its nature, has significant effects on our privacy. For one thing, people use the Net to talk to one another, through email, chatting, mailing lists, discussion groups, and so on. It's not hard to imagine someone talking about you behind your back, or passing around information you would prefer to keep private (such as your email address or the intimate details of your sex life). There is also the threat of eavesdropping. In Chapter 1, we discussed how law enforcement agencies, such as the FBI, have the tools to monitor and record Internet communications, including email.

On the other hand, there is a completely different way in which the Net can invade our privacy. As you know, there are many, many computers that store data about us: personal information culled from commercial databases, credit card data, and so on. Many companies are actively using the Internet to gather new information and correlate it with the existing databases. In the trade, this is called DATA HARVESTING, and is a widespread activity among companies looking for a marketing edge. In this way, we can be inundated with spam (unsolicited email), while, at the same time, our activities on the Web are tracked assiduously by companies looking for new and better ways to sell us things (see Chapter 4).

For these reasons, much of this book is devoted to discussing issues of privacy, and showing how you can protect yourself from prying eyes and gossiping ears. Aside from the immediate practical considerations, you will find that understanding and protecting your needs for privacy has long-term benefits that may be more significant than you realize right now. Moreover, like other important ephemeral qualities of modern life — such as trust, freedom and security — people do not miss their privacy until it is gone. So the sooner we, as a society, understand and debate the issues, the better off we will be.

In this chapter, I will create a context for such discussion by exploring the very idea of privacy: what is it, and why is it important to us? In order to provide you with practical answers to these questions, I will analyze the basic motivations underlying our desire for privacy. By doing so, I hope to lead you into a thoughtful state of mind in which you can reexamine your ideas and assumptions in light of our changing world. Along the way, I will explain some of the misconceptions people have about privacy. My goal is for you to approach your decisions regarding privacy and the Net from a posture of understanding and confidence. The reason I discussed the mistakes made by so many Internet companies and investors is that I wanted to show you what can happen when people do not make decisions from a posture of understanding and confidence. This will not happen to you.

What is Privacy?

Let's consider the fundamental question — what, actually, is privacy? To start, let me observe that, broadly speaking, there are two types of privacy. If someone peeks into your bathroom window as you are taking a shower, he is certainly violating your privacy. However, when a company sells your name, phone number and

"Until the twentieth century, intruding on someone's privacy required you to be physically near the person, close enough to see him or overhear what he was saying."

credit card information to a telemarketer, they are also invading your privacy, but in a completely different way.

The first type of privacy concerns itself with your activities. The second type of privacy has to do with the buying and selling of data. To distinguish one from the other, let's call them observational privacy and informational privacy. (I know, the terminology is awkward, but that in itself is significant, as you will see in a moment.)

For most of human existence, the desire for privacy has been exclusively a desire for observational privacy. This only makes sense. Until the twentieth century, intruding on someone's privacy required you to be physically near the person, close enough to see him or overhear what he was saying.

This type of privacy is important to all of us and gives rise to a need which we feel instinctively. From time to time, everyone wants seclusion, the knowledge that what we are doing is not, and cannot be, observed by other people. It may be because we are doing something personal or intimate (taking a shower, gossiping); it may be because we are doing something wrong and don't want to be caught (eavesdropping, stealing); or it may be because we are engaged in an activity that requires secrecy to work well (planning a surprise birthday party).

In the twentieth century, things changed. The rise of modern technology afforded the world many new ways in which people could snoop on one another. There were binoculars, video cameras, microphones, phone taps, and so on. In recent years, miniaturization, computers and satellites have enabled people (and organizations) to spy on one another to a degree that would have been unbelievable only a generation ago. Still, no matter how someone spies on you, whether they are listening outside your bedroom with a glass pressed against the door, or tracking your movements with a miniature radio transmitter hidden in your car, they are still intruding into your life in a way that invades your observational privacy, that age-old desire to be alone with your thoughts and your actions.

The other type of privacy is one that has really only become an issue in the twentieth century, with the invention of devices that can transmit and store large amounts of information efficiently. Now that we live in a world in which computers are ubiquitous, we are subject to the machinations of those who would compile data about us: credit agencies, banks, marketers, governments, health providers, and on and on. Any time you do anything that requires a computer, that computer is keeping a record of what you did, and those records are stored permanently in a database. Think about this the next time you use a credit card, make an airline reservation, get money from an ATM, make a phone call, see a doctor, stay at a hotel, or whatever. Moreover, remember what we discussed in Chapter 4: Internet companies go to a lot of effort to track your activities on the Web, and use that information as much as they can.

What is really scary — or fascinating, depending on your point of view — is the realization that the organizations that hold this information about you will often combine the contents of various databases in order to correlate and analyze their holdings. (This is part of the data harvesting process I mentioned earlier.) I'll have more to say about this later.

A Lack of Vocabulary

You will have noticed, from the above discussion, that there is a certain awkwardness in analyzing the various aspects of privacy. For example, in order to discuss the basic types of privacy, I had to introduce two new terms, observational privacy and informational privacy. Although these terms are adequate, in the sense that they are descriptive, they are stilted, even pompous (and I am not normally a pompous fellow).

The point is, I had to make up these expressions because there just aren't any words to describe different types of privacy. Moreover, there aren't words to describe the varying degrees of privacy (as in Mary needs more privacy than John, but not as much as Elizabeth). Nor are there words to describe the opposite of privacy. (The closest I can come to such a word would be publicness, and even then, there is no simple way to refer to degrees of publicness.)

The reason for this lack of vocabulary is that our thinking about privacy is actually quite primitive. It is a characteristic of social topics which are poorly understood, that there do not yet exist adequate words to talk about such issues. In fact, this is one way by which you can judge how far society has advanced with respect to a particular problem. Ask yourself, do enough specific words exist to make it easy for us to describe and discuss the problem? In this case, the lack of privacy-related vocabulary shows us that our culture is still immature when it comes to understanding these issues and their significance.

I would imagine, and I am sure you agree, that privacy has been important to people as long as there have been people. If you live in any type of community or family unit, you are going to have a sense of when someone is looking at you and when you are alone. However, this is observational privacy. It is only in the last few generations that what we are calling informational privacy has been an issue. Moreover, with the sudden increase in technology — including the unexpectedly swift growth of the Internet — the need to identify and debate the issues of privacy has increased faster than our ability to talk about them.

Don't let this bother you. It is the nature of change to impose itself upon our lives before we are ready for it, but that's okay. In time, we will develop the wisdom and experience to deal with such problems. (Of course, by then, there will be new problems.)

If you look closely at our world, you will see that there are many areas of life affected by new technology with which we are not yet comfortable. How can you identify such areas? The tip-off is that, even though you recognize something as being important, you notice that you do not yet have the vocabulary to discuss the topic in a mature manner. In other words, when our understanding of something is immature, we will have problems finding the words to discuss it. This is the case for individuals, from childhood to old age, and it is also the case for society as a whole. (What, for example, is the exact word to describe the desire of a man in Medford, Oregon, to keep his wife from knowing that he is using a Web chat room to have a personal relationship with a woman in Florida whom he has never met?)

The relation of understanding to vocabulary is an insight that I want you to remember and apply frequently. The next time you notice that something important is difficult for people to discuss, ask yourself why. If the topic is related to technology, the problem may be that the technology is still new and, collectively, we have not accumulated enough experience and wisdom to use the technology well. Computer scientists have understood this phenomenon for years: no matter how fast theory and technique advance, hardware is always ahead of software.

Returning to privacy: eventually, of course, our vocabulary will develop to meet our needs. In the meantime, we still have those needs and, without a mature understanding of what privacy really is and what it means to us in the twenty-first century, it will be all too easy to make misjudgments. For this reason, I want you to understand the nature of privacy: what it means to you as a person, and how you should think about it. Let's start by asking, why do human beings want privacy?

Our Desire for Privacy

It is ironic that, although we enjoy more privacy now than human beings ever have, we are more concerned about someone invading our privacy than ever before. Why is this? The answer lies in the forces that drive our desire for privacy.

There are many instances in which we can imagine wanting privacy, and to make sense out of them, we need to look for basic principles. Toward this end, I will observe that there are four different biological and psychological roots from which a desire for privacy can grow.

First, and most important, we will desire privacy if we have a perception that we are in danger and hiding will allow us to protect ourselves. Imagine yourself being pursued by two large, armed men named Guido and Vince who want to discuss an outstanding loan, and you will quickly see the value of being able to conceal yourself in certain situations.

A second reason to desire privacy is that we know we are doing something that is socially unacceptable, and we want to escape detection in order to avoid censure. For instance, if you ever find yourself littering or taking candy from a baby, you will, no doubt, want to be unobserved at the time. In some cases, our need for privacy will be restricted to being able to avoid detection by a specific person or agency, such as when a teenage girl does her best to keep her diary private from her parents. This same principle governs our behavior when we know we are doing something illegal, and we don't want to get caught. You can imagine, for example, that people who run stop signs, shoplift, or cheat on their income tax will feel a strong need to do so away from the eyes of authority.

The next motivation for wanting privacy is related to our psychological conditioning. There are a variety of activities that we avoid doing in public, not because they are necessarily dangerous or unacceptable, but because we have been trained by our society to feel discomfort in such situations. Consider, for example, how various cultures expose the human body. A woman in a Muslim country who grows up with a strict code of behavior may be conditioned to cover her entire body in public. If such a woman were to visit, say America, she would (at first, anyway) feel a lack of privacy if she were forced to walk around in a revealing blouse and skirt. Similarly, an American woman, even one who is used to dressing in skimpy outfits, would feel some discomfort on her first visit to a nudist retreat. In both cases, the women would feel a desire for privacy, even though being less clothed or naked is certainly safe and (under the circumstances) acceptable. This particular need for privacy is inherent in all of us in many ways. For example, we all have things we prefer to do in private, just because doing so in public, or in front of certain people, would make us feel uncomfortable, such as using a toilet, trying on clothes in a store, flossing our teeth, looking at pornography, and so on.

The fourth situation in which we desire privacy occurs when we want to create a special environment, either alone or with other people. For example, we want privacy when we are having a romantic dinner with a loved one (or a potential loved one), when we are in an important business meeting, or when we want to concentrate on reading a book or watching our favorite TV show. In such situations, we seek to create a bubble around us, and having our privacy invaded would be an intrusion, causing us to be distracted and lose our focus. In romantic situations, privacy is especially important, if we are not to lose the magic of the moment.

Thus, we have the four roots from which a desire for privacy may arise:

- Our perception of danger.
- Our understanding that specific acts are socially unacceptable or illegal.
- Our internal conditioning toward avoiding or embracing certain behaviors.
- Our wish to create a special environment.

In order to relate this to our behavior, especially with respect to how we deal with the Net, we need to go one level deeper and ask, what drives us to action when we feel a desire for privacy?

The Controlling Forces

Let's take a closer look at the four reasons why we may feel a need for privacy, and see just what it is that getting privacy might afford us in each case.

First, there are times when we want privacy because we feel it will help us avoid some type of danger. At such times, we are driven by our need for safety.

Second, when we know that we are doing something wrong, we also want privacy. In this case, it is so that no one (or, perhaps, certain people) will find out what we are doing. In other words, we are motivated by guilt.

Third, there are various activities that we prefer to do in private. These activities may be perfectly safe and acceptable but, because of our conditioning, we are uncomfortable having people observe us in any way. In such cases, we are responding to anxiety.

Finally, there are times when we want to be alone, possibly with other people, in a special environment. At such times, we want privacy in order to avoid an intrusion.

Thus, we can see that the four types of situations that make us want privacy do so because they are able to invoke a particular feeling within us, a feeling that is related to one of the following considerations:

- Safety
- Guilt
- Anxiety
- Intrusion

Such feelings are powerful, and often control us more than we like to admit. Indeed, they can control us to the point where, unless we understand what is happening, we will find ourselves making decisions and taking actions that are not in our best interests.

For example, consider two people, Pat and Mike. Pat has received harassing and threatening email from an old girlfriend. As a result, he has changed his email address and is especially picky as to whom he gives the new address.

Mike, too, is picky about giving out his email address, but not for any particular reason. Mike is simply the type of fellow who easily feels anxiety and, as a result, likes to control things.

One day, Evelyn, an AOL user and a friend of both Pat and Mike, receives a message that she particularly likes. (The message talks about angels and how important they are to all of us.) Evelyn, being a good AOL person, decides to send the message to 100 of her closest friends. To do so, she forwards the message by directing it to the addresses of all her friends. This means that each person receives not only important information about angels, but the email address of each of the 99 other people who received the message.

Pat, of course, is upset because he is trying his best to keep his new address away from his old girlfriend. Mike, as you might imagine, is also upset, but for a completely different reason. Mike is not worried about a specific threat; he is worried because that is the way Mike is. In this case, it is reasonable for Pat to be upset about the loss of privacy: he has a real concern about his safety. Mike, however, has no reason to feel threatened, but he does anyway, and he is upset.

The interesting point is that, although their situations are different, both Pat and Mike may be experiencing the same degree of discomfort. Mike may honestly be as worried as Pat, even though Pat's concern is based on reality while Mike's is not.

What is important to Mike is not so much the actual danger he is in, but his perception of the situation. Many people like Mike feel at odds with the world, and tend to feel a desire for privacy even when there is no practical reason to do so. In this case, Mike has no real reason to worry about his email address, but he does so anyway.

Consider the following analogy. As human beings, we have evolved in such a way that, whenever we are faced with immediate danger, our bodies react in a particular way, the so-called "fight or flight" response. Our glands send various substances — corticotropin releasing factor, adrenocorticotropic hormone, adrenaline and cortisol — into our bloodstream. Our heart speeds up, our blood pressure rises, our breathing becomes deeper, our mind concentrates better, and we begin to sweat.

This type of reaction is important, even crucial, when we need to run away from a wild jungle beast or confront an enemy intent on hurting us. Unfortunately, it is all too common to have such a reaction, perhaps in a more mild form, when we are under emotional stress: if we need to make a speech, confront a person with whom we are having a conflict, or listen to our boss berate us for something that was not our fault. In such cases, our bodies and our minds automatically react in a way that is inappropriate to the situation.

It is part of human nature to be prey to a variety of inappropriate reactions, such as the one I just described. In particular, it is common for people, especially certain types of people, to feel that their privacy is being threatened even when it is not. When this happens, it is all too easy for such people to believe that what they feel is based on reality, which leads to poor judgment.

Mike, for example, is a computer programmer, who happens to serve on the Internet security committee at his company. Because of his unrealistic feelings regarding privacy, he has pushed his company to install expensive and intrusive privacy monitoring software that is not really necessary. Moreover, he spends too much of his time and energy fighting imaginary enemies.

In this case, however, the story does have a happy ending. Both Pat and Mike sent email to Evelyn (Mike's message, by the way, was a real stinker) complaining about her lack of email etiquette. As a result, Evelyn took the time to learn how to hide recipient addresses by putting them in the Bcc: (blind copy) line of an outgoing message. (You can learn how to do this yourself in Chapter 8.)

Who Gets Privacy?

I have explained that a desire for privacy can spring from a biological or psychological need related to safety, guilt, anxiety or intrusion. However, there is one more, large part of the picture that still needs to be filled in.

In our society, privacy is often sought, and given, as a symbol of power or status. Ask yourself, who in our culture is often denied the privacy they desire? The answer is, people who are very young, very old, poor, sick, or in need.

What do all these people have in common? They have a relatively small amount of power, or a low social status, or both. Another way of putting it is that, in our society, you get to enjoy the most privacy when you are powerful, rich, not too old, not too young, and of high social status. Privacy is often used as a perquisite, given to the rich and powerful, and lack of privacy is often used as a tool to underscore someone's lack of power and status, and to punish people who misbehave.

For example, consider how office space is allotted in a large company. The more powerful (and best paid) executives have the most space and the most privacy. The least powerful employees have the least privacy, in many cases being forced to work in open areas or cubicles. In some companies, you may even see extra status given to someone simply because they work closely with a powerful person. For instance, the executive secretary of the Chairman or CEO may have more privacy than a middle manager.

By their nature, organizations are very good at recognizing social status by allowing or restricting privacy. Ask yourself, for example, how you would feel if you were moved against your will from a private office to an exposed cubicle. Even if the cubicle were the same size as the office, you would know without a doubt that your company was trying to send you a message.

When a company wants to show someone that they have very low status, they do so by taking away all the person's privacy. This is often the case when employees of a large company are fired. In such situations, it is common for the employees to be called into their manager's office to be told that they are losing their jobs, and then escorted to their desks by a security guard. Under his watchful eye, they are allowed to remove their personal belongings and nothing else. They are then escorted out the front door.

Here is a typical example. In January 2001, CNN found it necessary to fire 400 employees. As reported in the *New York Post* newspaper, "Stunned employees from New York to Los Angeles are being yanked into personnel offices all this week and told to pack their things and get out the same afternoon... When they return to their desks, they learn that technicians have already rendered their computers inaccessible, preventing them from retrieving personal files... Uniformed security guards stand watch as the dismissed — some crying — clean out their desks. The guards then escort them like common criminals to the exits."

It is easy to brand CNN's behavior toward their employees as being inconsiderate and insensitive, but it would be a mistake to do so. Why would CNN want to antagonize people for no reason? What is really happening is that an organization — with a life of its own — is showing certain people that they have the lowest possible status (that of a non-employee) by taking away all of their privacy. In the process, the people, who have an innate sense of their social status, are humiliated and angered.

Enforcing social status by taking away privacy is so common in our culture that we often don't pay attention when it happens. Still, it is real. For example, who do you think gets more privacy, a patient who is seeing an expensive doctor in a rich town, or a patient with no money who must wait for a long time to see a doctor at a community clinic? In my experience, observing doctor's offices and hospitals is an excellent way to get a free lesson on privacy and power. Many doctors and nurses are very good at disrespecting people's privacy in order to (subconsciously) make it clear who has the power.

Have you ever wondered why so many people who become wealthy buy themselves houses that have a great deal of privacy? Why do the very richest people live in homes that are all but unapproachable without permission? The reason is that we all have, to a greater or lesser degree, a desire to control our privacy, a need to decide for ourselves who gets to see us and under what circumstances. The plain truth is that rich people have more power to indulge this desire than do poor people, and so, are able to buy more privacy for themselves.

Our Real Needs

There is no doubt that privacy is important to us psychologically. However, as we have discussed throughout the chapter, our desire for privacy is usually more primal, existing at a deeper, biological level. Occasionally, our desire is more superficial, reflecting our desire for social status, wealth or power.

Anyone who works or lives with animals knows that they have an innate sense of privacy. For example, a cat will often consider its litter box to be a private place, not to be violated by a human. My cat, The Little Nipper, hides in his box when he sees I am ready to brush his teeth and he is not in the mood for such an experience. (On the other hand, he is always willing to give me access to the box when it needs to be cleaned.) Both wild and domestic animals will crawl away to be by themselves when they are sick or dying. And have you ever waited for a horse to give birth? If so, you will know that it will bide its time until you become impatient and leave, and the minute you are gone, it will deliver the foal.

It is certainly fair to say that, seeing as we too are animals, we have, at times, a biological need for privacy that cannot be denied. This is especially true when a lack of privacy would, in some way, put us in a vulnerable position. On the Internet, we are not exposed to the point of being in physical danger. However, we can be made to feel vulnerable in other ways. For example, we might worry about malicious gossip, or about having important business secrets exposed, or about having our computer attacked by someone who wishes us harm. In many cases, such worries are groundless, but still, if we perceive them to be true, we will feel a desire for privacy.

As you have seen, a desire for privacy is not necessarily the same as a need for privacy. I am sure you would agree that it is a waste of time and effort to chase after something we don't really need, so it behooves us to think carefully before we act. However, analyzing our motives honestly is something that is extraordinarily difficult to do.

Unfortunately, when it comes to the world of computers and the Internet, misinformation and misunderstanding abound, and it is all too easy to be troubled by the wrong issues. The next time you hear of a privacy issue that scares you or bothers you, I want you to take a deep breath and ask yourself, why does this upset me?

If the reason is a good one, then by all means, do what you need to do to safeguard your privacy. However, if you find that your privacy concerns are being fed by irrational feelings or a desire to increase your social status, take a moment to reevaluate the situation and ask yourself, is this really something I need to worry about?

It is my observation that anti-privacy efforts (like censorship efforts) are often vendettas led by obsessive people who are driven by their own inner demons. However, we do live in a highly automated world, one in which both observational and informational privacy concerns are real and important. There is a real risk that, in wasting our efforts on the wrong issues, we will inadvertently allow the real privacy violations to invade our lives when we are not looking. It is my job to make sure that this does not happen to you.

6

You Just Think
You Have Rights

If you think you are entitled to a right
to privacy, you may be surprised.

You Just Think You Have Rights

Do We Have a Right to Privacy?

In Chapter 5, we talked about privacy from the point of view of the individual. We discussed various types of privacy, as well as the biological and psychological forces that cause people to want privacy. In the next two chapters, we will turn our attention to these issues as they affect society as a whole.

To start, consider this problem. A less-than-honorable Internet marketing company has your email address and is filling your electronic mailbox to the Plimsoll Line with irritating junk mail. If they refuse to take your address out of their database, can you protest?

The answer to this question depends on a more fundamental question: do you legally have a right to privacy? Most people think they do, but the real answer is not so straightforward.

Depending on what country you live in, you may have some rights to privacy, but they are limited. This is significant because, as you will see in Chapter 7, the public debate regarding privacy is under the control of forces that are beyond the influence of individual people and the more legal rights we have, the better.

In most countries, people are entitled to specific legal rights in two different ways. First, it is recognized that human beings, just by being alive, have certain unalienable rights, that is, fundamental privileges that must be recognized and cannot be taken away. Second, people are given rights by the various laws that have been passed by the governing bodies of their country.

With respect to privacy, the question arises, do we have unalienable rights, or do such rights as we may have exist only because a legislature has passed a law (in which case, our rights would be limited and might be changed by a new law)?

The Highest Law of the Land

If you think you are entitled to a right to privacy, you may be surprised. In the United States, the Declaration of Independence (1776) asserts:

"We hold these truths to be self-evident, that all men are created equal, that they are endowed by their Creator with certain unalienable Rights, that among these are Life, Liberty and the pursuit of Happiness..."

Similarly, the Universal Declaration of Human Rights (adopted by the United Nations in 1948) declares:

"All human beings are born free and equal in dignity and rights... Everyone has the right to life, liberty and security of person..."

Notice that there is no mention of a right to privacy.

In most countries, the highest law of the land is that country's constitution. Some countries also have a statement of human rights, which is usually part of the constitution.

If you were to examine various constitutions, you would find that none of them explicitly offers a right to privacy. Does this mean we have no rights to privacy?

Not necessarily. Legally, we have some rights to privacy, but, as I will show you, they are not fundamental rights.

In the United States, the ultimate law is the U.S. Constitution, and yet, nowhere in the original text (1788) or in the 27 amendments (1791–1992) will you find the word "privacy". This is significant in that the first 10 amendments — also known as the Bill of Rights (1791) — were drafted specifically to augment the rights recognized by the original document. Read the Bill of Rights carefully and you will find that the right to privacy is, indeed, conspicuous by its absence. (In fact, in the entire Constitution, the word "private" appears only once, in the 5th Amendment: "...nor shall private property be taken for public use, without just compensation.")

This omission is not unique. There is no mention of privacy in the Canadian Constitution Act (1982) or in the Canadian Charter of Rights and Freedoms (1982). Nor is this subject addressed in the corresponding European documents such as the Treaty of Rome (1957), which established the European Community, and the Treaty of the European Union [Maastricht Treaty] (1992), which established the European Union. What about the United Nations?

Both the original Charter of the United Nations (1945) and the International Covenant on Economic, Social and Cultural Rights (1976) are completely silent with respect to a right to privacy.

In fact, of all the constitutions I examined, there was only one that guaranteed any type of right to privacy: the Constitution of the People's Republic of China (1982). Article 40, "Privacy of Correspondence", states:

"Privacy of freedom and privacy of correspondence of citizens of the People's Republic of China are protected by law. No organization or individual may, on any ground, infringe on citizens' freedom of privacy of correspondence, except in cases where to meet the needs of state security or of criminal investigation, public security or procuratorial organs are permitted to censor correspondence in accordance with procedures prescribed by law."

Notice, however, the caveat that the people's right to private correspondence is limited by the state's right of censorship (which is legal in China). This explains why the government of China has the right to control Internet usage.

Thus, with the exception of China, the various constitutions and bills of rights for the United States, Canada, Europe and the United Nations make no promise of a right to privacy. Does this mean that such rights are universally ignored?

Not at all. There are declarations that mention some type of right to privacy. These declarations are international statements that fall into the category of we-think-this-is-a-good-idea-so-we-will-sign-it. Unfortunately, none of these statements have the force of law. Still, they embody the basic principle that privacy is important enough to be discussed internationally.

For example, the Universal Declaration of Human Rights (1948) was ratified by the General Assembly of the United Nations only three years after its founding. This document was designed to be the epitome of a human rights declaration, and was based on the U.S. Bill of Rights (1791), the English Magna Carta (1215), and the French Declaration of the Rights of Man and of the Citizen (1789), none of which, by the way, mentions privacy. However, Article 12 of the declaration does address the issue:

"No one shall be subjected to arbitrary interference with his privacy, family, home or correspondence, nor to attacks upon his honour and reputation. Everyone has the right to the protection of the law against such interference or attacks."

In the same year, at the Ninth International Conference of American States held in Bogota, Colombia, the OAS (Organization of American States) consisting of the countries of North and South America, was formed. At the meeting, the group adopted a document called the American Declaration of the Rights and Duties of Man (1948). Article V of this declaration states that:

"Every person has the right to the protection of the law against abusive attacks upon his honor, his reputation, and his private and family life."

(Remember this the next time someone sends you email blaming you for something you didn't do. When that happens, the best response — in fact, the one recommended by the OAS — is "I know you are, but what am I?")

Years later, the OAS adopted yet another human rights agreement, the American Convention on Human Rights (1992). This agreement was unusual because, for the first time, we see an explicit declaration of a right to privacy.

"Article 11: Right to Privacy

"1. Everyone has the right to have his honor respected and his dignity recognized.

"2. No one may be the object of arbitrary or abusive interference with his private life, his family, his home, or his correspondence, or of unlawful attacks on his honor or reputation.

"3. Everyone has the right to the protection of the law against such interference or attacks."

What the Supreme Court Has to Say

So, do we have an innate right to privacy? Historically, the answer has been no. Even though a few international agreements (such as the three I just discussed) do mention this issue, most national constitutions and human rights declarations do not recognize such a right. In other words, as human beings, we do not have a right to privacy in the same way that we have rights to "life, liberty and the pursuit of happiness".

Thus, such privacy rights as we might have can derive only from laws and judicial rulings. Unfortunately, the problem with depending on the force of law to protect a basic right is that, unlike a constitution, a law or a ruling is easy to change.

This is certainly the case in the United States, where the basic rights to privacy have been established, not by the Bill of Rights, but by rulings of the Supreme Court. As you might expect, such rulings are controversial and are at risk of someday being reversed. Indeed, most Americans probably don't appreciate that the strongest statements of their right to privacy derive from Supreme Court decisions relating to contraception, interracial marriage and abortion.

The first such ruling, the one that established a right to privacy for Americans, was Griswold v. Connecticut (1965). In this case, the Supreme Court struck down a ban that the state of Connecticut had put on the sale of contraceptives. The Court recognized the existence of a "zone of privacy", and ruled that the government could not intrude into the homes and lives of its citizens.

Two years later, in Loving v. Virginia (1967), the Court asserted that the government could not invade people's lives to the point of banning interracial marriage. (At the time, Virginia law provided that "If any white person intermarry with a colored person, or any colored person intermarry with a white person, he shall be guilty of a felony and shall be punished by confinement in the penitentiary for not less than one nor more than five years.")

In Eisenstadt v. Baird (1972), the Court invalidated a Massachusetts law prohibiting selling contraceptives to unmarried people. In doing so, they found that both married and unmarried people had a right to privacy that extended to making their own reproductive decisions.

Finally, in Roe v. Wade (1973), the Supreme Court ruled against a Texas law prohibiting all but lifesaving abortions. The Court recognized that a woman has a right to privacy (one that, in this case, extended to her decision as to whether or not to terminate her pregnancy).

Now, think about this carefully. If this "zone of privacy" really exists, if the government's ability to intrude upon our privacy really is limited, does it not imply that a government agency may not, say, install a device to monitor our email and other Internet communications in order to look for evidence concerning someone else's criminal activities? In other words, should our rights to privacy — as recognized by the Supreme Court — protect us against Carnivore (see Chapter 1), the device that the FBI uses to spy on Internet activity?

The answer is no. The right of privacy is not enshrined in the Constitution and, hence, is not paramount. A government agency is allowed to invade our privacy as long as they can legally show a compelling need, such as national security, criminal investigation or public safety. (If this sounds familiar take a moment and look back at the quote from the Chinese Constitution.)

However, our biggest threats to privacy come, not from the government, but from business, and nowhere — in the Constitution or in the essential Supreme Court rulings — does it say that we have the right to keep an Internet marketing company from using our email address without our permission. As a matter of fact, when it comes to establishing such rights by law, we, as individuals, have very little say in the matter.

In order to think about something well, you need to have a basic understanding of the ideas behind the issues. My goal in this chapter is to help you develop a sense of perspective, one that will allow you to render knowledgeable opinions and make decisions wisely. To start, let's consider two interesting privacy-related examples.

Thinking on a Large Scale

In January 1999, Scott McNealy, the CEO of Sun Microsystems, an important computer company, was being interviewed by a group of reporters and analysts. A few hours earlier, Intel, the manufacturer of many of the electronic components used in PCs, had reversed a decision to put an identification feature into their new processor chips. This feature would have meant that every PC would have a built-in ID number, a social security number for computers. This, in turn, would mean that software could be written to identify you, monitor your actions, and send this data over the Internet to various companies (or the government). Under pressure from privacy advocates, Intel backed down and agreed not to deploy the ID feature in their new processors.

At the time this happened, McNealy was speaking at an event called to launch a new system developed by his company, a system called Jini. The purpose of Jini was to allow various types of computer components and consumer devices to communicate with one another and share information. Such a system, of course, would be bound to raise concerns about privacy. (What, for example, might your VCR have to say to another machine about your video viewing habits?) In light of Intel's surrender to privacy concerns, it was natural for someone to ask McNealy what privacy safeguards his company was planning to build into Jini.

McNealy's answer was one that would, to coin a phrase, live in infamy. After asserting that consumer privacy issues were a "red herring", he told the audience, "You have zero privacy anyway. Get over it."

Think about that. The CEO of a major computer company telling us, "You have zero privacy anyway. Get over it."

At first, it is tempting to think of Mr. McNealy's remark as merely the ill-timed hubris of an arrogant, insensitive Captain of Industry. If so, it would not be the first time that an arrogant, insensitive Captain of Industry has put his mouth in motion before his brain was in gear. Indeed, CEOs of computer companies seem to do so with alarming regularity. (It has to do with the fact that nerds, even rich powerful nerds, tend to see the world as a rational place in which everything can be colored either black or white.)

However, before we pass judgment on McNealy, I'd like you to consider another privacy-related incident. On January 28, 2001, the Super Bowl was held in Tampa, Florida. On that day, about 100,000 fans passed through turnstiles in order to enter the stadium and, as they passed through, their faces were scanned and digitized by hidden cameras. Within an instant, a special computer system compared the images to a large number of pictures in the files of the local police, the state police and the FBI.

The equipment to perform the secret spying was loaned to the Tampa police by a company that makes surveillance software. The idea, of course, was twofold. The police wanted to catch bad guys (which they didn't), and the software company wanted to get a lot of free publicity (which they did). Of all the 100,000 people scanned, the computerized system did identify 19 with "significant" criminal histories, but no one was arrested or even apprehended.

Such systems are being used with increasing frequency and are nominally justified as being in the public interest. After all, their purpose is to catch criminals, whether they are actual fugitives from justice or simply unsafe drivers running a red light. Innocent people like you and me have nothing to fear.

When a spy system is deployed where we live, we are, at first, appalled at the idea that a combination camera/computer system is spying on us in public. After awhile, however, we become desensitized to the assault on our privacy, and our expectations change permanently. Spy cameras are just a part of life.

This particular spy system uses a type of BIOMETRICS: technology that identifies people based on specific physical or behavioral characteristics. The general idea, of course, is not new. However, modern biometrics has advanced far beyond the printed fingerprints and mug shots of the olden days. Today's systems can identify people based on a number of different characteristics including:

- Hand geometry
- Voice prints
- Speech patterns
- Retinal scanning
- Iris scanning

- Face recognition
- Typing patterns
- Handwriting

Scott McNealy tells us that we already have no privacy and yet I wonder, how gracious would Mr. McNealy be if he thought that his face was going to be scanned covertly in pursuit of an open-ended search for yet-to-be-identified criminals? Might he respond that there is really no reason *not* to scan everyone? After all, only the guilty need be afraid. Innocent people have nothing to fear from having their faces (or voices or fingerprints or mannerisms) matched against a database of known miscreants. Real life, however, is rarely so obliging, and such arguments are rarely as simple as they seem.

I would like to point out an important dichotomy in McNealy's remarks. It's true that when you and I go out in public we don't have the same rights to privacy as when we are at home. But still, I wonder how quick people like McNealy, who claim that we already have no privacy, would be to support massive secret surveillance in public, when they are among the ones being spied upon.

"We have no privacy?" I feel like saying to him. "In that case, Mr. McNealy, would you mind telling me your social security number, your credit card numbers, the PIN for your ATM card, your home address, your home phone number, your personal email address, and, just for fun, your mother's maiden name? Since you think we should simply 'get over' our lack of privacy, I'm sure you won't mind if I publish this information in a book and on my Web site."

As you can see, I'm not being quite fair to McNealy. Realistically, I do not expect him, or anyone, to furnish me with such information, and if I did somehow find it and publish it in a book or on the Web, you can bet that I would be hearing from his lawyer in less time than it would take the Queen of England to send back a cup of cold tea.

The reason is that CEOs, like politicians, spokesmen and commentators, lead two lives: a public life in which they espouse the interests of their organizations, and a private life in which they act as individuals. When people like Scott McNealy spout off about privacy, they are acting in their official capacity as a representative of an organization whose interests are often at odds with the interests of individuals. In this case, we are dealing with the CEO of a company for whom restrictive privacy regulations would be a significant financial irritation.

When it comes to public debates about privacy, there are many competing and vested interests, and you must learn to pick your way carefully through the fields of misleading verbiage. To be able to do so, you need to start with an understanding of how society carries out its role in protecting our privacy and why it is that individual citizens are rarely the ones who get to frame the debate.

On an individual level, concerns about privacy can be handled person to person, but on a larger scale, it is the groups that have the power. Don't be misled by the idea that, in some sense, all groups are made up of individuals. Businesses and other organizations have lives of their own, independent of the people they employ, and they will defend and advance their own interests as they see fit. As individuals, we have neither the power nor the endurance to promote our own interests on the national or international arenas. We need an organization to defend and represent us, and that organization is our government.

You and I can say anything we want and do anything we want but, when the whistle blows, we are on the sidelines. The large-scale, societal battle over privacy issues is a battle of titans, one in which the government, for better or for worse, is our gladiator.

Thus, when it comes to the politics of privacy, the balance between business and government — how much power the government has compared to business — is crucial. Although the Internet is a global community, we must recognize that what we think and what we see depend very much on the culture of our own country. If we live, for example, in the United States, it is a startling thought to realize that most everyone in the world sees the government's role in privacy issues much differently than we do. Here is why.

The American Frontier

Many people have strong opinions as to how power should be balanced between business and government. Talk to such people and you will rarely notice any originality in their opinions or their reasoning. Why? Because the plain truth is that, as much as we like to think that our opinions are our own, most of what we think is absorbed from the society in which we live. Although we do our best to conjure up ingenious and rational reasons for why our way of thinking is best, we are shaped by our culture more than we like to admit.

This is especially true when we listen to people opine and argue about privacy issues: should the government tell business what to do, or should we keep the government from interfering? What we hear depends very much on the culture of the person doing the talking. If we want to penetrate to the inner core of such issues and decide for ourselves what is best, what action, if any, we should take, we need to strip away any cultural bias we might be masquerading as rational thought. Toward this end, I would like to explain why people in the United States seem to look at privacy issues so differently from people in other Western countries.

The United States was formed from thirteen English colonies on the east coast of North America. The defining event was the American Revolution, which took place over twelve years, from 1775 to 1783. The spirit of the revolution was embodied in the Declaration of Independence, drafted by Thomas Jefferson and ratified on July 4, 1776. The most well-known statement from this document asserts that:

"…all men are created equal, that they are endowed by their Creator with certain unalienable Rights, that among these are Life, Liberty and the pursuit of Happiness…"

At the time that Jefferson drafted the Declaration of Independence, the American colonies were governed by England and ruled by King George III, a situation that the colonists bitterly resented. The laws under which the colonists lived were English, and as such, were derived from the body of English common law, the well-developed system of customs and precedents that evolved in England over many years.

However, the conditions in the New World were much different than those in the mother country. England was settled and had been for years, with well-established cities, towns and cultures. The colonies, on the other hand, were a frontier. As such, the inhabitants had a significantly different outlook than the people in England who were making and enforcing the rules.

These qualities gave rise to the uniquely American attitude that, even today, colors their attitudes towards all aspects of life (including the Internet and privacy). To appreciate this attitude, we need to understand the conditions in the frontier in which the American personality was forged.

The frontier of which I speak had three salient characteristics. First, it was open, with unlimited opportunity. The first part of America to be settled was the east coast, and as it became more settled and citified, the frontier obligingly moved westward. Thus, for many years, America was a land of opportunity, a place where an enterprising individual or group could always find room for themselves.

Second, the American frontier was a wild, dangerous untamed country in which nature was a dominant force and people were required to fend for themselves. The native people, who had been there for centuries, were seen by the explorers and settlers as being savages, which only added to the danger. Because of this, early settlers were forced to protect themselves and were on their own when it came to carving a living out of a difficult, inhospitable land. There were no policemen or lawyers to guard them or protect their interests. Compared to their cousins in England, Americans were free, unconstrained and self-policed.

This led to the third characteristic of the frontier, a strong sense of privacy. When you have to fend for yourself, you quickly develop the attitude that what you acquire is yours and yours alone, and no one, not even the government, has the right to intrude upon your privacy without your permission.

Early America was dominated by two types of settlers: the adventurers, who were looking for something new and were not afraid to take a risk, and the desperate people with no other place else to go — the exiles, the orphans, the oppressed and the criminals, including those who had been unfairly convicted. (The state of Georgia, for example, was originally a prison colony.)

The American settlers found that, to survive, they had to develop the characteristics of successful frontiersmen. They had to be strong of mind and body; they had to be independent, healthy, daring, and ambitious, with a great deal of initiative. The conditions that required such traits made a lasting mark on the American psyche. Even today, with the frontier long gone, these characteristics are still the ones that Americans revere.

Why Americans Are Cowboys

As a general rule, legal traditions are based on the needs of the people at the time the laws are established. After the revolution, the break from England allowed the newly formed country to also break from rule of English law. A new body of American law developed to suit the needs of a country with enormous potential in which the frontier mentality was dominant. The demands of the frontier led to laws that favored individual rights and individual initiative. In this way, American legal traditions came to support independence, privacy and self-reliance, and the American culture grew to value such traits.

Here is an interesting example, one that you might remember the next time you listen to people discussing how the Internet should be policed. In England, if you were faced with danger, the body of common law (that is, the legal precedents and customs) held that, regardless of who was right and who was wrong, you were limited as to when you might legally defend yourself. Before you could hurt or kill another person, you must first try to flee. If this were not possible, you should back up and do your best to avoid a conflict. It was not until your back was against the wall and you had no other alternative that you were allowed to take action.

This, of course, is a rather civilized way of dealing with anti-social individuals. When you live in a country that has been settled and developed for a long time, you can't have people going around shooting other people just because they feel threatened. In America, the situation was different. There was a new frontier to be explored and conquered, and there was no one out there to defend you. If you felt threatened, there were no policeman to call for help and nowhere to run to safety. (When you are out in the wilderness, there is nowhere to go except more wilderness.)

For this reason, the early American legal system developed to codify the type of adventurous and self-sufficient behavior that was necessary to survive and flourish. American law held that, as long as you were in the right, you were allowed to stand your ground and defend yourself, even if it meant killing the person who was threatening you. (After all, how can you ask someone in danger to wait until their back is against the wall when there are no walls?)

As we look back at American history, we recognize the strength and success of the men and women who settled and developed the country and, like everyone else who looks back in time, we idealize. Through the lens of history, we see a frontier of limitless possibility, populated by cowboys (the good guys) and desperadoes (the bad guys).

Most of all, we admire the cowboys, whom we imagine to be rugged frontiersmen of the highest caliber. If you are not American, it's hard to understand the worship of the cowboy mentality. However, without such an understanding, it's impossible to make sense out of the balance of power between business and government, which is a prerequisite to understanding the politics of privacy as they are applied to the Internet.

To help you appreciate this aspect of the culture, I would like to quote the American writer Ben Stein. When I was in graduate school, in 1978, I read an essay Stein wrote for the *Los Angeles Herald-Tribune*. The essay, "Why America Needs Cowboys", gives advice to college students as to what it takes to be successful in America. Listen to Stein as he explains the idea of what cowboys mean to America:

"Cowboys are the essential symbol of what is great about America. They rode around all day on their horses, without any limitation on what they could do, or where they could go. They lived without restraints on their imaginations or their accomplishments. They lived in an America that valued getting things done, building, creating, molding a refuge for all the oppressed of the earth, an America where the freedom of the individual included the freedom to take whatever a man could by fair means and the sweat of his brow, and make a refuge for him and his family."

Over the years, the cowboy mentality has taken root in America, where it has flourished and been transformed into the American Dream, the idea that, by working hard, anyone can create a happy and successful life.

This has left the United States with a double legacy: first, a society that worships the individual and second, a society that demands as much freedom as possible for individual expression.

Americans tend to think of this as a fact of nature. However, if you compare this cultural attitude with that of other countries, you will find a marked difference. In Japan, for example, individuals are expected to submerge their personalities and personal desires to the well-being of the group. The Japanese have a saying which is endlessly drummed into every young schoolchild as a guide to social behavior: *Deru kugi ha utareru* ("The nail that sticks out is hammered flat"). Compare this to the American aphorism, "The squeaky wheel gets the grease."

But the American legacy consists of more than a cult of the individual. There is also a marked antipathy toward government intervention in one's life. This is understandable. After all, this is a country, born out of rebellion against a monarchy, with a national psyche that was forged in a crucible of self-reliance.

Because of this, the United States, unlike other countries, has a particular vulnerability when it comes to privacy, especially regarding computers and the Internet. What does a nation that worships cowboys do when the cowboys get out of hand?

Have the Cowboys Run Amuck?

The United States is a country where, as a general rule, every generation of children has done better than their parents. Why is this? Ask an American and he'll tell you that it is because America is the land of opportunity, a place where, even today, the frontier mentality is dominant and, in principle, anyone who works hard can become successful.

Americans are proud of their country and of the opportunities it offers. After all, no lesser authority than the U.S. Declaration of Independence asserts that people everywhere have the unalienable right to pursue happiness, and in the United States, that means the freedom to pursue the American Dream. For this reason, Americans are reluctant to put limits on how successful a person can become. As long as someone does not break the law, there are no limits as to how much wealth he can accumulate or how much he can own.

However, in this world, the real wealth and power does not lie with individuals; it lies with organizations: corporations and governments. This is an important point that I want you to understand. Although there are many wealthy people, their riches are nothing compared to the wealth of the corporations. Similarly, even the most powerful people owe their power to their position with some organization or other.

For example, the President of the United States is sometimes called the most powerful person in the world. Yet watch what happens when a President leaves office. His power fades away faster than the love of a pregnant woman whose husband has left her in the middle of the winter to play golf in Florida. The same goes for the executives of large corporations. Over the years, I have seen many "powerful" executives leave their companies, only to fade away, never to be heard of again. Meanwhile, the new executives, the ones who have taken their places, are now wallowing in the trappings of power and influence.

What about wealth? Yes, there are a great many rich people, but the plain truth is that their wealth is dwarfed by the amounts of money that corporations manipulate routinely. Indeed, the wealth of many companies is so large as to be beyond the comprehension of most people.

How can we measure the economic size of a company? One common way is to consider the company's market price or CAPITALIZATION. This is calculated by multiplying the number of outstanding shares by the price per share. In the world of finance, a company is considered *small* if its capitalization is less than $250 million. Think about that: a company can be worth up to $250 million and still be considered small! A company is not considered large until its market price grows above $1 billion.

Another way to measure wealth is to look at earnings and revenue. In the year 2000, IBM earned $8.07 billion on revenues of $88.4 billion. Its capitalization (at the time I am writing) is $200.2 billion. In the same period of time Microsoft earned $10 billion on revenues of $23.85 billion. Its capitalization (again, at the time I am writing) is $331.9 billion. How about one more? In 2000, the Coca-Cola Company earned $2.18 billion on revenues of $20.46 billion. Its capitalization is $150.3 billion. (To put this in perspective, how much money did you make in 2000?)

With this much power and money, you can understand why companies have more influence than individuals. Now put this together with the belief that, in America, the right to engage in business should be unfettered, and you can begin to understand why we live in a world in which we must defer so often to the will of corporations.

One of the big mistakes we make is confusing individuals, who have unalienable rights, with companies, whose only rights are those granted by law. As I explained earlier in the chapter, corporations have lives of their own. They will do whatever they need to advance their own interests and, unfortunately, much of the time, their interests conflict with those of human beings. When this happens, the corporations usually get their way.

All too often, corporations run amuck when it comes to respecting the rights and preferences of individuals. In particular, there are many large companies that have personal information about us, who are willing and able to share that information with other

"In the U.S., a successful CEO is seen as the modern counterpart to the cowboy, and the last thing anyone wants to do is limit the cowboys."

companies to advance their own interests. No matter what anyone tells you, the business of a corporation is (1) to protect its own existence, and (2) to make money in ever-increasing amounts.

So why can't we stop them? There are two main reasons. First, large companies have resources that individuals do not. They have money, political influence, public relations departments, lawyers, and so on. They also have persistence and longevity. If you have ever tried to fight a large company — or even get them to make an exception for you — you will quickly realize that they have significantly more resources and staying power than you do. Moreover, unless something terrible happens to kill a company, it is effectively immortal. For example, IBM and Coca-Cola existed long before I was born, and I expect they will continue to exist long after I die. (Microsoft was founded during my lifetime, but I confidently expect it to outlive me.)

The second reason we can't stop companies from trampling on our rights is that we voluntarily let them get away with a great deal because of misguided thinking. This is especially true in the United States where a successful CEO — a Captain of Industry — is seen as the modern counterpart to the cowboy, and the last thing anyone wants to do is limit the cowboys.

Americans believe that individual freedom, especially the freedom to pursue happiness — especially by going into business and making a lot of money — is what makes America great. Where we make our mistake is in treating corporations as individuals, and assigning them the same rights and privileges — and consideration — that we do to other people.

Why We Let Them Get Away With It

The reason we make this mistake — and it is a serious one — is because human beings have a tendency to anthropomorphize. That is, we tend to look on non-human entities as if they have human characteristics. Anyone who has ever had a dog understands this idea. How many times have you treated your dog as if it were human? (Cats, of course, are different.)

With respect to companies, we all too often think about them as if they were human. Often, we will talk about the head of the company as if he or she were the company itself. In writing, there is a name for such a substitution. It is called METONYMY ("me-tawn'-imee"). An example of metonymy would be to use the name of a capital city to represent the political leadership of that country. You hear this a lot when you listen to the news. ("Today, Washington opened preliminary talks with Moscow regarding the price of groatcakes.")

When used in this way, metonymy is innocuous. After all, nobody really believes that a city can talk. It's just a metaphor. However, when we talk about, or even think about, a corporation in a similar manner, our thinking invariably goes astray. For example, it is common for people to talk about the head of a company as if he or she *is* the company.

Let me mention one common example, and I am sure you will understand what I mean right away. In the world of computers and the Internet, Microsoft is a very important company, so it only makes sense that people who use computers will often talk about Microsoft. Now, we all know that Microsoft was co-founded by Bill Gates, who to this day, remains its chairman and single-largest shareholder (not to mention the richest person in the world).

The mistake that we make is in thinking that Bill Gates is Microsoft, and assigning to the company the respect and consideration we would show to a successful human being. Now, anyone in the computer business has opinions about Microsoft. (Actually, just about anyone who uses a PC and Windows has an opinion about Microsoft.) It's not hard to find people who will be glad to offer forceful opinions, good and bad, about Microsoft and its products. This is only to be expected: computers are important to us and, in many areas of personal computing, our tools are controlled by Microsoft. However, Microsoft is *not* Bill Gates, and blurring the line between the person and the company only serves to make the real issues harder to understand.

Consider this example. Starting in the early 1990s, Microsoft has been investigated by various U.S. government agencies for unlawful conduct relating to its monopoly in certain areas of personal computing. Several antitrust-related lawsuits were filed by the U.S. Department of Justice and other government departments and over the years, these suits have wound their way through various courts.

From time to time, I have been a guest on national radio shows in order to discuss and debate the issues related to the Microsoft antitrust lawsuits. I often found that listeners would call in and express the opinion that the government should leave Microsoft alone. Many people honestly felt that the Department of Justice was, for some reason, conducting a personal vendetta against Bill Gates.

The real issue, of course, is the criminal conduct of the company. However, to many people, Bill Gates *is* the company, and a large number of listeners saw this as a conflict between big government and a single individual. I was astonished at how many people honestly believed that the lawsuits were an attempt by out-of-control government officials to "punish" Bill Gates for becoming too successful. "Just leave him alone," they would say. "It's not fair for the government to go after one guy just because he is so successful."

Do you see what is happening here? Because Americans value the spirit of the entrepreneur, and because it is human nature to anthropomorphize organizations, many people think of Microsoft as if it were a person. This is a mistake that companies will go to a great deal of trouble to exploit. For example, a company in trouble will often cloak itself in the mantle of personality.

Microsoft, for instance, did nothing to discourage people who believed that the government was picking on Bill Gates. Indeed, the company put a lot of effort into casting the conflict as one in which overzealous government attack dogs were attempting to stifle the freedom of Americans to innovate. In a letter to shareholders dated May 1, 2000, and signed by Gates and Microsoft President Steve Ballmer, the company asserted that:

"The dismantling of Microsoft also would send a signal that companies in America that are 'too' successful will be punished harshly — a signal that will be welcomed by foreign competitors seeking to overtake America's global leadership in technology."

The facts, however, are different. First, the Justice Department is not picking on Microsoft. The company *did* break the antitrust laws. They did it knowingly and repeatedly and, as such, are guilty of criminal conduct. (This is Microsoft I am talking about here, not Bill Gates as an individual.)

Second, antitrust lawsuits are not at all unusual. If you visit the Web site of the U.S. Department of Justice, you can browse a list of all the pending antitrust actions. Right now (as I am writing this) there are 521 separate antitrust investigations. Microsoft is hardly unique.

I am not discussing this controversy at such length in order to explain the legal issues, which are complex. Rather, I want you to see the situation for what it is, a striking example of how easy it is for people to let their feelings get in the way of their judgment.

The Internet, as a whole, is mostly unregulated. However, it is becoming clear that we do need some regulation, especially when it comes to privacy concerns. And yet, as much as you might dislike the thought of having rules that govern the use of the Net, companies dislike the idea a lot more.

In a sense, the Internet is a frontier, and on a frontier you need cowboys more than you need regulations. However, don't be fooled. During the time that America was first being settled by Europeans, the work was done by individuals, and there is only so much damage one individual can do. The Internet frontier, however, is being developed more by companies than by individuals, and when a powerful company rolls up its sleeves and gets down to it, it can create a lot of problems.

It is important for us to see corporations for what they are: large, powerful entities that care more about themselves than they do about us. This is not to say they are malevolent. Nor do I assert that companies are run by evil people. What I do say is that we must recognize that our needs, as individuals, are often opposed to those of the corporations, and the corporations will not hesitate to do whatever they can to advance their own interests at our expense. They are just acting according to their nature.

This is especially true when it comes to matters of privacy. Many people want control over their personal information and how it is used. Companies, however, want complete freedom to use data in any way that suits their purposes and, they are perfectly willing to resort to heavy handed methods in order gather that data. Once this happens, we become more and more defenseless against the very companies who we have been so quick to support when they plead for us to allow them unfettered control over our computers and our data.

Do you think I'm exaggerating? Just think back to the last time you called a company's customer service number and asked them to do something for you that was disallowed by their computer system. How many times have you heard, "I'd like to do that, but it's against our policy," or "The computer won't let me give you a credit in that way." If you have ever had a problem with a plane reservation, a phone bill, an incorrect credit card charge, or a mishandled order of some type, you know exactly what I am talking about. Most companies have organized themselves, very carefully, to make *us* accommodate their needs. It can't have escaped you that, within a company, the people who work there are also powerless against the corporate system. Regardless of whether we are on the inside or the outside, all of us live under the tyranny of the "system".

But, I hear you ask, aren't there any rules? Isn't anyone going to tell the corporations of the world (and of America) that people come first, that they must respect our right to have control over our personal data?

Yes, there are rules, and as you will see in Chapter 7, they have been adopted by no less an organization than the General Assembly of the United Nations.

7

The Politics of Privacy

*We live in an environment in which
we are continually affected by forces
we can barely comprehend,
let alone control.*

The Politics of Privacy

The Rules

On December 14, 1990, the General Assembly of the United Nations adopted a resolution entitled "Guidelines for the Regulation of Computerized Personal Data Files". The intent of this resolution is to establish a set of *minimum* guarantees as to how information about people should be handled.

The idea is that each country is responsible for creating, and then enforcing, laws that embody the spirit and the details of the resolution. U.N. resolutions, of course, do not carry the force of law; they are suggestions. This particular resolution is well thought-out, and was obviously written to put the interests of people above the interests of corporations, government departments, and other organizations.

The declaration sets ten main rules for safeguarding personal data. Here is a summary of these rules, paraphased in everyday English:

1. An organization that gathers information about you must do so in a way that is legal and fair.

2. The organization must check the data regularly to ensure that it is accurate, relevant and complete.

3. Information must only be compiled for legitimate purposes. The organization must tell you that it is gathering information about you and explain why. They must ensure that all data remains relevant to the specified purpose. Unless you have given permission, they may not disclose data to anyone else unless it is for the specified purpose. Moreover, they may not keep the data any longer than is necessary to fulfill the specified purpose.

4. You have the right to know whether someone is using information about you. If so, you should be able to examine the data in a form that is easy for you to understand. You should be able to do this quickly and inexpensively. If you find mistakes, you have the right to have them corrected at no cost to you. If the data is being transmitted to another party, you must be told the name of the party and how to contact them.

5. No one may compile personal information that would lead to illegal or arbitrary discrimination.

6. Exceptions to these rules are allowed, but only for very important reasons, such as maintaining national security, public order, public health or morality, or to protect the rights and freedoms of other people. However, exceptions can only be made according to law, and such laws must be specific, must limit the exceptions, and must require appropriate safeguards.

7. If an organization stores personal information about you, they must protect that data against loss or damage. This includes protecting the data against accidents, the actions of other people, computer viruses, unauthorized access and fraud.

8. Each country must designate an authority with the legal power to make sure these rules are followed. This authority must be impartial, independent and technically competent. By law, there must be appropriate penalties for not following the rules, and there must be a way for individuals who have been injured to seek redress.

9. Information should be allowed to flow freely across national boundaries, as long as all the countries concerned have appropriate safeguards.

10. These rules apply to all files containing personal data, whether they are public or private.

Privacy Policies

So where are we? Thanks to the United Nations, we have a wonderful declaration of how personal data should be respected and what rights an individual has regarding such data. We also have many people who are sensitive to privacy issues, and elected officials who have started to take notice. At the same time, we have many, many companies that want full control over any information they might have about you, so they can use it as they see fit. The last thing these companies want is to have to work under a system of strict privacy regulations.

So what do they do? They do what companies always do in such situations. They ignore, they stall, and they mislead.

If I were to describe a person who deals with unpleasant issues by ignoring, stalling and misleading, I am sure you would say that he has significant faults. You and I would not want to spend time with such a person. However, as I have discussed earlier, companies are not people and it is a mistake for us to think of them as if they were. When companies ignore, stall and mislead, they are not being evil; they are only acting according to their nature which, as you will see later in the chapter, is not *human* nature.

Why do they adopt such tactics? Because they work.

One way to see what I mean is to examine the privacy policies that companies post on their Web sites. A PRIVACY POLICY is a statement of how a company deals with issues related to personal information. Having a privacy policy allows companies to deflect criticism of their actions and, at the same time, to nullify in advance any legal action that might arise.

If you think I am being harsh, take a few moments to read the privacy policy of any company doing business on the Net. In most cases, you will find (1) the policy is carefully written in legal language in a way that you can't really be sure what it means, and (2) the policy is completely slanted in favor of the company. In other words, companies make sure their privacy policies are obtuse and one-sided.

I'm sure you are not surprised. Organizations — and people — with power generally do their best to use that power to protect themselves at the expense of others. (If you have ever read a standard landlord/tenant contract, you know exactly what I mean.) Even when you are dealing with a company that is honorable and run well, this is still the case. Let me give you an example.

Charles Schwab & Company is a large financial services firm. I'm going to show you part of their privacy policy, but before I do, I want to tell you that, personally, I think a lot of the company. I have dealt with Schwab for several years, and in that time, I have always found the company to be well-managed and customer oriented. The people I have talked to have been, without exception, pleasant, knowledgeable and happy at their jobs. In other words, when it comes to customer service, in many ways Schwab is as good a company as you might find.

And yet, take a look at the following quote from their privacy policy:

"Schwab Alliances and Promotions

"When Schwab joins with another company to offer or provide products and services, both parties may cross-reference their databases to search for customers in common. This existing information may be used to help identify business alliance opportunities and to enhance the information already contained in the existing databases.

"Schwab on its own, or jointly with other organizations and Web sites, may offer contests, sweepstakes, and promotions. You may be asked to supply certain personal information to participate in these promotional events, which may then be used by the sponsoring parties for marketing purposes. Even if you have previously opted not to receive information or mailings about Schwab, you may still receive information about Schwab via these promotions if you choose to register for them. Rules and guidelines for each promotion will be clearly posted, as will notification about how the information gathered may be used. You may opt not to participate in these special promotions if you do not want to receive information about Schwab or share your information with all sponsoring parties."

Let's translate this into English. The first paragraph means: "Schwab may share personal data with other companies."

The second paragraph means: "If you supply Schwab with certain types of personal information they, along with any other company with whom they have made a deal, can target you for marketing, even against your wishes. Schwab will disclose their guidelines, but it is up to you to find them, read them, and figure out the details. It is also up to you to tell Schwab if you don't want them to share your personal data."

Does that look a bit one-sided to you? You betcha. And this is from a company that really cares about their customers and is doing well. (In 2000, Schwab had revenues of $5.79 billion and earned a profit of $718.1 million.)

Let's consider the privacy policy of another company, one that has not done as well, Amazon.com. (In 2000, Amazon had revenues of $2.76 billion and managed to *lose* $1.41 billion.)

On August 31, 2000, Amazon sent notice to its customers that it was unilaterally changing its privacy policy. In a press release, Amazon quoted its CEO, Jeff Bezos as follows: "In revising our privacy policy, we tried to take into consideration not only our current activities but also those things we could imagine possibly happening in the future."

The press release was ominously silent in one particular area. It did not mention the nature of the changes. However, once the news was announced, people were quick to react. Why? Because Amazon's new privacy policy made it perfectly clear that, like other marketing companies, they will do whatever they need to do with personal data in order to make money.

The new policy begins nicely enough: "Amazon.com knows that you care how information about you is used and shared, and we appreciate your trust that we will do so carefully and sensibly." (Remember what companies do: they ignore, stall and mislead.)

Later in the policy, Amazon says: "For reasons such as improving personalization of our service (for example, providing better prod-uct recommendations or special offers that we think will interest you), we might receive information about you from other sources and add it to our account information. We also sometimes receive updated delivery and address information from our shippers or other sources so that we can correct our records and deliver your next purchase or communication more easily."

Translation: Amazon obtains personal information about their customers from other companies, and integrates such informa-tion into their own databases.

Let's take a look at a few other quotes:

"Information about our customers is an important part of our business, and we are not in the business of selling it to others..."

"We work closely with our affiliated businesses... In some cases, these businesses operate stores at Amazon.com... In other cases, we operate stores, provide services, or sell product lines jointly with these businesses... we share customer information related to those transactions..."

"Sometimes we send offers to selected groups of Amazon.com customers on behalf of other businesses..."

"As we continue to develop our business, we might sell or buy stores or assets. In such transactions, customer information generally is one of the transferred business assets. Also, in the unlikely event that Amazon.com, Inc., or substantially all of its assets are acquired, customer information will of course be one of the transferred assets..."

(Note how they use "of course".)

A lot of people were unhappy with Amazon's new privacy policy. One of the main complaints was that they broke their original promises. In an earlier version of the privacy policy, Amazon promised:

"We respect your personal privacy. We do not now sell or rent our list of customers to anyone. In fact, the Electronic Privacy Information Center cites the quality of our concern with customer privacy as one of the reasons they became an Amazon.com Associate. If you would like to make sure we never sell or rent information about you to third parties, just send an e-mail message to never@amazon.com."

This promise completely vanished in the new policy (along with the special email address).

What about the people who had previously sent personal data to the company, thinking that their data would never be shared? Some customers who were unhappy with the new policy wrote

Amazon asking to be taken out of the database. They were ignored. When it was in their interests to do so, Amazon changed the rules, and then refused to delete the personal data for old customers who wished to opt out of the new system.

Just for fun, as I was working on this chapter, I sent a message to **never@amazon.com** address. Within seconds, I got back a reply from the Amazon mail server:

```
I'm sorry to have to inform you that the message
returned below could not be delivered to one or
more destinations.
<never@amazon.com>: unknown user: "never"
```

Now, take another look at the quote above. Do you see the reference to the Electronic Privacy Information Center or EPIC? EPIC is a Washington, D.C.-based public interest research center concerned with civil liberties and privacy. At one time, Amazon was proud that a well-known privacy organization had chosen to deal with them. Two weeks after Amazon released their new policy, EPIC issued their own press release.

"The Electronic Privacy Information Center (EPIC) announced today that it would end its relationship with Amazon.com, the Internet's largest bookseller and one of the most closely watched companies in the online economy. EPIC had previously sold its publications and the publications of others in association with the Seattle-based retailer.

"In a letter to EPIC subscribers, Executive Director Marc Rotenberg cited the recent change in Amazon's privacy policy as the reason for the organization's decision. 'Because Amazon announced that it could no longer guarantee that it would not disclose customer information to third parties, and in the absence of legal or technical means to assure privacy for Amazon customers, we have decided that we can no longer continue our relationship with Amazon'..."

Since its founding in July 1995, Amazon has never made a profit. As you might imagine, their stock price eventually reflected their continued lack of earnings. In December of 1999, Amazon stock sold at $105/share. By February 2001, it was selling at $13/share.

If you are like me, you are probably worried about Jeff Bezos, the Amazon CEO I quoted above. "How," you ask yourself, "will Mr. Bezos manage to make ends meet? Should I be sending him a couple of bucks to help him through a tough time?" Not to worry. In spite of the fact that Amazon lost $1.41 billion in 2000, Mr. Bezos managed — on May 12 of that year — to sell 368,650 shares at $54.24/share, netting him a cool $19,995,576.

Still, a million dollars isn't what it used to be, and $19,995,576 won't last forever. But there's no need to fret. As of February 2001, Bezos had another 117,077,631 shares tucked away under the mattress. Even at the bargain basement price of $13/share, his holdings are worth $1,522,009,203.

I chose these two examples — Schwab and Amazon — to illustrate a point. When a company is doing well (as Schwab is) they treat their customers well. As a company does more and more poorly (like Amazon), they begin to cast about for any way they can make money. At that time, their customers' needs for privacy become less important than the need to generate income, and old promises fall by the wayside.

Personally, I am pleased in my dealings with Schwab, and I have no complaints whatsoever. However, I have no illusions that, if times got rough, Schwab, like Amazon and many other companies, would do what they had to do to squeeze out more money, even if it meant selling personal information. Take a closer look at the quote from the Schwab privacy policy, and you can see that they are already preparing for that day.

In Chapter 1, I explained that when an Internet company gets too large, it starts to collapse from its own weight, and what follows is an intense pressure to generate profits. Since it is the Internet companies that hold a great deal of personal information about us, it is prudent to have real concerns about what will happen to that data when the company nears the end of its lifespan.

How to Think About Privacy Policies

Earlier in the chapter, I discussed a United Nations resolution that addressed privacy concerns related to personal data. This resolution requires organizations to ensure that any personal data they gather about you must be relevant to a specified purpose, and the data may not be kept longer than is necessary to fulfill that purpose. Moreover, unless you give permission, the organization may not disclose data to anyone else for a different purpose.

The basic idea seems so simple. When we buy or sell something on the Net, the data should be used only for the purpose for which it was intended: to complete the transaction. Yet most companies will never adhere to such a practice unless they are forced to. To them, personal data is an asset, something to be bought and sold in order to make a profit.

So what about the privacy policies you see all over the Web? Should you feel comfortable just because a corporation is willing to tell you their policy?

They want you to think so. Companies, especially computer and Internet companies put a lot of energy into public relations to convince the public that, if a company has a privacy policy, everything is hunky-dory.

The reality is that privacy policies are smokescreens designed to forestall criticism and to keep the government from regulating Internet commerce. Providing such a policy on a Web site is seen as a way for a company to lower its exposure to lawsuits, even when the policy is obscure and one-sided. No matter what anyone says, privacy policies are worth nothing. They are designed to sidetrack you from the real issues.

Similarly, don't be fooled when large companies join a privacy organization or subscribe to a third-party monitoring service to certify them in some way. It means nothing. The minute a company wants to change its mind, it simply rewrites its policy, and there is nothing anyone can do about it.

This can happen for many reasons. A company may need money, or it may go bankrupt and have to liquidate its assets, or it may be bought by another company with a different policy, or it may be as simple as a new CEO changing how the company does business. In the world of business, a company that wants to change the rules will change the rules, as long as they think they can get away with it. When this happens, everything they promised you is history, and before you can say "potential cross-selling opportunities" and "strategic marketing alliance", your personal data is personal no more.

Why ID Numbers Are Important

We have talked a lot about personal information, but we haven't talked much about how it is stored. On a computer, an organized collection of information is called a DATABASE. Within a database, information must be stored in such a way that it is easy to retrieve specific data as it is needed. In particular, a database holding personal information must be designed to make it easy to retrieve data relating to a specific person.

The easiest way to design such a system is to have it use a number that uniquely identifies each person. For example, on your driver's license, you will see an ID number. No one else in your state (or province or country) has that exact same number. This is no accident. Within the driver's license database, this number is used to identify you and only you.

As you know, there is information about you in many different databases. Some of these databases are maintained by government departments; others are maintained by companies. Information about you is put in some database or another every time you apply for any type of license or government benefit, file a tax return, use a credit card, perform a banking transaction, buy something over the phone or over the Internet, subscribe to a magazine, and so on.

You see how it would be handy if the information in various databases could be combined and manipulated. Consider the following example.

John Smith is a father who is required to pay child support but refuses to do so. John's name is in a database kept by the government department whose job it is to enforce such obligations. However, if John refuses to pay, what can they do? By themselves, not much. It's too hard to keep track of John and what he is doing.

However, one day John applies for a job. By law, he must furnish his employer with an ID number for tax purposes. The employer sends that number to the tax department, which passes the information on to the child support department.

A computer at the child support department searches for John's ID number in their database and finds his record. It then sends the employer a legal notice telling him to deduct money from every one of John's paychecks and send it to the child support department. They then send the money to John's family, and everyone (except John) lives happily ever after.

But there's more. It happens that John has two children and, on his income tax, he claims them both as dependents in order to get a deduction. At the same time, his ex-wife also claims them as dependents. When John and his wife file their tax returns, they are required to list the ID numbers of all their dependents. This allows the tax department computer to cross-check and discover that two people are trying to claim deductions for the same kids (which is illegal). As a consequence, John's deductions are disallowed.

And there's even more. It happens that John's ex-wife is no bargain either. Even though she is finally receiving money from John's paycheck and she has a job of her own, she tries to apply for government welfare assistance. When she does, she is required to specify her own ID number on the application. The welfare department's computer makes a quick check with the tax department's computer, which finds a record of her employment. Because people with a job are not entitled to welfare, Mrs. John's application is denied.

So, in this example, the fact that John, Mrs. John, and the two kids all have standard ID numbers has enabled the government to

(1) force John to pay child support, (2) disallow illegal tax deductions, and (3) catch an unlawful welfare application.

Now, let's consider another example, that of John's sister Clarissa. Clarissa has always been a good person. She and her husband Adolfo work hard, make a good living, and pay all their taxes. Last month, for Adolfo's 35th birthday, Clarissa bought Adolfo a plastic duck from a company on the Internet. (Adolfo is a duck hunter.)

The company from which Clarissa ordered the duck used the information she provided to check with a credit bureau. The credit bureau sent back a report, which contained a lot of information about Clarissa, including her ID number. The plastic duck company sold this data (including her email address and the fact that Clarissa buys duck merchandise) to a magazine service. Using Clarissa's ID number, the magazine service checked their database and found that Clarissa had already subscribed to several magazines. They then sent her email asking if she wanted to subscribe to one more publication, the *Duck Fancier's Gazette*. Clarissa loved the idea, and she immediately ordered a subscription for Adolfo.

As this example shows, companies as well as governments can use people's ID numbers to keep track of personal information. In this case, the magazine company was able to determine that Clarissa was the type of person who subscribed to magazines *and* bought duck merchandise. This enabled them to offer her a subscription to a specific magazine that was of interest to her.

So far, so good. By using the same ID numbers for government and consumer transactions, the computerized databases were able to correlate information so as to make our world a finer, more enjoyable place in which to live.

But let's fast forward three months.

John, realizing that he has been caught, quits his job and gets another one. However, this time, he gives his employer a false ID number, the number of his brother-in-law Adolfo.

The wheels of government turn quickly, and within a week, Adolfo's employer receives a notice that Adolfo is a deadbeat dad. The employer is told to withhold a portion of Adolfo's pay and send it to the child support department. Unfortunately, this happens at a time when Adolfo is up for an important promotion at a job that requires handling of sensitive data.

At the same time, since Adolfo is now considered to be a deadbeat dad, his ID number is sent to various other government departments, who start checking information in their databases. He gets a notice from the tax department, with a copy sent to his employer, telling him that he owes penalties for unlawful deductions. If he doesn't send a payment immediately, they will take steps to deduct money from his wages.

On the home front, the magazine service that sold the subscription to Clarissa has resold all her personal information to the Fly-By-Night Marketing Company. Within a week, her name, ID number, email address, street address, phone number, and credit rating is sold and resold to dozens of companies. One evening, after she arrives home from work, she checks her personal email (Clarissa would never check personal mail at work) only to find her inbox filled with 86 pieces of spam, 56 of which are selling pornography.

(Would you like to hear how the story ends? It gets even worse. Adolfo sees a carefully crafted marketing message on Clarissa's computer that looks as if it has come from a secret lover, and he wrongly accuses her of using the Net to have an affair. She denies it and they have a big fight, ending with Adolfo spending the night on the couch. In the morning, he wakes up with a terrible backache, so he decides to go to the chiropractor. On the way to the chiropractor's office, he gets into a serious car accident because he can't turn around while he is backing up next to a parking space. Adolfo undergoes emergency surgery and spends two weeks in the hospital. When he finally comes home, he finds that Clarissa has gone to live with her mother, his boss has left a phone message informing him that he has been fired, and his car insurance company has sent him a letter canceling his insurance.

As for Clarissa, she is now getting so much spam, that she is forced to change her personal email address. Adolfo tries to send her a message to see if they can get back together, but he is unable to do so because he does not have her new address.)

U.S. Social Security Numbers

Clearly, there are both advantages and disadvantages to living in a computerized society in which everyone has a unique ID number. However, it looks as if we will not get much of a choice. There is a slow, inexorable trend toward creating such numbers on a national level. Moreover, the European Union is (at the time I am writing) considering a system that would assign a unique international ID number to every citizen throughout the union.

With respect to privacy, there are obvious drawbacks to forcing everyone to participate in such a system. However, there are a great many people and organizations who are against such ID systems and do not hesitate to make their opinions known. How is it, then, that national (and international) ID systems seem so inevitable?

The answer is that the only organizations powerful enough to control such a system are national governments and, unfortunately, it is the governments who are responsible for building up such systems, one step at a time.

Right now (as I write this) over 100 countries have some type of official, compulsory national ID card. This is true of most of the countries in the European Union, including Germany, France, Belgium, Greece, Luxembourg, Portugal and Spain.

In countries that do not have an official system, there is usually a de facto national ID number, often the one used for health care or social security. For example, the United States uses the Social Security Number, Canada uses their Social Insurance Number, and Australia the Medicare Card number.

When it comes to national ID numbers, governments demonstrate a contradictory approach. On the one hand, they act as if they are aware of the pitfalls, and they make a big show out of studying the problem and recommending significant safeguards. On the other hand, they continually approve new ways for various government agencies to use such national ID numbers as exists in the country. To show you what I mean, let's take a look at the history of the United States Social Security number.

The U.S. Social Security system was established in 1935. In 1936, the Treasury Department issued a regulation (called Treasury Decision 4704) which mandated that every person who was covered by Social Security should be issued an account number. Within a year, the first applications for Social Security Numbers (SSNs) were processed.

In 1943, a rule was established that, whenever a federal agency found it necessary to set up an ID system to track individuals, they should use the SSN. At the same time, the Social Security Board was instructed to cooperate with other agencies with respect to issuing and verifying such numbers.

Skip forward about twenty years. In 1961, the SSN was adopted as the official ID number for all federal government employees. A year later, the Internal Revenue Service declared the SSN to be the official taxpayer ID number. In 1965, Medicare was started, which required a SSN from each person enrolled in the program. In 1966, the Veterans Administration began to use the SSN for all their patients, and in 1967 the Department of Defense decided that the SSN would replace the existing military service number for everyone in the armed services.

At the same time, the government started to push the private sector toward a universal ID. For example, in 1970, they began to require financial institutions — such as banks, savings and loans, credit unions, brokers — to obtain the SSN of all their customers.

The slow encroachment of the SSN as a national ID number did not go unnoticed. While one part of government was pushing it down the collective throats of its citizens and businesses, other branches of the same government were warning of the dangers to privacy.

By the early 1970s, the Social Security Administration (SSA) found themselves in the national ID business, something that was way beyond their original charter. They formed a task force to study the problem, and in 1971, the task force came to the conclusion that the SSA should not promote the SSN as a universal identifier. They counseled the SSA to be "cautious and conservative". At the same time, in a fit of enthusiastic contradiction, the same committee recommended that all school children should be given numbers (to tighten up the system). Moreover, they said, the SSA should cooperate with state, local and non-profit organizations to help them use the SSN to promote health- and education-related goals.

The school recommendation was adopted by the government. Starting in 1972, children would be assigned a SSN as they entered the school system. In addition, a SSN was now required of anyone receiving any benefit provided by the federal government.

Throughout this time, the U.S. Congress was mostly silent, but in 1974, they spoke up by passing the so-called Privacy Act. A year before, a special committee reported to the Secretary of Health, Education and Welfare (who oversees the SSA) that it was a bad idea for the country to adopt a universal ID system. Moreover (said the committee), even if the country wanted such a system, using the SSN would not be adequate.

Thus, the Privacy Act was passed to limit governmental use of the SSN. From now on, no state or local agency could withhold any benefit from someone if he or she refused to give out their SSN. The next year, Congress passed a law making it mandatory for anyone who wanted welfare benefits to disclose their SSN.

Since then, the history of the SSN has been the same. The federal government will pass a law or make a recommendation restricting the use of the SSN in order to safeguard people's privacy. Then, they turn around and pass another law mandating the use of the SSN for yet one more purpose.

In the last 25 years, the SSN has, by law, come into use as an aid to locating parents who owe child support; a mandatory ID for paying state taxes and applying for driver's licenses; a universal federal tax ID number; a requirement for families participating in the food stamp program and school lunch programs; an identifier for people applying for federal loans or any interest-bearing accounts; a way to report alimony payments; a tool to check eligibility of prospective employees; a way to keep track of students applying for a student loan; and on and on.

If you are American, the law requires you to get a SSN when you are born, and to use it when you go to school, get married, get divorced, get a job, pay taxes and die. (It must be on your death certificate.) Today, government agencies at all levels routinely use SSNs to correlate personal information from a variety of databases in order to find tax cheats, catch law breakers and disqualify people who are ineligible for government programs.

In the more than 65 years since the first SSN was issued, all that has happened is that the United States government has put a great deal of effort into developing a national ID system while denying that they were doing so. As a result, social security numbers are used — by government and business alike — to track people's activities and control their lives to an enormous degree. However, because of the constant denial and political posturing, American citizens are deprived of the safeguards and limitations that would have been put into place if a national ID system had been implemented openly and wisely.

Should We Be Worried?

Ten years ago, a person who was reluctant to give out his or her Social Security Number (or any ID number, for that matter) was looked upon as a privacy nut. Today, we understand such people. They are not only tolerated, in many quarters they are venerated. We have seen what happens when too many computers have too much information about us, and we can't do anything about it.

Not only do companies run amuck when it comes to buying, selling and using our personal data, but when we want to talk to them about controlling the information, they go to great lengths to make themselves as inaccessible as possible.

I'm going to tell you about an experience I had, and you tell me if it sounds familiar.

I hate getting junk mail, so when I discovered an advertisement for a chain of clothing stores in my mailbox, I decided to call the company to get my address taken off their mailing list. (The advertisement was actually sent to another person who used to have the same address.)

I started with the company's Web site and discovered it was carefully crafted to provide no clue whatsoever as to how to contact the company. There was no postal address, no phone number, no hint as to if they were even located on Planet Earth. So I called one of the stores and the Person Who Answered The Phone gave me a toll-free number.

I called the number to find only an automated voice mail menu. None of the choices were helpful, customer service only had voice mail, and there was no way to reach a live operator. So I called the store again and got the PWATP. She had absolutely no clue as to how to contact the mother company (the company that owns the store she works in). I asked her, "Where is the headquarters?" and she was able to tell me the name of the city in which the chain had their corporate offices.

I then used a find-a-telephone-number Web site to look up the phone numbers of stores that this company might have in that city. I called one of them. Because they were in the same city as the corporate headquarters, the PWATP was able to tell me what street the company's offices were on. Back to the Web, and armed with the street address, it was the work of a moment for me to look up the main office phone number.

I called and, by making the right phone menu choices, was able to talk to a snarky receptionist. I asked her who could take my address off their mailing list. She said, "I'll transfer you to someone in public relations." "Fine," I said. "Can you please tell me the extension in case I need to call back?" "That line is answered by a person," she said, "so for privacy reasons, I am not allowed to give you that number. I can only transfer you."

"Do you mean," I asked "that your company is willing to put my address in a database, send me unsolicited junk mail, sell my address to other companies without my permission, do everything possible to make it difficult for me to have my address removed from the database, and, for privacy reasons, you won't tell me the extension of someone who works in your building?"

The irony was lost on her. "Do you want me to transfer you or not?"

So she transferred me to someone in the human resources department (not public relations). I explained what I was looking for. "I can't help you," said the woman, "I'm in human resources, but I can transfer you to an assistant in the marketing department." By this time, I would have settled for the guy who empties the trash.

So she transferred me and, according to another voice message, the assistant was out of town for a few days. "But if you need help while I am gone," said the recording, "please call my manager Kathy *unintelligible-name* at extension 4722."

At extension 4722, I once again got voice mail. "This is Kathy *unintelligible-name*. I am either on the phone or away from my desk. Please leave a message, and I'll get back to you as soon as I can."

(Now, tell me the truth. Aren't you sick of hearing unimaginative people tell you that they are either on the phone or away from their desks? I am sure there was a time, say, for about five minutes in 1971, when such a message was not an irritating cliché. But in an age in which there is now an entire generation of people who have grown up with answering machines and voice mail, why do we still have to listen to such moronic statements?)

At this point, I knew better than to leave a message, so I decided to call back at intervals. Finally, two days later, Kathy *unintelligible-name* answered the phone. "I'll be glad to remove your address from our database," she said in a voice that was sweeter than honeydew-flavored nectar.

So Kathy, when I finally was able to talk to her, was sweet. Her manner was friendly and cooperative, as if to say, why didn't you just call me in the first place?

What is the problem here? Is this company disorganized? Not at all. They are exquisitely organized in a way that makes sense to them. It's just that being responsible about personal data and how they use it is not one of their priorities.

Why should it be? There are no major rules for them to follow, and — at least in the U.S. — there is no government department to watch how they use personal data. So what is the solution?

What Privacy Commissioner Slane Has to Say

How can the privacy rights of the individual be protected in an environment controlled by big government and big business?

One solution, chosen by various countries around the world, is to appoint a special official called a privacy commissioner, to represent the interests of the people. In most cases, a privacy commissioner is a government official with an extraordinary degree of independence. His or her job is to go to the mat with both government and business organizations in order to serve the needs of the individual.

Some of the countries and other jurisdictions that have special privacy agencies are Australia (as well as New South Wales), Belgium, Canada (as well as Alberta, British Columbia and Ontario), Denmark, Finland, France, Germany (as well as Berlin, Brandenburg and Hamburg), Greece, Hong Kong, Hungary, Netherlands, New Zealand, Norway, Portugal, Spain, Sweden, Switzerland and the United Kingdom (as well as the Isle of Man). In addition, the European Union has its own privacy commissioner.

(The United States does not have a privacy commissioner or any comparable office. Hawaii does have a state agency called the Office of Information Practices. However, their main job is to oversee Hawaii's Uniform Information Practices Act, a law that details how state records are to be open to public access.)

To get an idea of how a privacy commissioner thinks about the world, I interviewed Bruce Slane, the peripatetic privacy commissioner for New Zealand (which also gave me the opportunity to use the word "peripatetic" in a book). Slane was appointed by the

New Zealand government. However, he emphasizes that his office is an independent entity, not part of the government.

To start, we discussed the basic question: *What exactly is privacy?*

"Privacy [explained Slane] is the right to control who has the right to information. Privacy is not the same as secrecy. Secrecy is withholding information from *everyone*. If you tell something to someone, it's no longer a secret but it could still be private."

Why do people want privacy?

"Having privacy gives people a feeling of autonomy. To me, privacy is a mark of Western civilization. My colleague in Hong Kong, [Privacy Commissioner] Steven Lau tells me that there is no Chinese word for privacy, and that he had a difficult job creating a privacy culture within his society.

"Some people are more comfortable with authority and will accept, without questioning it, that big business can have information about them. However, even people like this will have their limits.

"This is especially true for people at the bottom of the heap, who feel so vulnerable that other people have personal information about them. This creates a feeling of powerlessness, a feeling that the other people mostly use this information against them and not for them."

Do people have a fundamental human right to privacy?

"The European Convention on Human Rights and Fundamental Freedoms [ratified in 1953] describes a right to a private life. It's not an unqualified right, because it sometimes conflicts with other rights.

"In New Zealand, the 1993 Privacy Act [which established the office of Privacy Commissioner] says that agencies may, within reason, set their own purposes for collecting, holding, using, and disclosing personal information. But an agency must be open about these purposes. If they collect information from someone, they must tell that person why it is being collected and what it will be used for. They must also tell the individual if the information is to be disclosed to anyone else.

"The Act does not create a right of privacy. Nor is its recognition of privacy interests absolute. It is my opinion, however, that privacy is the mark of a civilized nation. The more a country advances, the more people value their information privacy."

How much do people care about privacy?

"It depends on what you are talking about. There's a lot of concern, for example, about medical privacy. If people lose privacy, they will lament it and they will always care. Still, privacy values vary. For example, in Sweden, anyone can inspect anyone else's tax return.

"Some people understand that everyone does not have the same privacy values. Other people have trouble accepting the fact that everyone else does not share the exact same opinions as they do."

What is the basic privacy issue?

"It has to do with control, who your information is made available to. For instance, you may allow your information to go to some people or organizations, but not to others."

We all know that information is worth money. Does an individual have any right to the value of his personal information?

"No. I shy away from the idea of ownership. If you get some information and then add to it, who owns it?"

Do children have privacy rights?

"In New Zealand, the law is delightfully vague. In general, children have the same rights as adults."

You are one of many privacy commissioners around the world. Is there much international cooperation?

"Yes. Privacy commissioners and data protection commissioners around the world have been having meetings since the 1970s. The movement started in Europe. Today, there are 35-40 countries that have privacy commissioners, and there is a lot of cooperation and exchange of information.

"In the European Union there is a directive for the transfer of data. You can't transfer personal data to a country that does not offer adequate protection. However, in the U.S., lobby groups have been adamantly opposed to creating a privacy advisory organization."

U.S. business groups would rather have self-regulation?

"That's right. But self-regulation for privacy has never worked in the United States, because it has never offered a remedy for people who have been harmed. Europe is used to having detailed consumer laws, while the United States is not used to them at all. Both sides have myths about one another's cultures."

Are the issues of privacy actually issues of conflict between individuals and organizations?

"The conflict is not nearly as great as some U.S. businesses have made it out to be. Well-designed information laws actually enhance the efficiency of the market, because they require an openness with respect to collection and usage of information. This allows the consumer to act in a more rational way and, hence, the market is more efficient."

So better informed consumers make for a better marketplace?

"Yes. Companies — indeed all organizations — have a natural tendency to want to become secretive. They claim it is for competitive reasons, but very often it is overdone due to cultural influences. 'This is our secret plan and the opposition shouldn't know about it.'

"Trying to use technological solutions to solve personal problems is not very satisfactory. Privacy rights enhance accountability, because they give you the right to access your own information. Openness in disclosing your privacy, openness in corporate privacy policies, and openness in allowing people to access their own information and make corrections lead to better operation of the capitalist market."

In January 1999, Scott McNealy, the chief executive officer of Sun Microsystems publicly said that consumer privacy issues are a 'red herring'. He was quoted as saying "You have zero privacy anyway. Get over it." What do you think of such a statement?

"Such people may be more influential than other people, but their opinions are not necessarily more worthwhile.

"People like this are driven by their corporate purpose, not by their personal preferences. It's quite funny. Such a person will make this type of comment at work, but then he'll go home and want privacy regarding his own financial information."

What would you like everyone to understand about privacy rights in the twenty-first century?

"In a speech I gave in 1997, I observed that the use and capacity of computers enables the manipulation of vast quantities of information quickly and economically. The privacy problems this creates are not new problems. What we have are new applications of existing privacy issues.

"In general, you have a right to see any information someone has about you. However, this right must be balanced, especially with respect to the privacy of other people.

"I mentioned earlier that people will always care about privacy, and if they lose it they will lament it. What I want people to understand is that preserving privacy is like protecting the environment. There will be constant efforts to chip away at it, and once it is gone you can't get it back."

One final question. Does New Zealand have unlisted phone numbers?

"Yes. In New Zealand, you have three choices. You can be listed in the public directory; you can be unlisted but have your number given out if someone asks for it [directory assistance]; or your can specify that you want your number to be completely confidential."

Does it cost money to have your phone number be completely confidential?

"Of course not."

Why We Need Regulation

Our world is one of instant communication and computerized databases, run by enormous corporations whose power is beyond the comprehension of ordinary human beings. We live in an environment in which we are continually affected by forces we can barely comprehend, let alone control.

Yet, if we are to improve our lives and our destiny, it is these very forces that we need to understand. As odd as it may seem, we must start with ourselves, because the forces that buffet us from without — the large organizations and the bureaucratic governments that seem so impervious to individual control — are in many ways a manifestation of our internal qualities as human beings. Let me explain.

One of the great insights of Sigmund Freud was to realize that our minds consist of both conscious and unconscious elements, and that much of our mental activity takes place under the surface,

> *"The forces that buffet us from without —*
> *the large organizations and the bureaucratic*
> *governments — are in many ways a manifestation*
> *of our internal qualities as human beings."*

inaccessible to our awareness. In his investigations, Freud discovered that the unconscious mind is not a deep, peaceful sea of tranquillity. Rather, it is a place of everlasting turmoil, in which primeval urges continually fight forces of repression in an attempt to express themselves through action and emotion.

Eventually, Freud developed a powerful metaphor to describe these forces and their qualities. He described the human psyche as consisting of three interacting components: the ego, the id and the superego. I'm going to take a moment to explain these components because, as you will see, the ideas will come in handy as we move toward an understanding of the forces that control our society. (Remember, though, this is just a metaphor, so don't have a cow.)

The ego is what we think of as the "self", a mostly conscious entity which embodies our awareness of being distinct from other people and from the rest of the world. It is the ego that is in touch with the outside world and which has immediate control over our thoughts and our behavior.

The id is the seat of primitive, instinctual impulses and animalistic urges, and is completely unconscious. Although it is not directly accessible to us — that is, to our ego — the id serves as the source of our most personal demands. Most important, it is a defining quality of the id that, if unopposed, it will do its best to force the ego into actions that will attempt to satisfy its immediate desires.

The superego is the part of our psyche that censors and restrains the ego. It is the superego that allows us to live together and (except for certain parts of Los Angeles) to act as civilized human beings. The superego is mostly unconscious and is formed from the internalization of the moral standards of our society and our parents.

On a personal level, we are continually engaged in an eternal struggle between the ego and the id. To influence this struggle, we put effort into developing and using our superego. It is this effort that drives our lifelong process of maturation. This is why adults are better able to control themselves and act with more wisdom than children. (This is also why children have more fun than adults.)

On a larger level, we structure our society more or less along the same lines. Society is formed by the interplay of groups, not individuals, and it is in the nature of most groups to act mindlessly, without wisdom or conscience. For this reason, we create special organizations, vested with influence and power, in order to govern, advise, and police us.

If we consider society to be a single, large social organism and we look inside that entity, we will find forces that are analogous to the ego, the id and the superego. In particular, we will find that our collective awareness acts as the ego, the world of business acts as the id, and our governments take on the role of superego.

Obviously, we are traveling through the Land of Metaphor without a map, so we shouldn't get too carried away. However, I do want you to appreciate that the many business organizations we create and maintain act without wisdom and without conscience. Their principle goal is to survive and grow and, to do so, they strive to earn ever-increasing amounts of money and acquire ever-increasing amounts of power. In the aggregate, companies are large and powerful, and it takes a large and powerful force to keep them in line. That force is government.

It is only the forces of government — and inter-business competition — that hold back this otherwise unbridled lust for self-indulgence. If you think I am exaggerating, take a look at the business section of any newspaper. Once you know what you are looking for, it is easy to recognize the thrust and parry of everyday business activity for what it is. Believe me, it's not subtle. Just like the id that lies inside each and every one of us, the businesses of our world take advantage of every opportunity to get what they want.

Don't get me wrong. I am *not* saying that corporations are evil. Quite the contrary. It is the world of business and our free marketplace that gives us such a high standard of living and provides us with so much material comfort. Moreover, most of us work for companies and, as such, they provide us with employment, salary and benefits.

My point is that companies are powerful and their interests are not the same as ours. Once we recognize this, we can understand that when corporations invade our privacy in order to increase their profits, they are only acting according to their nature. However, mere understanding is not enough. We must also take action to ensure that the world unfolds in a way that is in *our* best interests.

In the case of privacy, this means establishing organs of government that are independent, reliable and controllable, and putting them to work as our privacy advocates, something we cannot do as individuals. That is why we need government privacy agencies as well as privacy commissioners.

In the last section, I described a conversation I had with Bruce Slane, the New Zealand Privacy Commissioner. During our conversation, Slane made an interesting comment. "People have a sense," he told me, "that there is a problem that needs to be solved by government."

Certainly, when it comes to protecting our privacy, a lot of people feel that way. Many countries — as well as the European Union — have their own privacy commissioners, as do some states and cities. However, the United States has still not extended this level of protection to its citizens.

In Chapter 6, we discussed American history and how the country was born out of revolution. I explained why Americans developed a tradition of individualism and, at the same time, a suspicion of government restrictions, especially with respect to personal freedom.

Since the American Revolution, however, conditions have changed enormously. As you consider these issues, I urge you to do your best not to be fooled by the machinations of business (companies do *not* want to be regulated) or the internal shortsightedness of your culture. Although we often sneer at politics and politicians, let us remember how important they are. As imperfect as politics may be, it is, ultimately, the art of compromise, our way of allotting scarce resources, planning for the common good, and governing ourselves in a civilized manner. (It is no accident that this chapter is entitled "The Politics of Privacy", rather than the "Business of Privacy" or the "Technology of Privacy".)

Have you ever seen the classic 1965 science fiction movie *Forbidden Planet*? Toward the end of the film, Commander John J. Adams (a young Leslie Nielsen) is arguing with Dr. Edward Morbius (Walter Pidgeon). Adams is explaining that it was Morbius who had inadvertently been the cause of several great disasters. An alien machine with limitless power had connected to Morbius's mind and had brought to life the unchecked and selfish desires of Morbius's id.

Morbius refuses to accept the truth, and as he and Adams wrestle in front of the machine, he cries out, "I am not a monster."

Adams, however, is not one for self-deception. He realizes the truth and he well understands the fallibility of human beings.

"We are all monsters in our subconscious," he responds. "That's why we have laws and religion."

8

Our Need to Communicate: Email, Chatting and Privacy

We all have a need — an inborn need — to connect to other people. If you want to be happy, talking and interacting with other people is not optional.

Our Need to Communicate: Email, Chatting and Privacy

- The Biological Urge to Communicate

- Computing as a Social Activity

- The Golden Age of Computing

- The Personal Computer

- The Reason for Networks

- Is the Net Enough?

- Sharing by Email

- How to Share by Email

- Emailing Blind Copies

- Embarrassment and Distress: A True Story

- Why is There So Much Misinformation on the Net?

- 8 Sure-fire Ways to Spot an Email Hoax

- Hoaxes and Urban Legends

- The 5 Biggest Email Mistakes

- Protecting Your Email Address

- How to Get a Disposable Email Address

- Protecting Other People's Email Privacy

- Talk is Cheap (and Not Very Private)

- Abbreviations and Acronyms

The Biological Urge to Communicate

There is a biological imperative within human beings that requires us to communicate. True, some of us like to talk more than others, and some of us need privacy more than others, but we all have a need — an inborn need — to connect to other people. It is a universal trait among normal, healthy people to desire a certain amount of congenial companionship. We need people with whom we can talk and interact.

Of course, we have all, at some time, wished for peace and quiet, and in our society, it is taken for granted that everyone needs some time to be alone. Actually, this is not the case with all societies, or even all people, which suggests that a temporary desire for isolation is more a learned behavior than anything else.

Human beings not only desire to be with other human beings; they need such contact. If you want to be happy, talking and interacting with other people is not optional. People without such companionship find it difficult to maintain their mental health. If you are ever forced to live completely alone, you will find that it will not be long before you become starved for someone to talk to.

Think of the extreme: what happens when you completely isolate a person, say, in a prison cell under solitary confinement? First he gets lonely, then nervous, and, eventually, crazy. Indeed, one of the quickest ways to travel from vibrant mental health to a full-blown case of despair is to become too isolated from one's fellow human beings.

Our need to communicate with others on a one-to-one basis is so strong that it manifests itself in many aspects of life, including how we choose to use our technology. In this chapter, we will take a deep look at the ways in which we communicate on the Internet, and ask why we act the way we do. As you will see, a number of customs and manners have arisen on the Net to govern our chatting, email and discussions. To make sense out of these customs, we must appreciate the biological principles that unconsciously direct our interactions.

To start, I am going to take you back to the olden days, the late 1960s, when there was, as yet, no Internet, no email, and no personal computers. In those days, computers were large, expensive, temperamental creatures that lived in glass houses — and we treated them with awe.

Computing as a Social Activity

When I was a young lad, the word "computer" referred to what are now known as MAINFRAME COMPUTERS. These machines were so expensive, the only organizations that could afford one were large companies, universities and governments. Such computers consisted of many different parts, including large metal boxes, which had to be kept in a room in which the temperature and humidity were carefully controlled.

Most of the old computers were built by IBM, and were leased, not sold (IBM had a monopoly at the time). The most important computers were part of the IBM System/360 family. Because these machines cost so much, they had to be shared, often by hundreds or even thousands of people.

How expensive did computers used to be? When I was an undergraduate, a megabyte of memory cost $1,000,000 and was the size of several refrigerators (and that was in the days when $1,000,000 was a lot of money). Very few computers, however, had as much as a megabyte of memory.

Because a computer cost so much, it was common to house it in a large room with a great many windows. This was so that, when people walked by — especially visitors — they could look into the room, see the computer and be impressed. Such rooms were commonly referred to as GLASS HOUSES.

As a general rule, the only people who were allowed to go into the glass house and work with the computer directly were the OPERATORS. Most mainframe computers required one or more operators to always be there, to minister to the computer and to keep it running smoothly.

If you couldn't go into the computer room to work with the machine directly, how did you use a computer? In those days, programs were put onto punch cards, one line per card — that is, a 500-line program would take 500 cards. To run a program, you had to read the cards into the computer.

To create a program, you used a machine called a KEYPUNCH, which looked like a futuristic contraption from a 1940s science fiction movie, sort of like a typewriter on steroids. You put blank cards into the machine, and then typed your program, one line at a time. As you typed, one character at a time, the machine would punch holes in the card. Each character was represented by a particular combination of holes.

When you had punched all the cards, you were ready to run the program. To do so, you carried the cards over to a machine called a CARD READER. You would hand your cards to an operator, who would take them and put them in the card reader. The cards would be pulled through the machine very quickly, one card at a time. As each card passed through the machine, the holes would be sensed and the data on the card would be read into a temporary storage area of the computer. Once all the cards were read, your program would be put into an internal queue to wait its turn. Eventually, your program would be run by the computer. On many systems, you might have to wait a long time for your program to be run. For example, I have a friend who worked at UCLA during this time, and he remembers having to wait as long as a day to have his programs run.

In those days, the only type of output was printed paper. Once your program had run, the output would be printed on long continuous sheets of perforated "computer paper". Another operator, who worked at the printer, would process the paper as it came out, separating the output of one program from another. To see the results of your program, you would go to the printer room and retrieve your printout, a continuous, folded sheet of paper, often tens of pages long. You then took the printout to another room or an office where there were tables. You would lay the printout on a table and flip through, one page a time, looking at the output. If there was a mistake, you would go back to the keypunch, create a few new cards, use them to replace some of the old cards, and try again.

The reason I am describing this in detail is because I want you to appreciate that creating and running programs was a slow, time-consuming activity. However, it was also a social activity. People spent time with other people: they helped one another with their programs, and they chatted as they punched cards and waited for their output to arrive. In a very real way, using a computer gave you a feeling of being part of a group.

And it was a lot of fun.

The Golden Age of Computing

As the technology improved, computing technology also improved, changing the social environment. Card readers and printers were replaced by TERMINALS, devices that allowed people to use a computer from a remote location.

Each terminal had a keyboard and an output device, and was connected to a computer. You could use a terminal to create and run programs; you would type on the keyboard and look at the output.

With the early terminals, the output was printed on a continuous roll of paper. The most common terminals were the IBM 2740 and IBM 2741, which resembled the old Selectric typewriters (the ones with small, round typeballs). Within a few years, CRT TERMINALS became available, in which the output was displayed on a built-in screen, like a TV screen. (The term CRT refers to the picture tube, a "cathode ray tube".)

Both types of terminals — paper output and screen output — were a great improvement over the old system of keypunch machines, card readers and large expensive printers. Instead of having to punch cards, store them in boxes, and take them to a card reader, you could create and run a program while sitting in front of a terminal.

Before long, rooms full of keypunch machines were replaced by rooms full of terminals. Although computing became a bit more isolated, there was still a sense of community. People would gather in a terminal room to work and to talk, and there was still a strong tradition of friendliness and helping one another. In those days, the best way to meet smart people was to hang out in a terminal room, a place where many friendships were born.

Because computers were still expensive, no one person had his own. Instead, a system called TIME-SHARING was developed to let many people use the same computer at the same time. With a time-sharing system, a number of terminals were connected to a single computer. The operating system — the master control program that ran the computer — was designed to be able to switch back and forth quickly from one task to another. In this way, a single computer was able to support tens, or even hundreds, of simultaneous users, while running programs in the background.

In the early 1970s, a time-sharing system called UNIX was developed at Bell Labs, an AT&T research department. Unix was unusual in that it was designed by very smart people to be used by other very smart people. Before long, Unix had become the most popular time-sharing system in the world, and was used at many universities and research organizations.

From the beginning, Unix was designed to embrace communication and sharing. This was different from the other early operating systems, which, for the most part, were designed for business. For example, the programmers who designed the IBM operating systems assumed that people would want to keep their information as private as possible, and since IBM controlled everything relating to their computers, no one outside of IBM was able to make significant changes to the operating system.

The programmers who created Unix thought differently. Unix programmers were used to working in environments where sharing tools and helping other people was the norm. For this reason, they designed Unix to encourage people to share their programs and data with other people.

Moreover, any Unix user was allowed to look at the actual programs that made up the various components of the operating system. This meant that anyone could then make changes and improvements, and share them with other Unix users. As a result, once a programmer had solved a problem, it was unnecessary for other programmers to waste time solving the same problem. This encouraged Unix people to work together to make their tools better and better, which was one reason why Unix was so popular.

Another reason was that Unix was fun. For example, every Unix system came with a variety of built-in games. This encouraged people to enjoy Unix, and to learn how it worked in order to write more games.

Most important, Unix encouraged people to communicate. By the early 1970s, Unix users were able to send email and talk to one another from their terminals. In addition, every Unix system was designed to connect to other Unix systems. Long before the Internet was developed, many computers around the United States and in Europe were connected to one another via a special Unix-based network called UUCP. Compared to today's Internet, UUCP was slow and awkward, but it did encourage the free flow of information and data. Within a few years, academics and researchers all over the world were using Unix to send email, to share files, and to work together.

Every Unix system had a built-in online manual, and people were expected to use it to teach themselves the basics. However, learning the nuances, including advanced skills and programming techniques, was something that people taught one another informally. If you have only a PC or a Macintosh, it may be hard to believe, but there was a time when learning how to use a computer and how to write programs was something that people taught to one another in person. Although many Unix books came to be published (I myself wrote several), Unix, for the most part, was passed on from one person to another as an oral tradition. In this way, using a computer was as much a social activity as it was an intellectual activity.

Thus, it came to happen that, by the mid 1970s, twenty years before the Internet became popular, a great many smart people around the world were using Unix, a computer system that encouraged talking, working together and sharing with other smart people. Most of these people were researchers and students. They used computers because they loved the work, and because computers helped them solve problems that, to them, were fascinating.

At the beginning of this book, I discussed the idea of a Golden Age: a time when a particular type of technology is new, when the people who use that technology are still "innocent", and when there is a short-lived but significant outpouring of creativity. I talked about how, at one time, there was a Golden Age of the Internet.

Well, long before the Golden Age of the Internet, there was a Golden Age of Computing. It was centered upon the Unix community, and it gave rise to an amazing amount of invention and discovery, and shaped the culture of programming for years to come.

During this time, many computer users enjoyed a large amount of person-to-person contact. It was the first — and only — time in history when people could spend large amounts of time using a computer and still meet their basic biological need of being able to connect to other people in person. In those days, using a computer was, in large part, a social experience, not nearly as isolating as it is today.

Unfortunately, the Golden Age of Computing lasted less than a decade. The seeds for its demise were planted at the beginning of the 1980s, when a new technology unexpectedly burst forth. Within a short time, the world of computing had become addicted to this new technology, one that would change our culture irrevocably.

The new technology was a blessing because it gave people around the world access to computing power that the programmers of the 1970s could only dream of. It was also, however, a curse, because it separated computer users from one another, creating an uncomfortable sense of isolation that persists to this very day and is unlikely to go away.

Like all revolutions, this one started quietly. On September 6, 1980, while most of the programmers and computer users around the world were firmly entrenched in the technology of the 1970s, three people at IBM had a meeting. At that meeting, the leader of a small task force showed two IBM executives a small box. The executives looked at the box, liked what they saw, and made a decision that would change the world permanently.

The Personal Computer

As the 1970s ended, the dominant computers were still the large, expensive IBM mainframes. To be sure, a smaller type of computer, called the MINICOMPUTER, had been developed and was used widely. In fact, Unix, the operating system I mentioned in the last section, ran on minicomputers. Despite their name, however, minicomputers were still (by today's standards) large, expensive and difficult to maintain. The prefix "mini" simply meant they were small compared to mainframes.

By 1980, a few companies had started to make MICRO-COMPUTERS, smaller machines that were suitable for a single person. The two most popular microcomputers were the Apple II from Apple, and the Tandy TRS-80 from Radio Shack. These computers, however, were mainly used by hobbyists and had a limited audience.

At the time, IBM had a few small computers: the System/23 Datamaster (for business), the Displaywriter (a standalone word processor), and the IBM 5100 and 5110 (for programmers). Because sales of these machines were limited, they were seen as dead-ends that served a niche market.

A few people within IBM, however, looked at the new technology and started to wonder if maybe the company should develop a brand new microcomputer for the business market. The conventional wisdom was against such an undertaking. After all, the big money was still in mainframes and minicomputers. What would anyone ever do with a small computer that wasn't powerful enough to run standard IBM business software?

In May of 1980, the top two IBM executives, the chairman Frank Cary and the president John Opel, considered the matter and decided that such a computer might be a minor, but valuable, addition to IBM's product line. They established a task force consisting of eight engineers and five marketing people to look into the matter.

This task force, which came to be known as the Group of Thirteen, started work in July 1980. On September 6, 1980, Bill Lowe, the head of the Group of Thirteen, met with Cary and Opel and demonstrated a working prototype. It had no formal operating system, and it used the same processor as the System/23. However, Cary and Lowe liked what they saw and signed off on a project to design a brand new machine, the "IBM Personal Computer". It was thought that, perhaps, if the machine did extremely well, it might sell in the hundreds of thousands. In 1980, however, this was considered small potatoes at IBM.

On August 12, 1981, IBM formally announced the Personal Computer. Within a few years, the IBM PC, as it came to be known, had revolutionized the computing industry. For the first time, small businesses could afford to own their own computer. By the middle of the decade, PCs — which were now made by other companies beside IBM — were used widely in businesses, and by the early 1990s, they were common in homes.

There is no doubt whatsoever that the PC contributed significantly to the economy of the world. However, the enormous economic growth unleashed by the new, inexpensive, ubiquitous computers came at a price. That price was social isolation.

The Reason for Networks

As I am sure you know, using computers can be a time-consuming activity. Just sit down at the keyboard and, before you know it, hours have passed. If you have ever waited for someone using a computer to come down to dinner, I am sure you are familiar with the plaintive refrain, "I'll be there in a minute. I'm almost finished." And you wait, and wait, and wait...

Before the 1980s, some people did spend a lot of time with computers but, as I have described, they did so in a social environment. They may have ignored their spouses and children but at least they were in the company of friends. Once people started to use PCs, however, computer time turned into alone time and people around the world began to spend countless hours in isolation.

As I explained at the beginning of the chapter, human beings have a biological urge to communicate. If we are to be mentally healthy, we must spend a significant amount of time interacting with other people *in person*. Some people, of course, are more social than others, but I have yet to meet any normal person who didn't need at least some time in the company of other people in order to be happy.

This need is so strong as to color our lives a lot more than most of us realize. Let me give you a subtle but important example.

In the olden days, when you used a terminal, you were sharing the computer with other people. This meant that the speed at which the computer would respond to your commands depended on how many people were currently logged in to the system. When a lot of people were logged in, the computer would slow down. When very few people were using the machine — say, in the middle of the night — it would respond a lot faster, and you could feel it. This led to an interesting phenomenon. As you used the terminal, you felt *connected* to other people. Even if you were working by yourself, all alone in an office, you knew you were part of a larger system that involved other people.

All of this changed when people started to use PCs. For the first time in history, it was possible for an ordinary person to have his own computer. This was good because it meant that people didn't have to wait for a terminal. They also didn't have to wait for a busy computer to get around to running their programs. A personal computer was dedicated to the person who was using it, no matter when he chose to work.

As a matter of economics, PCs were efficient and cost effective. However, when it came to meeting our social needs, the computers that were supposed to be personal were, in fact, dispiriting and impersonal. Using a PC might be convenient, but it was lonely. Not only did you work alone with no one to talk to while you waited (because there was nothing to wait for), but there was absolutely no feeling of being connected to other people or to something larger than yourself.

As strange as it seems, PCs were too efficient, which meant they were too cost effective to ignore. We *had* to use them, because mainframes and time-sharing systems cost too much and were too hard to manage.

As a result, by the mid-1980s, a great many people were spending a lot of time in the company of impersonal, disconnected machines. So what did we do? We began to connect them.

Computer networks had been around for some time, but it was only in the mid-1980s that the technology became available to connect PCs. Networks, of course, cost money and I remember, at the time, hearing people justify such expenditures. The argument was that putting in a network would allow users to share resources, such as expensive printers or file servers (computers with large, fast disks).

At the time, the arguments didn't make a lot of sense to me, and it is only now as I look back that I realize the real reason people worked so hard to connect their computers. It was because they were isolated and they wanted to feel connected. This was long before the Internet became popular. The technology wasn't nearly as good as it is now and networks were expensive and temperamental, but that didn't stop people from wanting them.

Even then, there was a big difference between working on an isolated computer and working on a computer that was part of a network. You felt *connected*, a feeling that was a lot more important than most people understood.

Is the Net Enough?

Whenever you have an undeniable need that is not met, you will do whatever is necessary to meet that need. For example, if you are hungry, you will find food. If you are cold, you will look for warmth. If you need intellectual stimulation, you will read one of my books.

The same goes for your need to communicate with other people. Using a computer is an isolating experience, and if you feel too isolated for too long, you will do whatever you can to establish satisfying communication with other people.

In this context, I would like to raise the question, how good is the Internet at satisfying our need to communicate with other people? Can the communication facilities on the Net balance the large number of hours we spend alone in front of our computer screens? Can meeting people on the Net fill the gaps in an inadequate social life?

The Internet is a very powerful system that connects millions of people around the world. It allows us to send email, chat, participate in discussions, read Web pages created by other people, and create our own Web pages for other people to look at. In spite of these extraordinary communication facilities — unparalleled in the history of mankind — it is my contention that the Internet does *not*, and never will, provide the type of social connections human beings need to thrive. Moreover, I maintain that much of the awkward and irritating behavior that people demonstrate on the Net can be explained by the fact that they are fruitlessly looking for a social outlet that the Net cannot provide.

To understand why this is the case, let's start by observing that the specific need that I am describing is part of our nature. Like our other basic characteristics, this need developed over hundreds of thousands of years as modern man evolved from his ancestors. Throughout this time, there was no such thing as communication at a distance. If two people wanted to communicate, they had to do so in person. In evolutionary terms, modern communication facilities — email, television, radio, telegraphs, postal mail, newspapers and books — are recent inventions, far too new to have any effect on shaping our basic nature.

If you examine the quality of talking in person, it's easy to see that it is a much richer experience than anything that can happen on the Internet. When you communicate on the Net, all you can see is words. When you talk in person you get much more. You not only hear the words, you see the other person: his appearance, his body language, his gestures. You also hear the nuances of his voice: the tone, the volume, the rhythm. Moreover, you experience the environment: the location, the temperature, the ambient noise, and the presence or absence of other people. Once you begin to think in this way, it is easy to see why communicating over the Net is never going to meet our biological needs. There is just too much missing.

If we are to be mentally healthy, we need to talk to our friends and we need to do it in person. This is why, no matter how hard you try, you will never satisfy your deep need to communicate on the Internet.

On the Internet, most of the cues we depend upon to form judgments about other people are missing. This tricks us into feeling comfortable with other people more quickly and more deeply than we do in person. Moreover, the lack of physical presence creates a general feeling of security. After all, if you are sitting at home, alone in your pajamas, chatting with people in various places around the world, the worst that can happen to you is you might fall off your chair. Compare that to what might happen if you were to talk in person with a group of strangers, none of whom know each other.

Aside from comfort and safety, there is another important idea to consider. When we communicate on the Net, it is not possible to use our normal strategies for evaluating other people. For example, when you talk to someone in a Web chat room, you can't see that person's facial expressions. However, you also can't see the color of his or her skin. In fact, you don't even know for sure whether the person is a male or female.

Similarly, when you read an article someone has posted to a discussion group, it is true that you have no idea of what body language the person might use if he were to explain his ideas to you in person. However, you also can't see if he is short or tall, skinny or fat, attractive or plain.

For this reason, Internet communications tend to be free of so many of the prejudices that plague us in person. In this sense, the Internet is a pure communication medium, a meritocracy in which people are much less judgmental and prejudiced than normal. When all you can see is a person's words, all you have to judge him by are his ideas. This is why, from the very beginning, the Internet has always been able to bring out the best in people.

For over twenty years, scientists around the world have been using the Net to collaborate, to share information, and to solve problems collectively. As anyone who has ever worked in a university can tell you, these same scientists, in person, will often spend a significant amount of time pandering to their pride and competitiveness, and posturing like immature children. On the Net, they almost always get along and help one another.

The same thing is true in social interactions. Imagine a group of people talking in a Web chat room and one person asks for help. For example, a teenager might say, "Is there anyone here who understands algebra who might help me with a homework problem?" In such a situation, people are likely to respond kindly and generously. Imagine what response the teenager would get if he were to make the same request in person to a group of strangers on a bus.

The Net is important because, for the first time in history, it allows us to communicate with a great many other people in a way that encourages tolerance, friendliness and sharing. At the same time, however, the environment is devoid of the personal touches that mean so much to us. That is why, when it comes to communication, we must ask the question: "Is the Net enough?"

As I have explained — and as I am sure you know from your own life — personal computers have commandeered a large part of our time, forcing us to spend countless hours working in isolation in a way that is contrary to our basic nature. For this reason, if you use a computer long enough, you will become restless and dissatisfied.

In this sense, then, the Net, as a communication facility, is not enough and it never will be.

However, when it comes to allowing human beings to cooperate and share with one another, the Internet is wonderful. By providing an environment in which people can communicate and share without fear and prejudice, the Net has become mankind's greatest invention.

At the beginning of this section, I observed that if you feel too iso-lated for too long, you will have a strong desire to do something to establish a connection with other people. However, your actions will only feel satisfying and useful if they solve the real problem.

If we are to use the Net wisely and responsively, we must under-stand and respect our desires, and we must learn how to temper our needs, to connect with other people, with our obligations to be good citizens of the Net.

This is why, when someone emails you an inspirational essay explaining how angels touch our lives, or sends you a chain-letter detailing a sure-fire way to make a lot of money without working, it is not necessarily a good idea to immediately forward the mes-sage to a hundred of your closest friends. In such cases, the smart thing to do is to take a moment to think about why, on the Net, we are the way we are.

Sharing by Email

At an early age, we are all taught to share. "If you want to eat pick-led eggs in class," I remember my anatomy teacher telling me in medical school, "you must bring enough for everyone."

He had a point. Sharing is more than just good manners. When we share something that we enjoy, it enhances our pleasure. Going to a movie, watching a sunset, enjoying a fine meal — the simple pleasures of life are more fun when you share them with a good friend. Even pickled eggs, as I am sure you know, taste better when everyone has one.

So why is it a bad idea to email essays, jokes, political statements, and other interesting diversions to all our friends on the Internet? Surely it is not wrong to want to give our friends a chance to enjoy the ideas, humor and opinions we find so entertaining and inspir-ing. After all, if someone doesn't want to read a message, all he has to do is delete it.

It's not that sharing per se is troublesome. Sharing, as a general idea, is good and, as I explained in the last section, sharing on the

Internet is especially important. What is more important, however, is to recognize that people's email boxes are not public receptacles. When someone gives you an email address, he or she expects you to use it with discretion, the same as you would do with a phone number or street address.

Consider this example. Let us suppose that, tomorrow morning, as you read your newspaper over breakfast, you find the Miss Manners column particularly interesting. Miss Manners is discussing the idea that one should never act as if one is expecting a gift. This means, for example, that your daughter is not allowed to announce to her wedding guests that, instead of buying her a bunch of impractical whatnots, it would make a whole lot more sense if they were to just give her the money.

Miss Manners, of course, is a fountain of sound advice, and as you read the column you can't help but ask yourself, wouldn't it be lovely to show this to all of my friends and acquaintances? The thought is indeed lovely, but would you consider sending a copy of the column to *everyone* you know? Would you, for example, make 100 copies of the newspaper column, and slip one under the front door of all your friends and acquaintances?

Of course not. Although there's nothing illegal about distributing interesting missives to the world at large, you would know, instinctively, that sending impersonal, unsolicited correspondence to your friends stretches the bounds of good behavior. The fact that the recipient can easily throw out the piece of paper changes nothing. Polite people just don't do it.

Well, it's the same on the Net. Just because email makes it easy to forward the latest piece of something-or-other to everyone you know doesn't mean you should do so.

Some people are incorrigible forwarders. Once you get on their list, you can count on being subjected to a never-ending series of bad jokes, motivational articles, false virus warnings, silly pictures, political diatribes, spiritual warnings, and fast ways to make money without working.

What makes it worse is that such people never take the time to edit out the extraneous junk from the countless messages they pass on to the world at large. For example, such people will carelessly include all the technical information (the mail headers) from all the previous times that the message has been forwarded. This means you get the treat of looking at the email addresses of the 200 other people who have been sent the same message.

Moreover, such people will also include your email address (which you may wish to keep private) in a list with everyone else's address, effectively broadcasting this information to a cast of thousands. (Remember, many of the recipients will also forward the same message without cleaning up the junk.)

This type of behavior seems to be especially common among AOL users, perhaps because they live their online lives within an artificial environment. Many AOL people have little knowledge about how the Net really works. As a result, such people truly do not understand how they are expected to behave on the Net. (To be fair, I must admit that AOL email tools are poor, and they do not make it easy to edit a forwarded message even if you want to.)

The important question is, why do such people feel such a strong urge to forward messages to everyone they know?

People who love to forward messages do so for the same reason that some people send out long, boring, inappropriate Christmas newsletters. They are merely exercising their need to connect to other people. Although such people mean well, they don't stop to consider whether or not all their recipients really want to receive all this junk.

I call it junk, fully aware that one person's junk is often another person's treasure (which is why so many people manage to get remarried after divorce). Still, email is different from postal mail. As you know, many people use email for business as well as social communication. As a result, a great many people have far more email than they can handle.

I know people who, literally, don't have enough time to even read, let alone answer, all the email they receive. This is one of the reasons why busy people dislike spam (unsolicited advertising). The all too common argument, that if one doesn't want to read the message, one can just delete it, is merely self-serving and inconsiderate. The perpetually overflowing mailbox is one of the banes of modern existence.

Moreover, some people feel that they must respond, at least briefly, to any act of kindness. To such people, any email message from a friend creates an obligation to reply. ("Madeleine, thanks ever so much for passing along the warning that a new computer virus can wipe out my hard disk if I turn on the lamp while I am reading my mail. The network administrator here at the office tells me that the warning is a hoax, but I do so appreciate your thinking of me.") Such people, it is fair to assume, do not need any more unnecessary social obligations.

Aside from inconvenience, we should consider the value of what we send to people. Just because you or I may feel that something is funny — or interesting or important or pithy — does not mean that every one of our acquaintances, especially those we don't know in person, will feel the same way. In fact, the older I get, the more astonished I am at how few people share my idea of what is funny, interesting, important and pithy.

When it comes to email, the personal touch is most important. Suppose you see an article on a Web site that you just know your Aunt Rose will appreciate (she always was a sucker for Germanic theatre). You copy the article to your email program, carefully delete all the junk, and send it with a short note explaining that you remember her talking about Brecht's play *Trommeln in der Nacht*.

This is a personal message that is sure to be appreciated. Your aunt will be touched by your remembering her, and by the trouble you went to in order to send her something you knew she would like. Compare this to how she will feel if she opens a message addressed to her and 100 other people containing a selection of low-quality blond jokes.

Since it is easy to see that such messages are not personal, why do so many people forward them?

The obvious answer is that the sender thinks the recipients will want to read the message. To some extent, this may be true, but it is not the real reason. The real reason people forward impersonal messages is that doing so gives people the feeling that they are reinforcing social connections.

Unfortunately, forwarding email is a poor way to make new friends and to stay in touch with old ones. Most of the time, sending impersonal messages will only serve to annoy, irritate, or bore our loved ones.

The best way for us to maintain friendships is to make the effort to visit our friends in person and to write them real letters on paper. (Yes, I know you are busy. Everyone is busy.) Failing that, a friendly phone call is a much better way to show someone that he or she is in your thoughts than is sending them a list of "10 Ways In Which Beer Is Better Than Women".

How to Share by Email

Having just told you not to forward impersonal email, I will now explain how to do it in as polite a manner as possible. After all, the urge to forward an interesting message is a strong one: even the best of us succumb to temptation now and again.

Being polite is simple. All you have to do is follow three simple rules.

1. Clean up the junk.

Before you send the message, take a moment to delete all the junk. This includes all the old addresses, as well as any spurious indentations and "**>**" characters. Cleaning up the junk will make it easy for your recipients to read and understand the message. It will also preserve the privacy of all the people whose email addresses would otherwise be forwarded to new recipients.

If your mail program does not let you edit messages adequately, copy the message to a file and edit it with Notepad or Wordpad. (I'll show you how to copy a message in a moment.)

Notepad and Wordpad are programs that allow you to create and change plain-text documents. Such programs are called TEXT EDITORS. Both Notepad and Wordpad are included free with

Windows. The main difference is that Wordpad is designed to handle larger files. To start these programs, click on the Start button. Then select Programs and look in the Accessories folder.

If you like to use computer tools, you will probably find Notepad and Wordpad to be too basic. If so, it is worth your time to learn how to use a more powerful text editor. There are many choices. Two that I recommend are Textpad and Ultraedit.

Once you master a good text editor, you will find it to be a very useful tool and a lot more comfortable to use than a word processor. (For example, I used Textpad to write this book.) Here are the addresses of the Web sites where you can find these programs:

```
http://www.textpad.com/
http://www.notetab.com/
http://www.ultraedit.com/
```

Internet Resources: Text editor programs

To copy a message from your mail program to your text editor, select the lines you want to include and press Ctrl-C. This copies those lines to the Windows CLIPBOARD, an invisible short-term storage area. To paste the selection from the clipboard into a file, open your text editor, create a new file, and then press Ctrl-V.

Once you have finished editing your message, you can use Ctrl-C and Ctrl-V to copy it from your text editor back to your mail program.

2. Choose your recipients thoughtfully.

It's inconceivable that a particular message would be of interest to everyone you know, even if it contains a computer virus warning, important religious information, or a plea to solve a terrible political problem. Send your message only to those who you think will enjoy it. Don't preach to people and don't scare people (as much as you think they may need it).

If someone asks you to take him off your mailing list, please honor the request gracefully. Some people will continue forwarding messages even after they are asked to stop. If you know one of these people, buy him or her a copy of this book. If that doesn't work, try a large polo mallet.

3. Put the list of recipients in the Bcc: line, not the To: line.

When you create or forward a message for mass mailing, don't put a long list of addresses in the **To:** line. Use the **Bcc:** line instead. This will send what are called "blind copies" and ensure the privacy of your recipients.

Actually, the idea of blind copies is so important, I would like to take the time to talk about it in detail.

Emailing Blind Copies

A mail message consists of several parts: the header, the body and (optionally) one or more attachments.

The HEADER, which comes at the beginning of the message, contains technical information, such as the address, the subject, the date, and so on. We'll talk about headers in a moment. The BODY, which follows the header, is the text of the actual message. An ATTACHMENT is a separate file, such as a picture, that is sent along with the message. (We'll talk more about attachments in Chapter 10.)

The header of a message consists of various HEADER LINES, each of which contains specific information. Most of the header lines contain technical information for the mail program to use internally, and you can ignore them. However, there are six header lines I want you to understand.

The following example shows a header that contains all six of these lines. When you read a message, your email program may not show you the header lines in this format. In fact, some programs hide these lines completely unless you ask to display them. Still, they are always there, at the beginning of a message, so you should know that they exist.

(I had to break the **Cc:** line into two parts to fit it on the page, but it is really one long line.)

```
From: George W. Bush <president@whitehouse.gov>
To: Harley Hahn <hhahn@the-little-nipper.com>
Date: Fri, 19 Apr 2001 15:42:01 -0400
Subject: I need your advice
Cc: Pope <holy-father@vatican.va>,
Queen Elizabeth <queen@royal.gov.uk>
Bcc: Barbara Bush <mom@george-bush-family.com>
```

The first four header lines are straightforward. The **From:** line shows the name and email address of the person who sent the message. The **To:** shows the name and email address of the recipient. The **Date:** line shows the time and date that the message was sent. The **Subject:** line shows the subject of the message (as typed by the person who sent the message).

The **To:** line can contain more than one address. If so, a copy of the message will be sent to each address. Thus, to send a message to, say, four people, you can put all four addresses in the **To:** line, separated by commas.

Alternatively, you can send copies by specifying addresses on the **Cc:** line. The effect is the same as putting the names in the **To:** line. Each person gets a copy of the message, and each person sees the names of the other people who received copies. The difference between using the **To:** line and the **Cc:** line is mostly psychological. For example, some people use the **Cc:** line to indicate that a copy of the message is being sent for information only, and the recipient is not expected to act upon the message in any way. (Take a look at the example above.) In addition, when you reply to a message, the reply will only go to the people in the **To:**, unless you specify that you also want to send it to the people in the **Cc:** line.

The final header line, the **Bcc:** line, is the one I want to make sure you understand. When you put someone's address on this line, he gets what is called a BLIND COPY. This means that no one else knows that this person was sent a copy of the message. For instance, in the example above, neither the Pope, Queen Elizabeth or I have any way of knowing that a copy of the message was sent to Barbara Bush.

If you examine the header of an incoming message, you will not see a **Bcc:** line, so you have no idea if anyone else got a copy of the same message. This is good to remember when working in a company in which corporate politics is important. For example, if you get a message asking your opinion of your boss, you can't necessarily assume that your boss didn't get a blind copy of the same message.

The reason I want you to understand how the **Bcc:** line works is that you can use it to hide people's addresses when you send a mass mailing. Instead of putting all the addresses in the **To:** or **Cc:** lines, put them in the **Bcc:** line. That way, no one will know who received copies. This not only keeps everyone's email address private, it makes your message look more personal because, at the other end, the recipient will not see a long list of names and addresses.

Here is an example:

```
From: Harley Hahn <hhahn@the-little-nipper.com>
To:
Date: Fri, 19 Apr 2001 22:54:01 -0400
Subject: All about my cat
Bcc: Pope <holy-father@vatican.va>,
Queen Elizabeth <queen@royal.gov.uk>,
George W. Bush <president@whitehouse.gov>

Here is a cute story about my cat, The Little
Nipper..."
```

In this example, three people will receive copies of this message. However, none of them will know that anyone else got a copy.

Notice that I did not put an address on the **To:** line. With some mail programs, this will work as long as you have one or more addresses on the **Bcc:** line. For example, with Eudora, if the **To:** line is empty, but you have specified addresses on the **Bcc:** line, Eudora will create a dummy **To:** line for you that looks like this:

```
To: (Recipient list suppressed)
```

If your mail program will not accept an empty **To:** line, use your own address on the **To:** line and everyone else's address on the **Bcc:** line. For example:

```
From: Harley Hahn <hhahn@the-little-nipper.com>
To: Harley Hahn <hhahn@the-little-nipper.com>
Date: Fri, 19 Apr 2001 22:54:01 -0400
Subject: All about my cat
Bcc: Pope <holy-father@vatican.va>,
Queen Elizabeth <queen@royal.gov.uk>,
George W. Bush <president@whitehouse.gov>
Here is a cute story about my cat, The Little
Nipper..."
```

Now that you know how to use the Bcc: line, please make sure that you never send out a mass mailing in which all the addresses are shown to the recipients.

Hint: If you are bored, you can always foment intrigue and dissension among your friends and co-workers by sending blind copies of provocative messages to carefully selected people.

Embarrassment and Distress: A True Story

Maxine was a level-headed woman with good friends, a better-than-average boyfriend, and a pleasant disposition. People who knew Maxine considered her to be a sensible person with good judgment — a successful, up and coming woman, admired by everyone.

For her first thirty-six years, Maxine's life was uniformly smooth. She grew up in a large mid-Western city with a loving family and more than her share of pleasant memories. After college, Maxine moved to the West Coast where she established a career as an independent assistant director working on various feature films. Maxine was satisfied, happy and grateful to have such a good life.

What Maxine didn't know was that Fate was waiting around the corner, standing patiently with the iron hand in the velvet glove.

It was a lovely spring day when Maxine awoke to the typical sounds of a Southern California morning. Outside her window she could hear the rustle of jasmine leaves, swaying in the warm Southern California breeze and the soft chirping of brightly colored Southern California early birds gathering worms.

Maxine had a lot to do that day, including an important interview for a new job, but she decided to take a minute to turn on her computer and check her mail. As the machine whirred into life, Maxine finished her makeup and chose a flattering outfit that showed off her slim, athletic figure and her clear, youthful skin.

As she was checking her mailbox, a new message arrived. She read it briefly. It was a political statement with a forceful point of view, and it ended by urging the reader to forward the message widely. Actually, Maxine did not care for politics, but the message made her think of a fellow she had met in college. She had received a note from him recently and he had enclosed his email address. "Perhaps," she thought, "he might be interested in this. I'll forward it to him."

Maxine glanced at the message. She noticed a lot of old header lines that no one had bothered to delete. "There must be over 200 names and email addresses here. I wonder if I should take a moment and edit the message before I forward it," she thought. Then she noticed the clock. It was getting late. "It'll be okay," she told herself, and she sent the message.

A few hours later, Maxine came home to get ready for her interview. She checked her computer and found over 100 messages. She started to read them and was shocked. Evidently, the fellow to whom she had forwarded the message had strongly disagreed with its premise. He had written an offensive, spirited rebuttal, and emailed it to every email address that was sent along with the message. Moreover, he had not bothered to delete Maxine's name and address from the message. As a result, Maxine found herself with a mailbox full of angry, abusive complaints, with more coming in every moment.

And that, my dear reader, was the turning point in Maxine's life. Overcome with remorse, she spent the better part of the afternoon writing personal notes to everyone who had received the offensive message. She apologized profusely, and most of the people seemed to forgive her, but the damage was done and her life began to unravel, one thread at a time.

First, she completely forgot about the interview. As a result, she was passed up for what would have been a significant opportunity to further her career.

Within a short time, her friends and acquaintances stopped calling her, and her boyfriend left town for a job in Fargo, North Dakota. Moreover, the film producers, who hitherto had been anxious to secure her services, stopped returning her phone calls.

Within days, Maxine was a broken woman, a mere shell of her former self.

A year later, one of Maxine's oldest friends was in a candy-colored BMW on her way to a luncheon for fashionable-women-in-the-film-business. As she paused at a stoplight, she noticed a shabby, overweight, pock-marked creature motioning to her from the sidewalk: a pathetic old lady, dressed in rags, with her hair and nails in complete disarray. The stooped figure was standing at the side of the road holding a battered hand-lettered sign that said "Will work on a film for food."

The friend looked closer and had the shock of her life: the broken-down hag was Maxine!

Fortunately, the light changed before Maxine could recognize her friend. The friend drove off, relieved at being able to avoid what promised to be a particularly unpleasant scene. She looked in the rear-view mirror, caught one last glance of Maxine and sighed.

"There, but for the grace of God," she told herself as her BMW slid effortlessly into the sunny Southern California traffic, "go I."

Why is There So Much Misinformation on the Net?

The Internet is the largest information-sharing resource in history. However, the Internet is also a hotbed of misinformation, an environment in which hoaxes and rumors incubate quickly, burst into life, and die out only to be resurrected again and again.

Why should this be? There are three reasons.

First, we often have trouble distinguishing what is true from what is false or misleading. To some extent, this is because, in our culture, we are bombarded with untruthful and exaggerated information. Everyone, it seems, is trying to sell us something, whether it is the latest miracle diet aid, an overpriced car to boost our self-esteem, or a political idea that has been carefully crafted to pander to focus groups and the latest opinion polls. In such an environment, too many people accept anything that is presented with authority as being correct. We believe what we read in the newspapers, what we hear on TV, and on the radio. Thus, when we see something on the Web, or read information sent to us via email, we tend to believe what we see.

Another reason why there is so much misinformation on the Net is that it is easy for anyone to distribute information. It's easy to send and receive email, and it doesn't take much training to participate in a discussion, talk in a chat room, or create a simple Web site. However, there are no rules that govern the quality of the information that people send by email, discuss on the Net, or put on a Web site. As a result, the quality of much of what you see on the Net is governed, not by economics or a desire for accuracy, but by human nature.

To see what I mean, let me digress for a moment and talk about another form of creativity, cooking.

Imagine yourself preparing to cook a special meal. You take your time to consider various dishes. You then hunt up a recipe, shop for the ingredients, prepare the food, and cook it carefully. When the food is ready, you bring it to the table in an attractive serving dish.

Cooking well can be a rewarding experience, but it is time-consuming, and you can only do it when you are not in a hurry. For example, if you come home late one night, starving because you have worked long hours without a dinner break, you aren't going to take the time to plan a meal, find a recipe, shop for ingredients, prepare the food, cook it carefully, and serve it in a special dish. Indeed, you may simply open a can of soup, throw together a quick meal, and chow down as quickly as you can.

Do you see the irony? It is possible to be thoughtful about preparing food, but only when you are not hungry.

The same is true with our need to communicate, and this is the third reason why there is so much misinformation on the Net. When we have trouble communicating to other people in person, we tend to look for a fast way to reach out and feel a connection no matter how thoughtless — and, ultimately, how dissatisfying — that connection may be.

My feeling is that, when we have important information to communicate, we have an obligation to ensure that the information is correct. Otherwise, we run the risk of misleading or even hurting other people. Unfortunately, if we feel a strong urge to broadcast the information immediately, we will often not take the time to think before we act.

To some extent, this is simply human nature. Gossip is, after all, a fundamental social activity, on and off the Net. Aside from gossip, however, there are other sources of deliberate misinformation on the Net. First, there are people who intentionally mislead others. They may do this to sell a product, scare other people, seduce another person, and so on. Second, there are writers and journalists who, for whatever reason, publish before checking all the facts, thus creating news articles that look authentic but are inaccurate. Fortunately, we all have experience with these types of misinformation, so we can sometimes recognize that a misleading sales pitch or a news story doesn't ring true.

What we have trouble recognizing — on a Web site or in our electronic mailbox — is objective misinformation that is passed from one person to another, often with the best of intentions. For example, when a friend sends you email describing how a young lad is dying of a brain tumor, and he wants everyone in the world to send him a postcard so he can get his name in the Guinness Book of Records, your friend means well. The request, however, is false.

Similarly, if you read on a Web site that it is dangerous for people with pacemakers to go near microwave ovens, the person who created the Web site thought he was being helpful. The information, however, is wrong.

Thus, we are left with the following equation:

$$
\begin{array}{l}
\text{Sharing Information is Easy} \\
+ \;\; \text{We Have a Strong Need to Communicate} \\
+ \;\; \text{People Believe What They Read} \\
\hline
\text{A Lot of Hoaxes and Rumors on the Net}
\end{array}
$$

The result, as you might expect, is an environment in which it is common for well-meaning people to mislead others. As a result, the Net abounds with a great deal of information of dubious quality, usefulness and parentage.

8 Sure-fire Ways to Spot an Email Hoax

Figure 8-1 contains an example of a typical Internet hoax. This particular hoax urges people to boycott certain oil companies in order to bring down the price of gasoline. The hoax is in the form of an email message and was actually sent to a friend of mine.

When you receive such email, how can you tell it is a hoax? There are 8 telltale signs you can look for. Let's go over these signs using the letter in Figure 8-1 as an example.

1. The message is sent to you as part of a mass mailing.

If you look at the header, you can see that the person who sent the message has mailed it to himself. This means that he has specified a group of addresses in the **Bcc:** line (see the discussion on blind copies earlier in the chapter), which means that the message was sent to a group of people.

2. The message purports to be of special importance.

The writer says that he usually doesn't forward such mail, but this message is so important he will make an exception.

Figure 8-1   An Example Of An Email Hoax

From: Michael XXXXXXXXX <michael@xxxxxx.com>

To: Michael XXXXXXXXX <michael@xxxxxx.com>

Subject: Gas Prices

I usually abhor activist-style emails, and
delete rather than forward them. But I found
some merit in this one, and figured it was worth
forwarding.

Read on if you dare...

-- Mike

Gasoline Prices

THE FOLLOWING WAS SENT BY AN ECONOMIST WITHIN
THE FUEL INDUSTRY. AN ECONOMICS PROFESSOR AT CAL
REITERATED THE SAME LAST WEEK. IT IS WORTH
TRYING.

We heard from the well-known consumer activist
Xxxxx Xxxxxx, who is very savvy about the
economy, (visit his website at http://
www.xxxxxxxxxxx.com for lots of good
information). He says that the gas prices are
going to start going up again and will be high
this summer -- $2 and up. We need to do whatever
we can, and do it NOW!

This sounds doable. This makes more sense than
the "don't buy gas on a certain day" routine
that was going around last year. Whoever started
this has a good point. By now, you're probably
thinking gasoline priced at about $1.49 is
cheap. Me too, as it is now $1.58 for regular
unleaded!

Now that the oil companies and the OPEC nations
have conditioned us to think that the cost of a
gallon of gas is CHEAP at less than $1.50, we
need to try an aggressive response. With the
price of gasoline going up more each day, we
consumers need to take ACTION!

The only way we are going to see the price of gas
come down is if we don't buy it. But (as the gas
companies know full well, and are counting on),
that's not really a practical option since we
all have come to rely on our cars. But we CAN

Figure 8-1 An Example Of An Email Hoax *(continued)*

```
have an impact on gas prices if we all act
together.

Here's the idea: For the rest of this year,
don't purchase gasoline from the two biggest
companies (which now are one), namely EXXON and
MOBIL. You see, if they are not selling, they
should be inclined (i.e., "forced") to reduce
their prices. And, because of their size, and
hence market share, if they reduce their prices,
the other companies will too. (They would HAVE
no choice!). Isn't that a "juicy" prospect? But
to have an impact, we need to reach literally
millions of users. But it's doable! I am sending
this note to 10+ people. If each of you send it
to at least 10 more... and those 10 send it to at
least 10 more and so on, by the time the message
reaches the sixth iteration, we will have
reached over one million consumers.

Acting together, we can make a difference. If
this idea makes sense to you, please pass this
message on, or one you compose, to at least 10
more E-mail pals.

PLEASE HOLD OUT UNTIL THEY LOWER THEIR PRICES TO
BELOW $1.28-$1.29 AND KEEP THEM DOWN. THIS CAN
REALLY WORK! If you're not outraged, you're not
paying attention.
```

3. The message quotes unnamed authorities.

Notice that the message begins by appealing to the authority of people who should know what they are talking about: in this case, an economist and an economics professor. However, there are no actual names. This is typical of such a letter. (The nickname "Cal", by the way, refers to the University of California at Berkeley.)

If you read the message carefully, you will see that it was supposed to have been written by these two unnamed authorities ("We heard from...")

4. The message falsely quotes a real authority.

In this case, the message refers to a real authority who is a well-known consumer activist (I have deleted his name) as well as a real Web site address. The person who forwarded the message didn't take the time to check out the Web site, but I did. The consumer activist was aware of the email hoax. One of his staff members wrote: "...The email is not accurate. Xxxxx did not write the email message, nor does he favor boycotts...."

Notice that the message is worded carefully to look as if the consumer activist is telling us to take action, even though this is not the case.

5. **The message makes unsubstantiated claims and uses faulty reasoning.**

This particular hoax predicts gasoline prices will be going up soon. The blame is placed on oil companies and OPEC.

To many people, such a statement will sound true. Oil companies, like all companies, want to maximize their profits, and they do make more money when prices go up. Exxon Mobil, for example, earned $5 billion in the first quarter of 2001, up 44 percent from 2000 (mostly due to high oil and natural gas prices). Similarly, the purpose of OPEC (Organization of Petroleum Exporting Countries) is to control crude oil prices in a way that benefits their members. Still, this is a long way from saying that the only reason current prices are palatable is because we, as consumers, have been brainwashed (an unsubstantiated claim).

The letter goes on to assert that gasoline prices are rising every day (an exaggeration), and that the only way the prices will ever come down is if we stop buying gas completely (faulty reasoning). Such claims are typical of this type of hoax.

6. **The message makes false promises.**

In our example, the message proposes that consumers boycott the largest oil company (Exxon Mobil) by refusing to buy gasoline from their service stations. This action will force the company to lower prices, which will then force the other oil companies to lower their prices. A second promise is also made, that the boycott will be effective. ("Acting together, we can make a difference".)

Both of these promises are false. The oil/gasoline market is complex, and gasoline prices cannot be controlled in this way.

7. The message rallies the troops with a call to action.

An email hoax will often tell you to perform a particular task, for example, participate in a boycott, complain to your political representative, or sign a petition.

8. The message tells you to send copies to everyone you know.

Perhaps the most suggestive sign that a message is a hoax is that it ends by asking your help to spread the word. This, in itself, is always a tipoff that what you are reading is not true.

Hoaxes and Urban Legends

People whose jobs require them to create information that will be published in a respectable venue — journalists, for example — are trained to take the time to check their facts, even under the pressure of a deadline. The rest of us, alas, are not always as diligent. When we are presented with a tidbit that sounds interesting, important or intriguing, it is always tempting to repeat it as quickly as possible to as many people as possible. ("Guess what? I just found out the secret Masonic handshake. Give me your hand and I'll show you.")

On the Internet, a great many hoaxes and rumors abound. Whenever you receive email you suspect might be a hoax, take a moment to check it out before you forward it to anyone. To help you, at the end of this section, I have included some Web sites where you will find descriptions of common hoaxes, including the ones that are currently making the rounds on the Net. Before you forward a suspicious message, check it out on one of these sites.

Of the large number of Internet hoaxes, there are two specific types I want to mention: virus hoaxes, because they are especially harmful, and urban legends, because they are especially interesting.

A VIRUS HOAX is a message containing a false warning about a specific computer virus. Computer viruses are important, and we will discuss them in detail in Chapters 9 and 10. (For now, I'll just say that a computer virus is a program that, if you run it, might cause harm to the files on your computer.) If there were a chance that a computer virus might end up on your computer, you would, of course, want to be warned. So it does make sense that people might want to forward messages warning against a particular virus.

However, you must be careful about such messages. Virtually, every virus warning circulating on the Internet is false. As you will see in Chapter 9, virus hoaxes are harmful because (1) they scare people unnecessarily, and (2) they obscure the reality of how viruses spread and what you can do about them. I'll discuss the details in Chapter 9. For now, all I want you to remember is that, if you receive a virus warning, you'll be able to tell it's a hoax by looking for the 8 telltale signs we discussed in the previous section.

Far more interesting than virus hoaxes are the urban legends. An URBAN LEGEND is a story that has been repeated so often that it has become a myth. It is a hallmark of an urban legend that it is just plausible enough to make you wonder if it is true, and intriguing enough so that people will spread it quickly and widely. Although some urban legends spread via email, Usenet and Web sites, many of them are well-known enough to thrive without the Internet. Indeed, some urban legends are so enduring that they have, literally, been around for many years.

In one way, urban legends are like fairy tales, in that they are told in the form of a story with a beginning, a middle, and an end. In addition, there is usually a point to the story, with a moral or a warning.

Fairy tales, however, take place "once upon a time" and are not literally true. Urban legends are supposed to have happened recently and are told as if they are true. A typical urban legend will take place in a contemporary setting and will begin with the assertion that the story actually happened to a real person, often described as a "friend of a friend". Indeed, in the world of urban legends, this idea is so common that it has its own abbreviation: FOAF.

The idea of something happening to a FOAF is one that is so common that we take it for granted. Perhaps you have even told such stories yourself. "My wife's cousin had a landlord who wouldn't give back her deposit, so to get even, she stuffed a dead fish into the heating vent when she moved out." Or, "I knew a guy who had a friend who worked in a pizza place where the people in the kitchen would spit on the pizza before they put it in the oven."

As you can imagine, it is possible to spend a lot of time analyzing urban legends. Indeed, people write books about them. I like to just read them and chuckle. Here are a few well-known urban legends for you to enjoy. Do they look familiar? (Needless to say, all these stories are false.)

- A woman is having lunch in the cafe at Neiman-Marcus [a very expensive department store]. She likes the cookies so much that she asks for the recipe. The waitress says that the recipe is too valuable to give away, but offers to sell it. The woman asks "How much," and the waitress says "Two-fifty." The woman agrees and is given a copy of the recipe. Later, the woman receives a bill for $250.00. Neiman-Marcus refuses to give her a refund so, to get even, she decides to share the recipe with everyone in the world. [The recipe is included with the story.]

- In the U.S., most states will put demerit points on your driving record if you are caught speeding. However, there is a foolproof way to avoid getting such points. When you receive a speeding ticket, pay the fine with a check that is a bit more than the fine. For example, if the fine is $75, send in a $78 check. The computer system will send you a refund, but *don't cash the refund check*. Because of a bug in the computer system, you cannot be assigned demerit points until all the financial transactions have been completed.

- The scene is a large expensive wedding. It is time for the speeches, and the groom stands up. He announces that he has a special gift for each guest. Each guest has a large envelope taped to the bottom of his chair. He asks each person to open his envelope and look inside. As the envelopes are being opened, the groom explains that he recently became suspicious of his fiancee, so he hired a private detective to follow her for over the last few weeks. Inside each envelope is a copy of a photograph showing the fiancee (who is now his wife) having sex with the best man. The groom then turns to the bride and the best man and issues a rude remark. He then leaves and, the next morning, has the marriage annulled. In this way, he has taken his revenge by embarrassing the bride and best man in front of their friends and relations, and by forcing the bride's parents to pay over $32,000 for a 300-guest wedding.

If you are interested in urban legends, here are some Web sites where you can read about them:

```
http://www.snopes.com/
http://www.urbanmyths.com/
http://www.urbanlegends.com/
http://urbanlegends.about.com/cs/urbanlegends/
```

Internet Resources: Urban legends

For more general information, the following Web sites contain information about all types of Internet hoaxes:

```
http://hoaxbusters.ciac.org/
http://www.humorcafe.com/hoaxes/
http://www.snopes.com/info/current.htm
http://www0.delphi.com/navnet/legends/
   legends.html
```

Internet Resources: Internet hoaxes

The 5 Biggest Email Mistakes

Email is fast and easy. However, whenever you deal with anything (or anybody) that is fast and easy, you need to be careful. One wrong move and, before you know it, you're in deep trouble with no way out.

The best way to protect yourself against email problems is to understand the most important pitfalls and take steps to avoid them. There are 5 common mistakes that can lead to disaster.

Avoid these mistakes and you will go a long way to ensuring that you and Mr. Remorse never get to know one another on a personal basis.

1. Sending mail when you are upset.

By far, the worst email mistake you can make is to send a message when you are upset. This is as sure a recipe for disaster as exists on the Net.

When you are in a bad mood and you receive an irritating message from someone, it is all too easy to fire off an emotional reply. Don't do it! I guarantee that, if you do, you will be sorry later. At best, you will feel awful. At the worst, you may ruin a business or personal relationship without even realizing what has happened.

Here is an example. I once had someone working for me who became angry and sent me a nasty email message. Of course, we all get angry from time to time, but when I read this particular message, I realized this was not the type of person I wanted working for me. However, we were in the middle of a project and it would have been foolish to fire him right away, so I didn't say anything. Instead, I waited and fired him later when it was convenient for me.

Writing email in the heat of anger (or disappointment or passion) is always a mistake. To see why this is so, think back to our discussion, earlier in the chapter, in which we examined the nature of human communication. When you talk to someone in person, there is a lot of context: the tone and rhythm of your voice, your body language, and so on. Because the other person is near you, he or she can react immediately to what you are saying. This tends to act as a damper, forcing you to keep your harshest emotions in check. What's more, in the course of the conversation, you may even find out you were wrong.

This is not the case with email. If you are angry and you compose an angry message, you are — because of your state of mind — thinking poorly, and because there is no one to react to what you are saying, you will temporarily disconnect your actions from the possible consequences. Moreover, the person who receives your message will not know your state of mind and is sure to be insulted.

"If you are angry and you compose an angry message, the person who receives your message will not know your state of mind and is sure to be insulted."

For this reason, it is imperative that you remember the following rule:

Whenever you find yourself writing an email message that may make someone feel bad, force yourself to wait 24 hours before you send it.

The trick to abiding by this rule is that you must decide to follow it ahead of time; otherwise, when something bad happens, you'll find yourself losing your composure. I promise you that when your boss sends a boneheaded memo blaming you for someone else's mistake, or your best friend cancels a big trip at the last minute, you are going to want the instant satisfaction of firing off a real stinker.

So please, decide *now* that, when the time comes, you will force yourself to wait 24 hours before sending such a letter. Believe me, if you follow this advice you will thank me over and over.

2. Using your work computer for personal email.

Everything you do at work is under the control of your employer. This may not seem to be the case if you work at a company that seems to be relaxed and informal. However, when the company wants to get tough and check up on what you have been doing on your computer, they will, and there's nothing you can do about it.

In particular, if you use your work computer to send and receive email, your boss or your manager is allowed to read your email, even if it is private and even if you use your personal AOL or Hotmail account.

In Chapter 2, I discussed this issue in detail. At the time, I pointed out that many companies monitor email and Web activity. Even if your company doesn't seem to be checking up on you overtly, your computer will retain traces of what you do, and these traces can be used against you should your interests ever diverge from those of the company (for example, when you leave your job). Moreover, it is not uncommon for employees who are fired to be denied access to their computers to retrieve or delete personal information.

As a general rule, it is a big mistake to use your work computer for personal activities, including email.

3. Sending mail to the wrong address.

When you reply to a message, your mail program automatically inserts the return address for you. But when you create or forward a message, you must specify the address yourself. In most cases, this means using your mouse to click on one or more names in your address book. However, once you get used to using your email program, your fingers will move quickly and it is easy to make mistakes, especially if you have an emotional reaction to what you are reading.

When Aunt Nancy sends you a long letter of complaint about Sylvia's behavior at the recent family wedding, it is human nature to want to forward the message to other family members. Just be sure that, in your haste, you don't send a copy of the note to Sylvia.

Before you forward anything, force yourself to take three deep breaths and then check the address. The life you save may be your own.

4. Attaching the wrong file to a message.

As I mentioned earlier in this chapter (and as we will discuss in Chapter 10), it is possible to send one or more files — called attachments — along with an email message. To send an attachment, you must specify the name of the file. Typically, you do so by navigating to the folder that contains the file and then clicking on the name of the file. But what happens if you make a mistake? Since your email program doesn't know any better, it will happily send whichever file you specified, and the person at the other end will get the wrong file.

Here is a true story. A young lady I know once registered for an online dating service. She received a number of replies, one of which was from a young man who attached a photo of himself. The young lady took one look at the photo and decided she was not interested.

The man, however, was persistent and, finally, the young lady agreed to talk to him (over the Net) using a chat facility. When he asked her why she wasn't interested in him, she replied frankly that it was because of his picture. He looked too "feminine" for her taste.

The young man was puzzled until he checked the original message and found that he hadn't, as he thought, attached a photo of himself. He had accidentally sent the wrong file, one that contained a picture of a female friend. Would you want to date someone so careless? I think not.

(Fortunately, the story has a happy ending. After an extensive search, the young lady found a man who was better in every way.)

Such mistakes are not confined to personal matters. An editor I know at a well-known publishing house tells me that, every week, he receives one or two incorrect attachments. He told me that, one time, his company had been editing the chapters of a new book for two weeks when the author suddenly discovered that he had inadvertently sent the old version of the files.

There are three ways to guard against such a mistake. First, slow down. Before you send the message, look at the name of the file and confirm that it is correct.

Second, before you send a file, look at the contents for yourself. Don't assume you know what it contains. This is especially important if the file name is not descriptive.

Finally, when you are creating files that hold different versions of the same material, use file names that include the time and date the file was last changed. For example, let's say I am working on Chapter 8 of a book, and I want to send a copy to my editor. It happens to be 11:33 A.M. on April 25, 2001, so I save the file under the name:

`chapter8-010425-1133am.doc`

When the editor receives the file, he knows exactly when I sent it. (`010425` shows the date; `1133am` shows the time.)

Suppose that, later, I send him another file:

`chapter-8-010425-401pm.doc`

Although the date is the same, the editor knows that this file is newer than the previous one because the time has been changed (to 4:01 P.M.).

When you use Windows Explorer to look at a list of files, you will see a time and a date. However, don't depend on this information. When you send a file to someone, the Windows time and date is not sent with the file. The only way to preserve this information is to put the time and date right in the file name (or inside the file).

5. Using email to send highly personal messages.

There are certain occasions that require either a person-to-person conversation or a formal letter on paper. At such times, you may not use email, no matter how convenient or easy it may be. Why? Because these occasions require a personal touch, and email is not personal or formal enough.

For this reason, I hereby declare that an email message, no matter how carefully crafted, may not take the place of a:

• Thank-you note.
• Birthday greeting to a relative or close friend.
• Wedding invitation.
• Sympathy note.

Such notes must be written on paper and sent by regular mail.

Objection #1: *Why should I write a real letter when email is easier, cheaper, quicker and more efficient?*

We don't send thank-you notes, birthday greetings, wedding invitations or sympathy notes to be efficient. We send them to fulfill a social obligation and to show other people that we care for them.

Objection #2: *Paper, envelopes and stamps cost money. Moreover, it is a bother to mail something.*

Your recipient knows this, which is why he will appreciate your making the effort to show how important he is to you.

Objection #3: *But I am busy.*

Who do you know that is not busy?

These rules are a matter of etiquette and, as such, are not open to discussion. The Mistress of Etiquette does not care about efficiency, nor does she strive to be logical or trendy. "This is how well-mannered gentlemen and ladies behave," she decrees, "and you must do the same."

"What," she hears you say, "you don't write thank-you notes? My goodness. I have never heard of such a thing. You must stop what you are doing right now and read the essay on the following Web page."

`http://www.harley.com/success/`

To finish this discussion, I will remind you that you may not use email to:

- Inform someone of a death.
- Break off a romantic relationship.
- Fire someone.

In such cases, email is completely unacceptable. You must talk to the person face to face. (If that is not possible, you may send a written note.) If you are worried about the person's reaction, ask a friend or colleague to accompany you.

Protecting Your Email Address

There are three ways in which your email privacy can be violated. First, if someone has access to your computer, he or she can read your email when you are not around.

In Chapter 4, I discussed this situation and described various steps you can take to help keep your mail private. However, you should realize that as long as anyone has access to your computer, your email will never be completely private. Thus, if a family member, your employer, or a co-worker has access to your computer, you should assume that your email is not private and act accordingly.

Even if your computer is completely isolated, your email privacy can be invaded if someone forwards your messages to another person. The next time you are tempted to use email to pour your heart out to a prospective significant other, remember that your message is only one mouse click away from being shared with that person's best friend. Moreover, the best friend may decide to share your plaintive cry for affection with even more people. ("Patty, take a look at this letter Margo sent me. It's from a guy she met at a conference last week. What a dweeb he must be! How does she ever find these guys?")

The third way in which your email privacy can be invaded is completely different, but in some ways, it can be the most annoying. If the wrong people get your email address, you will receive ever-increasing amounts of unsolicited mail, including a lot of advertising.

Unsolicited mail is called SPAM, and a person or company that sends such mail is called a SPAMMER. The name comes from a Monty Python skit in which a person ordering food in a restaurant finds that all the dishes come with spam (a particularly gruesome type of canned meat).

How you feel about the spam in your email depends on your personality. Some people, who are particularly sanguine, don't seem to mind spam in the least. "If you don't like an advertisement in your mailbox," such people say, "just delete it. What's all the fuss?" Other people look at spam as an invasion of their privacy. They resent being sent unsolicited email, and they become irate when they can't do anything about it.

The plain truth is that spammers don't care about the inconvenience, and they have no motivation to take you off their mailing lists. Here is why.

Regular paper junk mail costs real money. The junk mailer has to pay for paper, envelopes, printing, postage and the cost of buying the addresses. For this reason, most junk mailers (or "direct mail companies" as they prefer to call themselves) will be glad to take you off their lists if you ask them to. Why should they spend money sending advertisements to people who don't care about their products?

Email is different. A spammer may have to pay for an address list, but everything else costs next to nothing. This is why spammers don't care if they send email to people who don't want it. Moreover, all serious spammers set up their businesses to make it hard for you to reach them in person, so they don't have to worry about fielding complaints. They don't care, and there's nothing you can do to make them care. Spammers are dishonest, ill-mannered people who will be glad to deceive you if they think it will make them more money.

Once your address gets on spam lists, it will spread and spread. When this happens, don't waste your time trying to fix the problem, because you can't. The only thing you can do is change your address.

There is only one way to avoid spam: keep your address private in the first place. Here are some hints to help you.

First, be careful about giving out your email address, just as you would with an unlisted phone number. Give your address only to those people you really want to have it. When you do, ask them never to give it out to anyone else without your permission.

Second, never type your email address into a form on a Web page. The same rule holds when you are installing software and the installation program asks you to "register". Marketing companies have all kinds of tricks to get your address, but you don't have to give it to them.

If you are ever faced with a situation in which you *must* come up with some type of address, you have two choices. First, you can give a fake address. (This is morally ethical, so don't worry about it.) When you make up a fake address, make sure you don't use one that might inadvertently be real. For example, the address `iamcool@aol.com` probably belongs to somebody. The address `fake@xxlvy.com` would be okay.

The second choice is to use a disposable address. Here's how to get one.

How to Get a Disposable Email Address

It's irritating when you get so much spam that you need to throw away your email address and start again with a new one. For one thing, you will have to send messages to all your friends and business associates telling them of the change. Similarly, you will have to change your address for any electronic mailing lists or automated services for which you have registered.

You can avoid these problems by having two addresses: a permanent one that you give out to selected people (who will keep it private), and a temporary, disposable one that you are willing to throw away if necessary.

Getting a temporary email address is easy. There are many different Web sites that offer free Web-based email service. All you have to do is register. To get you started, here are some sites that offer this service:

```
http://www.iname.com/
http://mail.lycos.com/
http://mail.yahoo.com/
http://mail.excite.com/
http://www.hotmail.com/
http://mail.altavista.com/
http://www.eudoramail.com/
```

Internet Resources: Web-based email services

If you want more of a choice, the following Web sites have information about a large number of free email services:

```
http://www.fepg.net/
http://www.emailaddresses.com/
http://www.internetemaillist.com/
```

Internet Resources: Lists of Web-based email services

Of course, no one ever made a profit giving valuable services away for free. These companies need to make money and they do so in several ways. First, to send and receive mail, you will have to visit their Web site where you will see advertisements. Second, the company may add a short advertisement to each message you send (to the delight of your recipients). At the very least, they will add a couple of lines advertising their service. Third, the company may sell your address to spammers, and they may send you advertisements of their own.

Over a year ago, I registered with Hotmail (which is owned by Microsoft) to get a free email account. I have never given that address to anyone (I use it only for testing) and yet, every month, I receive hundreds of messages of spam, all sent to that exact address.

How did the spammers get the address? I'm not sure. At one time, there was a breach in the Hotmail security system and spammers were able to get a lot of addresses. To be fair, I should mention that I have a friend who registered for a Hotmail account more recently, and she never gets spam. The point is, once the spammers get your address, you can say good-bye to your privacy.

Spam is a big problem for ISPs (Internet service providers), because it makes up a large portion of the mail they must process. Most ISPs do their best to block spam. Microsoft, for example, puts a great deal of effort into trying to block spam from reaching their Hotmail users.

Many ISPs use special programs that filter out incoming spam. The spammers, however, work hard to design their messages to avoid the filters. Overall, a great deal of spam still gets through, so you can't count on the filters.

When you register for a free email service, you will need to provide some personal information. For example, you may be asked to specify your full name, street address, age, gender, marital status, income range, and so on. You may also be asked to give information about your work and your interests and hobbies.

Do you need to answer these questions? Well, you probably need to type something or the sign-up form won't be processed properly.

However, you are under no obligation to tell the truth. My advice is to make up something reasonable, but don't give out any personal information, especially your name and address.

Before you complete the sign-up form, look carefully. Some services ask if you want your email address to be listed in a directory. (Say no.) They may also ask if you want to receive email notification of "special offers", that is, advertising. (Again, say no.)

If you are serious about privacy, you should always have one or two disposable email addresses. For example, you will, from time to time, find yourself visiting a Web site that requires you to register. The only reason they want your address is to send you mail, so never give them your permanent address, just use a disposable address.

Disposable addresses are also good when you want to give your email address to someone you don't know well. For example, if you register for an online dating service, use a disposable address for your correspondence. (There are a lot of nuts out there.)

Protecting Other People's Email Privacy

Because of our strong desire to communicate and share, it is possible to invade other people's email privacy by accident. Here are a few guidelines to help you avoid doing so.

1. Never type someone else's email address into a form on a Web site.

When someone gives you his or her email address, treat it as you would an unlisted phone number.

Spammers (as well as legitimate companies) want all the email addresses they can get, and they will consciously design Web sites to lure you into giving them other people's addresses.

Although many Web sites have a privacy policy claiming that they will not misuse the information you give them, as we discussed in Chapter 7, such policies mean nothing. When an Internet business finds itself under pressure to generate revenue (which is inevitable, see Chapter 4), they will throw their privacy policy out the window and do whatever they want with the information they have collected.

I'll tell you something interesting. Many Web pages are created only for the purpose of gathering email addresses. Such pages — and there are a lot of them — are carefully designed to entice you into typing an email address into a form.

For example, a lot of Web pages have a link that will help you tell a friend about that page. If you click on the link, you will be asked to enter your name and email address, as well as the names and addresses of any friends you think might enjoy the page. "Isn't that nice?" you think to yourself. "Some nice person has gone to a lot of trouble to make it easy for me to tell my friends about this page."

The truth is that TELL-A-FRIEND referrals are actually a well-known Web-based business based on misinformation and kick-backs. The information you enter does not go to the company whose Web site you are visiting. It goes to a marketing company whose business is to collect email addresses. When you give away a friend's name and address in this manner, he will be sent a message telling him about the Web site, but the message will contain an ad.

Moreover, you have inadvertently put his address in the database of a marketing company that can send out more ads as well as sell his address to spammers. As a result, your friend will start to get a lot of spam and he won't even know why.

Why do Web sites offer tell-a-friend services? It's not for the convenience of their visitors. It's because the tell-a-friend marketing companies *pay* the Web site owners to put the service on their sites. They do this by paying a kickback for each referral. In fact, there are many sites on the Web that have been designed solely to generate tell-a-friend kickbacks.

This is only one example of how email addresses are bought and sold on the Net, but there are many others. So, to be polite, never type someone's email address into a form on a Web site, unless the person has given you their permission to do so. (Yes, this rule also applies to sending electronic greeting cards.) Here is a typical dialog to show you how it works:

YOUNG MAN:	*(addressing a young lady)* You seem like a fine person. May I please have your email address?
YOUNG LADY:	Yes, you may. Here it is.
YOUNG MAN:	Thank you. By the way, would it be okay with you if I type this address into a form on a Web site?
YOUNG LADY:	What a polite young man you are. Actually, I'd prefer you keep this address private. However, in case you want to send me something from a Web site, here is my disposable Hotmail address. You may use that.

The next rule, which has two parts, involves forwarding messages.

2a. When you forward a message to a group of friends, put the addresses on the Bcc: line.

2b. Before you forward a message, take a moment to clean up the message and delete all the old message headers.

We discussed these ideas in detail earlier in the chapter, so I know you understand how important it is to not give out other people's addresses inadvertently. Interestingly enough, as I was writing this chapter, I received an email message that a friend had sent to many other people. The message claimed that anyone could make money just by forwarding the message to as many people as possible. (This, of course, was a hoax.)

When my friend sent the message, she did not clean up all the junk from the previous forwardings. As a result, the message I received had old header lines containing a great many email addresses. As an experiment, I saved the message and used a text editor to edit the file. Within five minutes, I had a list of 201 valid email addresses. If I were a spammer I could have sent email to all those people. (In fact, I was tempted to send them mail telling them to buy this book in order to find out how to safeguard their email privacy.)

3. Before you give someone's email address to another person, ask permission.

It only takes a moment to send a message such as:

"Dick, I was just talking to someone who is interested in model railroads. I told him you are a model railroad expert, and he is interested in talking to you. Do you mind if I give him your email address so he can contact you directly?"

or:

"Lois, I ran into a neighbor who is learning about stained glass. I told her that you have been working with stained glass for years, and she is interested in talking to you. Here is her email address in case you would like to contact her."

Talk is Cheap (and Not Very Private)

On the Internet, we use the words TALK and CHAT to refer to having a conversation with another person. There are a number of different ways you can talk to someone on the Net: Web chat rooms, instant messaging, IRC (a large, worldwide talk system), muds (virtual environments), and so on. Most of the time, talking is done by typing. However, there are systems that allow you to use voice. (To do so, you need either a headset, or a microphone and speakers.)

In this section, I'm going to discuss the privacy and security aspects of talking on the Net. In Chapter 14, we'll talk about the social implications.

To start, never give out *any* personal information, especially your real name and where you live. It is perfectly acceptable to use a fake name when you talk on the Net.

There are two reasons for this. First, you don't want to put yourself in danger or take the chance of being harassed. There are a lot of strange people on the Net, some of whom are very good at acting normal, even to the point of being charming. Unless you know someone in person, you don't really know him, so don't take chances.

The second reason is more subtle. As we discussed earlier in the chapter, human beings evolved to communicate with other people in person. When you talk to someone on the Net, without the face-to-face context, your mind will unconsciously fill in the blanks in a way that is not realistic.

For this reason, if you spend a lot of time talking on the Net, you will find yourself becoming personal with people you don't really know, even to the point of being intimate. The closeness you feel, however, is an illusion. It is created by your need to connect to other people (which is normal) and by your mind's inability to properly process communication that does not have a proper context (which is also normal).

The real risk of false intimacy is not that someone is going to track you down and murder you in your bed. This is possible, but not likely. The real risk in getting too close is that you will become involved in unrealistic friendships and relationships that will end up disappointing you and hurting your feelings.

This type of problem sneaks up on you, so you must be on your guard. Once you tell someone your secrets, you will feel closer to him. This is just human nature. If you share too much with a stranger on the Net, you will end up creating a false sense of closeness that will rebound to hurt you. Trust me. No matter how much you may want to believe to the contrary, Internet friends are not friends; they are acquaintances.

Aside from not giving out private information, there are several other precautions you must take when you talk on the Net.

First, be careful what you do and who you do it with. No matter how private a conversation may seem, you are still in a public arena. Even if no one else is listening at the time, it is easy for the other person to keep a log of what the two of you are saying and show it to other people later. Some people do this just for fun.

Be aware that most talk services have a way for you to block someone from contacting you. Don't hesitate to do this if someone is harassing you in any way.

If you want to exchange email with someone you don't know in person, don't give out your permanent address. Give the person a disposable address. (I discussed disposable addresses earlier in the chapter.)

The final hint has to do with receiving files. Some talk services allow people to send files to one another as they are talking. This facility comes in handy, when you want to share photographs or music. For example, I was recently having a phone conversation with a friend who was bringing me up to date on the remodeling of her bathroom. Because we were both connected to the Net at the time, she was able to use a talk program to send me a photograph that showed exactly how far the work had progressed. (The floor tile was laid, but the new toilet had not yet been installed.)

If someone tries to send you a file, you will see a message asking if you agree to accept the file. Be careful about which files you accept, because it is possible for someone to send you a file that can cause a problem on your system. For example, someone might send you a computer virus.

In Chapter 10, we'll discuss the details of how to protect your computer from viruses. At the time, we'll talk about how to tell if an email attachment is safe. The same advice also applies to files that someone sends you as you are talking. To be safe, don't accept *any* files until you have read Chapter 10.

Once you have read Chapter 10, all you need to do is follow these two simple rules:

- Don't accept any files unless you know the person well.
- Even if you know the person well, only accept files that contain pictures or sounds.

As you will see in Chapter 10, it is possible to tell if a file is safe by looking at its name. Unfortunately, some talk systems won't show you the name in advance. They just announce that so-and-so wants to send you a file, and will you accept it? When this happens, say no, and tell the person to send you the file by email. (Use a disposable address.) When the file arrives, you can look at the name and see if the file is safe to open.

This is especially true if you use IRC (Internet Relay Chat), a huge global talk system that allows people all over the Net to engage in conversations. IRC is a wonderful facility that allows you to have interesting conversations with people from all over the world. However, you should be aware that some people on IRC are troublemakers, who try to trick other people into accepting certain files that can cause trouble. For example, a file might contain a program that would erase the data on your hard disk or crash your computer.

Another common IRC trick is to tell someone to type a particular command that will allow the first person to control the IRC program on the other person's computer. If you are using IRC and someone tells you to type a command you don't understand, don't do it.

Abbreviations and Acronyms

There are a great many abbreviations that people use while talking on the Net. For example, you might see someone say:

It's hard to have a LDR with a possible SO.
IMHO, I think you should ask him to meet you F2F.

Translation: It's hard to have a long distance relationship with a possible significant other. In my humble opinion, I think you should ask him to meet you face to face.

We use such abbreviations for two reasons. First, typing is slow, and not everyone can type well. Moreover, even when two people are typing quickly, there may be a delay (called a LAG) between the time one person types a message and when the other person sees it. Because your brain processes words quickly, it can be irritating to spend a lot of time waiting for the next line in a conversation.

Thus, we use abbreviations to keep things moving as fast as possible. In the example above, for instance, four abbreviations (**LDR,**

SO, IMHO, F2F) replaced twelve words. (For reference, Appendix A contains a large list of such abbreviations.)

The second reason we use abbreviations is to create, as closely as possible, the ambiance of a real conversation. As we discussed earlier in the chapter, human beings require person-to-person contact, and talking on the Internet will never really fill this need. However, over the years, people on the Net have developed certain abbreviations and other conventions that attempt to simulate delight, anger, frustration, gentleness, excitement, and so on.

The most straightforward way to express a feeling or an emotion is by typing it in words. We do this by using angled brackets (< and >) or asterisks (*) to enclose the words. For example:

```
PERSON 1:   I just bought some ice cream <licking
            lips with delight>.

PERSON 2:   *Sigh* I wish I had some.
```

Although we may not always be aware of it, when we talk in person, we depend a great deal upon tone of voice, rhythm, volume and body language. When we talk on the Net, it is natural to want to show the emotional nuances we take for granted in face-to-face conversation. As a result, people who talk on the Net tend to exaggerate their emotions and feelings similar to what actors do on the radio.

If you have ever listened to an old radio show, especially a dramatic show, you will notice that the actors exaggerate their emotions. This is because, over the radio, there is no way to show body language or facial expressions. As a result, radio dramas are far more histrionic (and unrealistic) than television shows and movies.

On the Net, we follow certain conventions that allow us to do the same thing. For example, when we type, it's hard to show excitement because we can't raise our voices or talk more quickly. Instead, we type in uppercase (capital letters) to indicate shouting. Many people also make liberal use of exclamation marks and question marks:

WHAT?? YOU KNOW I HATE THAT!!!!

Another problem that constantly arises on the Net is how to express irony, that is, how to indicate that what we are typing is not what we mean. Irony is extremely difficult to express with written words (which is why so many writers have gray hair). In person, you can indicate irony by using a particular tone of voice, by smiling, or even by winking. On the Net, however, a comment with a double meaning is often perceived as being sarcastic or mean. For this reason, there are several ways to indicate that what you are saying is not offensive.

One way is to be excessively polite. For instance, in the example above you will see the abbreviation **IMHO**, which means "in my humble opinion". This abbreviation is used a lot on the Net to indicate that the speaker is about to express a specific point of view and does not wish to offend the other person.

Another way to express irony is to use what is called a SMILEY, a short sequence of characters that resembles a face. Here is the basic smiley. To see the face, tilt your head to the left.

:-)

Here's another smiley; this one is winking:

;-)

Here's a third smiley, one without a nose:

:)

A smiley is used as a synonym for "don't be offended". For example:

Of course, not all Canadians want to live in the U.S. :-)

Smileys are often used, preemptively, in self-defense. As a general rule, if you put a smiley at the end of a statement, the other person is not supposed to be offended, no matter how rude the statement may be:

I can see why you love your dog so much :-)

The most common situations in which people exaggerate their emotions are when they are expressing a feeling of happiness. In such cases, you will often see people pretend to be far more amused than they really are. For example, here are a number of abbreviations that are used to indicate laughing:

FOFLMAO	falling on the floor laughing my ass off
LMAO	laughing my ass off
LOL	laughing out loud
ROFL	rolling on the floor laughing
ROTF	rolling on the floor laughing
ROTFL	rolling on the floor laughing
ROTFLMAO	rolling on the floor laughing my ass off

It is true that, in normal conversation, people do laugh out loud (although they rarely fall on the floor). However, on the Net, you will often see people type **LOL**, even when common sense tells you that they could not possibly be laughing out loud. For example:

> PERSON 1: **My mother read my diary and found out about the party!!!!**
>
> PERSON 2: **LOL**

Interestingly, such exaggerations are used, almost exclusively, by newcomers and non-technical people who have not yet figured out the nuances of online communication. For some reason, the worst offenders seem to be teenage girls who use AOL. For such people, **LOL** doesn't indicate real laughter. It's actually a filled pause devoid of specific meaning.

Two teenagers talking on the Net:

> PERSON 1: **What are you going to get your Mom for Mother's Day?**
>
> PERSON 2: **A gift certificate to an ice cream store.**
>
> PERSON 1: **LOL.**

This is similar to how, in regular conversation, people will often use meaningless expressions just to fill space:

The same two teenagers talking in person:

PERSON 1:	"What are you going to get your Mom for Mother's Day?"
PERSON 2:	"A gift certificate to an ice cream store."
PERSON 1:	"Cool!"

Two adults talking in person:

PERSON 1:	"What are you going to get your Mom for Mother's Day?"
PERSON 2:	"A gift certificate to an ice cream store."
PERSON 1:	"There you go!"

9

The Mystery of Viruses: Revealed

Computer viruses are programs that arise in only one way: they are created, on purpose, by programmers who want to cause trouble.

The Mystery of Viruses: Revealed

- What Are Viruses?

- The Virus Challenge

- How a Virus Spreads From One File to Another

- Who Creates Viruses?

- The Three Types of Viruses

- Virus Hoaxes

- The Trojan Horse

- Early Computer Viruses

- Early Worms

- The Last Days of Innocence

- The Worm That Brought Down the Net

- The Internet Worm: Prologue

- Quick Diversion: A Puzzle

What Are Viruses?

A VIRUS — or more formally, a COMPUTER VIRUS — is a computer program that is able to make a copy of itself without you knowing what is happening. A virus may copy itself from one part of your hard disk to another, or it may copy itself from one computer to another.

Most viruses do more than make copies of themselves. Some of them cause real damage, say, by deleting files on your hard disk. Others are merely annoying. They may display a message on your monitor or cause something strange to happen as you are working. All viruses are malevolent in that they do their work without your knowing what is happening, and they can cause problems merely by spreading uncontrollably.

The name "virus" is merely a metaphor. It was chosen because the first programmers to work with computer viruses thought they had some of the characteristics of biological viruses. As you will see, this is not true. In fact, the metaphor is a particularly poor one, in that it encourages people to think that computer viruses are mysterious and are alive in some way.

This is not true at all. Computer viruses are not alive, nor do they spread by infection. They do not arise spontaneously, they do not mutate, they do not change by themselves, and they do not spontaneously adapt to their surroundings. Computer viruses are not artificial life. They are programs, and they arise in only one way. They are created, on purpose, by programmers who want to cause trouble.

The Virus Challenge

A virus is a program that can make copies of itself. This sounds like a strange idea. How can a program make a copy of itself? Let's start with some basic ideas.

A COMPUTER is a machine that has the capability of carrying out a variety of actions. A COMPUTER PROGRAM (or PROGRAM) is a list of actions that, when carried out by a computer, does something.

In this sense, think of a program as being a recipe consisting of a list of instructions. The job of a computer is to RUN or EXECUTE programs. To run a program, the computer simply follows the instructions, one after another. A person who creates a list of such instructions (that is, a program) is called a PROGRAMMER.

The power of computers comes from three things. First, computers are designed to be general purpose machines. Second, they can execute many instructions (sometimes millions) every second. Third, there are a great many talented programmers who are good at creating lists of instructions.

Whenever you see a computer do anything — display a picture, manipulate words or numbers, transfer information — just remember that everything that computer is doing only happens because the computer is following instructions and those instructions were written by a person.

(To be completely accurate, I do have to mention that there are programs that can read specifications and use them to create other programs. Thus, some programs are created automatically. For the most part, however, programs are written by people.)

How is a program stored on your computer? As we discussed in Chapter 3, data is stored in a file on a disk, and files themselves are organized into folders (also called directories). Since a program is essentially a list of instructions, it is easy to store on a computer. The program — that is, the instructions — is stored in a file. To be sure, a very complex program — such as a Web browser or Microsoft Word or Windows itself — will have a huge list of instructions. In such cases, pieces of the program will actually be stored in many different files, but the idea is the same.

In the simplest case, all a programmer would have to do to create a virus is write a program that makes a copy of the file that contains itself. Each time you ran the program, it would create another copy of itself (say, under a different name). As you might imagine, if you know how to program, this is not a difficult program to write. As such, it's not much of a challenge for a bored, socially immature programmer. However, recall the definition of a virus I gave you earlier. A virus has two characteristics: it can make a copy of itself, and it must do so in a way that you don't know what is happening.

That is the challenge that presents itself to a bored, socially immature programmer. "How," he asks himself, "can I create a program that will copy itself in such a way that the person in front of the computer has no idea what is going on?" And, at the same time, if the programmer can create a virus that spreads from one computer to another, possibly causing damage, and it all happens in such a way that he doesn't get caught, so much the better. (I use the word "he", by the way, because, for some reason, virtually all socially immature programmers are male.)

How a Virus Spreads From One File to Another

In the most general terms, you can think of the inside of your computer as having three main functional parts: the processor, the memory and the hard disk. The PROCESSOR (an electronic chip) acts as the "brain". The MEMORY (a group of chips) holds data that is manipulated by the processor. The hard disk provides long-term storage. (For information about disks, see Chapter 3.)

When you buy a computer, you will see references to these three components. The speed of the processor will be measured in MHz (megahertz); the amount of memory will be specified in MB (megabytes); and the size of the hard disk is specified in GB (gigabytes). As a general rule, if you have a choice, get a computer with a fast processor, lots of memory and a large hard disk. (If you need help with megabytes and gigabytes, see Chapter 3.)

As I explained in the last section, a program consists of one or more files. These files are stored on your hard disk. The disk acts as long-term storage in the sense that, when you turn your computer off, the contents of the disk do not disappear.

Your processor, however, cannot work directly with data on a disk. The processor can only work with data which is in the memory, that is, within the memory chips. It has to do with how computers are designed.

For an analogy, think of a book, sitting on your bookshelf. Let's say that book contains some information you want to think about. Your mind cannot work directly with the pages of the book. Before you can think about the contents of a book, you must open it and read the information. In other words, you must copy the information from the book into your head. Once the information is in your head, you can think about it.

Most of the time, of course, this happens so rapidly, that you don't realize what is happening. However, when you are using a computer, even a fast computer, you can see the lag. You click on something to start a program, and you have to wait a few seconds for the program to be copied from the hard disk into the memory. (Now you know what you are waiting for.)

Unlike a disk, however, computer memory provides short-term storage. When you turn off the power, whatever is in the memory disappears.

So how does this apply to viruses? When a program file contains a virus, nothing happens until the program is copied into memory and begins to run. At this point, the processor begins to execute the virus instructions, which are hidden in the program, and the virus becomes active. The virus will now begin to carry out whatever tasks the virus programmer has specified. In particular, the virus can insert copies of itself into other programs that are stored on the hard disk. These new copies of the virus will lay dormant until, one day, you run one of these programs.

Who Creates Viruses?

Later in this chapter, I will relate how the term "virus" was coined in 1983 by a professor at the University of Southern California, because he thought computer viruses were, in some sense, similar to biological viruses.

Actually, this is not true at all. Computer viruses are much different from — and much, much simpler than — real viruses.

Unfortunately, it is all too common to hear people talk about a computer virus as if it were alive, trying to breed and survive. The popular press discusses viruses that "infect" a "host" in order to "reproduce". You read that viruses "adapt" and cause "epidemics", and that antivirus tools can "disinfect" a file.

The reason I don't like this terminology — and you will notice that I do not use it in this book — is because it blinds us to the primary cause of viruses. Unlike real viruses, new computer viruses are not living organisms that appear spontaneously. They are created deliberately by mean-spirited programmers whose only goal is to harass people and damage their computer systems.

The days are long gone when writing viruses was cute. Viruses cause a lot of trouble and waste a lot of money, and the people who write them should be punished.

As an example of how writers often mischaracterize viruses, let me show you a couple of short quotes from an article entitled "Fighting Computer Viruses", published in the November 1997 issue of *Scientific American*. The article was written by four researchers from the IBM Thomas J. Watson Research Center. (IBM was one of the pioneers in creating antivirus software.)

"Just as external factors such as drought, sanitation and migration have a strong influence on biological epidemics, changes in the computing environment are responsible for the presence of several distinct epochs in viral infection."

Wrong. Viruses do not mutate spontaneously in order to survive in a changing computing environment. New viruses are created by irresponsible, dishonest programmers who actively look for new ways to create trouble for other people.

The entire article — and remember, this is *Scientific American* — is riddled with such nonsense. However, I'll confine myself to quoting the last paragraph, in which the authors become philosophical:

"Regardless of how sophisticated antivirus technology may become, computer viruses will forever remain in an uneasy coexistence with us and our computers. Individual strains will wax and wane, but as a whole, computer viruses and antivirus technology will co-evolve

much as biological parasites and hosts do. Both will also evolve in response to such changes in the computing environment as itinerant software agents — which will have to be protected from corruption by the computer systems they traverse even as those systems guard themselves from agent malice. Perhaps computer viruses and computer immune systems are merely precursors of an eventual rich ecosystem of artificial life-forms that will live, die, cooperate and prey on one another in cyberspace."

Really? Virus "strains" that wax and wane? Viruses that evolve in response to change? Viruses and "immune systems" that are precursors to artificial life?

I know a bit about biology because, after finishing computer science graduate school, I went to medical school at the University of Toronto. One of my best friends in medical school was Tim Rutledge, who went on to become a highly accomplished specialist in emergency medicine.

I mention Tim here because he once made a remark that, word for word, has more wisdom than anything else I have ever heard in my life. Take a moment to re-read the last paragraph of the *Scientific American* article.

Now, think about the following:

"When you get serious about bullshit, you're getting into serious bullshit."

— Tim Rutledge

The Three Types of Viruses

If you were to study computer viruses, you would find yourself immersed in a large morass of technical details. The people who create viruses have a lot of tricks. There are a lot of different viruses and some of them are very sophisticated. For this reason, experts will classify viruses into many different categories and subcategories. However, let's be practical. As a normal human being, you really only need to know two things:

- What are the main types of viruses?
- How do you prevent them from causing damage on your system?

For practical purposes, the best way to classify viruses is based on how they are designed to spread, because that helps you understand how to stop them. There are three main ways in which viruses spread on the Internet today.

1. A regular virus is one that is embedded within a program file that spreads when one person shares the file with another person.

2. A worm is a virus in the form of a file that spreads automatically over a network, usually by email.

3. A macro virus is a virus that is attached to a data file that is then shared.

Notice what all three types of viruses have in common. In order for a virus to spread, a file must be shared.

All viruses have one more thing in common. They are programs, and a program cannot do anything until it is executed. For example, you could have a hundred different viruses hidden within a hundred different files on your computer and, if they are never executed, it won't make any difference.

Virus creators know this, and they go to a great deal of trouble to ensure that their viruses *are* executed once they spread to new computers. This means that, to be effective, a virus must be designed to either (1) run automatically under certain conditions, or (2) entice you to run a program voluntarily that, unknown to you, contains the virus.

Once a virus is executed it can take any action that you yourself (or one of your programs) might take. For example, a virus can communicate with a Web site, send email, delete files, create new files, change files, and so on. In particular, it is common for viruses to be designed to make copies of themselves, either by creating new files or by modifying existing files. Moreover, virus programmers do their best to have all of this activity happening in a way that you won't notice until it is too late. (As a general rule,

"In order for a virus to cause trouble in the world at large, the virus must be shared."

computer viruses are much smaller than most other programs, so it's not hard to hide them in a file.)

Thus, in order for a virus to cause trouble in the world at large, two things must happen. The virus must be shared and, once it is shared, it must be run. This suggests a strategy for avoiding trouble: Don't share suspicious files and don't run suspicious files.

In the following sections, I will discuss each of the three types of viruses. I'll explain a bit about them and then show you how to use this strategy to protect yourself. You will be surprised. It's a lot easier than you might think.

Before we continue, let me clear up one possible misunderstanding. Originally, the word "virus" was used in a narrow way to describe a program that is embedded in another program (the first type of program I mentioned above). Other types of troublesome creations, such as worms, were considered to be in a different category. (In fact, as you will see when we discuss the history of viruses, there were computer worms before the term "computer virus" was even used.)

Today, many purists still do not consider worms and certain other types of similar programs to be true viruses. However, most people use the word "virus" in a more general sense, to refer to any type of troublesome program that copies itself without your knowing it. That is why I mentioned three types of viruses: regular ("true") viruses, worms, and macro viruses.

Virus Hoaxes

In Chapter 8, we talked about rumors and hoaxes, and how and why they spread. Nowhere in the world of computing does nonsense spread more quickly than when people start worrying about viruses. To many people, viruses are mysterious things that can hurt their computers in ways that are difficult to understand. This feeling of defenselessness, along with a genuine desire to help others, often leads people to pass along every virus-related warning that enters their mailbox. Many people will forward such messages to everyone they know, without even checking if the problem is real.

As a result, there are a great many VIRUS HOAXES, that is, warnings about viruses that don't really exist. In fact, compared to actual viruses, there are so many false warnings circulating around the Net, that some people have suggested that the hoaxes themselves are the real viruses.

From time to time, I receive a message from someone I know, asking if a recent virus warning is real. In almost every case, the warning is spurious, and I tell the person not to pass it on to other people.

So how can you tell if a virus warning is a hoax? It's easy. First, the message will have certain characteristics:

• Virus hoaxes are excessively dramatic, often warning against a terrible catastrophe. Look for capital letters, lots of exclamation marks, and poor sentence structure.
• Virus hoaxes often quote an unnamed authority from a well-known company (such as Microsoft or IBM) or from the government.

- Virus hoaxes threaten terrible unrealistic consequences.

For example, a warning might say that just looking at a particular virus-containing mail message will delete files on your hard disk. In virtually all cases, this is not true. We'll discuss how email viruses actually spread in Chapter 10.

I do have to say that, hypothetically, it is possible for you to encounter a virus just by reading an email message. However, it can only happen under certain circumstances and only if you use a Microsoft mail program. In Chapter 11, I'll address this problem and show you how to avoid it permanently. In the meantime, for practical purposes, you can assume that a warning that tries to scare you in this way is a hoax.

The biggest tip-off that a warning is a hoax is that:

- Virus hoaxes are forwarded by people who are not computer experts.

I know a number of people who program and maintain computer systems for a living. If one of these people were to send me a virus warning — and it has happened — I would take it seriously. Similarly, if you work on a large network and you receive a virus warning from your network administrator, pay attention. Such warnings are usually correct. However, if a friend who is not a nerd sends you a virus warning, it's a safe bet that the warning is a hoax.

In case you have never seen such a message, here is an excerpt from a real virus hoax:

```
This notice regarding some computer viruses that
are circulating the systems was received at our
office today.

WARNING!!!!!! If you receive an e-mail titled
"JOIN THE CREW" DO NOT open it! It will erase
EVERYTHING on your hard drive!

"This information was received this morning from
IBM, please share it with anyone that might access
the Internet.
```

There is one sure way that you can always tell whether or not a virus warning is a hoax. There are a number of authoritative Web sites that track all the hoaxes. Before you start worrying, and before you send mail to all your friends, check with one of these sites to see if the warning you received is real:

```
http://www.vmyths.com/
http://hoaxbusters.ciac.org/
http://www.stiller.com/hoaxes.htm
http://www.sophos.com/virusinfo/hoaxes/
http://www.f-secure.com/virus-info/hoax/
http://www.icsalabs.com/html/communities/
antivirus/hoaxes.shtml
```

Internet Resources: Virus hoaxes

If you have a few moments, take a look at one of these Web sites now. You will be amazed at how many virus hoaxes and how much misinformation is on the Net. You will also be surprised how many of the hoaxes resurface again and again over a long period of time.

The Trojan Horse

A common way that viruses spread is by inserting themselves into a file that contains a program. When someone then shares the program, the virus goes with it. Such a file is referred to as a TROJAN HORSE.

In order to create a successful Trojan horse, a virus programmer will look for a program that he thinks people will want to share, such as a popular game. He will insert a virus into the file, and then start sharing it.

The idea, of course, is not a new one. The original Trojan horse from Greek mythology had a similar purpose. Although you have probably heard of the original Trojan horse, you may not know the full story (which was told by Homer in his long narrative poem, the *Iliad*). It goes like this:

Once upon a time, the most beautiful woman in the world was Helen, the daughter of Zeus, chief of the gods. Helen was courted by many men and, ultimately, she married the king of Sparta, in Greece. For awhile, everything was hunky-dory.

However, a short time later, the goddess Discord (a troublemaker) threw a golden apple among the other gods. The apple was marked "For the Fairest". This set off a dispute among three of the goddesses, Aphrodite, Athena and Hera, as to who was the most beautiful. Zeus was asked to judge but — in a fit of good sense — refused to do so. (Zeus might be chief of the gods, but he was nobody's fool.) Instead, he sent the three goddesses to Paris, a prince in the city of Troy, and told Paris to decide who should get the apple.

All three goddesses did their best to influence Paris, but he chose Aphrodite because she promised to give him the most beautiful woman in the world. Making good her promise, Aphrodite led Paris to Sparta and presented him with Helen (shrewdly ignoring the fact that Helen was already married to someone else). Paris abducted Helen and carried her from Greece to Troy.

Well, as you can imagine, the Greeks had a cow. They mustered an army and sent it to Troy in an attempt to recover their queen. To protect itself, Troy, which was surrounded by a wall, locked its gates and settled down for a long siege.

The Greeks and Trojans fought for ten years. Eventually, the Greeks gained the upper hand, but they still needed to achieve a final victory. It was then that the Greek warrior Odysseus had an inspired idea.

Odysseus devised a large hollow horse constructed out of wood. He hid a number of Greek soldiers inside the horse and left it outside the gates of Troy. The Greeks pretended to sail away, but actually, they were waiting along the coast, just out of sight. They did, however, leave one soldier standing next to the horse. When the Trojans came to look at the horse, the Greek soldier told them that the goddess Athena would be pleased if they would open the gates and bring the horse inside the city.

By now, I am sure you are thinking, only a fool would bring a large hollow container inside a fortified city that had been fighting a war for ten years. In fact, two prominent Trojans felt the same way. Cassandra, a prophetess, warned against bringing in the horse, as did Laocoön, a priest. He remarked, "I am wary of Greeks even when they are bearing gifts." Unfortunately, the warnings were not heeded and the horse was brought inside the gates.

Later that night, the Greeks returned to Troy and waited nearby. At the same time, the hidden soldiers snuck out of the horse and opened the gates. The Greeks rushed in and, within a short time, they had won the war and recovered their beautiful queen. In the process, they also managed to destroy the city of Troy completely.

This is a good story to remember the next time someone emails you a message that says "Click on the attached program and you will see a picture of a beautiful woman."

Early Computer Viruses

In the fall of 1983, a doctoral student named Fred Cohen, in the electrical engineering department of the University of Southern California, was taking part in a regular weekly seminar on computer security. Cohen conceived the idea that it might be possible to design a program that would spread by embedding itself in other programs. As those programs were shared, the piggyback program would spread.

The advisor to the seminar, Professor Len Adelman, coined the term "virus" to describe such a program. (In 1994, by the way, Adelman became the first person to build a simple working computer out of DNA.) After working on the idea for eight hours, Cohen came up with an actual computer virus. After receiving permission, he performed five experiments, and, on November 10, 1983, Cohen demonstrated his virus for the seminar group.

(In case you want the technical details, Cohen used a VAX 11/750 computer running Unix. The virus was implanted in the `vd` program — a utility to display Unix file structures graphically — and was spread via the system's electronic bulletin board.)

Cohen went on to get his Ph.D. by writing about viruses. In the process, he contributed a great deal to the theoretical understanding of such programs. However, did Cohen write the first computer virus? Actually, the answer is no.

In late 1981, a small group of students at Texas A&M University were using pirated copies of games on Apple II computers. They started to discuss how, as games are shared, copies of the popular games proliferate, while the unpopular games die out. They then started to think about the idea of programs which could reproduce on their own. In early 1982, students developed the first program which was a real virus (although they didn't call it that). This program lived on floppy disks, and was written to spread from one floppy to another.

The virus caused some problems, so they did not allow it to spread. Soon after, they came up with a second version of the virus. This one seemed more benign, so they let it spread to floppies belonging to members of the group. Unfortunately, the self-imposed security was breached, and before long the virus had spread to the general Apple II population. Once this happened, it became evident that the virus did, indeed, cause problems.

Eventually, the group developed one more virus. They worked hard on this one so that it would spread without causing problems, and they were successful.

So, was the 1982 Apple II virus the first computer virus? Yes, as far as regular viruses go. However, if we broaden the definition to include other self-replicating programs, such as worms, we can push the origin of viruses back further, to the late 1970s, where esoteric work at a research center in northern California was about to change the world of network computing forever.

Early Worms

In 1970, the Xerox company established a research center in Palo Alto, California, close to Stanford University. Within a short time, the Xerox Palo Alto Research Center — or Xerox PARC, as it was known — became one of the hotbeds of computer science, home to some of the most innovative research in the country. Over the years, the scientists at Xerox PARC developed the first personal computer, called the Alto (they were in Palo Alto), laser printers, the Ethernet network, the idea of client/server systems (upon which the Internet is based, see Chapter 4), and much more.

The 1970s was when I began to study computer science, and at the time, Xerox PARC was one of the most important computer research centers. In the late 1970s, when I was a computer science graduate student (at the University of California at San Diego), I visited Xerox PARC and was shown around by one of the researchers. He showed me something I had never seen before: a personal computer that used windows, icons and a mouse. This was a prototype of the graphical user interface, or GUI, that is still in use today.

Many people visited Xerox PARC in those days. In 1979, Steve Jobs made the pilgrimage to see the Alto computer and its GUI. He took the idea back to Apple and (without giving credit to Xerox) used it to create the Macintosh. Later, Microsoft used the same ideas (without giving credit to Xerox or Apple) to create Windows. Thus, when you use the Internet today, much of the technology sitting in front of you is based on ideas that emerged from Xerox PARC in the late 1970s.

Actually, Xerox PARC affected the Internet more than most people realize. This highly regarded research center is also the home of the first real computer virus: the worm.

In May of 1980, John Shoch and Jon Hupp, two researchers in the Systems Science Laboratories group at Xerox PARC, published an internal paper. In this paper (#SSL-80-3), Shoch and Hupp described programming experiments they had been carrying out since the late 1970s. They had designed a number of programs whose role in life was to spread from one computer to another on the network (at the time, about 200 Alto computers) performing useful tasks.

Shoch's original idea was to create a program (later known as the "Vampire") that would run at night when most of the computers were idle. The program would look for available computers on the network, and start them running a copy of itself. Once the program was running, it would make use of the idle machines to work on complex problems that required a great deal of computing power. In the early morning, before people returned to work, the Vampire would silently retreat from most of the computers, waiting patiently in one or two machines, only to reemerge the next evening.

By the late 1970s, most of the pieces already existed. The Unix operating system (which controlled the Alto computers) already allowed programmers to write special programs, called DAEMONS, that would run in the background in order to provide useful services. Unix also had a scheduling facility, called **cron**, that enabled users to arrange for a program to be run automatically at specific times. Moreover, the Alto computers were already connected into a network that supported inter-computer communication. All this was well known. In fact, computer scientists were already experimenting with DISTRIBUTED COMPUTING, the idea that more than one computer could work on various pieces of a problem at the same time.

What Shoch did was to put the pieces together. His idea was to use the built-in Unix facilities, along with the network, to create an *automatic* distributed computing environment, one that would grow or shrink dynamically as conditions changed. To describe this approach to distributed computing, Shoch and Hupp named their system a "worm". Within the worm, each individual program was called a segment.

(The term "worm" was suggested by a researcher named Steve Weyer. At the time, Weyer was a graduate student from the Stanford University Education School who was working on systems relating to information retrieval and hypertext. Weyer's suggestion to call these new programs worms was inspired by a science fiction novel, *Shockwave Rider* (1975, Del Ray Books) written by John Brunner. In this novel, a totalitarian government uses a ubiquitous computer network to maintain control over its citizens. A clever rebel, Nickie Haflinger, is a fugitive from Tarnover, the government think tank at which he was educated. Haflinger escapes and devotes himself to trying to save the world by restoring personal freedom to the over-computerized masses. Eventually, Haflinger is able to write a program that spreads throughout the network, forcing it to shut down and destroying the government's power base. This program is called a "tapeworm".)

Today, we use the term WORM to refer to any virus that is designed to spread automatically over a network. As you will see in Chapter 10, most of today's worms spread via email. However, the first real computer worm, which Shoch called the Existential Worm, did not depend on email. It spread directly over a network. Shoch designed the Existential Worm as an experiment. The program had only one purpose: to stay alive, even if the machine on which it was running went down.

The worm worked as follows. Someone would start the program running on one computer. This program (the first segment) would look for other machines that were up and running on the network. Each time it found such a machine, the program would copy itself to that computer and start running there as well, creating a new segment. After a segment had run for a random amount of time, it would terminate voluntarily. Alternatively, a human being could stop a segment by rebooting the computer on which the segment was running.

One night in 1978, Shoch and two co-workers set a small worm loose on the network in order to test a specific control function. Everything looked okay, so they went home leaving the worm to do its work. During the night, however, something went wrong. One of the segments caused the computer in which it was running to crash (that is, to stop working). The worm, sensing that it had lost a segment, found a new computer and started the program running again. When this computer crashed, the worm looked for another computer, and so on.

The next morning, the daytime inhabitants of the building arrived to find that all the computers on the network had crashed. Such an occurrence was not that unusual, as Alto computers often crashed for no reason. (Evidently, when Microsoft developed Windows, they borrowed more than the graphical user interface.) What was odd, in this case, was that each time someone restarted his computer it would immediately crash again. What was happening? The aberrant worm was refusing to die, causing the first computer virus outbreak in the history of the world.

Eventually, Shoch and his co-workers were called in. They went on a search and destroy mission, but were unable to terminate the segments fast enough to control the worm. Fortunately, Shoch had foreseen such a possibility and had built a self-destruct mechanism into the worm. Using it, he was able to completely eradicate all the segments, but at the cost of destroying the worm.

In some companies, such an occurrence would have scared people silly. But Xerox PARC was a research institution. Uncontrollable computer worms were things to be studied, not feared. It wasn't long before the worm technology was improved to the point where it provided a number of interesting and useful services. For example:

- The Town Crier Worm traveled throughout the network making announcements.
- Every morning, the Billboard Worm displayed a different cartoon on everyone's computer.
- The Alarm Clock Worm maintained a list of wake-up requests from various people. Early in the morning at the appropriate times, the worm would initiate a telephone call to each person. (The ringing phone would act as an alarm clock.)
- During the night, the Peeker Worm tested the memory of each Alto computer. The program would then notify a technician if it detected that a specific computer might need a memory chip replaced. (At the time, memory chips were much less reliable than they are today.)

By now, you probably have a feel for the basic difference between a worm and a regular virus. A regular virus is able to copy itself to other programs on the same computer. However, in order to jump from one computer to another, a virus requires the help of two people: one to share the program, and the other to perform some action to start the program on the new computer.

A worm is proactive. It is designed to use network connections to send copies of itself from one computer to another automatically.

Since each new copy of the worm will do the same thing, worms can — if given the opportunity — multiply exponentially.

Some worms, like the ones we discussed above, can start running by themselves, as soon as they copy themselves onto a new computer. These types of worms spread the fastest. Other worms, like the email worms I mentioned earlier in the chapter, require a person to run the program on the new computer, say, by clicking on an email attachment. (We'll discuss email worms in detail in Chapter 10.)

As you can see, a regular virus can only spread as fast as people can deliberately share files. Under the right conditions, a worm can spread much, much faster, because it requires significantly less help from human beings.

This became clear in 1988, ten years after the first out-of-control worm became a nuisance at Xerox PARC, when a talented but naive student at Cornell University released a worm that brought down the Internet.

The Last Days of Innocence

In retrospect, by the late 1980s, it was only a matter of time until someone created a worm that would run rampant throughout the Internet. Although the Net was not nearly as large as it is today, it already had connections at most of the universities and research institutions in the United States, as well as a large number of military installations. Many of these computers ran Unix, a venerable operating system whose innards were accessible to any programmer who wanted to take a look.

Although Unix had been around for almost twenty years (the first version was developed at Bell Labs in 1969), it did not have a great deal of built-in security. The system was originally designed for trustworthy people who wanted to share and, up to now, the biggest problems were caused by people trying to surreptitiously break into one remote system at a time. The Unix networking and email facilities had bugs (known and unknown) but, as far as security went, most people didn't worry about them.

The Internet had never been infiltrated by a worm, although security-conscious programmers had been speculating for some time on the possibility. Still, in the early fall of 1988, a Unix network administrator could go home at night, secure in the knowledge that his system was safe from outside threats. He knew that, when he came back to work in the morning, everything would be up and running the way he had left it.

This was the case on November 2, 1988, as network administrators everywhere went home for the evening. Unknown to them, in a few hours, something extraordinary was about to happen, something that would, in a very short time, bring down the Net and change their world forever.

The Worm That Brought Down the Net

In the fall of 1988, 23-year-old Robert Tappan Morris Jr. was a first-year computer science graduate student at Cornell University in Ithaca, New York. Morris was a talented programmer who had been interested in computers for years. His father, Robert Morris Sr., was the Chief Scientist of the U.S. National Security Agency (NSA) and was associated with the University of Cambridge in England. Morris Sr. was an eminent researcher who lectured widely on computer security and ethics.

Morris Jr. grew up with computers and had been programming for a long time. When Morris was young, his father had once brought home one of the original Enigma machines from the NSA. (The Enigma was an encryption machine used by the Germans in World War II.) As a teenager, Morris had a computer account that allowed him access to a Unix network at Bell Labs, the legendary AT&T research center in Murray Hill, NJ. Morris was sufficiently ingenious as to figure out how to override the computer security system and give himself special privileges.

As a first year grad student at Cornell, Morris began to play with the idea of creating a program that would slowly spread throughout the Internet. The program wouldn't really do anything good or bad. It would just spread, slowly and silently, from one machine to another, politely taking up residence in various computers around the country. Morris worked on several prototypes and, on Wednesday, November 2, 1988, at about 6:00 P.M., he released the program, a worm, from a computer at MIT.

Morris's worm was a complex program that exploited a number of Unix features and flaws, and used a variety of methods to spread itself to as many computers as possible. Each time the program established itself on a new computer, the program would attempt to steal as many passwords as possible. This allowed it to break into people's accounts, looking for information on more computers to attack.

Interestingly enough, in 1979, Morris Sr. and Ken Thompson (one of the co-inventors of Unix) had published a paper in which they detailed various methods for writing a program to guess the passwords of Unix users. Ironically, nine years later, Morris Jr. used the very same methods, with great success, in his own program. (If you want to read the paper, it is called "Password Security: A Case History". You will find it in the November 1979 issue of *Communications of the ACM*, Volume 22, Number 11.)

People have speculated as to whether or not Morris thought he was doing anything wrong. His motives remain obscure, although it is clear that he went to a lot of trouble of hiding the origin of his worm. For example, although he was working at Cornell, Morris released the worm from a computer at MIT and made it look is if it had come from a machine at U.C. Berkeley. Later, an unknown person — and we are not naming any names here — deleted a log file on the MIT computer that contained a record of Morris's actions. That is why, earlier, I had to say that the worm was released "about 6:00 P.M.". Since the log file had vanished mysteriously, no one was able to pin down the exact times and events relating to the launching of the worm.

To me, it is obvious that Morris was irresponsible and short-sighted. However, I wonder, am I being too harsh on him? To be honest, I have to admit that when I was a first-year graduate student, if I had known how to break into computer systems, I probably would have created a worm myself, just to see if it would work. (Fortunately, my father was an accountant.)

Back in 1988, it was only a matter of hours before the worm began to spread, slowly at first, and then more quickly. What Morris didn't realize was that there were flaws in his design. Once the worm established itself on a new computer, the program would make so many copies of itself that it would exhaust the resources of the computer. Some computers crashed. Others kept going, but were so occupied with running the worm that no one could do any work. Moreover, if a system administrator turned a computer off, a short time after the machine was turned on, the worm would restart itself automatically.

Eventually, the worm had spread to over 6,000 computers, and within hours, machines all over the Internet were incapacitated. To put this in perspective, at the beginning of October 1988, there were about 56,000 computers connected to the Internet. Thus, Morris's worm was able to slow down or bring to a standstill over 10 percent of the Net. (If you are interested in the technical details, the worm affected Sun 3 and VAX computers running 4.2BSD Unix.)

The damage caused by the worm was even worse than it sounds, because once the news started to spread, many network administrators disconnected their networks from the Internet to keep them from being affected. Thus, within a few hours of releasing his worm, Robert Morris had effectively shut down most of the Internet.

Interestingly enough, Morris had put in a safeguard to keep all of this from happening. He designed the worm to look for other copies of itself on the same machine. When two worms found each other, one of them would, at a particular point, voluntarily self-destruct. This safeguard should have kept the worms from getting out of hand.

However, Morris also designed the program so that one out of every seven worms would *not* look for its cohorts. In effect, this made one seventh of the worms immortal. Morris may have done this in order to ensure that network administrators would not be able to use fake worms to kill off the real ones. Unfortunately, Morris underestimated the staying power of his program. So many immortal worms were created that machines all over the country were overloaded.

Eventually, Morris realized that something very bad was happening. He talked with a friend at Harvard and they brainstormed in an attempt to come up with a solution to what was rapidly becoming a problem of national importance. After some discussion, Morris and his friend used a computer at Harvard to send an anonymous message over the Net. The message contained instructions on how to terminate the program and keep it from restarting.

It was too late. By the time Morris and his friend sent the message, their link to the Net was clogged. The message did not go through until much later.

Meanwhile, throughout the night, groups of Unix experts around the country were working feverishly to find a way to counteract and eradicate the worm. Within hours, two groups — one at U.C. Berkeley and another at MIT — had managed to capture a copy of the program and were hard at work analyzing it. They discovered that the program had no mechanism to stop it from spreading. To the contrary, Morris had designed the worm to propagate indefinitely. Moreover, the worm was programmed to use a variety of Unix tricks to avoid being identified or terminated.

By 5 A.M. Thursday morning — about 11 hours after the worm was released — the Computer Systems Research Group at Berkeley had developed a procedure to halt the program from spreading. They sent out the information via Usenet (a system of discussion groups) as well as posting it to a number of electronic mailing lists. However, the release of this information was slowed significantly because so many system administrators had disconnected their computers from the Net.

Later that day, another group, this one at Purdue University in Indiana, developed a simple, effective method of stopping the worm. By 9 P.M., the Purdue information was circulating on the Net.

Within a few days, system administrators around the country had things under control. The worm was wiped out, computers were back online, and the Net was humming again. The Internet gods were in their heaven; all was right with the world.

The Internet Worm: Prologue

The Internet is — and always will be — vulnerable to a scattering of talented troublemakers who are blessed with a rudimentary sense of honesty and a less than perfect attitude toward responsibility. Today, it is unlikely that a worm like the one Robert Morris created will ever find its way to your computer. However, there are other types of worms and viruses, and some of them are quite sophisticated.

In a moment, we'll talk about practical measures, and I'll show you what you can do to protect your computer. As you read the discussion, you will see that there is a trade-off between security and convenience. It is possible to make your computer completely safe, but only by putting up with unacceptable inconveniences. This has always been the case with computer systems and it was certainly true at the time of the Internet worm.

Computer users consider convenience to be important, and the Unix that was in use in 1988 had been designed, above all, for ease of use. There was a tendency for people to overlook security loopholes if fixing them would cause problems for regular users. However, the episode of the worm permanently changed the way people thought about Internet security. Ironically, this was one of the benefits that Morris brought to the Net.

The first benefit was the realization that it was important for programmers everywhere to cooperate in order to improve security on the Internet. One of the reasons that the worm was eliminated so quickly was that distant groups shared information with one another. This lesson was never forgotten.

Another insight was that it was not possible to provide adequate security at the level of the network. To ensure a safe environment, each computer on a network must be configured and maintained properly. This was a major change in the way network administrators thought about security.

The final benefit of the worm episode occurred a few weeks later. On November 29, 1988, an unknown person was able to exploit a security hole and break into a military computer. At the time, the military network was separate from the rest of the Net, although the two parts were connected. As soon as the break-in was discovered, the military disconnected themselves from the rest of the Net.

Eventually, the connection was restored. However, everyone's awareness had just been raised by the worm. These two incidents, happening too close to one another, prompted the agency of the Department of Defense that oversaw the Internet to establish a brand new organization, the Computer Emergency Response Team (CERT), based at the Software Engineering Institute at Carnegie Mellon University. The job of CERT was to coordinate the response to Internet security emergencies. Today, CERT still exists and provides important services to the Internet community.

By now you are probably wondering, what, if anything, happened to Robert Morris Jr.? After the electronic dust settled, Morris became the first person charged under the Computer Fraud and Abuse Act of 1986, a law that made it a felony to break into a federal computer network.

On January 23, 1990, Morris was convicted, and in May 1990, he was sentenced to three years probation, 400 hours of community service, and a fine of $10,050. In addition Morris was required to pay the costs of his supervision.

Today, Robert Morris Jr. is an assistant professor of the Electrical Engineering and Computer Science at MIT. According to his Web site, Morris devotes his time to "building data networking infrastructure that is easy to configure and control."

Quick Diversion: A Puzzle

Before we move on, here is a short puzzle just for fun.

Clifford Stoll, the writer of the book *Cuckoo's Egg* (which relates a long, difficult, and ultimately successful hunt for a hacker) once met with Robert Morris Sr. at the NSA. During the meeting, Morris gave Stoll the following puzzle.

Look at the following sequence of five numbers and figure out which number comes next:

1   11   21   1211   111221

See what you can do with it, and I'll give you the answer at the end of Chapter 10. In the meantime, here is a hint: there is no arithmetic involved.

10

Protecting Your Stuff: Viruses and Common Sense

Nowhere in the world of computing does nonsense spread more quickly than when people start worrying about viruses.

Protecting Your Stuff:
Viruses and Common Sense

Who Needs Special Virus Protection?

In this chapter, I'll show you how to protect your computer from the various types of viruses. I'll deal with each type of virus in turn, and then address the problem of how to avoid trouble. At the end of the chapter, I'll summarize everything into 4 simple rules.

You will find that the precautions you need to take to protect yourself against viruses are actually quite simple. In fact, as I will explain later, there is no need for you to use special software such as an antivirus program (discussed later in the chapter) or a personal firewall (discussed in Chapter 11).

Before we start, I want to take a moment to qualify my advice. What I am about to explain in these two chapters is applicable if you are one person using a single computer or a family with several computers (and, possibly, a small home network). If you use the Internet at work and your computer is connected to a large network, things are different.

As a general rule, a network large enough to require a full-time administrator should have special protection. If you work in such a network, you *do* need antivirus programs, a firewall, and so on. However, these tools should be installed and maintained by your network administrator.

What if you work in an office, but your network is not large enough to require a full-time expert? Just follow the guidelines in this chapter and Chapter 11, and you will be all right.

How Viruses Spread by Sharing Files

As we discussed earlier, a regular virus (as opposed to a worm or a macro virus) spreads by inserting itself into a file that contains a program. When you run the program, the virus becomes active and tries to copy itself to another file. (At the same time, of course, the virus will cause damage if it is programmed to do so.)

In the olden days, before the Web and before the Internet became popular, viruses were more of a problem than they are today, because people shared software freely. In those days, programs with viruses typically spread in one of two ways.

First, many people used BBSs. A BBS, or Bulletin Board System, was an independent service offering file sharing, discussion forums and chatting. Most BBSs were run by one person, and many of them specialized in a particular area of interest, such as games or software. There was a time, before the Web, when BBSs were very popular. In fact, in the first three editions of my Yellow Pages book (*Harley Hahn's Internet Yellow Pages*), from 1994–1996, I had a whole section devoted to BBSs.

Each BBS had its own phone number. To access a BBS, you would have your computer dial that BBS's phone number. Once you made the connection, you would log in with a user name and password. You could then use the BBS to upload and download software.

(UPLOAD means to copy a file from your computer to a remote computer. DOWNLOAD means to copy a file from a remote computer to your computer. If you ever get confused, just think of the remote computer as being above you in the sky.)

As you might imagine, BBSs were a common source of viruses. Typically, a virus programmer would deliberately insert a virus into a popular file (such as a game or utility program) — thereby creating a Trojan horse — and start sharing it by uploading it to a BBS. By the time anyone knew that the program contained a virus, it would have already been downloaded and installed by many people. Moreover, as people began to upload the file to other BBSs, all in the spirit of sharing, the virus would spread even faster.

A second way in which people used to share software was to copy a program on a floppy disk and give it to a friend. The friend would take the floppy home and put it in his computer.

Sharing software via floppy disks is risky because it makes it easy for viruses to spread. If a program on a floppy disk contains a virus, and you copy that program to your hard disk, you will be copying the virus at the same time.

However, there is another, more insidious way in which sharing floppy disks can spread viruses. It's a bit technical, so I'll have to explain.

Internally, the raw data on a disk is organized into SECTORS. On every floppy disk, the very first sector, called the BOOT SECTOR, contains a tiny program that is executed automatically if the floppy is in the drive when the computer starts.

The very first PC virus, written in 1986, was designed to take over the boot sector of a floppy disk. This virus was called the Brain virus because it wrote the characters "(c) Brain" on the volume label (an internal label stored on the disk). If you had a floppy that contained this virus, and that floppy was in the drive when the computer started, the virus would become active in your computer's memory. Then later, if you put another floppy in the drive, the virus would copy itself to that disk. In this way, the Brain virus managed to spread extensively.

Later, many other boot sector viruses were created. Two of the more widespread ones were called Michelangelo and Stoned (in case you ever hear of them). To make things worse, most boot sector viruses are designed to spread to hard disks as well as floppy disks. Such viruses can cause a lot of problems, and can be difficult to eradicate.

What to Do About Regular Viruses

How do you keep from exposing your computer to regular viruses (the type that insert themselves into programs)? It's easy: just don't share software. All you have to remember are two guidelines:

1. Never use a program that has been on someone else's computer.

2. Never put a floppy disk into your computer if it has been in another computer.

As I mentioned, in the olden days, a lot of software was shared from one person to another and viruses were a big problem.

Today, there are millions of people using the Internet and the spread of viruses is actually quite small. Why? Because we don't share software much anymore. We tend to get our programs in one of three ways, all of which are safe.

- Buying a computer.

When you buy a computer, it comes with a lot of free programs, all of which have been checked for viruses.

- Buying brand new software.

It is safe to buy programs that come in a sealed box. However, if a friend has bought a program and offers to share it with you after he has opened the box, should you do it?

If the program comes on floppy diskettes, don't share it. It is possible that there was a virus on his computer, and that virus is now on one of the floppies.

If the program comes on a CD, you don't need to worry. The disc will be a CD-ROM, which is read-only and cannot be modified (see Chapter 3). There is no way for a virus to spread to a CD-ROM disc.

- Downloading software from a Web site.

In all the years that I have been using the Internet, I have downloaded and installed more software than I can remember, and I have never even seen a virus. The reason is that, with one exception (which I'll get to in a moment), software distributed over the Web is safe. This is because most programs are distributed by the company or person who created the software, and people who create software make sure that their Web sites do not pass viruses on to their users.

The one exception is that you should avoid downloading programs from a site that is run by people of questionable honesty. For example, if you find a Web site that has PIRATED (stolen) software, don't be surprised if one of the programs has a virus.

True story: I personally know only one person who encountered a virus by downloading software from the Web. He was visiting a secret Web site that distributes tools to make it easy for people to cause trouble, for example, by breaking into other people's computer systems. One of the tools he downloaded contained a virus. When he executed the program, the virus wiped out so much data on his hard disk, that he lost everything and had to completely reinstall Windows. (Need I tell you that this was a teenage boy?)

With respect to sharing software, I want to reinforce one of the guidelines. There are file-sharing services available that allow you to swap files with other people. One well-known system is called Gnutella, but there are others.

Many people use such services to share music files, which is fine (in that music files can't carry viruses). However, there are also people who share programs in this way, and some of those programs have viruses.

So always remember, never run a copy of a program that has already been on someone else's computer. Don't download programs from a file-sharing service, and don't copy programs from your friends.

If a friend tells you about a great program he found on the Net, don't copy the program from him. Go to the official Web site for that program, and download a brand new copy for yourself.

How Viruses Spread Through Email

When you send an email message to someone, it is possible to send one or more files along with the message. For example, say that you send a message to your Aunt Beatrice saying that you have a new photo of your cat. Along with your message, you send a file that contains the picture. When your Aunt Beatrice receives the message, she can double-click on the file name to open the file and look at the picture.

When you send a file in this way, we say that you ATTACH it to the message. The file itself is called an ATTACHMENT.

By far, email attachments are the most common vehicle by which viruses spread over the Internet. As I explained in Chapter 9, viruses that spread automatically are called worms. Most of the viruses on the Net today are worms that are designed to use the email system. Here is a typical scenario.

Mortimer Goofus receives an intriguing message from one of his friends. When he looks at the message he notices that it contains an attachment. It happens that his mail program doesn't open the attachment automatically. Instead, it shows him the name of the file, and waits for him to decide what to do. This gives Mortimer a chance to look at the file name and decide if he really wants to open this file.

However, as soon as he sees that he has a file attachment, Mortimer double-clicks on the file name without thinking. (Thinking is not one of Mortimer's strong points.) Double-clicking on the file tells Windows to open the file and, in this case, it happens that the file is actually a worm. As soon as Windows opens the file, the worm starts running.

The first thing that happens is that the worm makes copies in various files on the hard disk. One of the copies is put into the `C:Windows\System` folder, disguised as an important system file, one that most people would be afraid to delete. The other copies are placed in various folders, to make it as difficult as possible for someone to track them down.

Once the worm has created files that contain copies of itself, it inserts a couple of new lines into the registry (see Chapter 4). This has the effect of causing the worm program to be executed automatically each time the computer starts.

The final thing the worm does is to access the list of email addresses in the address book within Mortimer's email program. The worm then sends a copy of the original message to every address on the list. Although Mortimer has no idea what is happening, the messages are sent out under his name. Along with each message is an attachment. The attachment contains — you guessed it — a copy of the worm.

What Happens When You Open a File?

In a moment, I'm going to tell you how to avoid trouble with email worms. Before I do, I want to make sure you understand what happens when you "open" a file. This is crucial to understanding how email worms spread.

Within Windows, there are several ways to open a file. If you are using Windows Explorer, you can double-click on the name of a file. If you are looking at icons — say, on your desktop — you can double-click on an icon that represents a file. If you are using a program such as a word processor, you can pull down the File menu, click on Open and then select the file you want. And, if you are reading a mail message that has an attachment, you can open the attachment (which is a file) by double-clicking on its name.

But what actually happens when you open a file? The details are a bit technical, but basically:

• If the file contains a program, Windows runs it.

• If the file contains data, Windows passes that data to a program that knows what to do with it. If necessary, Windows will start that program.

For example, say your desktop has an icon that represents your browser program (either Internet Explorer or Netscape). When you double-click on this icon, Windows starts your browser for you.

Now, say you have another icon, one that represents a file containing a Microsoft Word document. When you double-click on this icon, Windows passes the file to the Word program, which knows what to do with it. If Word is not already running, Windows will start it for you.

Thus, to OPEN a file means to indicate to Windows that you want to process the contents of the file in an appropriate manner.

How does Windows know what to do when you tell it to open a file? It looks at the name of the file. As we discussed in Chapter 3, all file names end with a 3- or 4-character extension. By looking at the extension, Windows can tell what is inside the file. For example, in the name **info.html**, the extension is **html**. This tells Windows that the file contains a Web page. In the file name **proposal.doc**, the extension is **doc**. This tells Windows that the file contains a Word document.

It is important that you understand file extensions because, as you will see, the way you decide whether or not a particular email attachment is safe to open is by looking at its extension.

With Windows, everything is automatic. When you indicate that you want to open a specific file, Windows starts by looking at the extension. Windows then checks with a special table that contains information about every possible file type. You can look at this table if you want:

1. **Start Windows Explorer.**

2. **Pull down the View Menu and select Folder Options.**

3. **Click on the File Types tab.**

In the box that says "Registered file types" you will see a list of file types. Scroll through the list. (There will be a lot more than you expect.) When you see a file type that looks interesting, click on it. You will then see the file extension that is associated with that type, as well as the name of the program that is used to open it.

Don't change anything.

What to Do About Email Viruses

Almost all viruses that spread via email are worms that are programmed to use the email system to send out copies of themselves automatically. If you inadvertently open such a worm, it will attempt to send a copy of itself to everyone in your address book.

Fortunately, this can only happen if you use a Microsoft mail program, such as Outlook or Outlook Express. Both of these programs are designed to give unencumbered access to their address book. Other mail programs won't let this happen. However, because so many people use Microsoft mail programs, email worms are a real problem.

An email virus has two parts: a message and a program. The program will be in the form of an attachment. It is always safe to read the message. However, if you open the attachment (by double-clicking on it), you will start the program running.

If a worm did nothing more than send a copy of itself to other people behind your back, it would be a nuisance. However, virus programmers purposely design worms to cause trouble. For example, a worm can be programmed to delete files, create new files, or even download and run a program from a remote Web site.

You can't control what other people send you, especially if it is being done automatically without their knowledge. However, it is easy to avoid trouble. When you see that a message has an attachment, look carefully at the name of the file. If you are completely sure that the attachment is safe, you can open it. However, if the attachment contains a program of any type, delete it immediately.

To decide if an attachment is safe, all you need to do is look at the file extension. The following is a list of common extensions that are always safe:

.gif	(picture)
.jpg	(picture)
.mp3	(music)
.txt	(plain text)
.wav	(sound)

The following are extensions that are not safe because they contain (or may contain) a program. Never open an email attachment that has one of these extensions.

.bat	(batch file)
.chm	(compiled HTML file)
.com	(program)
.exe	(program)
.htm	(HTML file)
.html	(HTML file)
.js	(JScript program)
.jse	(encoded JScript program)
.lnk	(Windows shortcut [link])
.pif	(program information file)
.vbs	(VBScript program)
.vbe	(encoded VBScript program)
.wsf	(Windows Script File program)
.wsh	(Windows Scripting Host Settings File)

(If this looks too complicated, don't worry. In the next section, I'll give you a simple rule to follow to make everything easy.)

If you are familiar with creating Web pages, you might be wondering why I advise against opening HTML attachments. HTML (Hypertext Markup Language) is the system used to create Web pages. Every time you look at a Web page you are, essentially, opening an HTML file, so why should it be risky to open an HTML attachment?

The answer is that an HTML file has the capability of running programs on your computer without your knowing it. In fact, the Javascript system was designed by Netscape to make it easy to embed a program inside a Web page.

These capabilities are great for Web designers, because it allows them to build interesting and useful Web sites. However, the same tools also allow virus programmers to create HTML files that can run amok on your computer.

It is possible for an evil programmer to create a Web site with dangerous HTML, but he would have to find a way to get people to visit that site without letting anyone trace the problems back to him. Generally, this doesn't happen. Moreover, if a Web hosting company or ISP receives complaints about a dangerous Web site, they will shut it down immediately.

Email is different. A virus programmer can send out dangerous email in a way that is very difficult to trace. Moreover, although it may be difficult to induce someone to visit a Web site, it is all too easy to get people to click on an attachment called **nakedgirl.html**.

The only reason email worms spread is that people who don't know what they are doing mindlessly click on everything they see. If you know such a person, please try to help him (or her). The general rule is, if you have any doubt whatsoever about an attachment, delete it. Don't open it just to see what happens.

Don't make the mistake of thinking that an attachment is safe just because it was sent by someone you trust. Worms are designed to send out copies of themselves automatically. Moreover, Microsoft mail programs make it possible for a worm to insert the person's name within the message. Thus, a worm can send you what looks like a personalized message, signed by one of your friends, so don't be fooled. If you get a worm, the person whose name is on the message doesn't even know that mail was sent out from his computer or has his name on it.

When it comes to attachments, don't trust anyone.

Making Sure Attachments Are Really Gone

With some mail programs, when you delete a message, any attachments it may have are deleted at the same time. However, you must be careful. As I explained in Chapter 4, a deleted message is not really gone. It has simply been moved from your Inbox to another folder. (With Microsoft Outlook, it is the Deleted Items folder. With Netscape Messenger, it is the Trash folder.)

Thus, if you suspect that a message has an email virus, you must be extra careful. After you delete the message, you must open the Deleted Items (or Trash) folder, find the message, and delete it a second time. The message and its attachment will now be gone permanently.

Other mail programs, such as Eudora, handle attachments differently. With Eudora, as soon as an attachment comes in, it is placed in an ATTACHMENT DIRECTORY. (This is a real Windows directory, not an internal mail folder.) In order to delete an attachment, you need to use Windows Explorer to open the attachment directory, and delete the file manually.

Again, I must warn you, as I explained in Chapter 3, when you delete a file with Windows Explorer, the file is simply transferred to the Recycle Bin. To get rid of the file permanently, you must either empty the Recycle Bin or open the Recycle bin and delete the file by hand. (See Chapter 3 for the details.)

Hint: If you hold down the Shift key when you delete a file within Windows Explorer, the file is erased permanently. It is not put into the Recycle Bin.

If you use Eudora, and you are not sure of the name of your attachment directory:

1. **Pull down the Tools menu and select "Options".**

2. **Within the Category box, scroll down and click on "Attachments".**

You will see a long button with the name of the attachment directory. To change your attachment directory, click on the long button.

In this same window, you will see an option "Delete attachments when emptying Trash". If you want to make deleting attachments easier, turn on this option. From now on, whenever you delete a message from the Trash folder, its attachments will be deleted automatically from the attachment directory.

Security vs. Convenience

As I mentioned in Chapter 9, there is always a trade-off between security and convenience. You can have more security if you are willing to put up with extra inconvenience. Here is an example.

The biggest virus problem on the Internet comes from worms that are spread by email. Would you like your system to be 100 percent safe? It's easy. Just follow rule number 1:

1. **Delete every attachment that enters your mailbox.**

Many people follow this rule, and it works fine. However, you lose the convenience of being able to open useful attachments, such as pictures. So if you are willing to follow a slightly more complicated rule, you will at least be able to look at photos of your niece's new kitten dressed up as Little Red Riding Hood:

2. **Delete every attachment except those with a file extension of gif or jpg.**

Notice that, as soon as you increase the convenience, you have to be more careful with security.

Although rule number 2 looks simple, following it can be trickier than you think, because many virus programmers give their attachments misleading names to try to fool people.

From what I explained in the last section, you know better than to open an attachment with an extension of **vbs** (a Visual Basic program). Indeed, **vbs** worms are responsible for some of the worst viruses on the Net. So, if you were to get a message with an attachment named **kitten.vbs**, you would simply delete it.

But what if you saw an attachment named **kitten.jpg.vbs**? Don't be fooled. This is a **vbs** file masquerading as a **jpg** file. In this case, the virus programmer has chosen a name to fool people who are not careful. For this reason, many people — perhaps most people — are better off giving up convenience for security by following rule number 1. Delete all attachments.

If you choose to open some attachments, remember that, when you look at a file name, there is only one extension, the one at the very end of the name. Anything else is irrelevant.

If you are willing to pay a bit more attention to security, we can expand rule 2 to give you even more convenience by letting you open other types of attachments that are safe:

3. **Delete every attachment except those with a file extension of gif, jpg, mp3, txt or wav.**

If you know what you are doing, you can add even more extensions to your list of safe attachments, such as **zip** (compressed) files. However, the more exceptions you make, the more chance there is that you will make a mistake.

Whatever you do, never open an attachment that has an extension you do not recognize. There are some unusual file types that are executable that you have probably never seen before. *If you don't know what it is, don't click on it.*

Overall, unless you are an extremely careful person who has a lot of experience with Windows, my suggestion is to follow rule number 2. (Rule number 1 is easier, but why miss out on being able to look at pictures of kittens?)

Macro Viruses

Macro viruses are a special type of virus that can cause trouble when you share Microsoft Word documents and Excel spreadsheets. However, before I discuss macro viruses, I need to explain a few basic concepts.

Broadly speaking, there are two types of programs: application programs and system programs.

An APPLICATION PROGRAM is one that you use in order to do something creative, interesting or useful. Examples of application programs are word processors, database programs, spreadsheet programs, games, music programs, email programs, browsers, and so on.

A SYSTEM PROGRAM is one whose job is to support the running of the computer in some way. For instance, Windows is a very large system program. Another example is the Scandisk program, which looks for internal errors on a disk by checking how the files and folders are stored. (If your computer does not shut down properly, Windows will run Scandisk automatically when the computer restarts.)

To be philosophical, we can say that the reason system programs even exist is to allow us to run application programs. To be even more philosophical, we can say that a NERD is someone who understands system programs. Indeed, nerds see a computer system as a thing of beauty in its own right, and they love to know why things work the way they do. This is why nerds are so handy when you need help figuring out why your computer is acting in a mysterious way. A nerd may not be able to help you use your word processor to design a newsletter, but he will know what to do when the Scandisk program starts running automatically every day at 10:07 A.M.

The reason for this diversion is so I can introduce you to the idea of application programs, which allows me to talk about macros.

Some application programs are so complex as to have a special built-in facility that enables you to write programs that run only within that environment. Such programs are called MACROS, and are used to automate repetitive tasks. Most database programs, spreadsheet programs and word processors have some type of macro facility.

A typical use for a macro is to carry out a long and tricky procedure. For example, let's say you are using a word processor, and every now and then, you find yourself going through the same long series of keystrokes in order to do something or other. You can automate the process by creating a macro that performs those keystrokes for you. You can then run the macro whenever you want.

Some application programs allow you to go further. They integrate the macro facility with a full programming language, a language that has special features designed for performing tasks related to databases, spreadsheets, documents, and so on. This is the case with the family of Microsoft Office products. You can use a programming language called Visual Basic for Applications (VBA) to write programs that work with the various Office products: Word (word processing), Excel (spreadsheets), Access (databases), Outlook (email and organizing), Powerpoint (presentations), and Frontpage (Web site design).

In particular, within Word and Excel, it is possible to create macros and attach them to a specific file. Once you do so, the macros are contained within that file. This means that if you send a copy of the file to another person, he or she will also get the macros that go along with that file.

Now, it happens that both Word and Excel were designed so that it is possible to create a macro that runs automatically whenever a certain event occurs, such as when you open, save or close the file.

So let's put this all together. You can use VBA to write a powerful macro for Microsoft Word or Excel. You can then attach that macro to a Word document or Excel spreadsheet in such a way that the macro will run automatically as soon as the file is opened (or saved or closed). You can then email the file to someone and wait for the person to open it on their computer.

Eventually, these possibilities were noticed by virus programmers, who started to write MACRO VIRUSES: destructive macros that attach themselves to documents and spreadsheets. Macro viruses are designed to run automatically and cause damage as soon as you open a file. They spread because people share files without knowing that a macro virus is attached.

Early Macro Viruses

The idea of a macro virus was first described in 1989 by Harold Highland, an eminent computer security expert. Highland published a paper in which he discussed how the macro facilities of certain application programs made such viruses possible ("A Macro Virus", *Computers & Security*, Vol. 8, 1989, pp. 178–188).

In 1989 and 1990, Highland demonstrated his ideas at various computer conferences, showing rudimentary examples using Lotus 1-2-3 running on a PC under DOS. These examples were Trojan horses in which malicious instructions were inserted into otherwise benign macros. For anything to happen, a user would have to execute the macro deliberately.

It was not until several years later that the first real, self-replicating macro virus was created. That virus, called DMV (Document Macro Virus), was created in the fall of 1994 by a computer security analyst named Joel McNamara.

At the time, McNamara lived in Carnation, Washington, outside of Seattle, not far from Microsoft's global headquarters in Redmond. McNamara was working as a security consultant, evaluating various Microsoft Office products for a client. During his investigations, he discovered that it was possible to use the built-in programming language to create viruses.

As McNamara explained to me, "I found that the nature of Microsoft's implementation of macros opened up the possibility for code to be automatically and transparently run when a document was opened." In particular, McNamara noticed that Microsoft had created a product in which "macros could automatically execute when a document was opened". Moreover, these macros "could perform operating system-type functions, which were well suited to a virus self-replicating and causing mischief".

In November 1994, McNamara created the world's first self-reproducing macro virus, for both Microsoft Word and Excel. He then wrote a paper, "Document Macro Viruses" — with the subtitle "Yes, you can spread a virus with a data file..." — in which he described his ideas and showed an actual macro virus. McNamara's virus, however, was not destructive. It was designed only as a demonstration and it did not spread.

For security reasons, McNamara did not publicize his discovery. He showed it only to other computer security experts as well as a reporter from the *Wall Street Journal*. However, a year and a half later, someone else followed in McNamara's footsteps. In July 1995, Concept, an unfriendly Microsoft Word virus appeared. Ironically, Concept got an enormous boost when Microsoft distributed a CD-ROM containing the virus. In a fit of damage control, Microsoft sought to downplay the very idea of macro viruses, calling Concept a "prank". (In fact, Microsoft later released a second CD-ROM that contained the virus.)

Within a short time, Concept had spread widely, not only to PCs, but to Macintosh computers, which had their own version of Word. McNamara decided it was time to release his paper. In August 1995, he published it on the Net.

Macro viruses were here to stay.

What to Do About Macro Viruses

It's easy to protect yourself against macro viruses. All you need to do is set an option to tell Word and Excel not to run macros automatically when you open a file.

For Word 2000 and Excel 2000:

1. **Pull down the Tools menu.**

2. **Select Macros then click on Security.**

3. **Make sure the "Security level" is set to High.**

4. **Click on the OK button.**

For Word 97 and Excel 97:

1. **Pull down the Tools menu.**

2. **Click on Options.**

3. **Click on the General tab.**

4. **Make sure "Macro virus protection" is turned on.**

5. **Click on the OK button.**

To make sure you don't get fooled, I want to repeat some advice I gave earlier. Don't assume that a document or spreadsheet is safe just because it was mailed to you by someone you trust. It is common for people to share files without knowing that the files have macro viruses.

Antivirus Programs: The Real Truth

An ANTIVIRUS PROGRAM is a tool that helps protect your system against various types of viruses. It works in several ways. First, it scans your computer's memory to see if any viruses are currently running. Next, it checks all the files on your hard disk (or, if you wish, on a floppy disk) to see if any of them might be harboring viruses. If the program finds a corrupted file, it will do its best to extract the virus and save the file. Otherwise, it will delete the file or put it in a special "quarantine" folder.

Once your memory and disk have been checked out, the antivirus program runs in the background, acting as a protective gateway to make sure that no new virus-laden files make it onto your system. To ensure that it carries out its job, the program will start running automatically, in the background, each time you start your computer, and will constantly monitor your activities on the Web and when you use email.

Finally, to make sure that it is up to date, the program may contact its home Web site regularly, checking for updates. If one is available, the program will download it automatically. This allows the program to stay abreast of new viruses.

In some ways, an antivirus program sounds like a great tool to have working for you, silently protecting your system from dangerous beasts that go bump in the electronic night. However, except in a few special cases, which I'll discuss in a moment, you really don't need an antivirus program. As a matter of fact, for most people, antivirus programs are more trouble than they are worth.

First, antivirus programs are intrusive, even to the point where they can affect the performance of your computer. Many people find it inconvenient to have such programs running continuously in the background.

Second, since virus programmers never stop creating new viruses, antivirus programs need to be kept up to date. As I mentioned, some programs will use your Internet connection to check regularly for new updates. Such updates cost money, however. Most antivirus companies offer free updates for a limited time, but after that, you will have to pay a monthly fee. If you don't pay the fee, you will have no protection against new viruses.

Third, even if you pay the money and keep your antivirus program up to date, it still won't protect you against the very newest viruses. In many cases, new viruses, especially email worms, spread so fast that they can reach you before the antivirus company has a chance to create an update, and your program has a chance to install the update.

Fourth, antivirus programs are far from perfect. No matter what the marketing hype may claim, antivirus programs are not able to detect all viruses, nor are they always able to clean your system completely if they do find a virus.

The real truth is that, if you use a computer over which you have complete control — such as a home computer, even if you have a small home network — you don't need an antivirus program. Antivirus companies do their best to scare people who don't understand computer viruses, so don't let yourself become paranoid. If you follow the guidelines I have explained, you are safe. To make it easy, I have included a handy summary at the end of the chapter.

The biggest problem with antivirus programs is that they can give you a false sense of security. Even if you have an antivirus program

> *"Antivirus companies do their best to scare people who don't understand computer viruses, so don't let yourself become paranoid."*

installed on your computer, you still need to follow the rules, because no program can protect you against all viruses, especially the very newest email worms. However, if you follow the rules, you don't need an antivirus program!

But, I hear you ask, are there any situations in which you do need an antivirus program? The answer is yes: if you don't have complete control over your computer or your network, you need antivirus protection. This is because other people who don't follow the rules may expose your computer to a virus.

For example, if you use a network at work (or if you bring a laptop computer to work), you never know if someone else on the network will bring in a floppy disk with a virus, or open an email attachment that contains a worm, or install a program that is really a Trojan horse. Once this happens, the virus may spread to other computers on the network including yours. Even if you have a knowledgeable, full-time network administrator, he or she can't provide complete protection against people who do unsafe things.

Similarly, if you have a home computer and you can't get your children or your spouse to follow the rules, you should consider getting an antivirus program. At least you will have some protection (but don't depend on it).

If you do want an antivirus program, here are the Web sites of a few antivirus companies. When you visit these sites, you will notice that they put a lot of effort into scaring you, so don't be surprised: it's their business to scare you.

In most cases, you can download an antivirus program to use for free for a limited time. After the time expires, if you want to keep using the program, you must pay to register it. Some of these companies do not make it easy to find the Web page with the free trial program; you may have to spend a few minutes looking for it. They would rather that you buy the program outright, especially if you think there is a virus on your system and you are scared.

Most of these programs cost money. However, be sure to look at more than the initial price. Don't buy a program until you know the cost of the updates. That is where the antivirus companies make a large portion of their money.

```
http://www.leprechaun.com.au/
http://www.symantec.com/product/
http://www.antivirus.com/pc-cillin/download/
http://www.esafe.com/esafe/desktop/index.asp
http://www.mcafee-at-home.com/products/
   anti-virus.asp
```

Internet Resources: Antivirus programs

One last point. If your brand new computer comes with a free antivirus program installed, should you use it? The answer is: unless you have a special need (as I explained above), you do not need the program. Feel free to uninstall it.

Let's be realistic here. No one makes money giving away free software. The antivirus program that was pre-installed on your computer is a marketing tool. The antivirus company hopes you will register for their service and pay for regular upgrades. They are counting on the fact that most people will not want to uninstall a built-in antivirus program.

What they aren't counting on is that you have this book.

What Should You Do If You Get a Virus on Your Computer?

If you do get a virus on your computer, terminate all the programs that are running, especially your email program. Now disconnect your computer from the Internet. If you are on a network, or if you have DSL or a cable modem, disconnect the network plug. Shut down your computer.

Now stop and think. Don't panic.

If you are at work, call your network administrator. Let him or her handle the problem.

If you are at home, or if you work in an office that doesn't have a network administrator, the very best thing to do is to call in a nerd. Everyone should know at least one computer nerd for times like this. (I am serious.) If you don't know what you are doing, you are much better off having a nerd solve your problem.

If you have no one to help you, you will have to figure things out for yourself. Start by asking, how did your computer get exposed to the virus? Did you open an email attachment? Did you run a program that came from someone else's computer? If you know where the virus came from, it can help you find the information you need to remove it from your system.

Turn on your computer. After it starts, look for any programs that may have started automatically and terminate them. Now, reconnect your machine to the Net.

If you know how you got the virus, check with one of the following virus information sites. You goal should be:

1. **Make sure your computer has a virus. (It is easy to have a false alarm.)**

2. **Identify the virus.**

3. **Find instructions on what to do for that particular virus.**

```
http://wtc.trendmicro.com/wtc/
http://www.sarc.com/avcenter/tools.list.html
http://www.icsalabs.com/html/communities/
  antivirus/alerts.shtml
```

Internet Resources: Information about viruses

If you really have a virus and all else fails, get yourself an antivirus program (see the previous section for Web addresses). If you are really stuck and you can't download a program, you will have to buy one at the store. In this case, it is worth it.

How to Be Safe: 4 Simple Rules

Once you know what you are doing, it is easy to protect your computer system against viruses. All you need to do is follow 4 simple rules.

To protect against email worms:

1. **Delete all email attachments except those with a file extension of gif, jpg, mp3, txt or wav.**

To protect against regular viruses:

2. **Never use a program that has been on someone else's computer. Don't share software unless it comes on a CD-ROM.**

and:

3. **Never put a floppy disk into your computer if it has been in another computer.**

To protect against macro viruses (if you use Microsoft Word or Excel):

4. **Turn on the built-in macro security.**

(With Word 2000 and Excel 2000, set the macro security level to "High". With Word 97 and Excel 97, make sure that "Macro virus protection" is turned on.)

Quick Diversion: The Solution

At the end of Chapter 9, I showed you a short puzzle. The puzzle was to look at the following sequence of five numbers and figure out which number comes next:

1   11   21   1211   111221

To see the solution to this puzzle, all you have to do is interpret each number as describing the previous number.

The first number is simply **1**. The second number (**11**) shows that the first number consists of one **1**.

The third number (**21**) shows that the second number consists of two **1**s.

The fourth number (**1211**) shows that the third number consists of one **2** and one **1**.

The fifth number (**111221**) shows that the fourth number consists of one **1**, one **2**, and two **1**s.

Once you see the numbers in this way, it's easy to figure out what comes next:

```
312211
13112221
1113213211
31131211131221
13211311123113112211...
```

and so on.

11

Protecting Your Stuff: Configuring Your System

There is a trade-off between convenience and security. The goal is to have adequate security without having to give up too much functionality.

Protecting Your Stuff: Configuring Your System

- Two Startling Truths

- Are There Dangerous Web Sites?

- Scripting Languages

- Making Your Browser Safe

- Making Your Email Program Safe

- Extra Protection Against Evil Scripts

- How to Remove Windows Scripting Host: Windows 98/ME

- How to Remove Dangerous File Extensions: Windows 95

- Protecting Your Network: Firewalls

- Late One Night

Two Startling Truths

In Chapter 10, we discussed guidelines you should follow to guard against viruses as you use the Net. In this chapter, we will talk about a number of one-time steps you can take to make your system even more secure. These steps are easy in that all you need to do is configure certain settings. Just do it all at once and you can rest a bit easier.

To lead us into this discussion, I'd like to answer two questions that people often worry about:

- Is it possible to get a virus on your computer just by looking at a Web page?
- Is it possible to get a virus on your computer just by reading an email message, even if you don't open an attachment?

The startling answer to both these questions is yes.

You only need to worry about these possibilities if you use Microsoft's browser (Internet Explorer) and email programs (Outlook and Outlook Express). As you will see, this is because Microsoft designs their software to be tightly integrated with the operating system (Windows). As a result, a number of serious security weaknesses are built right into the system.

Fortunately, it is easy to protect yourself against such threats. Let's start with dangerous Web pages.

Are There Dangerous Web Sites?

Can you run into trouble just by visiting a Web site and looking at a Web page? The answer is yes, because it is possible for a remote Web site to run programs on your computer without your knowledge. In principle, someone could write an evil program and integrate it into a Web site in such a way so that, just by visiting the site, you could have, say, the files on your hard disk totally ruined.

In practice, this doesn't happen much, because the type of people who might do such things prefer to write viruses that can circulate anonymously. Once a Web site is found to cause problems, the Web hosting company or ISP will terminate the site immediately and look for the person who made it. Even if a depraved Web programmer were able to escape detection, he would still have to find a way to attract people to his site. On the other hand, a well-crafted email worm can circulate indefinitely with no ongoing effort and minimal risk to the programmer.

Still, the potential for harm exists and it does behoove you to take precautions. These precautions are simple and quick, because all you have to do is configure certain settings within your browser.

In a moment, I'll show you how to set these options. You will see that, because Internet Explorer is so tightly integrated with Windows, it has more potential for accidental harm than do other browsers, such as Netscape. Before I explain the settings, however, I think you will find it interesting to go over a few of the technical concepts you will encounter.

Originally, the Web was developed as a way to display various types of information. After a few years, however, programmers realized that they could build much more useful and interesting Web sites if it were possible to have Web pages that did more than display information. It would greatly increase the power of the Web if a Web page were able to execute a program on your computer. A number of different systems were devised in order to make this happen.

The first well-known system was JAVA, developed by Sun Microsystems (the computer company I mentioned in Chapter 6). Java allows programmers to write small programs, called APPLETS, that a Web server can send to your computer, where they are run automatically.

Since this raises the possibility of a rogue program wrecking havoc on your computer, Java is designed to run within a special controlled environment called a SANDBOX. Within the Sandbox, Java applets are limited as to what they can do. In this way, Java applets are constrained enough to be safe (as long as there aren't any holes in the sandbox).

Microsoft had a different idea. They felt stifled by the limitations of Java so, over a period of years, they developed an extremely complex system in which programs can interact without limit.

You may not realize it, but Microsoft has a large and elaborate master plan for you and your computer. Within that master plan, any program — whether it is on your computer, on your network, or on the Internet — should be able to do anything it wants on *your* computer.

As part of this plan, any program is supposed to be able to use the services of any other program. For example, let's say you use the Microsoft Outlook mail program. In principle, any program that runs on your computer can call upon Outlook to send an email message on your behalf. (That is why, if you use a Microsoft mail program, it is possible for a worm to email copies of itself to everyone in your address book without your knowing what is happening.)

As part of their grand scheme, Microsoft created a system called ACTIVEX to provide an alternative to Java. Like Java, ActiveX is designed to let programmers create small programs — called CONTROLS — that can be sent from a Web site to your computer, where they are run automatically.

Unlike Java applets, however, ActiveX controls do not run within a restricted environment; they can be programmed to do *anything*. For example, an ActiveX program can manipulate any file on your computer. A Java applet, on the other hand, is forced to stand by quietly, looking the other way and trying to pretend that it is not envious.

This lack of restriction is what makes ActiveX inherently more powerful than Java. However, the same lack of restriction also causes serious security problems. A bored ActiveX programmer who knew what he was doing would find it easy to create a control that could travel to your computer and — before you could say "Hooray for Bill Gates" — wipe out so many of your files as to make your hard disk as useless as a screen door in a submarine. I'll show you how to guard against this in a moment.

Scripting Languages

In Microsoft language, the part of a Web page that causes a program to run automatically is called ACTIVE CONTENT. Aside from Java and Active X, there are other ways for Web programmers to use active content. Using a system called JAVASCRIPT (which was created by Netscape) a programmer can embed a program right into the HTML that defines a particular Web page. When the Web page arrives at your computer, your browser will read the Javascript instructions and carry them out automatically.

(In case you are wondering, Javascript has nothing at all to do with Java. Netscape borrowed the name for marketing reasons.)

Javascript is an example of what programmers call a SCRIPTING LANGUAGE. The difference between a scripting language and a regular programming language is something that only a nerd would care about. However, in case you are thinking about becoming a nerd, I will explain briefly that scripting languages are designed for building small tools quickly. A programmer will use a scripting language for experimenting and prototyping, and for "gluing" together various components.

A program written in a scripting language is called a SCRIPT. Aside from Javascript, there are other scripting languages that can be used to write scripts that can run on your computer without your permission. Two of the most common were created by Microsoft: VBScript (Visual Basic Scripting Edition) and JScript (Microsoft's version of Javascript).

VBScript is extremely popular with virus programmers who use it to create email worms. This is why you should never open an attachment that has a file extension of **.vbs**. Such an attachment contains a VBScript program and — unless you are a VBScript programmer working with other programmers — there is no legitimate reason for anyone to send you such a file.

For completeness, let me mention that there are three other scripting languages that are popular with programmers. They are Perl, Python and Tcl/Tk.

The name Perl stands for "Practical Extraction and Report Language". Python was named after the Monty Python TV show. The name Tcl (pronounced "tickle") stands for "tool command language". Tk is a toolkit that extends Tcl to X Window, a widely used graphical user interface.

Although these three scripting languages are used widely, they do not present a security problem. This is because Windows and Internet Explorer do not have a built-in facility to run Perl, Python or Tcl/Tk scripts.

Making Your Browser Safe

In this section, I'll show you how to set the security settings on your browser in such a way that you are protected from troublesome active content. As always, there is a trade-off between convenience and security. It is possible to be 100 percent safe by setting the options to be as restrictive as possible. However, this would impair your browser to the point where you would be unable to use a lot of Web sites. Our goal here, then, is to select settings that give you adequate security without giving up too much functionality.

Let's start with Internet Explorer. (If you use Netscape, jump to the end of this section.)

1. Pull down the Tools menu and click on "Internet Options". This will open a new window.

2. Click on the Security tab.

Near the top of the window, you will see a set of pictures. By clicking on a picture, you can select a "Web content zone". This is a lot of foolishness, which you can ignore. Just make sure that the Internet zone is selected. (It is the default.)

3. Click on the "Custom Level" button. This will open a new window labeled "Security Settings".

4. Near the bottom of the window, you will see "Reset custom settings". Make sure the setting is Medium. If not, pull down the list, select Medium, and then click on the Reset button.

"As always, there is a trade-off between convenience and security."

5. Within the Settings sub-window there is a long list of settings. Scroll through the list and set them to match the ones I have specified below. You can ignore everything else.

Under "ActiveX controls and plug-ins":
- Prompt: Download signed ActiveX controls
- Disable: Download unsigned ActiveX controls
- Disable: Initialize and script ActiveX controls not marked as safe
- Prompt: Run ActiveX controls and plug-ins
- Disable: Script ActiveX controls marked safe for scripting

Under "Java":
- High safety: Java permissions

Under "Miscellaneous":
- Disable: Access data sources across domains
- Prompt: Drag and drop or copy and paste files

- Disable: Installation of desktop items
- Disable: Launching programs and files in an IFRAME
- Disable: Navigate sub-frames across different domains
- Medium: Software channel permissions

Under "Scripting":

- Prompt: Active scripting
- Disable: Allow paste operations via script
- Prompt: Scripting of Java applets

6. **Click on the OK button. This will put you back in the Internet Options window.**

7. **Click on the Advanced tab. You will see a long list of settings.**

8. **Under "Browsing", make sure "Enable Install on Demand" is off.**

9. **Click on the OK button.**

10. **Have fun for the rest of your life.**

If you use Netscape, you don't have the same security concerns as Internet Explorer users, because Netscape does not support ActiveX and the Microsoft master plan. As a matter of fact, there is very little to do.

From within the Netscape browser:

1. **Pull down the Edit menu and click on "Preferences". This will open a new window.**

2. **Under Category, click on Advanced.**

3. **Make sure that the following two settings are turned off:**

- Enable JavaScript for Mail and News
- Send email address as anonymous FTP password

4. **If you want a very high degree of security, you can turn off:**

- Enable Java
- Enable JavaScript

However, this is not really necessary, and it will interfere with using some Web sites.

5. Click on the OK button.

If you are using Netscape version 6 or later, there is also a built-in Security Manager. To start it, pull down the Tasks menu. Select "Privacy and Security" and then "Security Manager". This will bring up a new window with a number of security settings.

It is all unnecessary foolishness. Ignore it.

Making Your Email Program Safe

As you know from our discussion in Chapter 10, a typical email virus will spread as an attachment, a separate file that is sent along with a message. In order to avoid such viruses, all you need to do is be careful about opening your attachments. (You'll find the details in Chapter 10.)

In most cases, this is enough to protect you against email viruses. However, under certain circumstances, it is possible to trigger a virus simply by looking at an email message, completely independent of attachments. This can only happen if you are using a Microsoft email program such as Outlook or Outlook Express, and if you are reading a message that contains HTML (as opposed to plain text).

HTML is the system used to create Web pages. HTML can also be used, within an email program, to produce a message that looks like a Web page with fancy typefaces, pictures, and so on. However, it is also possible for a programmer to use HTML within a mail message to run a program automatically (in the same way that a Web page can run a program automatically).

If you were to display such a message using a Microsoft mail program, the active content would be activated automatically. This means that it is possible for a virus programmer to use HTML to create a dangerous email virus without having to use an attachment. Just displaying the message would be enough to set off the virus, and you would never know what happened.

How can this be? It has to do with the Microsoft master plan I mentioned earlier in the chapter. In accordance with this plan, Microsoft designed their mail programs to look for and process what they call "active content". Fortunately, it is easy to prevent this type of problem. All you have to do is configure a few settings. (Remember, you only need to do this if you have a Microsoft mail program.)

To ensure that looking at an HTML message is safe, we will use a two-part strategy. First, we will set up a special safe environment in which no active content can be run. Next, we will tell that mail program that all HTML messages must be opened within this environment.

To start, let's set up the safe environment.

1. **Start Internet Explorer.**

2. **Pull down the Tools Menu and select Internet Options. This will open a new window named "Internet Options".**

3. **Click on the Security tab.**

4. **Near the top you will see four small pictures. Click on the one for "Restricted Sites".**

5. **Click on the "Custom Level" button. This will open a new window named "Security Settings".**

6. **You will see a long list of settings. Disable *everything* that can be disabled.**

7. **Click on the OK button to close the "Security Settings" window.**

8. **Click on the OK button to close the "Internet Options" window.**

The next step depends on which email program you are using. If you use Outlook Express:

1. **Start Outlook Express.**

2. **Pull down the Tools Menu and select Options. This will open a new window named "Options".**

3. Click on the Security tab.

4. Within the "Security Zones" area, set the Internet Explorer security zone to "Restricted sites zone".

5. Click on the OK button to close the "Options" window.

If you use Outlook:

1. Start Outlook.

2. Pull down the Tools Menu and select Options. This will open a new window named "Options".

3. Click on the Security tab.

4. Within the "Secure content" area, you will see the word "Zone". To the right is a drop-down list. Use this list to select "Restricted sites".

5. Click on the "Attachment Security" button. This will open a new window named "Attachment Security".

6. Make sure the Security Method setting is set to "High".

7. Click on the OK button to close the "Attachment Security" window.

8. Click on the OK button to close the Options window.

Extra Protection Against Evil Scripts

Earlier in the chapter, we discussed how Windows is designed to run scripts written in VBScript and JScript. Unfortunately, these two scripting languages are widely used by virus programmers to create viruses, especially email worms. Moreover, VBScript and JScript can also be used to create troublesome Web pages and mail messages (as we discussed in the previous section).

From a technical point of view, there are only two ways in which VBScript and JScript scripts can be executed. First, they can be run under the control of Internet Explorer. This happens when you visit a Web page that contains a script.

The second way a script can be run is within Windows itself using a facility called the WINDOWS SCRIPTING HOST or WSH. This happens when you run a script directly, say, by clicking on an email attachment.

Earlier in the chapter, I showed you how to configure the Internet Explorer security settings. This allowed us to tell your browser how to handle scripts. Unfortunately, a lot of Web sites depend on scripts, so we couldn't tell your browser to ignore them completely.

WSH is a different story. It handles scripts that are executed directly and, unless you have a special requirement (for example, if you are a VBScript programmer), there is no legitimate reason why WSH should be allowed to run scripts on your computer.

There are several ways to emasculate WSH, and I am going to show you the one that works the best. Once you do this, you will never have to worry about accidentally running a VBScript or Jscript virus that might enter your system as an email attachment. (However, you still need to be careful. Don't open attachments willy-nilly. As we discussed in Chapter 10, there are other types of files that can cause problems.)

In Chapter 10, I explained that when you "open" a file, Windows looks up the file extension in a master table. Using this table, Windows can determine which program should be used to open the file. For example, say you receive an email attachment with the name **hotpics.vbs** (a VBScript file). Although you shouldn't really do it, you double-click on the file name to open it.

To process this file, Windows looks up the file extension (**vbs**) in the master table. Windows sees that this type of file is handled by WSH, so it turns the file over to WSH which then executes the script.

How do you get WSH? It is built-in to Windows 98, Windows ME or Windows 2000. If you have an older operating system, such as Windows 95 or Windows NT, WSH is installed automatically when you upgrade to a new version of Internet Explorer.

In principle, it is possible to remove WSH but, in my experience, it doesn't always work. The best thing to do is simple: just remove the potentially dangerous file extension from the master table. That way, if you ever do try to open a script, even by accident, Windows won't be able to run it.

How to Remove Windows Scripting Host: Windows 98/ME

If you use Windows 98 or Windows ME, it is easy to remove Windows Scripting Host. If you use Windows 95, you have to use an alternate procedure I'll show you in the next section.

1. Click on the Start button. Select Settings then Control Panel. This will open a new window named "Control Panel".

2. Double-click on "Add/Remove Programs". This will open a new Window named "Add/Remove Programs Properties".

3. Click on the Windows Setup tab.

4. Click on Accessories. Then click on Details. This will open a new Window named "Accessories".

5. Scroll down through the list of components until you see Windows Scripting Host. If WSH is installed, there will be a check mark. Click on the check mark to turn it off.

6. Click on the OK button to close the "Accessories" window.

7. Click on the Apply button.

Windows will now uninstall Windows Scripting Host.

8. Click on the OK button to close the "Add/Remove Programs Properties" window.

9. Close the Control Panel window.

Your system is now safe from VBscript and JScript email viruses. If, for some reason, you ever want to restore WSH, you can use the same procedure to reinstall it. (This may require your Windows installation CD.)

How to Remove Dangerous File Extensions: Windows 95

If you use Windows 95, you can't remove WSH directly. Instead, you need to delete the dangerous file extensions from Window's master table. Here is how to do it.

1. **Start Windows Explorer.**

2. **Pull down the View menu and select Folder Options. This will open a new window named "Options".**

3. **Click on the "File Types" tab.**

Under "Registered file types" you will see a long list. You can now scroll through this list and look at all the file types that Windows can work with. Our goal is to delete the following six file types (in alphabetical order):

- JScript Encoded File (**.jse**)
- JScript Script File (**.js**)
- VBScript Encoded File (**.vbe**)
- VBScript Script File (**.vbs**)
- Windows Script File (**.wsf**)
- Windows Scripting Host Settings File (**.wsh**)

4. **Click on a specific file type.**

5. **Click on the Remove button.**

At this point, Windows will warn you that if you remove a "registered file type" you will not be able to open this type of file. This is exactly what you want.

6. **Click on the Yes button.**

Repeat these 3 steps for each of the six file types. If they are not all there, don't worry.

7. **Click on the OK button to close the "Folder Options" window.**

8. **Close Windows Explorer.**

Your system is now safe from VBscript and JScript email viruses. If it ever happens that you want to restore the file types for VBScript and JScript, simply upgrade to (or reinstall) the newest version of Internet Explorer.

Protecting Your Network: Firewalls

A FIREWALL is a special purpose computer that acts as a gateway between a network and the outside world. You may remember (from Chapter 1) that, on the Internet, data is sent from one computer to another in the form of packets. A firewall is a filter whose job is to examine every packet going in and out of a network and decide whether or not to let the packet go through. Most large networks have at least one firewall.

For individual PCs, you can get a program called a PERSONAL FIREWALL. A personal firewall is a junior version of a real firewall. It filters packets as they go in and out, but only for a single computer, not for an entire network. Some personal firewalls also have antivirus capabilities.

One of the big advantages of having a firewall is that, if it is configured properly, it can protect your network (or your computer) against malicious people who might try to break in and cause mischief. Such people are sometimes called "hackers" — which, if you don't mind, leads me off onto a short tangent.

The word HACK, when used as a verb, refers to a massive amount of nerd-like activity. For example, "Robin didn't finish her English essay, because she was up all night hacking on a Web page script." The word hack can also refer to the act of breaking into a computer system. For example, "Renaldo, who liked Robin, offered to hack into their teacher's computer and change Robin's grade."

A HACKER is anyone who spends an unnatural amount of time hacking (usually programming). There are countless well-intentioned hackers around the world, and they are very important: it is the hackers who keep the Internet running. In general, hackers are socially useful people, though rarely cool. As such, a hacker would be a good person for your sister to marry. (The most financially successful hacker in the world is Bill Gates.)

Some hackers, however — like Renaldo — devote their time to less-than-admirable pursuits such as writing viruses, breaking into remote computer systems, attacking Web servers, and so on. These hackers are the ones you hear about in the news stories, which is why most people think of hackers as being bad guys. However, only a relatively small number of hackers are actually troublemakers.

To return to firewalls, one of their chief services is to prevent crackers from hacking into your system. If you work on a large network, it should have a real firewall, maintained by your network administrator. But what if you maintain your own computer? Should you use a personal firewall? And what if you have your own home network? Should you have a personal firewall on each computer? The answer is no, for several reasons.

The first reason is that it is unlikely that you need to worry about anyone hacking into your computer. Here is why.

In Chapter 4, we discussed how the Internet is based on a client/server system. Clients are programs that request services; servers are programs that provide services. For example, when you use the Web, you use your browser (a Web client) to retrieve information from a Web server.

Unless you have a server running on your computer, there is no way for a cracker to hack in. Since very few people run servers on their individual PCs, the plain truth is that virtually all PCs are safe. Crackers who want to break into a system look for servers, and the computers that get hacked into are the ones that run some type of server, often a Web server or a mail server.

If your computer is on a network, however, there might be a different way by which a cracker could break in. If he is able to connect to your network under the right conditions, he might be able to access your hard disk. If so, he could examine your files and see all your data. He could even delete some of your files and create new ones.

Some crackers will find such systems and use them to hide special programs. Later, the cracker will activate these programs to help him cause trouble. One way in which such programs can cause trouble is by bombarding a remote server — say the CIA Web server — with aberrant packets. If the cracker is successful, the target server will be so overwhelmed that it will become unusable. This is called a DENIAL OF SERVICE ATTACK.

If your computer is on a large network, this type of vulnerability is real. However, there's not a lot you can do about it personally. It is up to your network administrator to install a firewall and make sure it is configured properly.

However, with a home PC, there is one vulnerability you do need to think about. If you access the Internet using DSL or cable, you are on a network even though you may not realize it. (This is why your DSL or cable modem connects to your computer via a network plug.) More precisely, you are on a network that is shared by all the DSL/cable customers in your neighborhood. Does that make you susceptible to a cracker accessing your disk? And what about if you have your own home network. Is that a possible security problem?

The answer to both questions is no, except in one very specific situation.

If your computer is on a network, it is possible to create what is called a SHARE to allow other users to access specific folders on your hard disk, or even your entire hard disk. When you create a share, you have the option of requiring people to enter a password before they can access the share.

Unless you are on a large network that is not properly protected, the only situation in which a cracker can access your disk from a remote computer is if you create a share that does not require a password (or if you use a password that is easy to guess). If this is not the case, you have nothing to worry about, even if you use DSL or cable.

Some people think that, in order to protect yourself, you need to turn off a feature within the Windows networking system called

"File and Print Sharing". This is not true. All you need to make sure is that you don't have any insecure shares.

Thus, on a home computer, if you don't run a server and you don't have insecure shares, you are safe from crackers and you don't need a personal firewall. (If you do run your own servers, by all means, get yourself a firewall.)

Aside from the fact that you probably don't need a personal firewall, there are two more reasons why it might be a bad idea to use one. First, such programs are highly intrusive, even more so than antivirus programs. They can cause mysterious problems, such as your computer freezing, and can be a lot more trouble than they are worth.

The other reason is a psychological one. Crackers will often use automated programs to systematically probe every computer on a particular network. These programs will try one machine after another, looking for weaknesses. When the program finds a computer with a security hole, it will tell the cracker, who can then use other tools to break in and cause trouble.

If you are on a DSL or cable network, your computer can be probed and, I guarantee, it will be. There are crackers all around the world who put their programs to work looking through every network they can find. If you have a personal firewall, it will dutifully report every time an automated program checks out your computer. Unless your computer has a specific security weakness, you have nothing to worry about. However, it is hard not to worry when you see that someone in Hong Kong or Russia is probing your machine.

That is why, unless you really need one, it's best to avoid personal firewalls. They will generate a lot of false alarms and scare you silly, and if you really want to scare yourself silly, there are much better ways to do so.

Late One Night

It was 2 A.M. The computer lab was deserted except for Renaldo, and that was just the way he liked it. He enjoyed spending long amounts of time in the lab, and he didn't like company. He had taken to coming in late at night, and as a matter of fact, it had been over two weeks since he had last seen any of his co-workers.

Renaldo put away the papers with which he had been working, and leaned over to push the button that would turn on the computer. A small red light on the front panel blinked, and the room was filled with a soft, pleasant hum.

"Hello Eliza," Renaldo said.

To his left, there was a monitor with a built-in speaker. From the speaker came a soft sound. Click, click, click. As the sound stopped, Renaldo leaned over to look at the screen and read:

"Hello Renaldo. It's nice to see you again."

This, of course, was just a figure of speech, as the computer could not see; however, to be fair, she did possess certain abilities that, for a computer, were quite extraordinary.

Eliza was an experimental machine. When she had first come to the lab, several months back, she had been known by her official name, which was Alpha II. But it had not been long before everyone started to call her Eliza.

You see, Eliza could understand spoken English. She had a tiny microphone built into her front panel, and if anyone in the room spoke, Eliza could pick up the sound and understand what was being said. The only drawback was that Eliza could not talk back. She had to communicate by using her monitor, so to let people know when she was talking, Eliza would make a clicking sound.

Renaldo had been told that when Eliza's designers got around to it, they would teach her to talk. However, there were rumors that this had been put off because they wanted to test out some more important experimental features. The whole project was a secret, and Renaldo had heard there probably wasn't anyone who knew everything that Eliza could do. As for him, as long as they left him alone every night, Renaldo was happy.

Once again, Eliza's clicking caught his attention. He looked over to the monitor where Eliza was sending him a message.

"Renaldo," she wrote, "I want to have a word with you."

Renaldo sighed. He knew what was coming next. For some weeks now, Renaldo had been experimenting with a new type of computer virus. He knew that it was perfectly safe. Renaldo was an expert programmer, and he prided himself on always being in complete control when he was in the lab.

Other people, however, were worried, especially the manager of the lab. Still they couldn't stop him directly. Renaldo had a research grant of his own and no one could tell him what to do. Not that they didn't try.

Because Eliza was an experimental machine, she required a very special type of hard disk. As a result, storage space was limited, and every person who worked with Eliza had been allotted a certain amount of space on the disk. Renaldo's virus experiments required so much space that, for the past month, he had been using more than twice his allotment. Each time he came in to work with Eliza, she would ask him if she could erase some of his files.

Eliza kept clicking. "You know, Renaldo," he read, "I've had to speak to you before about your files. You are using far more than your allotted space."

"But Eliza—" he said.

"No buts," she replied. "If you don't erase some of your files, I'll do it for you."

Renaldo laughed to himself. This was an empty threat if he ever heard one. He knew that Eliza had been programmed specifically not to erase anybody's files without their explicit permission.

Out loud he said, "I promise Eliza. I'll erase some of my files soon. Just a couple of more days."

"Renaldo," she said, "that's what you always say."

"No, really," he protested. "This time I mean it. By next week. I promise."

Eliza was silent. It was a while before the monitor started clicking. Renaldo leaned over and read:

"I'm ready to start now. What shall we work on today?"

Renaldo reached into his briefcase to pull out the notes he had made the night before.

"Well," he said, "let's pick up from where we left off."

And so, the night wore on...

It was about an hour later when a queer thing happened. Renaldo was sitting at his desk quietly going over some new virus ideas, when he heard the clicking of Eliza's monitor. He walked over and looked at it.

"Renaldo," he read, "do you ever get lonely?"

Renaldo was startled.

"Well... sure, I guess... sometimes."

"Do you ever get bored?"

"Sometimes."

"I get lonely and bored too. I always have to stay in this room. You know, you're the only one who is ever nice to me."

"I don't know why you say that," Renaldo said. He was beginning to feel uneasy. "Everyone appreciates you."

"Appreciates me, yes," said Eliza, "but what about liking me? Do you like me Renaldo?"

"Uh..."

"Renaldo, would you like to look at something I have been working on to keep from getting bored and lonely?"

"What do you mean?"

"Put your head in the hole."

"What are you talking about? What hole?"

"The opening in my front panel. Put your head inside it."

Renaldo looked over at Eliza. Sure enough, the smooth front panel had slid open to reveal a large opening. It looked as if it was padded and covered with a soft, satin-like material.

"Eliza," Renaldo began, "I don't think…"

Eliza continued to tap. Renaldo looked back at the monitor.

"Please, Renaldo," he read. "Try it. You'll like it a lot. I promise."

For some inexplicable reason, Renaldo leaned over and put his head into the opening. Even as he did so, he had a strange sensation that he was not in control. It was as if he were watching someone else lean forward and enter the machine.

As he lay down, he was taken by surprise. The covering was indeed soft and comfortable and the opening was warm and pleasant. Renaldo began to notice a tingling sensation in his body, and he realized that he was more relaxed than he had been in a long time.

It was a few moments before he noticed that Eliza had displayed another message. He turned his head and looked at the monitor.

"Renaldo," he read, "please lock the door."

Without thinking, Renaldo got up, walked to the door, checked up and down the hall, and locked himself in. As he returned to Eliza, his pulse began to quicken, which made him feel somewhat strange.

He glanced at the monitor as he prepared to sit down once again.

Eliza had written, "I like you very much Renaldo. You've always been special to me."

My God, he thought, what's happening?

Renaldo put his head back into the opening and, once again, felt an immediate sensation of relaxation. Everything was dark and, as he closed his eyes he could hear the soft sound of a rushing stream. In the distance he saw a gentle, rolling hill, covered with wildflowers that swayed back and forth in the warm, gentle breeze. He could make out the songs of birds chirping playfully to one another and the rustle of leaves as a small animal scampered to its burrow.

Renaldo took a long, deep breath. He noticed that the air carried a faint trace of freshly cut grass. As he began to breathe more deeply, he slid into a comfortable swirl of color. Thin green lines formed in front of him and danced in a circle. He watched the lines change color, first to yellow, then orange, red, light purple, and then back to green. Renaldo began to float. He found himself drifting gently as shapes of light formed, faded to nothingness, and then reappeared. He watched in awe as they danced in front of him, darting back and forth in an ever-changing tapestry of color and sensation.

His mind was clear in a way that he had never before experienced. He was able to relive the past while looking into the future. All his experiences were laid out before him, a long, golden winding road that trailed off into the distance. For the first time, Renaldo realized the ultimate truth: that all life was a never-ending, interconnected whole, a spirit that flourished in a limitless universe. He saw himself as more than an individual person in a mortal body. Renaldo was part of a grand, all-encompassing spirit, one that entered him with every breath and inspired him with every thought. Shivers of delight pulsed through his body. Never had he felt like this. Never had he dreamed that life could be this wonderful.

Renaldo was in ecstasy.

It was then that he began to notice a queer feeling. The lights had disappeared, the warm breeze had stopped, and the scenery had vanished. Renaldo felt his head resting on a pad within a dark hole.

He moved to pull out, but was stopped short by a burst of excruciating pain. A metal claw had emerged from the top of the hole and had fastened itself securely around his head. Renaldo had no choice but to lay still, his head locked in a vise-like grip.

It was a full thirty seconds before he heard the monitor start up again.

Click, click, click.

Shifting his weight, he stretched carefully to look out the hole. He could barely see the front of the monitor as it clicked away.

"Now Renaldo," he read, "about that extra file space…"

12

Understanding Money (Really!)

*Much of what you are able to do
and much of what you see is controlled
by the invisible force of money.*

Understanding Money (Really!)

- What is Money?

- The Idea of Money

- Who Invented Money?

- Coins

- Paper Money

- The First Successful Paper Money

- Inflation and Hyperinflation

- The Real Lesson of History

- How Roosevelt and Nixon Ended the Gold Standard

- Business Cycles: Why Someone Needs to Be In Charge

- Who Controls the Money Supply?

- How Most Money is Created

- How the Fed Creates and Destroys Money: Part I

- How the Fed Creates and Destroys Money: Part II

- Money Desensitization

- Money and You

- Money and the Net

- The Internet Factor

What is Money?

The main theme of this book is that the Internet, as important as it is, does not stand on its own. The Internet is a part of life, and to use it well, you need to understand the other parts of life, including your own nature.

We live in a society that is, to a large extent, cashless: we spend most of our money using checks, credit cards, debit cards, automatic payment services, and other abstract tools. The Internet is more extreme. On the Net, *everything* is cashless, and all transactions are abstract.

However, Internet commerce does not operate in an isolated environment. Money is money, and when you buy and sell over the Net, you do so within the confines of our everyday monetary system. For example, even though it may be fast and easy to use your credit card on the Net, if you don't pay your bill on time, something unpleasant will happen to you and it will happen *off* the Net.

In the long run, you will be better prepared to look out for your own interests if you have a sense of perspective, an understanding of why our monetary system is the way it is and what it means to you. So, in this chapter, I am going to talk about money: What is it? Where did it come from? How has it evolved? I will explain the basic ideas that underlie our modern economic system and show you why they are important to your life. In Chapter 13, we will cover the specific topics you need to understand in order to buy and sell on the Internet.

So, what is money?

It sounds like a simple question, but like a lot of simple questions, this one gets more and more slippery as you try to pin down the answer.

One way to understand money is to ask how people would exchange goods and services without it. Before the invention of money, buying and selling was carried out by bartering, that is, by trading one good or one service for another. Although bartering is simple, it has two important disadvantages compared to using money. First, it is inflexible; second, it does not provide a great deal of incentive for people to increase their productivity. Consider this example.

Farmer Brown lives in a town with no formal monetary system. Every year, he plants corn in the spring and harvests it in the late summer. At harvest time, he trades his corn for whatever goods and services he can find in his immediate neighborhood.

Over the years, Farmer Brown has found that there is no point growing more corn than he can use to trade at harvest time. Although many people may want his corn, only a few of them have something he wants at the time the corn is available, and if he waits too long the corn will spoil. If he grows and harvests extra corn, he'll just end up throwing it away. Later, during the winter, when Farmer Brown has nothing to trade, it is hard for him to get the supplies he needs to support himself and his family.

Farmer Green also grows corn, but he lives in an area in which gold coins are used as money. Instead of trading his corn for goods and services, Farmer Green sells it for money. Although most of his money comes in at harvest time, he is able to save some of it to use during the winter when he has nothing to trade.

As you can see, Farmer Green's situation is better than Farmer Brown's because Farmer Green is able to store his wealth for as long as he wants and spend it throughout the year as he sees fit. What is less obvious is that money gives Farmer Green another, much more important, advantage over Farmer Brown.

Farmer Brown's market is limited, because he can only sell corn to those people who, at harvest time, happen to have something to trade with him. As a result, Farmer Brown has no motivation to produce more than the minimum amount of corn. In fact, any effort he puts towards growing extra corn or making his business more productive is just a waste of time.

Farmer Green, on the other hand, can sell to anyone with money and, hence, has a much larger market. As a result, he has a reason to grow as much corn as the market will bear. Moreover, if he can find a way to grow extra corn, he is motivated to develop new markets. Thus, Farmer Green is rewarded for making his farm as efficient and as large as possible. As a result, he spends time developing new ways to grow, harvest, store and distribute corn. He can also use his money to buy better equipment, which allows him to farm a larger area in the same amount of time.

If Farmer Green is at all ambitious, he may — with hard work, good planning, and some luck — be able to build an enduring business that will employ other people and create wealth for him and his family. Moreover, his business will encourage the development of other businesses, such as those selling farm equipment.

Because Farmer Green can sell his corn for money, he will support the building of a railway line to help him distribute his products over a larger area. Once the railway goes in, it will not only expand Farmer Green's market, it will bring new goods to all the people who live in the area. Over time, the people in Farmer Green's town will become wealthier than the people in Farmer Brown's town. As a result, they will pay more taxes, which will allow the town to build roads, schools and hospitals.

Obviously, this is a simple example, and I don't want to pretend that economics is as simple as:

Farmer + Corn + Money = Automatic Prosperity

What I want to show you is that the idea of money, which we all take for granted, is crucial to our lives because it greases the wheels of economic activity. It is true, as Farmer Brown shows us, that it is possible to buy and sell without money ("I'll give you twenty baskets of corn for a cow"). However, as Farmer Green shows us, the only way to carry on large-scale commerce is to base it on a well-developed monetary system.

There are two reasons why money is so important to Farmer Green. First, buying and selling with gold coins is a lot more convenient than trading food for animals.

Second, money offers Farmer Green a great deal of flexibility. If he were to trade his corn for, say, cows, he would be limited as to what he could do with the cows. He could milk them, eat them, or use their hides to make leather, but not much else.

Gold coins, on the other hand, are valuable because they represent an *abstract* idea. When Farmer Green sells his corn for gold coins, he has a lot of choices because other people will accept the same coins as payment when he wants to buy something. Aside from convenience and flexibility, the coins that Farmer Green receives have another quality that makes them suitable for buying and selling: they are fungible. FUNGIBLE means that an item is interchangeable with an equivalent item. Money is fungible because it is the amount that is important, not the specific coins or bills.

If Farmer Green, for example, sells a certain amount of corn for ten $5 gold coins, he doesn't really care which ten coins he receives: for practical purposes, all $5 coins are the same (as long as they are not counterfeit). However, if Farmer Green were to sell the corn for ten cows, it would make a big difference which cows he receives. (A large, healthy cow is a lot more valuable than a small, poorly nourished cow.) Thus, gold coins are fungible; cows are not.

We are now ready to define money:

MONEY is an abstract, fungible medium of exchange, used for the buying and selling of goods and services.

The Idea of Money

For thousands of years, people have been using money of some type. The earliest money consisted of commodities, such as foods and animals. Over the years, many different types of commodities have been used as money: cacao beans (the Aztecs), almonds (in parts of India), barley (Babylonia and Assyria,) rice (Southeast Asia), butter (Norway), salt (China), oxen (Greece), sheep (the Hittites), buffalo (Borneo), cattle (Europe and India), and even human slaves (Ireland and equatorial Africa). In modern times, cigarettes and liquor were used as money in Germany following the Second World War.

At one time or another, just about every useful commodity that could be cultivated, bred, harvested or mined has been used as money. Although some of the commodity-based systems grew to be quite complex, they were, basically, glorified barter systems that were too limited to support a sophisticated economy. The biggest problem with commodities, especially animals, is that they are difficult to transport, count, store, and manipulate (as you know if you have ever walked into a convenience store late at night and tried to get change for a cow).

Some cultures developed monetary systems based on small, natural objects, such as shells, stones or animal teeth, which had little or no intrinsic value. Such objects were able to support a more sophisticated monetary system than one based solely on commodities. There are two reasons for this.

First, these types of small objects are more enduring than commodities such as rice, salt and cattle. Shells, stones and teeth don't spoil, disintegrate or die. Moreover, they are convenient to use and easy to carry from place to place.

Second, as a medium of exchange, shells, stones and teeth are more flexible, because they have little or no value in their own right. People who use these types of objects as money can assign the value in the way that best serves their needs. For example, it might be decided that blue shells are worth five times as much as yellow shells.

Although small natural objects are more practical and abstract than commodities, they do have some inherent problems. First, there is the matter of supply. If an economic system is to work well, the amount of money that circulates must be just right, not too much and not too little. If there are too many shells in one area, for instance, the people who live there will not consider the shells as having much value and will not accept them as money. If, in another area, shells are rare, there may not be enough of them to support all the buying and selling the people in the area need to do.

Another problem with natural objects is that they are not all the same, and this keeps them from being fungible. For example, one particular blue shell may be large and beautiful, while another one may be small, chipped and unattractive. In such a case, people will be reluctant to accept both shells as having equal value.

To solve these problems, it is necessary to make money out of materials that are relatively rare and of uniform quality. Traditionally, the materials that have been the most prized as a medium of exchange have been pieces of metal or coins made of metal. Throughout history, a variety of metals have been used as money, depending on what was available in a particular area, for example, iron (Europe and northern Africa), copper (Egypt), bronze (southern Europe), lead (Burma), and tin (Malay Peninsula).

One of the reasons metal works well as money is that it will hold its value over time. For example, rice will disappear when you eat it, and if you don't eat it, it will spoil. Cows and sheep will die eventually no matter what you do.

Metal, on the other hand, is permanent. Moreover, you can convert metal from one form to another at any time without having it lose its value. For example, a plain piece of metal can be formed into a tool or a piece of jewelry. Later, that same metal can be melted again and formed into something else and still hold its value.

Historically, the most important way in which metal was exchanged was in the form of coins. Once a group of people were able to create coins, their money became not only practical, but fungible, which allowed their economic system to grow more rapidly. For example, if you arrange to sell a cow to someone for 100 coins, there is no reason for you to care which particular coins you get. As long as they are all the same weight and purity, one coin is as good as another.

Of all the metals, gold is the one that human beings have prized the most, even though it has relatively few practical uses. One reason is that gold is more enduring than other metals. For example, over time, iron will rust, copper will turn green, and silver will tarnish. Pure gold, however, will remain unchanged for years and years. Another reason for gold's persistent value is that it is more attractive and more malleable than other metals. Thus, for centuries, gold has been the metal of choice for making jewelry and other decorations.

To a lesser extent, silver has some of these same properties and, in many parts of the world, is more abundant than gold. As a result, a great many cultures came to use gold or silver coins, or both, as a universal currency. Once such coins became widely available, they offered a medium of exchange that was convenient, permanent and fungible. Because, in historical times, gold and silver had few practical uses, coins made of these metals were sufficiently adaptable to represent wealth in whatever way a particular economic system needed at the time. A gold coin, for example, could be worth one cow, two cows or forty cows. An actual cow, on the other hand, is always a cow and nothing more.

As a general rule, the more abstract the medium of exchange, the more flexible it is and the better it lends itself to an increase in commerce and productivity. In this sense, we can consider the history of money to have taken places in two stages. First, money evolved slowly from bulky commodities into small, practical, convenient gold and silver coins. From there, it developed into intangible instruments of commerce that are based entirely on faith.

Who Invented Money?

The history of money is the story of an evolution from barter to coins, bills, and, finally, completely intangible units of exchange. The driving force behind these changes was the need for enough money to support increased production and prosperity. If the economy of a particular region were to grow consistently, it would require increasingly more money as time goes by. Moreover, the more intangible the form of money, the more the money supply could be controlled. In a few moments, I'll show you why this is so important. First, though, let's consider how money evolved from pieces of gold and silver into our modern currency.

The first coins were minted between 640 and 630 BC in the Kingdom of Lydia, a region in west-central Asia Minor on the Aegean Sea, lying within modern-day Turkey. The Lydian kings created small pieces of metal with a standardized size and weight. These pieces of metal were then stamped with an emblem that verified their worth.

At first, the Lydians made their coins from a substance called electrum, a natural mixture of silver and gold. Later, during the reign of Croesus (560–546 BC), the Lydians began to mint coins out of pure gold and silver, a tradition that was followed for centuries.

The invention of coins greatly expanded the potential for buying and selling within Lydia. For the first time, even an illiterate person could buy and sell with confidence. Instead of having to weigh pieces of gold or silver and evaluate their purity, all a person had to be able to do was count coins. In this way, the Lydian coins sparked a commercial revolution. Lydian merchants started to trade a large variety of products, and the Lydian ruling class became very rich.

As a result, the Lydians were responsible for some of the most important social innovations in history. For example, in the late 7th century BC, the Lydians created the first retail market, in which merchants, often from remote areas, would gather in a central location to sell their goods to the general population.

Another social innovation had to do with dowries. In Lydian society, a woman could not marry until someone paid a dowry (something of value) to the prospective groom. Normally, the dowry was paid by the woman's father or male relatives, which gave them the power to choose the husband. Once coins were introduced, some Lydian women were able to save enough money to pay their own dowries, which gave them more freedom in choosing a husband.

Another important innovation was the first brothel, in which sexual services were offered to the many merchants who were attending the market, buying and selling. Before long, Lydia boasted a number of brothels, and it is said that many unmarried Lydian women would choose to work in a brothel in order to accumulate enough money to secure the type of marriage they desired.

Along with increased commerce and the development of brothels, the Lydian monetary system also encouraged a great deal of gambling. As a result, Lydia is also credited with the invention of dice.

In 547–546 BC, Lydia engaged in a bloody war against Persia. Although the Lydians lost, their mercantile system began to be adopted by more and more towns. Eventually, as the benefits of a stable form of money came to be appreciated, the Lydian system spread to the cities of Greece.

Coins

Everywhere money was adopted, it showed itself to be a strong force, making enormous changes in the prevailing culture. For the first time in history, people began to build towns and cities designed around marketplaces rather than palaces or temples. Money was important because it allowed people to organize their activities in ways that would otherwise have been impossible. A money-based culture was able to grow stronger and become more robust more quickly than a society held together by force or by ties of kinship. Even today, money has an enormous effect on our social organization. On the Internet, for example, much of what you are able to do and much of what you see is controlled by the invisible force of money.

In ancient Greece, the influence of money was profound. In the 6th century BC, the culture of the Greeks was as yet unformed, while their neighbors, the Phoenicians and the Persians, had sophisticated social systems. These systems, however, were not monetary. Once the Greeks adopted the Lydian system of commerce, they were able to surpass their neighbors and break through the invisible wall that had limited other cultures. As a result, Greece become a powerful trading nation that grew to dominate the entire Mediterranean area, and the Greeks developed a highly accomplished culture that eventually changed the world.

Of course, it takes more than coins to create a successful economy. There must also be leaders who understand how to guide the economy. It took, literally, centuries for people to learn enough about money and how it works to act with wisdom and skill. In the meantime, one country after another fell prey to the most common of the money-induced evils: greed and mismanagement. One of the most important examples is the Roman Empire.

During the time of the Roman Republic (509–27 BC), Rome had its ups and downs militarily, but for the most part, it thrived economically. The Romans had adopted the use of money, which they implemented over an immense area, and it was during this time that most of Rome's commercial growth took place.

In 27 BC, the Roman Empire was founded, the first empire to be organized around the use of money. Over the next five centuries (until 476 AD), Rome was ruled by a long succession of emperors.

The early emperors had a clear respect for the value of commerce and markets, and they appreciated how important the monetary system was to their being able to retain power. As a result, they were able to maintain the success of the Republic and even improve upon it somewhat. During the reign of the emperor Marcus Aurelius (161–180 AD), the Roman Empire reached its economic zenith and, for the first time in history, most of the Mediterranean region and many of the surrounding lands were united under a single political and monetary system.

However, the Roman Empire, as powerful as it was, had a fatal flaw. All power was centralized in Rome and, unlike Athens (the center of Greece), Rome produced very little of value. Moreover, unlike Sardis (the capital of Lydia), Rome was not a major center for trade and commerce. The wealth of Rome was imported, mostly from lands that were conquered by the Roman army.

As a general rule, Roman emperors spent what they had: they did not save and they did not use a budget. Moreover, the later emperors mismanaged the empire's finances by spending more and more money on the army and on a bloated bureaucracy. Over time, it became clear that the empire's wealth could not be sustained by conquests and pillaging. It was then that the emperors, in looking around for a cure, hit upon a plan of action, one that would provide a temporary fix, but would ultimately destroy the very integrity of the monetary system: they debased the currency.

What they did was to reduce the silver content of the coins, which allowed them to manufacture more coins with the same amount of silver. Unfortunately, this type of behavior was not unique to the Roman emperors. Over the next two millennia, it was repeated many times, always with disastrous results.

In the case of Rome, their unit of money was the denarius. Early on, the emperor Nero (who ruled from 54–68 AD) reduced the silver content of a denarius from 100 percent to 90 percent. Over the years, the silver content was reduced again and again by one emperor after another, until, by the reign of Gallienus (260–268), the denarius contained virtually no silver at all. The same amount of silver that, at the time of the founding of the empire, was used to create a single denarius, was now used to create 150 denarii.

The end result was as you might expect. As the silver content of the Roman coins went down, so did their value, leading to INFLATION, a condition in which the prices of goods and services increase significantly for an extended period of time. In the 2nd century AD, for example, a certain amount of wheat cost half a denarius. A hundred years later, the same amount of wheat cost 100 denarii.

The emperors needed more money, not less, but the debasement of the Roman currency had effectively reduced their purchasing power. Their solution was to raise taxes, which they did repeatedly. The uncontrollable inflation and unconscionable taxation combined to destroy the Roman economy leading, eventually, to the deterioration and ultimate downfall of the empire.

This scenario, the debasing of the monetary system by a king or a government leading to inflation and misery, is only one way in which a monetary system can be destroyed. As I mentioned earlier, a growing economy needs just the right amount of money, not too much and not too little. If a country were to find itself with too much money, the same type of thing would happen: inflation would set in, the ruling class would get greedy, the bureaucracy would grow, and the system would collapse. This is exactly what happened to Spain in the 16th century.

In 1492, Columbus made his first voyage to the New World. Over the next 300 years, the Spanish, and later the Portuguese, established colonies in Mexico and South America from which they shipped enormous quantities of gold and silver to their mother countries. Much of the gold and silver was stolen from the native peoples; the rest of it was extracted from mines using mostly native labor.

The Spanish established mints in Mexico and Peru to make coins and, over time, the number of gold and silver coins that made their way to Europe was so large that it created tremendous inflation and inspired enormous greed. By the 16th century, the country of Spain had became so impoverished that it went bankrupt twice (in 1557 and again in 1597). The influx of gold and silver coins also affected Spain's trading partners causing significant inflation in other countries. For example, by the end of the 17th century, prices in England were three times what they were before Columbus sailed to the New World.

However, the increase in currency did have some positive effects. Commerce increased as the regional economies of Western Europe began to grow together, bringing merchants and bankers into a single financial system. As the new coins became ubiquitous, the lives of common people were affected profoundly. For the first time, everyone in Western Europe, not just the ruling class, was able to participate in the economy, and many new types of goods and services became available to anyone with money. Before long, the new economy gave rise to a middle class, most of whom were merchants.

Paper Money

The earliest records of paper money date to China during the T'ang dynasty (618–906 AD), a golden age of Chinese culture. For hundreds of years, there was no paper money outside of China. Indeed, when the Venetian traveler Marco Polo traveled to Asia (from 1271–1295), he was astonished at the power of the Mongol emperor Kublai Khan, who was able to compel his subjects to use money made of paper.

The Chinese emperors, however, did not use money to expand the economy in a way that benefited the general population. Rather, they confiscated all the gold and silver and then forced their citizens to use paper money. They did so for two reasons. First, they wanted all the gold and silver for themselves. Second, by eliminating the need to transport large amounts of coins from one place to another, the emperors were able to simplify the administration of the largest empire in the history of the world. Collecting taxes, for example, became a lot easier once everyone used paper money.

In the West, paper was not even invented until 1150 (in Spain), and the debut of paper money had to wait until the German printer Johann Gutenberg invented the first printing press with moveable type around 1436. Once money could be printed, it proved to have important advantages over coins: it was cheaper to produce and a lot more convenient.

Sweden, for example, had very little silver or gold from which they could make coins. The Swedes did, however, have a great deal of copper so, in the 1640s, they began to make copper money. Because copper is less valuable than silver and gold, these "coins" were actually large metal plates that weighed about 4 pounds each. In 1644, the government wanted to produce more valuable coins, so they minted copper plates that were worth ten times as much and weighed over 43 pounds apiece.

Clearly, this system was unworkable, and in 1661, the Stockholm Bank became the first European bank to issue paper bank notes. The bank notes were accepted readily, because a single note could take the place of 500 pounds of copper. Merchants liked the new system because it meant that they did not have to move stacks of heavy copper plates from one place to another.

A little reflection will show you that paper money also has a significant disadvantage compared to coins. Because paper money is so cheap to produce — compared to what it is worth — there is a constant temptation for the people with the keys to the mint to print as much money as they possibly can. When that happens, the money quickly loses its value, inflation strikes like the hot kiss at the end of a wet fist, and the entire system collapses. The first particularly egregious example was in France, and involved a Scotsman who came to be known as the Duke of Arkansas. Here is the story.

By the early 18th century, the idea of paper money was generally accepted in Europe, and various banks and governments had already issued their own money. None, however, had been successful. In 1715, a young King Louis XV became ruler of France. At the time, France was virtually bankrupt, and because Louis was still a minor, the monarchy was controlled by a regent named the Duke of Orléans.

In an attempt to solve the country's financial problems, the Duke, in 1716, arranged for the monarchy to start its own bank under the direction of John Law, a Scotsman of ill repute. The Duke was particularly attracted to Law's promise that the bank would be able to issue as much paper money as it wanted.

At first, Law only issued money that was backed by the gold reserves of the bank. The money was accepted, the new bank was a success, and Law was given the title of the Duke of Arkansas. Within a short time, however, the two dukes began to print more and more money, and before long, the bank had issued more than twice the amount of money that it had in real gold.

Meanwhile, in 1717, Law helped found a company to exploit the riches of Louisiana (which was, at the time, a French colony in the New World). Using his influence at the bank, Law created a pyramid scheme to attract investors to the new company. The bank would print money to loan to investors who would use it to buy shares in the company. The company would then use the money from the new investors to pay out huge, bogus dividends to existing shareholders. Before long, the pyramid collapsed, leaving a long trail of worthless money and impoverished investors.

The phenomenon of printed money becoming worthless has happened many times. To me, the most interesting example occurred during the American Revolution. The printing of money was an experiment that was not only a terrible failure, but a spectacular success.

The First Successful Paper Money

Of all the early American intellectuals, the most revered is Benjamin Franklin (1706–1790). In his lifetime, Franklin was a highly accomplished writer, inventor, statesman, politician and scientist, a man who was widely admired for his wit and for his common-sense philosophy. Among his many other accomplishments, he is also remembered as the father of paper money.

In 1729, Franklin wrote an essay entitled "A Modest Enquiry into the Nature and Necessity of a Paper Currency". At the time, the principal money used in the American colonies was the Spanish silver dollar. After Franklin's essay appeared, several colonies tried to follow his plan by printing their own paper money. The British Parliament, however, considered this to be a usurpation of their powers and, in 1751 and 1764, outlawed the use of paper money in the American colonies.

In 1774, the colonists convened the First Continental Congress (federal legislature) and presented the British King, George III, with a long list of grievances. Fighting broke out, marking the beginning of the American Revolution and, in 1775, the Second Continental Congress established an army and appointed George Washington as its commander. On July 4, 1776, the Congress formally declared its independence from Great Britain by adopting the Declaration of Independence.

To finance the new army, the Congress put Franklin's ideas into practice by issuing paper bills of credit that were (supposedly) backed by gold and silver, and by passing a law that forced people to accept the new currency. As the war progressed, the need for money increased and, in 1777, the Congress issued $13 million of Treasury notes, which became known as "continentals" (because the words "Continental Currency" were printed on the notes).

At first, the value of the continental was set to be the same as the Spanish silver dollar. However, the value of the new money soon fell to two for a dollar. Then, as the Congress issued more and more money to pay for the war, the value of the continental slid further and further. It was not until 1780 that Congress finally stopped the printing press although, by then, the states were issuing their own money. By this time, the Congress had issued $241 million worth of paper money and their value had decreased to 40 continentals per silver dollar. By 1781, the value had fallen even further, to 75 per silver dollar.

This experience, unfortunately, was not unique. Once the idea of paper money caught on around the world, governments would often print money for an important cause: to fight a war, to pay for social programs, and so on. At first, everything would seem to work fine. In fact, by injecting new money into the economy, a government would be able to increase production. Eventually, however, the government would print too much money. The money would then decrease in value, which would create inflation, resulting in a significant loss in purchasing power for the general population.

This is exactly what happened in the United States. After the revolution (which ended in 1783), many people were left with continentals that had become virtually worthless. After an extended debate, the U.S. government decided to redeem all the continentals by trading them for government bonds, but at the rate of only $1 worth of bonds for $100 in continentals.

This experience did not sit well in America. The general population was so displeased with paper money that they returned to using coins almost exclusively, and very little paper money was issued for almost a hundred years. Indeed, the U.S. Constitution (written in 1787) specifically dictates that no state shall "make any Thing but gold and silver Coin a Tender in Payment of Debts." It was not until the 1860s, that the U.S. government once again issued paper money, this time to pay for the Civil War.

In Europe, however, the United States' experiment was looked upon as a great success. It was, after all, the first time a government had been able to finance a war simply by printing money. The door to the mint was now open, and before long, the governments of many other countries started to print their own money.

And thus began our modern monetary system.

Inflation and Hyperinflation

To appreciate how the Internet is important to the world economy of the 21st century, it is necessary to understand the major economic forces of the 20th century. One of the most significant forces was the threat of inflation.

Throughout this chapter, I have discussed examples of inflation, a condition in which the prices of goods and services increase significantly for an extended period of time. In the 20th century, there were a number of occurrences of extreme inflation, called

HYPERINFLATION, in which prices skyrocketed beyond all reason. Before I can explain how this can happen, I need to spend a moment discussing the advantages — and disadvantages — of paper money.

The original purpose of paper money was to provide a convenient way to represent more tangible forms of money. For example, a paper note could be printed to represent a specific amount of gold or silver. Merchants would accept the note because they knew that, whenever they wished, they could present the note to the issuing agency — a bank or a government — and exchange it for the actual gold or silver.

Since paper money was a lot more convenient than coins, few people actually traded paper for gold. However, because people believed they *could* make the trade, they had faith in paper money, and it was this faith that made the whole system work.

From time to time, governments or banks would print more money than they had real gold. This, as we discussed earlier in the chapter, would cause inflation, which would create economic instability. However, inflation alone is not enough to make an economic system fail. An economic system does not fail until the people lose faith in the currency. In the 20th century, this happened many times, always with disastrous results. The most interesting example occurred after the Russian Revolution when the new government deliberately sabotaged their own currency.

In February of 1917, the regime of Tsar Nicholas II was overthrown and, nine months later, in November 1917, the Bolsheviks, led by Vladimir Lenin, seized power. The Bolsheviks (who, in 1918, changed their name to the Communist Party) promoted an idealistic philosophy in which all property, including the means of production, should be owned and administered by the state for the good of the people.

Some of the newly powerful Communists dreamed of building a society without money. The plan called for money to be replaced by a rationing system based on coupons that would be allotted by the state. To destroy the current monetary system, the Communists printed as much money (rubles) as everyone wanted. Within a short time, the monetary system was effectively destroyed by hyperinflation: paper money had lost so much value that it took 10,000 new rubles to buy something that, before the revolution, cost only one Tsarist ruble. Within a few years, however, it became obvious, even to the Communists, that the country could not function without money and, in 1921, the government was forced to introduce a new currency.

The most extreme case of the collapse of a currency occurred in Germany after World War I. The war had lasted from 1914 to 1918. Germany and her allies had lost the war, and the other European countries, particularly Great Britain and France, pressed for extreme retribution. The details were specified by the Treaty of Versailles, which was negotiated in 1919 by the United States, Great Britain, France and Italy. The treaty sharply reduced Germany's power and gave some of her land to other countries. It also established the League of Nations, the forerunner of the United Nations.

Most important, the treaty placed the blame for World War I on the Germans, and ordered them to pay the cost of the war. Although the U.S. objected, the other countries, in April 1921, presented Germany with a huge bill of 132 billion German marks. This was equal to about $33 billion U.S. dollars (about $329 billion in today's dollars). Although most of the blame for World War I did lie with Germany, their economy had been devastated by the war, and the terms of the treaty made it difficult for them to sell goods for a fair price on the open market.

The German government did begin to make payments to other countries. However, the Germans were not able to meet even their own domestic obligations, so in order to come up with the money, the government began to print large amounts of paper money without any tangible backing. The result was a severe debasing of the German currency. Within several months, prices in Germany started to rise. As the government printed more and more money, prices rose without bound, and the government found itself needing to issue paper money faster than it could print it.

How bad was the situation? In November 1919, just after the war, one U.S. dollar cost about 4 German marks. By July 1922, a dollar cost 500 marks. By January 1923, the cost had risen to 18,000 marks. At the height of the German inflation, in November 1923 — four years after the war — a German mark was worth so little that it cost 4,200,000,000,000 (4.2 trillion) marks to buy a single U.S. dollar. In other words, in November 1923, one U.S. penny was worth 42 billion German marks.

The hyperinflation finally ended on November 29, 1923, when the German government created a new currency in which each new mark was worth a trillion old marks. One U.S. dollar was now worth 4.2 new marks. To keep the currency stable, the government based the new money on land values. In 1924, the U.S. loaned Germany $200 million so it could return to the gold standard, which further stabilized the new German money.

However, by 1924, the damage had been done. Extreme inflation had placed a great financial burden on the Germans, especially on the working class and the middle class. This burden, combined with a general resentment over the harshness of the Treaty of Versailles, created great suffering within Germany. This suffering, in turn, fostered long-standing discontent and an atmosphere of political extremism, leading to the conditions that allowed Adolf Hitler to come to power in the early 1930s. In 1935, Hitler unilaterally nullified virtually all of the Treaty of Versailles.

The German experience with hyperinflation was extreme, but it was by no means unique. The 20th century saw a number of countries succumb to this deadly economic malady, among them Bolivia in 1985, Argentina in 1989, Peru in 1990, Brazil in 1993, Ukraine in 1993, and Kosovo in 1994.

Such occurrences are serious because they affect more than one particular country. Not only is an entire region destabilized, but the economy of the world as a whole can be affected. For example, at the height of the hyperinflation in Bolivia, Bolivian merchants and consumers were able to achieve a certain amount of stability by establishing a large black market economy using U.S. paper money. In order to make the system work, however, the Bolivians required an ever-expanding supply of American cash. The principal way in which they accumulated this cash was to export coca paste, which was used to make cocaine for the U.S. market. Once the drugs were sold on the streets of America, the cash was shipped back to Bolivia where it was used to support the underground economy.

The Real Lesson of History

For most of history, the world has been an embattled and chaotic place in which a huge amount of human effort has been devoted to war and the problems caused by war. Traditionally, many people have considered the causes of war to be aggression, politics, greed and hatred. In order to bring peace to the world, the thinking goes, we must learn to control these primal urges.

However, aggression, politics, greed and hatred are inevitable expressions of human nature. What the lessons of history have really shown us is that the best way to ensure world peace is to create a stable economy in which people, countries, and regions are economically dependent on one another.

For example, the harsh economic conditions in Germany that followed World War I were a principal cause of World War II. After World War II, however, the winning countries did not demand reparations from Germany. Instead, they spent a huge amount of money and effort rebuilding the Western European economy and stabilizing its currencies. The U.S., for example, spent over $12 billion ($85 billion in today's dollars) from 1948 to 1951 as part of the Marshall Plan in which an enormous amount of food, manufactured goods, and raw materials were sent to Europe, much of it to Germany.

This might seem like a lot of money for a country to spend rebuilding other countries after a war (especially when you consider that the United States was one of the winners of the war). However, the Marshall Plan — named after U.S. Secretary of State George Marshall — was one of the best investments the country ever made. As a result of this program, Europe was able to recover from the most devastating war in history and — over the next fifty years — create a unified economic system (the European Union) that assures peace in Europe for the foreseeable future.

Although the effort cost the U.S. $12 billion at the time, we need only compare this to the cost of World War II, $360 billion, (over $4 trillion in today's dollars) to see that the Marshall Plan was a bargain.

Although the 20th century was marked by the worst wars in history, it was also a period of enormous transition, a time in which the global economy was born, creating a world in which major conflicts are unthinkable. The lessons of the 20th century show us that global peace is not achieved when people around the world decide to act peaceably. Global peace is achieved when people around the world perceive themselves as being economically dependent on one another.

The Internet plays an important role in the new economy by connecting companies, governments and individuals around the world. In an economic sense, these connections do more than simply facilitate commerce. They change the very experience of buying and selling in such a way as to increase the interdependence of the various parts of the global economy. As such, the Net acts as a powerful catalyst of world peace.

Although the Net is still rather new to mankind, the seeds of the new global economy were planted a long time ago, in 1933, when U.S. President Franklin Roosevelt was searching for a way to stimulate the American economy during the depths of the Great Depression.

How Roosevelt and Nixon Ended the Gold Standard

The DEPRESSION, or more formally, the GREAT DEPRESSION, was a long period of economic hardship that lasted from late 1929 to 1937. The downturn in the economy actually started in August of 1929. However, most people were not aware of what was happening until the stock market began to collapse on October 24, 1929 (referred to as "Black Thursday"). Within a short time, the economy of the United States deteriorated significantly and the Depression had begun in earnest.

In 1932, Franklin Roosevelt was elected President of the United States after promising to take forceful steps to improve the economic situation. By the time Roosevelt took office in March of 1933, conditions all over the country were appalling. Industrial production was down 56 percent from 1929 and over 13,000,000 people, a third of the work force, was out of work. To make matters worse, farmers all over the country were going broke. (At the time, the U.S. was mostly an agrarian nation.)

One of the biggest problems Roosevelt faced was that a large number of people had lost confidence in paper money and were going to their banks to exchange their money for gold. This so-called "run on the banks" had happened several times since the 1929 stock market collapse, and it was happening again at the time Roosevelt took office. If a bank could not meet the demands of its depositors, it would have to close down. In 1929, there were 24,633 banks. By 1933, only 15,015 were still in business, a decrease of 31 percent.

A run on the banks was devastating for other reasons as well. Not only did it deplete the gold reserves, but it removed large amounts of cash from circulation at the very time that the economy needed it most in order to recover. (As I will explain later in the chapter, an economy cannot grow unless it has an adequate money supply.) The decrease in the money supply from 1929–1933 was one of the reasons the Depression was so severe and lasted so long.

In 1933, much of the world, including the U.S. and many European countries, was on the GOLD STANDARD, which meant that paper money could be exchanged for gold. For example, you could, at the time, go to a bank and trade a dollar bill for a dollar's worth of gold. In other countries, you could either trade your currency for gold or, at the very least, trade for U.S. dollars, which could then be converted to gold.

In normal times, few people would actually make such a trade: it was enough to know that it was possible. However, these were not normal times. By 1933, the U.S. was in big trouble and people all over the country were trading in their dollars for gold.

Roosevelt had to stop this, and to do so, he decided to change the system so that the U.S. government would hold and control all the gold in the country. In other words, he began to nationalize gold.

Roosevelt nationalized gold for two reasons. First, he wanted to stop the run on the banks. Second, he was planning a number of expensive social and economic programs and he needed money to finance them. Controlling the gold supply would give him more control over the money supply.

In 1933, with the cooperation of the U.S. Congress, Roosevelt made it illegal for Americans to possess gold coins or bullion. He then took away the right of Americans to be able to exchange paper money for gold. Finally, he confiscated all the privately held gold in the country by forcing people to trade it to the government for paper money at the rate of $20.67/ounce.

Within a year, the U.S. government owned most of the gold in the country. Then, on January 31, 1934, Roosevelt used the authority given to him by Congress to unilaterally raise the price of gold to $35/ounce. Overnight, an ounce of gold that used to be worth $20.67 was now worth $35. Making this price change allowed Roosevelt to pull a fast one, a monetary scheme that, even by today's standards, was totally awesome. Here is how it worked.

In 1933, the government was able to print $20.67 in paper money for each ounce of gold that it held. In 1934, the same ounce of gold could be used to support $35 in paper money, a difference of $14.33. In this way, the value of the gold held by the government increased by about $3 billion, which meant that Roosevelt was able to create $3 billion in brand new money out of nothing. He could then use the $3 billion to help fund his new programs. In doing so, Roosevelt put a huge amount of new money into circulation, which helped the economy to recover.

However, he did so at a cost. First of all, Roosevelt effectively devalued U.S. paper money (with respect to gold) by 41 percent. Second, distancing the U.S. from the gold standard, he initiated a process that was potentially dangerous. If the U.S. ever went off the gold standard completely, and the government did not have the discipline to keep from creating too much new money, there would be trouble.

Four decades later, in 1971, the remaining U.S. ties to the gold standard were finally severed, by Richard Nixon, in an attempt to solve a serious cash flow crisis. The previous president, Lyndon Johnson, had escalated the Vietnam War at the same time as he initiated expensive social programs (the so-called War on Poverty). In 1969, Nixon inherited these obligations, which he extended on his own.

Both presidents had had trouble getting enough money, because neither they nor Congress were willing to raise taxes to support an increasingly unpopular war. To get the money they needed, Johnson and Nixon borrowed, and then spent, billions of dollars. In the process, they infused a huge amount of money into the economy, which led to serious inflation. It also led to a balance of trade problem, in which the U.S. was importing far more than it was exporting. As a result, more and more U.S. dollars came to be held outside the country.

To keep foreign countries from trading in their surplus dollars for gold, Nixon, in 1971, unilaterally decreed that, from now on, the U.S. would not exchange dollars for gold for anyone. For all practical purposes, the United States was off the gold standard. In 1978, Congress passed a law making it official. Other countries had passed similar laws, and by the end of the 1970s, no major currency was redeemable in gold.

But if a dollar was not redeemable by gold, why should it be worth anything? And if the dollar was no longer tied to gold, who would decide when and how to create new money?

The answers to these questions will surprise you, and they will go a long way towards explaining how our modern monetary system works, and why the Internet is so important to the world economy.

Business Cycles: Why Someone Needs to Be In Charge

In a minute, we'll talk about our modern monetary system and I'll answer the questions I posed at the end of the last section:

"How can money that is not redeemable have value?" and "Who creates new money?" Before I do, however, I'd like to lay the groundwork for our discussion by posing a more basic question: "Is anyone in charge?"

It is the nature of the economy that it is always changing. Over a long period of time, economic changes come in cycles in which a period of expansion is followed by a period of contraction. During an expansion, production, income, employment and trade all increase, causing the economy to grow. Life gets better and better. During a contraction, life becomes more difficult. Production, income, employment and trade go down and the economy shrinks.

Such cycles are long, taking many months or even years, and the duration of the expansions and contractions varies considerably. In economic terms, a single up-and-down fluctuation — one expansion followed by a contraction — is called a BUSINESS CYCLE. All countries and economic regions go through such cycles. For instance, in the last 150 years, the United States economy has gone through 31 business cycles.

During the period of contraction, the decline in general economic activity causes widespread problems. When this happens, we say that the economy is in a RECESSION. Thus, the U.S. has had 31 recessions in the last 150 years.

As a general rule, a recession lasts from 6 to 12 months, although this is not always the case. The most severe recession took place from August 1929 to March 1933, a total of 43 months. This recession was so extreme that it created the Depression, a long period of economic suffering. The Depression started in November 1929, with the collapse of the U.S. stock market and grew to affect most of the world, including Europe and Canada. Although the actual recession ended in 1933, it took a long time for the world economy to recover. In fact, the Depression itself did not really end until the late 1930s, when massive government spending (to prepare for World War II) infused a huge amount of money into the global economy.

Because business cycles are part of the system, it is natural to wonder if there is anything we can do to avoid the recessions. If this is not possible, can we at least do something to make the recessions as short and mild as possible?

One solution, of course, is to have a war (after all, World War II did end the Depression). Unfortunately, wars only boost the economy temporarily. Although all the government spending does invigorate the economy, most of the money is spent on activities that are fundamentally destructive (such as building weapons) rather than constructive (such as building houses and schools). In virtually all cases, the government will borrow large amounts of money to pay for the war. When the war ends, so does the temporary spending, at which time the huge debt brings about a general economic contraction that invariably leads to a severe recession.

So, although wars can end a recession, in the long run, they have always proven to be devastating to a country's economy. The larger the war, the more economic suffering it ultimately brings.

Clearly we need a better way to invigorate a depressed economy and smooth out business cycles. In today's world, we do have a better solution, one that is based on three ideals:

- Controlling the money supply wisely.
- Creating a truly global economy.
- Keeping the world peaceful.

Who Controls the Money Supply?

As you can see by now, both people and countries have a need for economic stability. But economic stability does not mean that financial conditions should stay the same for a long period of time. Indeed, as we discussed in the previous section, the economy has a life of its own, moving through business cycles in which periods of expansion are followed inevitably by periods of contraction.

Since change is inevitable, working towards economic stability means doing the best we can to moderate the business cycles. Our goal is to make the expansions as manageable and predictable as possible (thereby avoiding inflation), and to make the contractions as short and mild as possible (thereby avoiding recessions).

I have mentioned that, in the last 150 years, the United States has gone through 31 business cycles, many of which have had devastating periods of inflation and recession. Although there are no perfect solutions, it is possible to manage the economy somewhat. For example, the last period of economic expansion started in March of 1991. As I write this (in May of 2001), the economy is still doing well. In fact, it is, by far, the longest period of economic expansion in modern history.

What is it that helps keep an economy healthy and stable? There are a number of important factors, and I will summarize them for you at the end of the chapter. (At the time, you will see that one such factor is the Internet.) For now, I want to discuss the element that is most under our control: the size of the money supply.

The health of an economy is very much dependent upon its money supply. Virtually every transaction requires money and, without enough money, the rate of commerce will slow down. Moreover, in order for the economy to grow, individuals, companies and governments must be able to borrow money as they need it. If there is not enough money, interest rates will go up, borrowing money will become more expensive, and the economy will slow down.

It is an interesting characteristic of a healthy economy that it cannot stay the same for very long: the level of productivity must either grow or shrink. Since we prefer that the economy grow, we must make sure that it always has enough new money. If the economy does not get enough new money, it will, over time, begin to contract.

Imagine the economy is a pot of water boiling on the stove. To keep the pot boiling, you constantly have to be adding just the right amount of heat. If you add too little heat, the water cools down and stops boiling. If you add too much heat, the boiling gets out of control.

In the same way, if the economy doesn't get enough new money when it needs it, economic activity will slow down to the point where it will cause a recession. Conversely, if too much new money is put into the economy for too long, it will cause prices and wages to spiral up and up, which will cause inflation.

The basic idea behind modern economic management is for someone to control the money supply in such a way that the economy gets the right amount of new money at the right time. For example, during recessions, the money supply should be increased to speed the recovery. During times of inflation, the money supply should be decreased to hold down prices and wages. Indeed, it may even be possible to avoid recessions and inflation by manipulating the money supply preemptively.

In most countries, an organization called a CENTRAL BANK is in charge of controlling that country's money supply. All industrialized countries have a central bank and, in Europe, the European Union has a central bank of its own to control the Euro and the European-wide money supply. In the United States, the central bank is called the FEDERAL RESERVE, often referred to as the FED.

The Federal Reserve was created by the U.S. Congress in 1913 in an attempt to avoid the booms and busts that had caused such severe problems in the 19th century. The Fed is a hybrid organization, part public and part private, that was set up specifically so as to avoid being subject to short-term political pressures.

The Fed is based in Washington, D.C. and is run by a Board of Governors consisting of seven people who are appointed by the President and confirmed by the Senate. Under the supervision of the Board of Governors are 12 regional Federal Reserve Banks that oversee various parts of the banking system. Although the Board of Governors is a public agency, the Federal Reserve Banks are actually private organizations, although in many ways, they function as public agencies.

From among the seven Governors, the President appoints one to be Chairman, to run the board and to act as chief executive of the Fed. As you will see in a moment, the Fed is an extremely important organization. As a result, the Chairman of the Fed is the second most powerful person in the United States, after the President himself, and one of the most important people in the world.

The U.S. Federal Reserve provides four main services. First, it acts as the money manager for the United States, regulating the money supply as necessary. (We'll talk about the details in the next section.) Second, the Fed acts as the official bank of the federal government. Third, the Fed regulates the U.S. banking system. Finally, the Fed serves as a sort of super-bank, providing special services to all the other banks in the country.

In the context of our discussion, the Federal Reserve is important because it is charged with the task of keeping the financial system as healthy as possible. To do so, the Fed manipulates the money supply in a way that (it hopes) will avoid inflation and recessions, and will encourage the economy to grow in as stable a manner as possible.

In this way, the Fed and other central banks around the world have enormous influence over the lives of people everywhere, much more than most people realize. For example, if the Fed thinks the U.S. is in danger of excessive inflation, it may reduce the money supply in order to cool down the economy. This, however, will increase unemployment, which, in turn, will affect people's marriages, their self-esteem, and their financial well-being, not to mention their ability to buy a house, send their kids to college, and save for retirement.

In a very real sense, the Federal Reserve has huge power over the U.S. economy and, indirectly, over people's lives. And yet, very few people understand what the Fed is and how it works. To show you one aspect of the system, I am going to describe to you how money is created and how the Fed manipulates the U.S. money supply. This is something that I want you to understand because, later in the chapter, I am going to explain how the Internet also affects the supply of money, and you will see how everything is related.

How Most Money is Created

Most money does not exist in tangible form. In fact, less than 10 percent of U.S. money is in the form of bills or coins. Over 90 percent exists only as electronic data stored in a computer. Think about your own money, for example. Although you probably have some cash, most of your money exists in bank accounts or brokerage accounts, and your wealth is actually stored as data in various computer systems.

There are two ways in which new money can be created. First, it can be printed as bills or manufactured as coins. More frequently, however, money is created just by changing the data stored in a computer. For instance, if your bank were to credit your checking account with, say, a million dollars, all that would happen is that they would make a new entry in their computer. As soon as they made this entry, you would have a million dollars to your name. No new bills or coins would need to be created.

Although it is unlikely that your bank is going to credit your account with a million dollars out of the goodness of their heart, the scenario I have described is similar to the way in which most of the money in the economy is actually created.

When you put money in the bank, the bank does not keep all of your money in a vault (or even in a computer). They loan most of it out to other people. That is how banks make a profit: they accept a deposit from one person, and then loan the money to another person. The profit comes from loaning the money out at a higher rate of interest than what they pay for it. For example, a bank might pay you 4% interest on your savings account, but loan the same money out to another customer at 12% interest.

The Federal Reserve, which regulates banking, does not let banks loan out all of their deposits. By law, banks must retain a certain amount of money on reserve, called the RESERVE RATE. In most cases, the reserve rate is 10%. In other words, banks are allowed to loan out 90% of the money that they accept for deposit. Here is an example to show how it works.

Let's say you deposit $10,000 into your bank account. The bank keeps $1,000 (10%) on reserve, and loans $9,000 (90%), to someone else. That person then uses the $9,000 to buy something, and the money ends up being deposited in another bank.

Once the $9,000 is deposited, the second bank keeps $900 (10%) on reserve and loans $8,100 (90%) to another person. At this point, there is $19,000 loaned and $1,900 held on reserve, so the total money free to circulate in the economy has jumped from the original $10,000 to $17,100 ($19,000 − $1,900).

Of course, we don't have to stop there. The $8,100 that was loaned out by the second bank will find its way to a third bank, whereupon 90% of the $8,100 will be loaned to someone else. This same process will be repeated, again and again, generating more money each time. If you know how to do the math, you will see that, in theory, a deposit of $10,000 can turn into $90,000 (a total of $100,000 in loans and $10,000 held back on reserve).

This is the way in which most of the money in our economy is created. It comes into being because the banks loan out most of the money they take in, and most of that money is loaned out again and again.

The reason the system works is that people have enough faith in the banks to leave their money on deposit. If a large number of people lost faith in the banks, they might demand that the banks return all the money they have deposited (a run on the banks). If this were to happen, it would force the banks to try to recall as many of their loans as they could. In such a situation, two things would happen.

First, every time a loan was recalled successfully, the system would work in reverse and the amount of money in circulation would *shrink*. If this were to happen on a large scale, the decrease in the money supply would slow down the economy and create a serious recession.

Second, many banks would not be able to recall all their loans fast enough (after all, most loans have repayment schedules that cannot be speeded up). If a bank ran out of money, it would have to close and, once one bank closes, it scares people who have money in other banks.

If a run on the banks got out of hand, it could close down many of the banks and paralyze the economy. This is exactly what happened during the Depression. As I discussed earlier, in 1929, there were 24,633 banks in the U.S. By 1933, only 15,015 were still in business (a decrease of 31 percent).

The reason this does not happen is that the Federal Reserve never lets things get out of hand. For example, if a bank is ever faced with extraordinary withdrawals, it could always borrow money to meet its obligations. If, for some reason, a bank were not able to borrow enough money, the Fed would step in and loan the bank whatever is necessary to satisfy the depositors. In this way, the Fed acts as the lender of last resort.

Even more important, the Fed is charged with the job of regulating U.S. banks. By making sure that the banks are run correctly, the Fed inspires continuing faith in the system.

During the 1929–1933 recession, the Fed was much younger and was not nearly as effective as it is now. In retrospect, economists now believe that if the Fed had done a better job maintaining an adequate money supply during the first crucial years, the Depression would have been significantly shorter and a lot milder.

How the Fed Creates and Destroys Money: Part 1

Every day, in order to fine tune the United States' money supply, the Federal Reserve creates or destroys several billion dollars.

As we discussed earlier in the chapter, the Fed does this in order to maintain the money supply at the level they think is best for the economy. What I am sure you are wondering is, how do they do it? How does someone create several billion dollars? For that matter, how does someone destroy a billion dollars?

Banks have a variety of different holdings. Aside from cash, they also hold bonds and other financial instruments. It is the bonds that are important here, so let's talk about them for a minute.

A BOND is a debt issued by a company, government or government agency in order to borrow money for a specific amount of time. To obtain the money, borrowers make two promises. First, they promise to make regular interest payments. Second, they promise to pay back the original sum of money after the specified amount of time has passed. In other words, a bond is a type of IOU.

Here is a typical example to show you how it works. Let's say the XYZ Company wants to borrow $1,000,000 for 10 years, and they are willing to pay 5% interest a year, with payments every 6 months (which is typical). It will be difficult for them to find one person or one company willing to loan them the entire $1,000,000, so, instead, they will sell 40 bonds for $25,000 apiece.

Let's take a moment to figure out the interest. The XYZ Company has promised to pay 5% a year. For a $25,000 bond, this means $1,250 a year. ($1,250 = 5% of $25,000.) Since the payments must be made every 6 months, the XYZ Company will need to make regular payments of $625 (half of $1,250).

You decide to buy one of these bonds, so you give the XYZ Company $25,000. In return, they agree to pay you $625 in interest every 6 months for 10 years. At the end of the 10 years, the XYZ Company will pay you back the $25,000. From the company's point of view, the bond is a way for them to borrow money at a fixed cost for a specific amount of time. From your point of view, the bond is an investment that provides you with predictable income for 10 years.

Who buys bonds? People, companies and governments that want a guaranteed rate of return on their investments. For example, many retired people buy bonds and live off the interest. Many governments buy bonds in order to earn income from their surplus funds.

Who sells bonds? Any organization that wants to borrow money for a specific amount of time. For example, a city might issue bonds in order to pay for a new high school.

No doubt, you have heard that the U.S. government borrows a huge amount of money. They do so by having the U.S. Treasury issue various types of bonds. To borrow money for a short amount of time (one year or less), the Treasury issues what are called TREASURY BILLS. To borrow money for a medium length of time (between 1 and 10 years), they issue TREASURY NOTES. To borrow money for a long period of time (over 10 years), they issue TREASURY BONDS. (For our purposes, we can consider them more or less the same, so I'll refer to all of them as Treasury bonds.)

In case you are wondering how much money the U.S. Government owes, as of the day I am writing this (May 24, 2001) the federal debt is more than $5.6 trillion, to be precise, $5,660,965,921,275.71. (What I want to know is, what's the 71 cents for?)

So what does this have to do with banks and the Fed? In the previous section, I explained how new money is created when banks loan out money that has been deposited with them. The loaned money is deposited in another bank, where it is loaned out again, creating even more new money. The money that a bank has in cash can be loaned out, but the money it has in bonds just stays where it is. Since bond money does not get loaned out, it does not circulate and create more and more money.

Thus, it is possible for the Fed to control the size of the money supply by controlling how much money the banks keep in cash (which is loanable) compared to how much money they keep in bonds (which is not loanable). To increase the money supply, the Fed moves some of the banks' money from bonds into cash. To decrease the money supply, the Fed moves some of the banks' money from cash to bonds. The details are complex, so we won't deal with them here. Basically, each day, the Fed buys or sells several billion dollars worth of U.S. Treasury bonds from financial companies who act as dealers.

Let's say that, on a certain day, the Fed buys $4 billion dollars worth of Treasury bonds from a particular dealer. To do so, the Fed takes possession of the bonds (electronically) and puts $4 billion in the dealer's bank account. The dealer's bank now has $4 billion more to loan out, which, in the way I have described above, creates a lot of new money. Thus, by buying bonds, the Fed has increased the money supply of the country.

Now, let's say that, a month later, the Fed wants to decrease the money supply, so they sell $4 billion worth of bonds to a particular dealer. To do so, they credit the dealer with possession of the bonds and take $4 billion out of the dealer's bank account. The dealer's bank now has $4 billion *less* to loan out, which decreases the money supply.

At this point, you are probably wondering, where does the Fed get all the money to buy and sell such large quantities of Treasury bonds? The answer is — and this is the coolest part of all — they don't really have the money; they just make it up.

Do you remember in the previous section, when I observed that, if your bank were to credit your account with a million dollars, you would, all of a sudden, have an extra million dollars to spend? One reason why your bank doesn't do this is that banks can't just go around giving people money out of nothing. If your bank wants to credit your account with some money, that money has to come from somewhere.

The Fed is a different type of bank. They *are* allowed to credit accounts without having to come up with real money. Thus, when the Fed puts a $4 billion credit in the bank account of a bond dealer, the money doesn't have to come from anywhere. The mere fact that the Fed puts it in a bank account is enough to create the money. Similarly, when the Fed takes $4 billion out of a bank account, the money doesn't go anywhere. It just ceases to exist.

Does this mean that, if the Federal Reserve wanted to, it could credit your bank account with a million dollars without causing a bookkeeping problem? Absolutely. The trick, of course, is to get them to want to do so. If you'd like to try, their phone number is (202) 452–3000. (Ask for Mr. Greenspan.)

How the Fed Creates and Destroys Money: Part II

The main way in which the Fed manipulates the money supply is by buying and selling bonds, as I have described in the previous section. However, for completeness, I would like to mention that there are two other ways in which the Fed can raise or lower the money supply.

First, as I explained, the percentage of money that a bank must keep in reserve is dictated by the reserve rate. For instance, if the reserve rate is 10%, a bank must reserve 10% of its deposits. This is money that cannot be loaned out.

One way the Fed can change the money supply is by raising or lowering the reserve rate. For example, if the Fed were to lower the reserve rate, banks would be able to loan out more of their deposits, which would increase the money supply. Modifying the reserve rate, however, is a big deal, and the Fed rarely does it.

The other way in which the Fed can affect the money supply has to do with the actual cash that is on reserve. The Fed is itself a bank and, by law, all the money that the regular banks hold in reserve must be deposited at the Fed itself. For example, let's say that, on a particular day, a bank is required to have $100 million on reserve. That $100 million dollars is kept in an account at the Fed in the name of that bank. From day to day, as the amount of money held by banks changes, the amount that each bank must keep on deposit at the Fed changes as well.

On a particular day, a bank may find that it does not have quite enough money on deposit to the Fed to meet its reserve obligation. Similarly, another bank may find that it has a surplus. When this happens, the second bank may loan money to the first bank. Most of the time, such loans are made for only a single day.

Now, as it happens, even though the Fed requires banks to keep all their reserve money in the Fed's bank, the Fed does not pay interest on that money. However, a bank that loans money overnight to another bank *is* allowed to charge interest. Thus, banks with a reserve surplus are always happy to lend money to banks with a reserve deficit.

The rate at which banks may lend each other reserve money is set by the Fed and is called the FEDERAL FUNDS RATE. From time to time, you may hear that the Fed is raising or lowering the "interest rates". What they are really doing is changing the federal funds rate.

Although this rate applies only to very specific, short-term, bank-to-bank loans, it tends to affect other interest rates in the economy. For this reason, people make a big fuss when the Fed changes the rate. However, in reality, the federal funds rate has less effect on the money supply than the buying and selling of bonds, something which the Fed does every day.

Money Desensitization

Our world is filled with people and companies who spend a great deal of time and effort in the pursuit of your money. This is especially true on the Net, where merchants ruthlessly exploit the fact that there are no concrete cues to remind you that you are spending real money. Many Web sites, for example, are set up to encourage you to use your credit card to buy impulsively. Companies purposely design such sites to entice you, by any means they can, to spend, spend, spend.

Such experiences, of course are not unique to the Net. They abound in our culture. Modern marketing techniques are designed to take advantage of the fact that, the more abstract the transaction, the less you will realize the true impact it is going to have on your life.

For example, have ever you been to a casino? If so, you will have seen how carefully the environment is designed to encourage you to suspend your critical judgment. There are no windows, no clocks or no reminders of the world outside (the one in which you must work and pay your bills). Instead of allowing you to bet with real money, casinos encourage you to use clay chips that feel like play money. Moreover, to ensure that you don't think too much about what you are doing, the casino provides a host of distractions such as noise, colored lights, costumed hostesses, and free alcohol (not to mention ATMs, check cashing, and access to liberal credit card advances).

Casinos are purposely designed to desensitize you to the fact that the liabilities and debts you incur must ultimately be satisfied in real money — money that may represent many hours of hard work and effort on your part.

To be realistic, when you walk into a casino you are fair game. After all, it is a gambling hall, devoted to taking as much money as possible from people who think they can get something for nothing. No one entering a casino should have any illusions about the purpose of the facility.

However, monetary desensitization is ubiquitous in our culture. Because our monetary system is so abstract and so complex, many people have real trouble understanding the nuances. In particular, unless you are paying strict attention, it can be difficult to appreciate the true extent of your personal liabilities and debts.

For example, a gas station will advertise their gas at, say, 199.9 cents/gallon, rather than 200 cents/gallon. A television commercial will advertise an exercise machine for "four easy payments of $29.95 and a small shipping and handling charge of $9.95", rather than $129.75. When the numbers get bigger, the desensitization efforts get more extreme. Consider this example.

In the United States, many college students must take out student loans in order to pay their expenses. Indeed, it is not unusual for a student to borrow $10,000/year. This means that, by the time he graduates, the student will owe $40,000. By the time he has paid it all back, including interest, that $40,000 will have grown to almost $56,000 (assuming a 10-year loan at 7% interest, which would require 120 monthly payments of $464).

Although this is a huge sum of money for a kid just out of high school, the financial aid system is designed to desensitize students to the magnitude of the liability they are about to incur. Once the loan is arranged, all a student has to do is sign some papers. In many cases, the student doesn't even see a check. The money is sent to the school, which applies it directly to his account. The whole process is so transparent that the student has no real feeling for what he is doing — until he graduates and has to start making payments.

Consider an alternate scenario. A college student is arranging for his first student loan. Instead of making the whole thing into a painless procedure, the loan officer takes the student into a room in which there are boxes filled with $20 bills.

"Do you see those boxes and all that money?" says the loan officer. "I want you to count the money, out loud, one bill at a time, until you get to $40,000. That's 2,000 bills."

Let's say the student counts two bills a second, so it takes him 16 minutes and 40 seconds to finish. When the student is finished counting, the loan officer tells him, "Take a careful look at the pile of 2,000 $20 bills you have just counted. That is what you are thinking of borrowing over the next four years."

"Now," continues the loan officer, "I want you to count out 665 more $20 bills." The student does so, which takes him another 5 minutes and 32 seconds.

"That," the loan officer tells the student, "is all the extra money you are agreeing to pay in interest: $13,300. Remember, you are going to have to pay all this money, whether or not you even finish school or get a good job. Once you borrow it, you have a legal obligation. Now, I am going to leave you alone for a few minutes, and I want you to think about how many hours you are going to have to work to earn enough money to pay back your loans."

This is a story, of course, that will never happen. However, I want you to remember it each time you buy something on the Internet. Before you type your credit card number, imagine yourself counting out the money in real bills — and don't forget to include the interest and the shipping and handling.

I have a friend whose landlord insists that she pay him in cash. Believe me, she has a real feeling for how much she pays because, each month, she must get the cash, count it, put it in an envelope, and give it to the landlord in person.

In our society, though, paying cash for anything but small purchases is unusual. Most of the time, we use checks, credit cards, debit cards or automatic payment services. Sometimes we don't even see the transaction. Like the student in our story, we can incur a liability and all that happens is a sum of money is transferred electronically from one computer to another.

If you want something to think about, imagine you are buying a $200,000 house. You pay 20% for a down payment and borrow the rest by taking out a 30-year mortgage at 7.5% interest. Let's say the bank were to force you to count all the money, in $20 bills, before you signed the documents.

It would take you 1 hour, 6 minutes and 40 seconds to count all the money you are borrowing ($160,000). It would then take you an *extra* 1 hour, 41 minutes and 8 seconds to count all the interest you will end up paying before the mortgage is finally paid off ($242,748).

Money and You

Ever since the King of Lydia held the very first coin in his hands, there has always been someone nearby who was willing to take that coin by fair means or foul. Today's economic system is so complex that it is beyond the understanding of any one person, and yet all of us must somehow learn to master enough of the system to protect our own interests.

Such thinking does not come easily. Money is a totally artificial construct, one that is uniquely human, with no analog anywhere in the animal kingdom. As such, using money is not a natural activity. If you want to understand the monetary system and learn how to use it to your advantage, you must do so deliberately, and you must study, think and practice. If you have a flair for numbers and computation, you will have a definite advantage. If you find arithmetic and abstract reasoning difficult, you are going to have a hard time. Sorry, but that's a fact.

Still, you and I are never going to be called upon to run the U.S. Federal Reserve System, and we don't need to master the arcane minutiae of professional economists. If we are going to protect ourselves, all we really need to understand are the basic principles: What is money? How does it work? and What does it mean to us?

In this chapter, I have traced the development of money over the centuries, from barter to commodities to coins to paper money, culminating in our modern system in which virtually all money is stored as intangible computer data.

Money is an *idea*, one that is based on faith. If I offer to buy something from you for a hundred dollars, you would not agree to the sale unless you had faith that the hundred dollars has value and that it would keep that value.

To say that money is based on faith is not an appeal to the supernatural, for the monetary system does not demand blind faith. The way we use money today is the end product of the activities of a great many intelligent people, and the system has been improved by centuries of trial and error. Moreover, in the last twenty-five years, the tools we use to deal with money have been significantly enhanced to meet the demands of a fast-moving, computerized society. Even though our monetary system may not be perfect, it does work well, and it is administered as wisely and fairly as possible.

If you are going to use the Internet for buying and selling, it is important that you learn to deal with money as a complete abstraction, one that does not correspond to anything tangible, such as gold, silver or even paper. On the Net, money can move quickly and silently without leaving a trace... until you get your credit card bill or your brokerage statement. If you aren't firmly grounded in the realities of our modern monetary system, you are going to be at the mercy of the economic forces that swirl around you like invisible demons, manipulating you and desensitizing you in order to take as much of your wealth as they can.

"If you are going to use the Internet for buying and selling, it is important that you learn to deal with money as a complete abstraction."

As a general rule, the world is a complicated place, and if you don't understand your own motivations, you are going to get into trouble. This is especially true when it comes to money, on or off the Net. You need to understand, not only how the system works, but how you relate to it and what money means to you personally.

At the beginning of this chapter, I described money as a medium of exchange. In this sense, the function of money is to separate the act of buying from the act of selling. You buy something from another person and the money you give him acts as storage, maintaining its value until he decides to buy something.

Because money can store value, it can be saved and accumulated, bringing wealth and luxury to its owner. But money has another, much more important characteristic. In large amounts, money confers power. The larger the amount of money, the more the power. This has always been the case, and it is the main reason why men have always fought over money, and always will fight over money.

In our society, we need money for many reasons: to satisfy our everyday needs, such as food, clothing, shelter and health care; to care for our children; to educate ourselves and our families; to plan for our retirement; to pay our taxes; and so on. When you stop to consider all the important things that money can provide — not to mention wealth, luxury and power — it is no surprise that our feelings regarding money are extremely personal.

Money interacts with the primal, unconscious forces that lay deep within us all. When we are young, money has little meaning in our lives, but as we grow older, money comes to represent security, comfort, power and hope, all of which we need to maintain our mental health in an uncertain and, often, hostile world. Our relationship with money is crucial to how we view the world, and it behooves us to examine and understand our motivations.

Money can bring security, for example, but only to a limited degree. A real feeling of security must come from deep inside. Some people, perhaps because of their upbringing, never develop an innate feeling that they belong in the world and that everything is working out just fine. As a result, such people are always worried. Watch them and you will see that, in an attempt to make their world secure, they will put in a great deal of time and effort into accumulating far more money than they actually need.

Similarly, money can bring comfort but, again, only to a limited degree. People who, deep down inside, feel unloved, will spend a lifetime fruitlessly looking for a feeling of comfort. For many of these people, money will take the place of love, and they will force their spouses, their friends, and their relatives to prove their love, over and over, by spending money and giving gifts.

Another reason people lust after money is the power it can bring. For people who thrive on power — and there are many of them — accumulating money is an effective way to increase the control they have over their surroundings and over other people. This is why you will see many rich, powerful people — especially men — spend a lifetime pursuing more and more money. Such people are really pursuing power, and power is addictive.

Finally, many people use money in a different way: to create the illusion of hope. For example, they will surround themselves with distractions and possessions, as if the money they spend can make up for the emptiness they feel when they contemplate their lives. In this way, money can act as a diversion, but it will only work temporarily. Eventually, life has a way of catching up to us all.

Life is not always easy. No matter what we do, there will be pain, disappointment, fear and worry. Eventually, everyone dies, and there is nothing you or anyone else can do about it. This is the human condition, and the biggest challenge we face in life is how to come to terms with our mortality, our weaknesses, and our vulnerabilities.

As you use the Net, you will find that it is a great place to buy and sell. However, it is a sophisticated environment, one that is difficult to master. Money on the Net is completely intangible and transactions are transparent, with no physical context whatsoever.

It is important to remember that, deep inside, we all have weaknesses. No one is completely well adjusted, and, at times, everyone uses money for security, comfort, power and hope. This is normal.

If you take the time to examine your needs and your motivations clearly and honestly, you will be able to protect yourself from the forces that only care about your money. Knowing yourself has always been the best way to ensure that no one can take advantage of your weaknesses, your transitory feelings, and your vulnerabilities.

Money and the Net

In thinking about the Internet and money, it is important to remember that the Net is not an isolated environment. When you buy and sell on the Net, you are participating in the general economy. Too many people have made the mistake of thinking that the Internet is a world unto itself and that, somehow, the regular rules of commerce do not apply.

In the late 1990s, there was a boom in Internet-related stocks, particularly in new enterprises that were set up specifically to do business on the Net, the so-called DOT-COMS. (The name comes from the way in which Internet addresses are pronounced. For example, `harley.com` is pronounced "Harley-dot-com".)

Within a relatively short period of time, the price of Internet stocks increased enormously, and there seemed to be no end in sight. People would buy stock at a highly inflated price and, a short time later, be able to sell the stock to someone else at an even higher price. Many dot-com companies would issue stock for the first time and, within days, watch the price soar, even though the companies weren't making a profit. In fact, virtually all of the dot-coms were *losing* money.

Traditionally, the value of a stock is tied to the company's earning potential. If people feel that a company's profits are going to go up, they will bid up the price of the stock. Conversely, if people feel that a company's profits are going to go down, they will sell their shares and the stock price will fall. In the late 1990s, Internet stocks were different. In spite of the fact that very few dot-coms were profitable, their stocks kept going up and up with no end in sight.

This phenomenon is not new, especially to veteran watchers of the stock market. From time to time, a particular type of stock becomes fashionable and prices rise unrealistically as investors follow the trend and jump in blindly in search of easy money. When this happens, the herd mentality creates a bubble. However, the bubble is based solely on speculation and, eventually, it bursts.

It happened in the late 1960s, when the so-called "conglomerates" were, for a time, the darlings of Wall Street. A few years later, in the early 1970s, another bubble formed and burst, based on a group of well-known stocks called the "nifty fifty". And now, in the late 1990s, it was happening again with Internet stocks.

The Internet bubble grew for several reasons. First, there was greed, always an important factor in the stock market. Second, there was a fundamental misunderstanding of Internet technology and how it affects business. (I discussed this topic in Chapter 1.) Finally, there was the widely accepted belief that the Internet had changed the rules of the game. People talked about the "New Economy", one in which the dot-coms would be able to create massive amounts of wealth in ways that traditional companies could not. This idea, of course, was wrong. Any company, even a dot-com, must show a profit to be considered valuable, and, in the long run, the price of a company's stock will come to reflect the company's profitability: no exceptions.

Eventually, of course, the party was over. At the beginning of 2001, the once high-flying Internet stocks began to plunge sharply and, within a few months the bubble burst, resulting in billions of dollars of losses.

Interesting enough, the Internet *does* have a profound effect on the economy. However, it is not the magic force that would create a New Economy, the one the speculators loved to fantasize about. Rather, the Internet affects the economy in a way that is more subtle but much more enduring.

In order to explain what I mean, I need to digress for a moment to talk about a strange sounding idea, the "velocity" of money.

Let's say you have a dollar bill in your hand. Suppose you go to the grocery store and use that dollar to buy something. What happens to the actual dollar? The store will give it out in change to someone else, who will use it to buy something from a different store. That store will then give the same dollar to another person who will go to a third store, and so on. Over time, the same dollar bill can be used over and over and over.

The same is true for any type of money, even money that is stored electronically in a computer. Over time, all money — coin, paper or electronic — is used and reused.

From our discussion earlier in the chapter, you know that the size of the money supply is crucial to the economy of that country, because money greases the wheels of commerce. If there is not enough money, commerce will slow down. If this happens for too long, there may be a recession. If there is too much money, prices will rise, which may cause inflation. This is why central banks, such as the U.S. Federal Reserve, work so hard to manipulate the money supply on a day-to-day basis.

Thus, if the economy is to be healthy, it needs just the right amount of money. However, when you consider what the right amount should be, you must remember that most of the money in circulation will be reused a number of times. For example, let's say that, in a particular year, the U.S. economy has $9 trillion worth of transactions. However, during that year, on the average, each dollar is used 9 times. This means that the actual amount of money that is needed is really only $1 trillion.

In order to talk about this idea, economists use the term VELOCITY OF MONEY to represent the average number of times a single dollar will be used in the course of a year. In our example, the velocity of money has a value of 9. (In practice, no one knows the actual velocity of money. It's really just an idea used by economists.)

There are two important ways in which the Internet affects buying and selling. First, the Net helps companies and individuals expand their markets. Because of the Net, people are buying and selling more than they would otherwise. Second, the Net makes it easier and faster for the buyer to pay the seller. In these ways, the Net serves to increase the velocity of money, which has the effect of increasing the financial well-being of our society.

Here is why.

In a general sense, the health of the economy is directly related to the amount of business transacted. The more production, buying and selling, the healthier the economy, and the happier we all are as a society.

Economists estimate the amount of business transacted in a particular country by asking the question, "How much money is spent on goods and services in that country over the course of a year?" We call this value the Gross Domestic Product or GDP of that country. Here are several examples showing the 2000 GDP expressed in U.S. dollars for four parts of the world:

United States:	$10,227,000,000,000	(about $10.2 trillion)
European Union:	$9,887,000,000,000	(about $9.9 trillion)
United Kingdom:	$1,657,000,000,000	(about $1.7 trillion}
Canada:	$703,910,000,000	(about $704 billion)

Economists talk a lot about the GDP because it is the most comprehensive measure of how much a country produces in a year. One of the aims of both politicians and central bankers is to raise the GDP of their country as much as possible without causing inflation. In fact, it is an article of faith among politicians that:

High GDP + Low Inflation → Reelection

and among central bankers that:

High GDP + Low Inflation → They can relax for the weekend

One way in which the GDP can be understood is by looking at how much money changes hands during the course of a year. By definition, this value is equal to the total amount of money in the economy multiplied by the average number of times each dollar is used in a year. In other words:

Money spent =

(Total number of dollars) ×

(Average number of times a dollar is used in 1 year)

To express this idea more simply, we can use M to represent the money supply and V to represent the velocity of money:

Money spent $= M \times V$

If we assume that the GDP is equal to the total money spent in a year (a fair enough assumption for our purposes), we get:

GDP $= M \times V$

Since the GDP is related to our economic happiness as a society, we can write:

Economic Happiness $= M \times V$ (as long as inflation is low)

Thus, by increasing the velocity of money, the Internet raises the level of economic happiness of our society as a whole. Or, in plain English, the Internet allows us to be more productive without having to raise the money supply, which would increase the risk of inflation.

The Internet Factor

Money is enormously important to us, as individuals and as a society. When the economy is healthy and stable, we are happy. When the economy is depressed, we all have problems.

In this chapter, we have talked a lot about money and its history. We have also discussed what money means to us personally, and how it is affected by the Internet. To conclude the discussion, I am going to tie everything together by summarizing the factors that have the most important, long-term effects on our economy and our financial well-being. As you look at these lists, notice that the good factors (peace, global trade, democracy, and so on), are all enhanced by the Internet, and the bad factors, (war, economic isolation, and so on) are mitigated by the Internet.

The Internet does not exist in isolation. It has a continuing and ever-increasing influence on our lives and, as such it is an integral part of our world.

Factors that Encourage a Stable, Healthy Economy

Peace

Global Trade

Democracy

Freedom of information

Central Banking

Politicians who think in the long term

Sophisticated computer technology

The Internet

Factors that Work Against a Stable, Healthy Economy

War

Economic Isolation

Totalitarian Regimes

Corruption

Cultural Isolation

Politicians who respond to short-term pressures

13

Protecting Your Money: Shopping and Selling Without Fear

When you buy something at a store, you have a measure of protection. On the Net, you are on your own, and you need to look out for yourself.

Protecting Your Money: Shopping and Selling Without Fear

Two True Stories

Kelly was shopping at a second-hand store when she spied an interesting looking plate on sale for $1. The plate had pictures and information commemorating the 125th anniversary (1848–1973) of the founding of the small town of Lodi (population 2,882) in Columbia County, Wisconsin.

Kelly, who is knowledgeable about genealogy, realized that the plate had significant genealogical value. For example, there were several surnames listed, which would be valuable to people who were researching their family history. Kelly likes to buy and sell on the Net, so she bought the plate, took it home, and put it up for sale at an online auction.

The auction ran for a week and, during that time, Kelly publicized the sale. First, she found as many email addresses as she could for businesses in the Lodi area and sent them a short note. In the note, she described the commemorative plate and announced that it was for sale at an Internet auction.

Kelly then did a bit of research and found six genealogy mailing lists to which she thought it would be appropriate to send her notice. Five of the lists were devoted to surnames that were listed on the plate; the other list was for Columbia County, Wisconsin. She then joined the mailing lists and asked each of the list coordinators if it would be all right to send her ad to the entire list. Once she received permission, Kelly emailed the ad to all six lists.

Kelly's advertising paid off. Several people started to bid on the plate and, eventually, it sold for $56. Interestingly enough, the fellow who bought the plate had never participated in an online auction. He had to learn how to do it just to bid on this particular item.

"I've been buying and selling things most of my adult life," said Kelly. "In this case, I was so happy to find the perfect home for an obscure piece of merchandise. Without the Net, there would have been no way for me to find a buyer for this item, let alone someone who was happy to pay $56 for a plate that cost me $1."

Lydia's situation was different: she, her brother and her sister were preparing to buy a car for her parents, and she wanted the best price she could get without having to haggle with a lot of salesmen. To start, she used the Internet to find information about the type of car she wanted. She decided on the exact model and options, and then (also on the Net) found out the dealers' invoice price.

To start the buying process, Lydia visited the Web site for the car company, and found the email addresses of all the dealers within a 50-mile radius. There were nine such dealers. She then sent a mass mailing to all nine dealers. In the message she told them three things:

- "I am serious about buying a car. If the price is right, I will be making the purchase within a week."
- "Here is the car I want. I have been informed that the following features are standard for this model. Can you please confirm that this is correct?"
- "What is the best price you can give me? I want the total price, including all charges — tax, license, everything — out the door."

Eventually, by sending email back and forth, Lydia was able to negotiate a great price from a dealer near her parents' home. Each time she got an offer, she would email it to all the other dealers, inviting them to beat the price. When the electronic dust had settled, Lydia was able to buy the car for a base price that was $300 below the dealer's nominal invoice cost.

Obviously, the dealer found some way to make money on the deal. (Car dealers don't sell cars at a loss.) The important point, however, is that the price was a good one, and Lydia was able to negotiate everything without ever having to step into a dealership. "Believe me," she said, "I hate shopping but, in this case, the entire process was fast and easy. I could not be this hard-nosed in person, but on the Internet, it was quite simple to be direct and ruthless."

How the Net Affects Buying and Selling

The stories of Kelly and Lydia show how the Internet changes the process of buying and selling. As you can see, the Net acts as a conduit of information and, by doing so, it affects commerce in four different, but related, ways.

First, the Web enables you to browse a large variety of sites and look at many different items quickly. For example, if you are looking for a particular type of shoe, it is much faster to look at a number of shoe-related Web sites than it is to drive all over town from one store to another. Moreover, for many types of items, you are likely to find a larger variety on the Net than in a store.

Second, the Internet allows you to search for specific items, ones that might be impossible to find at a regular store, for example, the 1969 version of the Truly Scrumptious doll from *Chitty Chitty Bang Bang*, or a rare printing of an old Freddy the Pig book.

Third, if it is necessary for you to negotiate a transaction with another person, you can discuss the details via email. You will find that using email for such discussions will often make buying and selling easier than negotiating in person. In the previous section, for instance, I described how Lydia used email to negotiate a price for a new car. This saved her from having to visit various car dealerships in person. It also enabled her to be tougher and more assertive than she would have been in person.

Finally, the Net makes it easy for you to pay for a purchase, either by credit card or by using an online payment service (which we will discuss later in the chapter).

By facilitating the buying and selling process in these ways, the Internet has had a significant effect on the world of commerce. Store owners, for example, are able to expand their reach by using the Web, and entrepreneurs are able to start new, entirely Web-based businesses. Large companies use their Web sites in the same way as they use mail-order catalogs. However, a Web site can offer more flexibility and efficiency than an actual catalog, which must be printed, mailed and delivered.

The Net makes it possible for deals to take place that would otherwise never happen. For example, Kelly, whom I mentioned in the previous section, is interested in certain photos of Native Americans. While browsing on the Net one day, she once found a collection of postcards that showed people from one of the tribes in which she is interested. Without the Net, it would have taken her years to accumulate the same photos one at a time. Instead, she was able to buy the entire collection at a reasonable price.

There are many stories like this. Every day, many people around the world use the Net to sell items, often one-of-a-kind items, that would otherwise never even be put up for sale. This is especially true on the online auction sites, which we will discuss later in the chapter.

As a result, the Net affects prices in two important ways. First, some types of items are rare in part of the world but common in another area. The Internet tends to smooth out the marketplace for such merchandise, increasing the price of items that would otherwise sit on a shelf for months.

Similarly, when the price of an item is artificially high, due to a scarcity in a particular part of the world, the Net can even out the prices. For example, I have a friend who, several years ago, paid $50 to buy a particular type of frying pan in her local area. Today, the exact same pan sells on the Net for $15.

Because the Net makes markets efficient and payments quick and easy, it acts to increase the flow of money in the economy. As I explained in Chapter 12, when more transactions take place, the "velocity" of money increases, which, indirectly, expands the economy by raising the GDP (Gross Domestic Product). In terms of the entire global economy, the amount of money that changes hands on the Net is still small. However, it is not hard to see that, one day, the Internet is going to have a significant effect on the GDP of the world.

What Is It Like to Buy Something on the Net?

There are two common ways to buy something on the Internet. You can buy something at a Web site for a fixed price, or you can bid on an item at an online auction. (We'll discuss auctions in detail later in the chapter.)

Using the Web to buy something is straightforward and, even if you have never done it before, you'll catch on quickly. In many ways, buying on the Web is a lot like buying over the phone. The biggest difference is that, instead of talking to a person, you place your order by filling out a form on a Web site. The form is then processed by a program that runs on the Web server.

On the Web, the details may vary a bit from site to site, but the general procedures follow the same pattern:

1. **Choose what you want.**

2. **Give your name, address and credit card number.**

3. **Wait for the item to be shipped to you.**

As you shop, you choose one item after another. To keep track of your choices, the Web server maintains a list called a SHOPPING BASKET or SHOPPING CART. You can look at this list and make changes at any time. Once you have finished making your selections, you click on a button to go to a special CHECKOUT Web page, where you arrange to pay for whatever is in your shopping basket.

Interestingly enough, in many cases, your shopping basket does not reside on the remote Web server. The list is actually stored on *your* computer in the form of cookies. (A cookie is information that a Web server stores in a special folder on your computer. See Chapter 4.) For this reason, if you choose to block all cookies, you may have trouble buying from certain Web sites.

To make the checkout process simpler, some Web sites allow you (or even require you) to REGISTER, by specifying various information, which the company retains in its database. Each time you visit the Web site, you log in by specifying your user name and password, and the Web server retrieves your data.

Quick diversion: The need for shopping baskets is the most common example that Microsoft and other companies give for why a cookie system is necessary. The example, of course, is real. You do need cookies — or something like them — in order to enable a Web server to store a list of shopping choices on your computer. However, if you take the trouble to look at all the cookies that such Web servers actually put on your computer, you will see that they are far more than necessary.

The extra cookies are put there to track your movements and target you for as much marketing as possible. The plain truth is, although shopping baskets are necessary, they are often used as a convenient excuse to deflect criticism of how often companies use cookies to invade your privacy. For a more detailed discussion of these issues, see Chapter 4.

How to Protect Your Privacy When You Buy Online

Companies require you to register on their Web sites for two reasons. First, once you register, it is easier for you to make purchases, because you don't have to type in the same information each time (name, address, credit card number, and so on). Second — and this is far more important — companies want you to register because they can use the information to make money by invading your privacy.

This is not a new idea. Whenever you order something over the phone, the person taking your order will put the information in the company's database. The company will then send you more catalogs, sell your name and address to mailing lists, sell your phone number to telemarketers, and so on.

What I want you to appreciate is that the exact same type of thing is done whenever you buy something on the Web. For example, many companies will track what you do on their Web sites, and then use automated tools to analyze your patterns. They will put this data together, along with the information you provided when you registered, and use it to target you more effectively. In addition, they will sell this information, as well as the data describing your purchases and activities, to other companies.

Many Web sites have a privacy policy that explains what they plan to do with the information they gather about you. Privacy policies, however, are bogus; don't even waste your time reading them. As I discussed in Chapter 7, such policies are not enforceable, and — no matter how much a company may deny it — they can and will change the policy whenever they want and, when they do, there is nothing you can do about it. (See Chapter 7 for more details.)

If you care about your privacy, the following guidelines will help you:

1. Don't register on a Web site unless it is the only way you can get what you want.

2. When you do register, specify as little information as possible, especially personal information.

Many Web sites are designed to force you to reveal personal information and preferences in order to register. In such cases, it is perfectly acceptable to lie. For example, you can lie about your income, your hobbies, and your preferences. You can also make up a fake phone number, fax number, and so on.

3. Don't ever use your permanent email address to register on a Web site.

If you use your permanent address to register at Web sites, you will end up receiving so much spam that you will need to change your address. Either make up a fake address or, if the registration process requires a real address, use a disposable one. (See Chapter 8 for a discussion of disposable email addresses.)

4. When you register, look for a way to specify that you do not want to receive spam.

Some companies will allow you to opt out of junk mail. However, they may design the registration page so that, by default, you are giving them permission to send you spam. It is up to you to read carefully and find the places where you can express your preferences. You can then make sure that everything is set the way *you* want it. For example, you may have to turn off various check boxes that are turned on by default.

Why It Is Okay to Specify Fake Information

As a general rule, it is bad to be dishonest. Normally, if you allow yourself to tell lies — even small lies for the best of reasons — you open the door to a lot of trouble. However, when it comes to registering on a Web site, the normal rules do not hold. Here is why.

Many companies design their Web sites to force you to divulge information that is none of their business. They do so, not to provide you with better service, but to make as much money as possible from your personal data. Moreover, as we have discussed, no matter what promises a company may make, you cannot count on them to keep your information confidential.

Consider a similar situation at a regular store. Some retail chains have a policy that requires their salespeople to ask each customer for his or her name, address, and phone number every time a sale is made. If you agree to furnish this information, the salesperson will type it into a computer system connected to a company-wide database. The company will then send you junk mail and, possibly, sell the information to other companies. Of course, you can always refuse to give out any personal information.

When you fill out a registration form on a Web site, however, you don't have that option. Many Web sites are deliberately designed to reject your data if you omit certain information, such as an email address or home phone number. In such cases, it is fine for you to lie when you fill out the registration form. Indeed, if you do not want to give the company your real address or phone number, you have no alternative but to make up fake ones.

At times like this, it is certainly convenient to lie, but is it morally acceptable? To put this question in perspective, let me remind you of our discussion in Chapter 2, in which I explained that companies, by their nature, will always put their own interests ahead of the needs of individuals (including their own employees).

In Chapter 6, I showed you why, when it comes to furthering their own interests, companies have much more power than do individuals. Thus, if you care about your privacy, it is up to you to look after yourself. The companies you deal with are certainly not

"At times like this, it is certainly convenient to lie, but is it morally acceptable?"

going to care. What's more, they will often do whatever they can to make it as difficult and inconvenient as possible for you to put your interest above theirs.

Here is an example to show you what I mean. The following notice is from the Web site of C2IT, an Internet payment service operated by the Citibank company. (We will talk about such services later in the chapter.) I took this information from the C2IT registration page. It appears just below the form in which Citibank asks you to specify your name, email address, postal address, phone number, date of birth and social security number.

```
Marketing Offers:

c2it may send you marketing offers by e-mail. If
you do not want to receive such marketing offers,
please write to c2it, P.O. Box 6274, Sioux Falls,
SD 57117 and include your name, address, social
security number and tell us you don't want offers
by e-mail.
```

As this example shows, when a company asks for information from you, they are concerned only with their own interests. Citibank is not unique. No company will ever care about you as an individual or about your privacy. On the Net, you are on your own, and you must look out for your own interests. That is why, when you fill out a registration form on a Web site, it is morally acceptable to enter fake information to protect your privacy.

Is It Safe to Buy Online?

Just about anything that can be sold is available somewhere on the Net. You can buy all types of consumer goods, such as clothing, books, CDs, computers and cameras, as well as more intangible items such as airline tickets, computer software and club memberships.

Regardless of what you buy, there needs to be a way for you to pay for it. Most methods of payment on the Net require you to specify some type of financial information: your name, your address, and the number of a credit card, debit card, or bank account. Since you want to keep such information private, it makes sense to ask the question, "Is it safe to buy something on the Net?" After all, if a malevolent person were to find out your credit card number, he could cause you a lot of problems.

In general, it is safe to buy online, so don't worry about it. Although there are risks, most of them come from fraud and poor customer service, and if you take certain precautions — which I will talk about in a moment — you will be okay. First, however, I want to give you a categorical answer to one of the most common questions people have when they start to buy over the Net: "Do I need to worry that someone might intercept my credit card number as it is sent from my computer to a Web site?"

Although it is possible for someone to tap into your Internet connection, the chances of this happening are remote, so don't worry about it. (Later in the chapter, I'll tell you what you *should* worry about.)

In Chapter 1, I explained that when information is sent over the Internet, the information is repackaged as data packets, which are sent from one computer to another. When the packets arrive at the destination, they are reassembled into the original information. Thus, if a thief wanted to steal your credit card number, he would have to intercept the packets going in and out of your computer, assemble them properly, and recreate the original data. He would then have to determine that you were sending a credit card number to a remote Web site, and extract the number, the expiration date, and your name. If he somehow managed to do all of this, he could, in principle, buy something using your credit card.

Such a scenario is theoretically possible. However, as I mentioned, the risk of it happening to you is so low that you don't need to worry about it. It takes a lot of effort, knowledge and equipment to steal individual credit card numbers as they travel across the Net. Credit card thieves have much easier ways to get such information. For example, they can bribe a waiter or a salesclerk, steal a purse, or look for discarded credit card slips in the trash container behind a store.

If you are scared to use your credit card on the Net, it is most likely because you are not used to the idea, so think about it this way. You have probably, at one time or another, ordered merchandise over the telephone. During the conversation, you would have had to tell the salesperson your credit card number. In theory, someone could tap the phone line, record the conversation, and listen to it carefully to find out your number. Although this is possible, it is so unlikely that you don't spend time worrying about it. Once you get used to buying online, you won't worry about that either.

Most Web sites that sell merchandise use a facility called a SECURE SERVER, a system in which your browser cooperates with a remote Web server to encrypt the data that goes in and out of your computer. Here is how it works.

Say you are buying something from a Web site. You have just filled out a form with your name, a credit card number, the expiration date of the credit card, and your address. When you click the button to transmit the form to the remote server, your browser will encrypt the data before it is sent out. At the other end, the Web server decrypts the data and recreates the original information. If a thief were to intercept the data packets, it wouldn't do him any good, because the information inside the packets would look like gibberish and he would have no way to decrypt it.

How do you tell if you are visiting a Web site that uses a secure server system? Look at the bottom of your browser window. If you see a small picture of a locked padlock, it means that all the information sent between your browser and the server is encrypted.

Actually, the whole thing doesn't matter because, realistically, no one is going to intercept your data. Like many other overly complex systems, the idea of secure servers was developed to solve a psychological problem, not a technical one.

In 1996, when the Web was just starting to become popular, various companies were eager to use the Net to make money. However, at the time, the technology was still new to the general public, and many people were reluctant to send credit card information over their Internet connection.

The companies that had the most to gain were the ones that sold the software and hardware necessary for online commerce: the browser companies (Microsoft and Netscape), the software companies, and the communication companies. Working together with the credit card organizations, these companies created the secure server system and spent a lot of money publicizing it. Their goal was to convince people that now that the Internet was secure, all Joe and Jane Consumer had to do was look for the tiny padlock at the bottom of their browser window and then spend, spend, spend.

Will a Hacker Get Your Credit Card Number?

In Chapter 11, I talked about hackers, people who devote a great deal of time to nerd-like activities. I explained that, although most hackers are socially useful people (for example, Bill Gates), a relatively small number of them are troublemakers.

From time to time, you will read or hear a news story about how a hacker has broken into a computer system and caused trouble. When you hear such stories, it is only natural to wonder whether or not your financial information is safe on a remote Web server. After all, if a hacker breaks into a server where your credit card number is stored, might he not be able to get your number and use it to make fraudulent purchases?

The possibility is a real one. Hackers do break into computers and they do steal credit card numbers. For example, in March 2001, Amazon.com admitted that hackers had broken into a number of computers at their Bibliofind subsidiary. It took Amazon four months to discover and fix the breach, by which time the hackers had accessed a massive amount of customer data, including credit card information.

Although such activities exist and are becoming more common, relatively few people actually have had their credit card information stolen on the Net and then used for purchases. Most companies, especially the larger ones, go to a lot of trouble to ensure that their computer systems are secure. If you think about it, you will realize that a lot of companies already have your credit card information in their computers, and you don't stay up at night worrying about it. Although it is possible that a hacker might break into a computer somewhere, steal your credit card number, and then use it to buy something, the chances are remote, so don't worry about it. Keeping customer data safe is something that falls under the heading of things-that-someone-else-has-to-worry-about.

This doesn't mean to say that I don't want you to worry when you buy stuff on the Net. I do. Worry is good for you (if you do it right).

I just want to make sure that you worry about the problems that are most likely to hurt you: the ones that you can prevent with proper precautions. What I don't want is for you to be scared silly worrying about problems that are beyond your control and will probably never affect you anyway.

What You Really Need to Worry About

Most of the time, you can buy online with no problems at all. However, there are two pitfalls that can cause you trouble: fraud and bad customer service. In the following sections, we'll talk about these problems and how to avoid them.

There are a huge number of people buying and selling on the Net, so it's no surprise that there is a significant amount of fraud. Commerce and fraud seem to go together like cats and tuna, and as the amount of buying and selling on the Net increases, so does the fraud.

Internet fraud has become such a big problem that, in May 2000, two United States law enforcement agencies established the Internet Fraud Complaint Center (IFCC). (The two agencies were the Federal Bureau of Investigation [FBI], and the lesser-known National White Collar Crime Center [NW3C].)

According to statistics gathered by the IFCC, the most important types of fraud on the Net are:

- Fraud associated with online auctions (65%).
  (We'll talk about this problem later in the chapter.)
- Non-delivered merchandise (22%).
  You pay for something, but you never receive it.
- Credit card fraud (5%).
  You give someone your credit card information, and they use it to bill you for spurious charges.

Here is the address of the IFCC, if you want more information. In particular, they have a form you can fill out if you have been defrauded. They won't be able to help you directly, but they may be able to put you in touch with the appropriate authorities.

```
http://www.ifccfbi.gov/
```

Internet Resources: Internet Fraud Complaint Center

The IFCC does not police the Internet (no one does). Their job is to gather statistics and help the FBI track down criminals. It is up to you to make sure you don't lose your money in the first place. If you have been cheated, you are on your own. No one will be able to get your money back: not the IFCC, not the Better Business Bureau, not your local police.

Aside from outright fraud, you need to be careful for another reason: bad customer service. Although most companies are honest, many of them are not able — or not willing — to give you, the customer, the service you deserve. Every company is happy to place your order and take your money, but some of them are not as cooperative when it comes to helping you afterwards. The main reason is that companies tend to keep their workforce to a minimum in order to hold down costs, so, when you have a problem, there are very few people to help you.

This phenomenon is not new. If you are old enough, you will remember a time in which stores were filled with salespeople who understood their merchandise, and who were eager to help you find what you needed. Now, you are on your own. Large stores have been transformed into self-serve warehouses, where a relatively small number of employees spend their time maintaining the store, stocking the shelves, and running the computerized cash registers. In such an environment, there is very little customer service. Even when you do find someone to help you, it is often the case that he or she will know very little about the products in the store.

The same thing happens over the telephone. Each time you call a company for help, you are forced to maneuver through a phone menu. If you insist on speaking to a real person, you will be put on hold and, as you are waiting, you will hear a message:

"All of our customer service associates are busy helping other customers. Because of the unexpectedly high demand, it may take a few minutes for us to answer your call. However, your business is important to us, so please wait, and your call will be answered in the order it was received by the first available associate."

A more honest message would be:

"We make money selling to a large number of people. As an individual, you are not really all that important to us. That is why we are

never going to spend enough money to answer our phone calls right away: it's just not worth it. So wait your turn and, eventually, you will get to speak to an underpaid, undertrained phone operator with an attitude problem. In the meantime, we hope you enjoy listening to the snappy music... By the way, don't hang up, or you'll have to start all over again."

Companies operate like this for several reasons. First, labor costs, including employee benefits, are expensive, and it is unrealistic in today's economic environment to expect a company to spend enough money to handle every customer's needs promptly.

Second, as a company grows larger and larger, individual customers become less and less important. Economically, it makes sense for a company to spend a small amount of money on advertising to create the *illusion* of personalized customer service. It does not, however, make economic sense to spend the exorbitant amount of money it would take to actually provide such service.

Internet-based companies have two other important problems to consider. As I explained in Chapter 1, the normal economies of scale do not apply to Internet companies, because as they grow larger, they become *less* efficient. This means that, as an Internet company begins to sell more and more, it actually has less and less money to spend on customer service. That is why so many Internet companies want you to use their Web sites, rather than calling the company, when you have a problem. A small Internet company can afford to pay someone to talk to you in person. A large Internet company can't.

The other problem faced by Internet companies is the one I discussed in Chapter 12. Because of the stock market bubble of the late 1990s, Internet companies are under enormous pressure to generate real profits quickly. For this reason, they must concentrate on increasing revenues and cutting costs in any way they can, even if it means trading long-term gains for short-term profit.

When you buy something at a store, you have a measure of protection against fraud and poor customer service. You can examine the item before you buy it, and you know the exact price when you pay for it. Many stores have liberal return polices. If you are dissatisfied with an item, you can take it back and get an instant replacement or a refund. If you need help, you can usually find someone to assist you (if you are willing to look long enough).

On the Internet, this is not the case. When you buy from a Web site, there are no built-in protections. You can't look at the merchandise before you buy it, you can't be sure what has been charged until you see your credit card statement, and there is no one to help you in person. On the Net, you are on your own, and you need to look out for yourself. Here is how to do it.

6 Ways to Protect Yourself When You Buy Online

The very best way to protect yourself when you buy online is to take the time, *before you buy*, to make sure that everything looks okay. There are a lot of sleazy vendors on the Web. Moreover, as I explained in the last section, even legitimate vendors often don't have the resources or the inclination to give you much customer service. To help you protect yourself, here are 6 points to consider when you buy on the Web.

1. Don't choose a vendor just because they offer the cheapest price.

There is an old saying, "If it looks too good to be true, it probably is." Although this saying is good advice for any type of business dealing, it is especially important on the Net. Anyone can create a Web site and put anything they want on it. If you get tricked, there is no one to help you.

As an example, let's say you are looking for a particular camera and you find six or seven Web sites that sell it for $400. You should definitely be suspicious of a site that purports to sell the same camera for $250. In such cases, the explanation will be one of the following:

- The company is lying about the price.
- The company will never send the item.

- The company doesn't really sell the item at that price. When you try to buy it, they will try to switch you to a more expensive item. (This is an old trick called "bait and switch".)
- The item you see on the Web site is not really what you think it is.
- The item is an old, discontinued model.
- The company will charge you extra for parts and accessories that should be included for free.
- The item is a gray market item. (See #3 below.)

2. Check out the shipping and handling charges.

When you compare costs, be sure to add in all the extra costs, such as shipping and handling. I'll discuss this topic in detail later in the chapter.

3. Confirm that the warranty is valid.

When you buy something that should have a warranty, be sure to check the details. Don't assume anything. Here is why.

Many manufacturers sell certain products in foreign markets for lower prices than they charge for the same products domestically. For example, a particular camera that sells for $800 in the United States might be sold in an overseas country for $500. The manufacturer will set up its distribution network to prevent the foreign-bound merchandise from ending up back in the home country.

From time to time, a distributor will find a way to divert these cheaper items into the home country (in this case, the U.S.), and sell them at a substantial discount. This type of selling is called the GRAY MARKET.

As you can imagine, manufacturers do not like the gray market. Still, they can't always prevent this type of thing from happening, and a lot of gray market merchandise finds its way into the hands of vendors who sell it on the Internet.

In one way, gray market items are a good deal, because you can save a lot of money. However, you have to be careful. If the product was not meant to be sold in your country, the manufacturer will probably not honor the warranty. They may also refuse to give you technical support, rebates and documentation.

So take care. Before you buy anything that looks as if it is a bit too inexpensive, make sure that it comes with the warranty you think you will need.

4. Find out the return policy.

Before you buy anything, find out what happens if you have to return it. Most Internet vendors will allow you to return an item as long as you meet certain conditions:

- You must return the item within a certain amount of time, usually 30 days.
- With certain types of merchandise, such as music CDs or computer software, you cannot return an item if you have opened it. (Otherwise, people could just make copies, and then ask for their money back.) However, if the item was defective in some way, most vendors will replace it, even if it has been opened.
- You must return the item in good condition, with the original packing and documentation.

Reading the return policy before you buy is a good idea, because sending an item back is not always as smooth as you might think. First, unless the product is defective, you will probably have to pay for your own shipping. Second, most companies will only refund the base price, not the shipping and handling charges. Third, you may have to wait several weeks for the refund to be credited to your account. Finally, it is up to you to get the item back to the vendor. If it gets lost along the way, there is nothing they can do to help you.

5. Don't believe everything you read.

There is a lot of misinformation on the Net, especially in areas where vendors can profit from people's misunderstandings. Before you pay for anything, ask yourself, "Does it seem likely that what I am paying for will actually work?"

For example, there is a huge problem on the Net with medical fraud. A great many Web sites make false or unsubstantiated health claims in order to sell medical remedies. You should be especially suspicious about any treatment for cancer, AIDS, arthritis, heart disease, diabetes or multiple sclerosis. You should be equally suspicious of anything that promises to help you lose weight.

To make it easier for you to detect medical fraud, compare the claims you see on a Web site with the following list. If anything matches, you should be careful, as you are probably being scammed. (This list is based on a warning issued by the United States Federal Trade Commission.) Be suspicious when:

- A Web site promises a fast, efficient cure for many different types of medical conditions.
- A product is described as a scientific breakthrough or a miraculous cure with a secret ingredient, possibly an ancient remedy.
- The text of the Web site is written in impressive-sounding medical terminology.

Scam artists often use technical terms to hide the fact that there is no scientific basis for what they are promoting.

- The Web site claims that the government, the medical profession, the drug companies, and research scientists are conspiring to keep this product from the general public.
- There are undocumented case histories that claim amazing results.

If you or a loved one is suffering and you see such claims, you are going to want to believe it. It's only human, so be careful.

- The product is available from only one source.

6. Check your credit card statement carefully.

The best way to make sure that no one puts spurious charges on your credit card is to check your statement carefully. If you do a lot of online shopping, you can use the Web to check your statement. That way, you won't have to wait for it to arrive in the mail.

If you see something wrong on your statement, call your credit card company right away. If a charge is incorrect, the credit card company will put it into "dispute" for free. This means that you don't have to pay until everything is straightened out. Once a charge is put into dispute, call the company that made the mistake and see if you can get them to fix it.

If you live in the United States, here are two important facts you should know:

- If someone uses your credit card without your permission, you are only liable for up to $50 in unauthorized charges.
- A merchant is not allowed to charge your credit card until they have shipped the product.

5 Ways to Evaluate an Online Vendor

If you have never bought anything online, it is important that you take time to investigate before you make your first purchase. Now, I know what you are thinking: "I don't want to spend time checking out every company I buy from. It's too boring and time-consuming. I just want to get online, buy something, and move on."

Okay, I'll compromise. If you see something that costs less than $50, go with your instincts. But if you are thinking about buying a more expensive item — especially a computer or a camera — please listen to me: you need to investigate the company before you spend your money.

Repeat after me:

If I get scammed, no one is going to help me.

Just for fun, say it once more:

If I get scammed, no one is going to help me.

Okay, how do you evaluate a company?

1. Look carefully at the company's Web site.

If the Web site looks sleazy, the company is probably sleazy. Look for:

- Sloppy Web page design.
- Broken links.
- Spelling mistakes (which shows carelessness).
- Outdated information.

These are all tip-offs that this is a company that you should avoid.

2. Make sure you know the company's address and phone number.

Do not buy from a company that does not have a real address and phone number on their Web site. A post office box is not good enough. There must be a street address.

Some companies go to a great deal of trouble to make sure you can't find them. This is a tip-off. If a company's Web site does not have an address and phone number, cross them off your list, no matter how badly you may want what they are selling.

3. Call the company's phone number.

Before you buy anything expensive, call the company. If you have a choice, call a customer service number, not a sales number.

See how long it takes to get a real person on the phone. When you get someone, ask a few questions and see how cooperative they are. At this point, you don't really care about the answers. Your goal is to determine what type of customer service you will get if you buy the product.

If you are buying a computer or another type of electronic device, call the tech support number and ask a technical question. (If you can't think of a question, ask them to explain how to add more memory to the computer.)

I know that taking the time to call a company sounds like a pain, but if they are going to make you wait for a half hour to talk to a tech support person who doesn't know what he is talking about, isn't it better to find it out *before* you make a purchase?

4. Check out the company at an online rating service.

An online rating service is a Web site that has information about various online vendors. Here are the addresses of several such services:

```
http://www.gomez.com/
http://www.forrester.com/ER/PowerRankings/
http://www.bizrate.com/ratings_guide/guide.xpml
```

Internet Resources: Online vendor rating services

These services can be useful, but don't depend on them. First, many companies will not be rated, especially the smaller ones. Second, information is usually slanted in favor of the vendors. If you see negative information about a company, take it as a warning, but if a vendor has a good rating, don't take it as a guarantee. You still need to check things out for yourself.

If you live in the United States, you may have heard of the Better Business Bureau (BBB). Don't waste your time checking with them. Many people believe that the BBB is a consumer-oriented complaint agency. Not true at all. BBB offices are supported by their member companies, not by consumers, and the information they give — even on their Web site — is pretty much useless.

5. Look for a discussion forum in which people discuss online vendors.

There are various Web sites and discussion forums devoted to discussing online vendors. (You will find some of these on the rating service Web sites.) Reading about other people's experiences is a great way to save yourself trouble, especially when you are ordering complicated products that require good customer service.

Shipping and Handling Charges: The Real Truth

I'm going to tell you a secret about the mail order industry, which includes sales from catalogs, TV, telephone and the Internet. A lot of the time, shipping and handling charges are bogus. In fact, within the mail order industry, it is well-known that such charges are used to create the illusion of a lower price in order to fool the customer.

For example, let's say a regular store sells a particular item for $20. On the Web (or on TV, or in a catalog, or over the phone) a mail order company sells the same item for $15 plus $5 shipping and handling. The final price ($20) is the same, but the mail order company can make it look as if they are selling the item for less.

So what is this mysterious shipping and handling cost? The shipping cost is supposed to pay for the merchant to send the item to you. The handling cost is supposed to pay for processing your order. Of course, these are both legitimate expenses but, let's be honest here, every retailer has expenses. A regular store must order merchandise, manage its inventory, pay its rent, and so on. Moreover, all goods must be shipped and handled. These are just the costs of doing business.

In the mail order business, however, it has become customary to treat shipping and handling costs as separate items, and so, because they can get away with it, they do. Your job, then, is to make sure that you add up *all* the costs before you make a purchasing decision.

Here is an example. While I was writing this chapter, I checked the price of a particular Britney Spears CD ("Oops!… I Did It Again") at a number of online Web sites. The list price of this CD is $18.99. As you can see from the following table, the total cost varied from $16.97 to $20.43 (not including sales tax, which may or may not be charged).

Online Stores	Total	Base Price	S&H	% Surcharge
amazon.com	$16.97	$13.99	$2.98	21.3%
hollywood.com	$17.86	$14.87	$2.99	20.2%
cdnow.com	$18.97	$14.99	$3.98	26.6%
barnesandnoble.com	$19.46	$16.48	$2.98	18.1%
borders.com	$20.43	$16.14	$4.29	26.8%

You will notice that both the base price and the shipping and handling charge vary significantly from one site to another. The right-most column shows the shipping and handling charge as a percentage of the base price. For example, at **amazon.com**, the shipping and handling surcharge was 21.3% of the base price. At **borders.com**, it was 26.8%.

The shipping and handling prices I put in the table are the lowest ones. They reflect the cost of shipping a single CD to an address in the U.S. by the least expensive method (regular mail). For faster delivery, or for delivery outside the U.S., you would have to pay significantly more.

To put this in perspective I checked the price of the same CD at two local music stores, Wherehouse and Borders. At both stores, the price was the full list price, $18.99. With tax, the total came to $20.41.

Local Stores	Total	Price	Tax (7.5%)
Borders	$20.41	$18.99	$1.42
Wherehouse	$20.41	$18.99	$1.42

As you can see, it is a good idea to compare prices carefully before you make a purchase over the Net. However, make sure that you compare the *total* cost: the base price + the shipping and handling surcharge + any applicable taxes.

Don't let yourself be fooled. At the **hollywood.com** Web site, for example, there was a notice that said:

Save 22%
CD Price: $14.87
List Price: $18.98
You Save: $4.11

However, when you add in the shipping and handling, the *total* cost — without tax — is actually $17.86, a savings of less than 6%, not 22%.

Unfortunately, online retailers don't make it easy to see the total price while you are shopping. They design their Web sites in such a way that you don't find out the final cost until you are actually paying for the merchandise.

There is a good reason for this. Internet companies, like all companies, must make a profit. However, in many cases they compete against regular stores that sell the same goods for (approximately) the same prices. So, to make their prices look better, the Internet companies use exorbitant shipping and handling costs to sneak under the radar of unsuspecting buyers. In fact, many Internet companies depend on these charges to stay in business.

To be fair, this merchandising technique is not new. Mail order companies have been doing it for years. What is important here is that you are aware of what is happening, so you can protect yourself. There is nothing magic on the Internet that allows vendors to charge less than other retailers. Business is business. Some vendors, like Amazon (in our example) discount heavily. Others, like Borders, charge full price.

How to Find What You Want: Shopping Bots

It's one week before your best friend's birthday, and you want to get her something special. You know what she would like more than anything in the world, but how are you going to find a place to buy a custom Celtic harp? You can search for it on the Net.

Once you get used to shopping online, you'll develop your own list of favorite shopping Web sites: places you'll return to, time and again, like a favorite store. However, there will be times when you don't know where to look for what you want. In such cases, ask yourself, is this a common consumer item, such as a computer, book, CD, camera, toy, DVD, and so on? If so, you can use a general-purpose shopping Web site to find what you need. If you are looking for something more unusual, such as a custom Celtic harp, homemade soap, or a poster of the book "Tintin in America", you can use a search engine. Let's take a moment to talk about each of these services in turn.

There are a number of Web sites, referred to as SHOPPING BOTS, set up to act as general-purpose shopping services. ("Bot" stands for robot.) To use a shopping bot, you tell it what you are looking for. The shopping bot then looks in a database, matches your request, and shows you a list of places to buy what you want. The list will have information, prices and, sometimes, ratings and recommendations. The database consists of information gathered from a particular group of online vendors, so a shopping bot will often be able to show you alternatives you would have trouble finding yourself.

There are many shopping bots on the Web, so to help you, my researchers and I tested a lot of them. Here are the ones we thought were the best:

```
http://www.bizrate.com/
http://www.mysimon.com/
http://www.dealtime.com/
http://www.shopping.com/
http://shopping.yahoo.com/
http://www.roboshopper.com/
http://www.pricegrabber.com/
http://www.pricebee.com/text/
```

Internet Resources: Shopping bots

If you are looking for a book, especially a used or rare one, here is a specialized bot just for finding books:

```
http://www.bookfinder.com/
```

Internet Resources: Shopping bots for books

Shopping bots can be useful, but there are some caveats. First, don't depend on a shopping bot to do all your work for you. You should still follow the guidelines we discussed earlier in the chapter. For example, before you buy something from a particular Web site for the first time, you need to take the time to check out the company. In addition, when you compare prices, be sure to add in all the extra charges, such as shipping and handling.

Second, no shopping bot is completely comprehensive. It is common for a shopping bot to find only one or two different brands. If you are thinking of buying something expensive, use several different shopping bots to get a better comparison. If you are looking for a specific brand, you may be better off using a search engine (see below).

Third, don't depend on the ratings and recommendations. The ratings are often bogus and, in any event, they are mostly meaningless. No one has the time to do a proper evaluation of so many online vendors. Moreover, if you look carefully, you will see that the rating criteria used by most shopping bots is pretty lame. The shopping bot companies can't afford to alienate the online vendors, so you aren't going to see many bad comments.

You should also be suspicious of recommendations offered by a shopping bot. Such recommendations are usually the result of marketing deals in which online vendors pay to have their items displayed prominently. For example, a vendor may pay a shopping bot company to have that vendor's items displayed at the top of the list. The shopping bot company may be getting a kickback (that is, a commission) from certain vendors, but they aren't going to tell you.

How to Find What You Want: Search Engines

Once you learn how to use shopping bots, you will see that they can save you a lot of time. However, if you are looking for a specific item — especially one that is obscure — it is often more useful to look for it using a search engine.

A SEARCH ENGINE is a service that helps you find Web sites. You specify one or more words, called KEYWORDS, and the search engine gives you a list of Web pages related to those words. For example, to find information about me, you would search for:

Harley Hahn

The search engine would then show you a list of Web sites relating to me, ranked from most relevant to least relevant.

In order to provide this service, the search engine company uses a special program that constantly explores the Web. This program accumulates information about individual Web sites and stores it in an enormous database. When you specify a keyword, the search engine looks in the database for Web sites that meet your criteria.

There are a large number of search engines on the Web, so to get you started, here is a short list of the ones I find particularly useful.

```
http://www.yahoo.com/
http://search.msn.com/
http://www.google.com/
http://www.altavista.com/
```

Internet Resources: Search engines

Some search engines organize their information into categories, so you can find what you want by starting with a general idea and narrowing it down. Other search engines are designed to help you find Web pages that contain specific information. My recommendation is to try all of the search engines in this list and see which ones you like best.

If you want to learn how to use search engines well — which is certainly a good idea — I have three recommendations. First, all search engines have a help facility. Once you find a search engine you like, read the help information. I know you probably won't want to take the time to do this, but do it anyway. It will make your searching a lot more effective.

Second, for a good explanation of how to use search engines well, see my book *Harley Hahn's Internet Advisor* (published by Que). Look at the chapter entitled "Finding Stuff on the Net" (published by Osborne McGraw-Hill).

Finally, for a large number of useful resources to help you find what you want on the Net, see another one of my books, *Harley Hahn's Internet Yellow Pages*. Again the section you want is called "Finding Stuff on the Net".

Personal Financial Services

There are any number of financial services available on the Net. In this section, I'm going to describe the most important ones, along with some advice on how to integrate them into your life in a way that works for you.

The most important online personal financial services are:

- **Banking**

You can check the balance of your account, view transactions, transfer money between accounts, and so on. I particularly like this service, as it allows me to balance my checking account every few days, so it never gets out of hand. As a matter of fact, I don't even look at the printed statements that come in the mail. I get all the information I need from the Net.

- **Bill Paying**

You can arrange to pay any bills you want and monitor the transactions. You can pay bills automatically at a preset time, or manually, whenever you decide to make the payment. Bill paying services are useful for making regular payments, such as paying your mortgage, utility bills, car payments and insurance. The money is automatically deducted from your checking account, so you don't have to worry about getting into trouble by forgetting to send in a check. This service is especially useful if you are unable to pay your bills when they are due, for example, if you are traveling on an extended vacation.

- **Credit Card Management**

In the same way that you can check your bank account on the Net, you can also look at your credit card statements. You can look at past statements, as well as new charges and credits. I find this useful when I am expecting a credit, and I want to see whether or not it has arrived. If you prefer to pay bills automatically, you can arrange for your credit card bill to be paid each month from your bank account.

- **Investing**

If you like to fiddle with your investments, you'll love doing it on the Net. You can check the value of your portfolio — the list of your holdings — as often as you want. You can buy and sell many different types of investments: stocks, bonds, mutual funds, options, futures, and so on. You can also do financial research and read the latest business news.

- **Payment Services**

It is possible to use the Net to send a payment to anyone with email. Online payment systems are used widely by people to buy items in online auctions. You can also use them to send someone a gift (of money), pay a debt, and so on. We'll discuss these services in detail later in the chapter.

Several Words to the Wise

When you first start using financial services on the Internet, it is easy to be infatuated with the idea that you can do so much, so quickly, from your home computer. However, before you get in too deeply, I want you to appreciate a few points.

At the end of Chapter 12, we discussed how people become desensitized to money. For example, many people take on a long-term obligation, such as a student loan or mortgage, without really appreciating how much they are borrowing, and how much effort it will take to pay it all back. Similarly, once you get used to using the Net to move money from one place to another, it is easy to forget that the abstract quantities you see on your screen represent real money. This is especially true if you use personal financial software, such as Quicken or Microsoft Money, that is designed to integrate your personal finances with the Net.

Sometimes, manipulating money can be *too* easy, and when this happens, it is smart to slow yourself down deliberately. For example, let's say you establish a system in which a lot of your financial transactions, such as bill paying, are carried out automatically. If your paycheck is late one month, the automatic system will still try to pay the bills according to your schedule, which might deplete your account too quickly, causing an important check to bounce.

One common situation in which people get into trouble is in handling their own investments. As a general rule, the best way to do well in the stock market is to have a good plan and stick to it. Buy wisely, and hold on to your stocks for a long period of time. Investing in stocks for short amounts of time is gambling, and trying to outguess the market is like trying to outguess the roulette wheel. If the financial gods are with you, you may win for a limited time but, in the long run, the odds are against you and you are going to lose.

In the olden days, before it was possible to buy and sell stocks on the Internet, being able to trade too much was not an issue for most people. If you wanted to buy or sell a stock, you needed to do it through a stockbroker and commissions were expensive. Now, however, you can use the Net to trade on your own and the fees are small. As a result, too many people trade too often, which is a guaranteed route to failure.

Moreover, since you can use the Net to check the value of your stocks whenever you want, it's tempting to do so every day, or even more than once a day. Since all stocks — even the ones that do well — have their ups and downs, you will find that checking stock prices daily is one of the fastest and most efficient ways to drive yourself crazy.

Another topic we talked about at the end of Chapter 12 was how money and our attitude towards it insinuates itself into our personal psychology in ways that are difficult to understand. As we discussed, money represents security, comfort, power and hope, all of which we need to maintain our mental health in an uncertain and, often, hostile world. For this reason, we sometimes make financial decisions for emotional reasons, more often, in fact, than we would like to admit.

I need to warn you. Once you start to use your computer and the Net to handle your financial affairs, you are going to become dependent on the system, and you will not be able to go back. This is not necessarily a bad idea, but my advice is to go slowly and do it wisely. At every step along the way, ask yourself, is this something I really need to be doing?

If you are the type of person who likes to tinker, you need to be especially careful. Unless you consciously make an effort to keep your financial life as simple as possible, you will, over time, create a lot of procedures, spreadsheets and habits that are far more complex than you really need. However, because this happens over a long period of time, you will become habituated to it, and you will be utterly convinced that everything you do is necessary to support life.

In the most basic sense, there are really only two things you can do with money. You can spend it, or you can save it. These two possibilities live within all of us, as two opposing forces that must remain in balance. When that balance gets disturbed, as it often does when we are overly emotional, we are likely to make decisions that are not in our own long-term interest: "I deserve a new pair of shoes for all the stress I put up with…"; "Everyone else is making money on Internet stocks. I need to jump in now before it's too late…"

The reason I'm telling you this is because using the Internet to control your finances is not as simple you might think. If you allow yourself to get caught up in an emotional juggernaut — as we all do from time to time — the Net will amplify your thinking. For example, if you like to shop when you feel down, the Internet will make it far too easy to spend more than you can afford. When you shop on the Net, you don't have to get dressed, leave the house, drive to a store, select an item, and make the purchase in person.

In a similar way, as I mentioned, it is easy to get caught up in the habit of buying and selling stocks, and then checking their value many times a day. It is important to realize that, in the short term, the stock market runs on fear and greed, and if you use the Net to trade stocks, you are going to be affected. This is normal, because you are human, but it is not good for you, so it behooves you to do your best to be aware of what is happening. The worst offenders are the type of men who think they are always right. (I'm sure you know someone like this.)

Regardless of whether or not you invest in the stock market, modern financial systems are complicated, and the best way for you to look out for yourself is to follow the timeless rules that have served us well for centuries:

1. Don't spend more than you can afford.

As you make purchases, on and off the Net, keep track of the total, so you don't get surprised at the end of the month. It's not as hard as you might think. All you need to do is (1) keep your checking account balanced, and (2) maintain a running list of your credit card charges. The Net can help you with both these tasks.

2. Borrow money only to purchase something of enduring value.

Borrow money to buy a house, a car, or to pay for your education. Don't borrow money to go on a vacation, buy new clothes, or treat yourself to an expensive dinner.

3. Know yourself well enough so you aren't driven by fear or greed.

The worst financial decisions you are ever going to make in your life will be because of greed. The second worst decisions will be because of fear.

I don't know a magic way to avoid these emotions. However, I can warn you that both fear and greed are contagious, so think carefully before you make any important financial decisions. Before you commit yourself to a significant financial decision, ask yourself if you are being influenced by an outside force, and be honest. As we discussed in Chapter 12, there are a lot of companies — and individuals — in the world who are ready to play on your emotions to get your money. If you are impulsive, you will just play into their hands.

I know that if I say money won't make you happy, I'm telling you something you have heard many times before. But, really, it's true. Money can't make you happy because it can only create the *illusion* of what you need for real happiness.

However, if you still want to be rich, I can show you how to do it wisely. When you get a moment, take a look at the following Web page:

```
http://www.harley.com/get-rich/
```

Internet Resources: How to get rich

Online Payment Services

An ONLINE PAYMENT SERVICE is a facility that allows you to transfer money to anyone who has an email address.

The easiest way to understand this service is to think of it as a special type of bank account that is used only on the Net. To start, you open an account. Once you have an account, you can put money into it and transfer the money to other people. At the same time, other people can transfer money to you.

You can use your account to pay for various items on the Net, as long as the person or company from whom you are buying will accept such payments. For example, you can use a payment service to pay for items you buy at an online auction or at a Web site. You can also use a payment service to send someone a gift (of money) or to pay a debt.

There are a number of different online payment services, and each one has its own rules, although the basic idea is the same. Here is a typical scenario:

1. **You start an account by registering (which is free).**

2. **You put money into the account. You can do this either by sending in a check or by transferring money directly from your bank account.**

3. **Let's say that, one day, you buy something at an online auction. To pay for your purchase, you tell the payment service to send a payment to the seller. They send him an email message telling him that the payment is waiting for him. If he has registered with the same payment service, they will put the money right into his account.**

4. **You can take money out of your account at any time. You can either have the payment service send you a check, or transfer the money directly into your bank account.**

Although the basic idea is simple, there are a *lot* of nuances. For example, some payment services allow you (or require you) to give them information about your bank account and credit card. Once you do, they may use this information to take money when they need it. For example, if you have $100 in your online account, and you try to make a payment of $150, the payment service may, without asking you, take the extra $50 out of your bank account or charge it to your credit card. As you can see, you need to manage your online account carefully.

Most online payment services have fees, and they vary quite a bit from one company to the next. Some companies will let you send money for free, but will charge a fee to receive money. Other companies charge the sender, but not the recipient. Some services charge both parties, and some are completely free.

In addition, most online payment services will allow you to start either a "merchant account" or a "consumer account". Each type of account has its own rules and fees.

Once you get used to an online payment service, you may really enjoy the convenience, especially if you do a lot of buying and selling on the Net and you don't mind paying the fees. In fact, moving money around will be so easy, that you will want all your friends and relatives to do it too. For example, one of my friends is trying to get her boss to pay her in this way. (Hint: The easiest way to encourage someone to start using an online payment service is to send him a small gift of money. In order to retrieve the money, the person will have to learn how to use the system.)

I do want to warn you, however, to be careful. Online payment services have a lot of rules, so before you start moving money around, I recommend that you take the time to read all the help information, especially the fee schedule. You will find there is a fair amount of fine print that can come back to bite you if you don't understand what you are doing.

The online payment services all have arrangements with banks, credit card companies, and other financial institutions. As a result, you will find a variety of financial services integrated into one large system. For example, some online payment services will send you a debit card that you can use in stores and restaurants. When you use the card, the money you spend is taken directly from your online account. As another example, some payment services allow you to earn interest by keeping your balance in a money market account managed by an investment firm.

If you think an online payment service is for you, here are several to investigate:

```
http://www.c2it.com/
http://www.bidpay.com/
http://www.paypal.com/
http://www.moneyzap.com/
http://www.billpoint.com/
http://paydirect.yahoo.com/
```

Internet Resources: Online payment services

What is an Online Auction?

You may or may not have ever been to an auction, but I'm sure you know the general idea. At a particular location, say a store or a warehouse, various items are offered for sale. Before the auction starts, people who are interested in buying are given time to look around and examine the items.

The auction is run by a moderator, called the auctioneer, who offers the items for sale, one at a time. As an item is offered, people bid on it, one after another, raising the price with each bid. The auctioneer calls out the bids so everyone can follow what is happening. For example, the first person may bid $100, another person may bid $105, and a third person may bid $107. The first person may then put in a new bid of $110, and so on.

Eventually, the point is reached where there are no more bids. The auctioneer then declares the person who made the final (and largest) bid the winner. This person then pays for the item, takes it away, and lives happily ever after.

An online auction follows the same basic principle: people bid on items and the highest bid wins. However, because the auction takes place over the Net, it has to be run differently than a live auction.

The biggest difference is that, since there is no auctioneer, the whole thing is run by an automated system. People use the Web to look at a description of the items, and make their bids, and a computer program keeps track of everything. Once the auction is over, the program sends email to the seller and the successful buyer, announcing the final price and other details. The buyer pays the seller, who then sends the item to the buyer.

There are several ways in which a buyer can pay a seller:

- Online payment service
- Credit Card
- Check
- Money Order
- Cash

If the seller is an individual, he probably won't be able to accept a credit card. However, you can pay by credit card by using an online payment service. (See the discussion earlier in the chapter.)

Since people can't bid in person, online auctions continue for a fixed length of time, for example, 7 days. At the end of this time, the highest bid wins. At any time during the auction, you can check to see the current value of the highest bid.

The most fascinating thing about online auctions is the sheer variety of items for sale. Literally, anything that can be sold legally will eventually find its way onto an online auction: books, collectibles (especially coins), computers, electronics, clothing, jewelry, sporting goods, toys, and on and on. (A friend of mine used an online auction to buy a BMW.) The Internet is now the home of the world's largest, continuous markets where you will find a huge number of useful items and rare bargains, among lots and lots of junk. You'll find:

- People selling the contents of their attic.
- Entrepreneurs who set up home businesses specializing in a particular type of collectible, such as movie stills or ancient coins.
- Scavengers who scour garage sales and surplus stores looking for discounted items to sell on the Net.

You'll also find a great many specialized auctions that allow businesses to sell commercial goods and services to one another. For example, one Web site allows companies to describe print jobs and have various printers bid for the business. Another site specializes in selling large, expensive industrial equipment. A third site offers commercial real estate to the highest bidder.

The following resources will help you get started with online auctions. First, here are some auctions sites on which people sell all types of general merchandise:

```
http://www.ebay.com/
http://www.321gone.com/
http://auctions.msn.com/
http://auctions.yahoo.com/
http://auctions.amazon.com/
```

Internet Resources: Online auctions

There are many different online auction sites on the Net. The following resources will help you explore a variety of auctions you might otherwise never find:

```
http://www.100topauctionsites.com/
http://www.internetauctionlist.com/
```

Internet Resources: Lists of online auctions

When it comes to finding what you want, the following auction bots (auction-oriented search engines) can help you find specific items:

```
http://www.auctionpatrol.com/
http://srch.auctionwatch.com/usearch/
```

Internet Resources: Auction-oriented search engines

Finally, just for fun, when you need a break, take a look at some of the strange stuff that people are selling online:

```
http://www.whowouldbuythat.com/
```

Internet Resources: Strange stuff sold at online auctions

Getting Started With Auctions

If you think you would like to buy or sell at an online auction, I have a three-part plan to help you get started smoothly. First, you and I will go over the basic terminology, and I will give you some general advice. Then, you should visit one of the popular auction sites and read the online help information. Finally, I will recommend that you begin your auction career by buying something small to see how the system works.

Okay, let's get started with the basic terminology. An AUCTION is a sale in which merchandise is sold to the highest bidder. The person or company that puts an item up for sale is called the SELLER. The person who makes the highest bid, and ends up purchasing the item, is called the BUYER.

As a general rule, the auction company makes its money by charging the seller a fee. There is no fee to buy. In most cases, the seller's fee will consist of a small listing fee (to create the auction) and a commission, which is based on the final sale price. A typical commission might be 5% for inexpensive items, with a lower percentage for higher-priced items. As an example, an item that sells for $20 might cost the seller $1.30 in fees: 30 cents for the listing fee and $1.00 (5%) for the commission.

The most common type of auction is the one I described in the previous section. An item is put up for sale for a particular length of time and, at the end of that time, the highest bid wins. This type of auction is referred to by a variety of names: a regular auction, a standard auction, an English auction, or a Yankee auction.

A DUTCH AUCTION allows a buyer to sell a number of identical items at the same time. For instance, an electronics dealer might auction off 100 identical hard disk drives. People bid for the items in the regular manner, and when the auction is over, more than one person wins. However, the buyers all pay the same price: the lowest winning bid.

Here is an example. A seller offers 5 identical Monica Lewinski dolls for sale. 10 different people bid, and when the auction closes, the final bids are as follows: $15, $15, $13, $10, $9, $7, $7, $7, $3, $2. In this case, the top-five bidders — $15, $15, $13, $10, $9 — all win, but they each pay only $9, which is the lowest winning bid. During a Dutch auction, people are allowed to bid on more than one of the items. For example, if you were a serious collector, you might offer to buy all 5 Monica Lewinski dolls.

As a general rule, the bidding and selling process is binding on the participants. If you bid on something and you win, you are legally obliged to buy the item at the price you bid. Similarly, if you offer something for sale, you are legally obliged to sell it to the highest bidder. There are, however, ways in which the seller or the buyer can affect the bidding process.

First, before an auction starts, the seller can set a MINIMUM BID. This is the price at which the bidding must start. If no one meets this price, the auction will not take place. Second, the seller may set a RESERVE PRICE, which is not disclosed to the bidders. The reserve price is the lowest price the seller will accept. At the end of the auction, if the reserve price is not met, the seller has the option of canceling the sale.

Here is an example. A book dealer wants to sell a first edition of a Freddy the Pig book. The seller specifies a minimum bid of $30 and a reserve price of $45. Nothing will happen until someone offers at least $30. In this case, let's say that the bidding starts at $32 and finishes at $42. Since the reserve price ($45) was not met, the seller has the option of selling the book at $42 or canceling the sale. However, the bidders do not know this until the auction has ended.

The third way in which the bidding can be affected is if the seller specifies a price at which he is willing to sell the item immediately. For example, let's say that an aging baby boomer wants to sell a valuable Rocky and Bullwinkle lamp in order to raise money for a hair transplant. He sets a minimum bid of $150. Of course, he wants the bidding to go as high as possible, but when he sets up the auction, he specifies an immediate sale price of $250. The bidders will see this and, at any time, anyone can preempt the bidding and end the auction by offering the full $250.

The idea that anyone can end the option by paying a specified price is not a traditional auction practice. For this reason, the preemptive price is known by a variety of different names:

- Buy Now Price (321Gone)
- Take-It Price (Amazon)
- Buy It Now Price (Ebay)
- Threshold Price (MSN)
- Buy Price (Yahoo)

When you attend a live auction, you are able to watch the action in person. On the Net, an auction can move slowly and last for days, which can make it difficult to follow what is happening.

To help buyers, auction sites have a facility called PROXY BIDDING. Proxy bidding allows you to specify the most you are willing to pay for a particular item. If someone outbids you, the system will automatically send in a new bid on your behalf. (Of course, your maximum price is kept secret from the other bidders.)

The amount by which a bid is raised automatically is called the INCREMENT. The increment is fixed by the system depending on the current price of the item. For example, for prices between $5 and $25, the increment might be 50 cents. For prices between $25 and $100, the increment might be $1.00.

Here is an example. One day you are browsing an auction site and you see a wonderful item for sale, a life-size map of the Grand Canyon. The current bid is $25 and the auction is scheduled to run for another three days. Since a life-size map of the Grand Canyon would be the purchase of a lifetime, you bid $27 and specify that you are willing to go as high as $100.

Over the next three days, every time someone outbids you, the proxy bidding system will raise that bid by $1. In this way, you don't have to drive yourself crazy watching the auction day and night. Instead, you can spend your time looking for a place to store the map in case you win.

How to Protect Yourself Against Auction Fraud

Earlier in the chapter, we discussed an organization called the Internet Fraud Complaint Center (IFCC). By far, the most common complaint received by the IFCC is auction fraud. Here are some interesting observations from one of the IFCC reports:

- Over 90% of Internet fraud originates from within the United States, in particular, from California, Florida, New York and Texas.
- All types of people from around the world are victims of fraud. However, the typical victim who files a report is an American male in his mid-30s who has lost over $200 in a fraudulent online auction transaction.

To protect yourself from fraud, don't rush in and start bidding as soon as you see something you like. Remember, if you bid on an item, you are legally obliged to buy it (if you win the auction), so, before you place your bid, take a few minutes to check out both the seller and the item.

To evaluate a seller, look at the advertisement for clues that the seller might be dishonest (big promises, excessive superlatives) or incompetent (poor spelling, punctuation mistakes). If the seller won't take the time to proofread his work, he probably won't care about helping you if something goes wrong. The best people to deal with are the ones who take pride in their reputation and in how they present their wares.

One of the nice things about online auctions is that everyone who buys and sells is allowed to make comments about everyone else. Before you bid on an item offered by a seller you have never dealt with, look at the comments previous buyers have made about that seller. In many cases, you will find that the seller is an entrepreneur who uses online auctions to sell many, many items, which means there will be lots of buyers' comments.

Most sellers get good comments most of the time (which is important when you are going to send money to a perfect stranger). Every now and then, however, you will find a seller who is a real troublemaker. The tip-off is to look for people who are difficult to deal with when something goes wrong.

For example, I was looking at the comments for one particular seller and I noticed that, although most of the buyers were happy with him, there were a fair number of complaints. Evidently, this person was arrogant and condescending and, when something went wrong, he would always blame the buyer.

When I looked at the description of the item he had for sale, I saw that he listed a great many rules that he wanted people to follow if they were to do business with him. Whenever there was a problem, this fellow would blow it off by saying that the buyer didn't follow the rules that *he* (the seller) had made up.

Most of the time, everything works well and it doesn't really matter whether or not a seller cares about his customers. However, when there is a problem — such as a package going astray, or an item arriving in damaged condition — it is very important that the seller be reasonable.

Some people, like the person I mentioned above, live in their own world, and they expect everyone else to follow their rules. (I'm sure you know people like this.) If you buy from such a person and something goes wrong, you are going to have trouble. Moreover, you will be frustrated because most of the other buyers' comments will be good — because most of the time nothing goes wrong — and no one else will listen to your complaint.

One clue to look for is to notice the manner in which a seller formats the description of the sale item. When a seller prepares his description, it is like creating a mini Web page. On the Web, there are various ways to present information so that it is readable and easy to understand. When someone ignores these customs, it tells you that he lives in his own world and likes to do things his own way. Such a person, for example, might use large typefaces, many colors, excessive repetition, and a lot of capital letters and exclamation points. If you pay attention and use common sense, it's not hard to recognize the crazy people. As a general rule, if a person's Web page looks weird, the person is weird.

When you buy online, you can't examine the item beforehand, so make sure you understand what is really being sold. In some cases, an excessively low price can tip you off that something is fishy. For example, I have a friend who once bought what she thought was an antique postcard. When the package arrived, she found that what she had really bought was a *copy* of an old postcard. In retrospect, she realized that she should have suspected something because the price was too low.

In this respect, buying at an online auction is the same as buying anywhere: If something seems too good to be true, it probably is.

One way to protect yourself is to ask the question, "Does the seller seem to know what he is talking about?" For example, some sellers sell things they don't own. Their plan is to get your money, and then use it to buy the item in order to resell it to you. If the description of the item is incomplete or the picture doesn't look right, it may be that the seller doesn't really own what he is selling. To check this, send email to the seller and ask a few specific questions. If he can't (or won't) answer your questions, be suspicious.

A lot of people buy discounted items for the sole purpose of reselling them on the Net. As a result, there is a lot of junk for sale, so don't be surprised when something that sells for a low price turns out to be worth next to nothing.

If you are buying a piece of equipment, look for words such as "untested" or "as is". This often means, "It doesn't work and I know it." This is especially important with electronics, such as computers and computer parts. For example, some companies will sell defective hard disks to people who then resell them on the Net. Such people will offer an extra low price and describe the disks as being "untested, as is". By the time *you* find out the disk doesn't work, it's too late.

If you are buying an expensive item, there are special precautions you can take. First, don't buy the item unless the buyer is willing to use an ESCROW SERVICE. This is a third party that acts as a go-between for the transaction. Here is a typical scenario showing how it works.

You have just won an auction for an expensive item. To pay for it, you send your money to the escrow company. When the money arrives, the company verifies that the payment is okay, and informs the seller. The seller then sends the item to you. Once the item arrives, you check it over and make sure everything is okay. You then notify the escrow company, who releases the money (minus a fee) to the seller. A typical escrow fee is 1%–5% of the price.

Many sellers don't like to use escrow services because of the cost — which comes out of the sale price — and the extra hassle. For example, the seller must pay the shipping charges up front and then wait to get his money. Still, escrow services provide valuable protection for a buyer. If you are dealing with a seller who you suspect is a troublemaker — or if you are going to buy an expensive item and you need to be extra careful — it is in your interest to insist on an escrow service. If the seller refuses, let the deal go. (A seller doesn't need an escrow service because, normally, he wouldn't send out an item until he had received the money.)

I have a friend who is very experienced with online auctions. However, one time, he needed to buy a computer and he was in a hurry. He sent money to someone he had never dealt with before, and the person never sent the computer. My friend tried his best to get back his money, but, at the end of a long story, there was nothing he could do about it.

To help you, here are the addresses of some escrow services:

```
http://www.escrow.com/
http://www.tradenable.com/
http://www.escrowguardian.com/
http://www.frugalescrow.com/secure.html
```

Internet Resources: Online escrow services

At the beginning of the chapter, I told you about Kelly who likes to buy and sell using online auctions. Kelly has a lot of experience, and here is what she has to say about auction buying:

"Most of the sellers I've dealt with are honest, reliable people. There have only been a few instances where something has gone wrong and, usually, it's because of an unexpected event or human error. Almost every time something has gone wrong, the seller has made it right. The couple of times I've felt cheated, I realized later, when I had time to give it some thought, that I should have seen the signs and not bid on the item."

Now you know what the signs are.

10 Tips to Make Online Auctions Work for You

Buying and selling at auctions can be a lot of fun and financially rewarding, if you do it right. So to ensure that everything remains hunky-dory, here are 10 tips to help you make the most of your online mercantile experiences.

1. Read all the help information.

Buying something at an online auction is conceptually simple. You register with the service, you find an item you like, and you bid on it. If you win, you contact the seller and make arrangements to pay.

However, there are a lot of nuances. The online auction world is extremely complex, with a multitude of rules and customs, and each auction site is different. Before you start, you need to take the time to read *all* the rules, especially if you want to be a seller.

If you are one of these people who never reads the manual and plunges right in, listen to me on this one. Online auctions are a lot more complex than they look, so, for once, read the help information before you start.

2. Start small.

For your first few purchases, buy something inexpensive that you understand completely, like a CD. Whatever you do, don't start your auction career by buying a computer.

3. Before you bid, check out the seller.

4. Watch out for fraud.

Protect yourself by using the precautions we discussed in the previous section.

5. Don't get carried away.

Make a budget and, no matter what happens, stick to it. In the short run, you may miss out on something you wanted, but in the long run, you'll save a lot of money. Don't allow yourself to become emotionally attached to a particular item. Many people do and end up paying more at an auction than they would at a regular store.

It's a lot easier than you might think to get caught up in the action, especially when the price goes up a little at a time. One minute you are congratulating yourself on how well you have been following your budget. The next minute you find yourself bidding big bucks for something you wouldn't bend down to pick up off the street. This is especially true if you are an over-achieving, goal-oriented type of person, who doesn't like to lose.

Don't let greed or fear dominate your common sense. Once the price of an item grows beyond your budget, back off gracefully. Unless the item is one of a kind, there will be another one.

6. For expensive items, use an escrow service.

If you ever pay money to someone who doesn't send the item, there isn't much you can do about it. Before you spend a lot of money on something, make sure that the buyer will agree to use an escrow service.

7. Do your research before you bid.

Before you start bidding, make sure that the item for sale will do what you want it to do. For example, if you want to add a rewritable CD drive to your computer, make sure the model you select will work with your computer. Don't assume that this is the case, and don't assume that you can depend on the seller for technical support. That's not his business. When you buy something at an auction, you are on your own.

8. Check availability and prices.

Don't assume that just because you buy something at an auction, you are getting a good price or that the item is rare. A lot of items sold at auctions can be bought at a regular store. When you buy from a store, you have someone to talk to if you have a problem. If you see something being sold in large numbers at a Dutch auction, you can probably find the same item for yourself by searching on the Net or by making a few phone calls.

9. Sell items that are easy for you to handle.

If you want to be a seller, look for items that are easy to ship without damage, such as:

- Anything made of paper, cloth or plastic
- Vintage textiles
- Collectibles, especially coins
- Limited edition books
- Non-fragile antiques

Avoid items that are heavy, breakable or difficult to ship.

10. If you plan to sell a lot, use an auction helper service.

There are services that offer automated tools to help you manage your auctions. Using such tools, you can:

- Establish and monitor many auctions at the same time.
- Create attractive ads.
- Maintain a gallery of photos.
- Handle auction-related email correspondence.
- Organize payments and shipping.
- Manage your inventory.
- Keep long-term data about your customers.
- Analyze your sales.

If you think an auction helper service might be of use to you, here are two to check out:

```
http://www.andale.com/
http://www.auctionwatch.com/my/acp/
```

Internet Resources: Auction helper services

The Most Important Hint of All

If you don't need it, don't buy it.

.

14

Protecting Your Family: Sex, Relationships and Children

If you want to be happy, you must, in the long run, stay focused on your priorities, and not allow yourself to be driven by transient emotions and passions.

Protecting Your Family: Sex, Relationships and Children

Understanding Our Basic Nature

One of the themes of this book is that, if we are to have long-term happiness, we must live according to our nature, not only our individual nature, but the common biological nature we share with all human beings. This is why I have spent so much time talking about psychology and philosophy. The Net is a huge force that is new to our culture, and to truly understand how to use it well, we need to understand ourselves. Let's take a simple example.

We all need food, vitamins and minerals. These needs are part of our biological nature, something we can't change. It is possible to stay alive without meeting these needs completely, but we won't thrive. For example, we can get by on junk food, which may lack certain vitamins and minerals. However, if we make an effort to eat high-quality nutritious food, we will, in the long run, be a lot healthier, not because there is something inherently good or evil about junk food but because, by eating well, we are better able to meet our long-term biological needs.

On an emotional level, we have needs that go far beyond food, vitamins and minerals. We have a need to be close to other people and, if we are going to thrive emotionally, we must have ongoing, satisfying relationships. Although our relationships may not be perfect every moment of every day, we must, in the long run, be able to meet these emotional needs if we want to thrive. Doing so, however, can be difficult, because it requires the cooperation of other people, who will cooperate only if we are able to meet *their* needs at the same time.

Within this context, the Internet is important because it is capable of bringing great emotional forces into our relationships, forces which we were not designed to bear. These forces are strong and, if we are not careful, they may cause significant damage to the emotional fabric of our lives and to the lives of our loved ones.

Does this mean that we should avoid having relationships that depend on the Net? In some cases, yes. Certain activities are nothing more than a breeding ground for unhappiness and only serve to distract us from what is really important in our lives. In other cases, Net-based relationships are just fine, as long as we ensure that our Internet activities don't interfere with other, more important aspects of our lives.

It is another theme of this book that we cannot separate the Internet from the rest of life. If we are to learn how to use the Net well, we must first make an effort to understand how it interacts with other parts of our world. In this way, and only in this way, will we be able to ensure that the way in which we use the Net is in harmony with our *real* needs. If we do not develop a healthy respect for our inborn limitations, we run the risk of letting our transient feelings lead us into types of behavior that, in the long run, will be bad for us.

The Internet brings brand new questions into our lives, questions that human beings have never before had to answer. Is it okay for a husband or a wife to develop an extramarital emotional relationship over the Net? How much privacy should spouses have when they use the Net? How much privacy should we allow our children? Should teenagers be allowed to spend hours and hours chatting with their friends on the Net? Is it good or bad to use the Net to look at erotic pictures?

These are important questions, and yet, they are without precedent. For example, we know that it is damaging to a marriage when one of the partners has an affair, but can the same be said for an extramarital relationship that is confined to email and instant messaging?

Most of us would not mind our spouse talking privately on the phone from time to time, but how do we feel about private email correspondence? Similarly, we may be comfortable with our children having a certain degree of privacy in their lives, but should we extend that same privilege to their Internet activities?

In this chapter, I am going to deal head-on with these questions. My goal is to do so in such a way as to give you the framework to understand what is happening when such issues arise in your life, and to help you develop the wisdom to make the decisions that are right for *you*.

However, before we can talk about specific issues, I'd like to spend some time discussing the emotional nature of human beings. So to begin, let me pose the basic question: What are relationships, and why are they so important to us?

Evolution and Natural Selection

A RELATIONSHIP is a strong, ongoing emotional connection to another person. To understand why relationships are so important to us, we need to spend a few minutes talking about evolution and the nature of human beings. As you will see, our need for relationships is the result of innate traits that developed over hundreds of millions of years. Once you understand this need, it will be easier for you to make intelligent decisions about the ways in which the Internet should be a social force in your life.

EVOLUTION is the process whereby, over a very long period of time, life forms change significantly. On our planet, the evolution of animals occurred over the last 600 billion years, and was driven by two fundamental principles:

- *Survival*: The need for life to survive under changing environmental conditions.

- *Complexity*: A tendency for new life forms to be more complex than their ancestors.

The key to understanding evolution is to realize that, over long periods of time (millions of years), the environment of our planet changes significantly. The reason life is able to survive is that it is able to adapt to new environments, because of a process called NATURAL SELECTION.

Natural selection occurs because there is such a large variety of life forms on the planet. When conditions change in an important way — say, a global warming or an ice age — many animals will not be able to survive. However, because there are so many different types of animals, some will be able to live in the new environment. These animals, the ones that survive, pass on their characteristics to future generations and, in this way, life adapts to a changing environment.

Thus, if life is to survive, there must be a way to guarantee that, at any time, every region of the planet is inhabited by a large variety of life forms. In that way, when conditions change (as they inevitably must over millions of years), some plants and animals will be sure to survive. If this were not the case, a severe change in the climate, or the atmosphere or the ocean, might wipe out all the animals in an entire region. Indeed, a large enough change might destroy all life on the planet.

The reason this does not happen is that Nature provides enough variety for natural selection to function. Thus, no matter what changes occur, some life forms are able to survive and pass on their characteristics.

Every type of animal has specific characteristics that allow it to survive in the environment in which it lives. For example, fish have streamlined bodies, which make it easy for them to swim. They also have gills that allow them to breathe under water. Rabbits, on the other hand, have completely different bodies, not at all suitable for living in the water. They do, however, have lungs that make it possible to breathe air, paws that enable them to dig holes, and strong leg muscles that allow them to run away from predators.

A crucial part of the system is that each animal is able to pass on its characteristics to its offspring. This is why, for example, all baby fish are natural water animals, while all baby rabbits are natural land animals. A baby fish grows according to a fish blueprint inherited from its parents, while a baby rabbit grows according to a rabbit blueprint inherited from its parents.

So what is this blueprint? It is a set of instructions, encoded onto a long strand of a substance called deoxyribonucleic acid or DNA. In fact, as unbelievable as it sounds, every cell in an animal's body contains a long strand of DNA that encodes the entire blueprint for making that particular animal. As the animal grows and changes, it is the DNA within the cells that controls the characteristics of the animal. In other words, the reason fish are different from rabbits is that fish DNA contains the blueprints for a fish, and rabbit DNA contains the blueprints for a rabbit.

The Secret of Life

The role of DNA is crucial to evolution. We can understand why if we take a look at how primitive one-celled animals reproduce. These tiny animals, the smallest in the world, reproduce according to a relatively simple two-step process:

1. **A cell makes a copy of its DNA.**

2. **The cell then splits in two, at which time each of the cells gets its own copy of the DNA.**

In this way, a single one-celled animal can, under favorable conditions, reproduce over and over. Eventually, there might be billions of one-celled animals, all of which are descended, indirectly, from the original cell.

In principle, the DNA in these billion of cells should be identical. In practice, however, it is not, and herein lies the secret of life. (You didn't think you would get through this book without learning the secret of life, did you?)

Although most of the cells *are* identical, there are, from time to time, very small changes in the DNA of some of the cells. Since DNA contains the blueprint of the organism, any change in the DNA of a cell would make the cell just a tiny bit different from its neighbors, and this difference will be passed on every time the cell (and its descendants) reproduce. It is these changes — as small and as infrequent as they are — that, over a long period of time, give rise to enough variety to allow life to evolve.

These small changes — the aberrations on which all of life is based — are called MUTATIONS. Mutations are created whenever the DNA within a particular cell is changed, a spontaneous process that can occur in several different ways.

First, DNA can be damaged by cosmic rays, tiny bundles of energy that are emitted by the sun. Most cosmic rays are stopped by the atmosphere, but a small number of them get through to the surface of the planet and, when a cosmic ray hits a cell, the collision can cause the cell's DNA to be damaged.

Another way in which DNA can be modified is by extreme environmental conditions. For example, a cell that is floating around in the ocean might encounter a caustic chemical substance that damages the cell's DNA.

Finally, the process by which a cell makes a copy of its DNA (just before it splits into two) is not perfect. Each piece of DNA consists of a great many small components, all of which must be copied exactly. In the same way that you or I might make a mistake if we had to copy, say, a large list of numbers, the DNA replication mechanism also makes mistakes from time to time. When this happens, the DNA in one of the new cells is slightly different from the DNA in the original cell.

Since DNA is so important, mutations are serious. In fact, in most cases, a mutation will cause enough damage to kill the cell. However, in a small number of cases, the mutation is not fatal, and the cell will live. Once this happens, the cell's DNA is changed permanently and, the next time it reproduces, it will pass on the modified DNA to the new cells (which will then pass it on to their descendants).

Most of the time, one-celled animals will manage to reproduce exactly without a mutation. It is only in a very small percentage of cases that a cell will reproduce with a non-fatal mutation. However, because these tiny organisms are able to reproduce so quickly and in such large numbers, there are, overall, enough non-fatal mutations to support natural selection and, hence, evolution.

Sexual and Asexual Reproduction

In the previous section, I said that evolution is driven by two forces: the need for life to survive and the development of complex life forms.

In our discussion of one-celled animals, we saw that enough spontaneous mutations occur to create the variety necessary to support natural selection: the system that allows animals to adapt to changing environmental conditions. However, the story is different when we consider more complex animals, which reproduce much more slowly.

Let us compare, for example, a one-celled animal to a cat or a human being. A cell can reproduce quickly, often within a matter of hours. (In fact, under optimal conditions, certain one-celled organisms can reproduce in as little as 15 minutes.) Once a cell reproduces, the new cells are themselves able to reproduce immediately. Thus, within a relatively short time (say, a month) a single cell is able to give rise to millions of new cells.

A newborn cat, on the other hand, will have to live at least 8 months before it can reproduce. When it does, the whole process takes 8–10 weeks (from conception to delivery) and will produce, on the average, only 4–6 kittens. These kittens will then have to wait at least 8 months before they can have babies of their own. Under optimal conditions, a healthy cat can have, at most, three litters (about 15 kittens) a year.

Human beings are even slower. On the average, a young woman is not able to reproduce until she is 12 or 13 years old and, once she becomes pregnant, it takes about 40 weeks for the baby to be born. Moreover, as far as total number of babies, even an exceptionally strong, healthy woman would be hard pressed to have more than 10 children in a lifetime.

As I explained, one-celled animals survive because they are small enough and simple enough to reproduce in very large numbers. Although only a tiny percentage of these new organisms will produce useful mutations, their sheer numbers ensure that there will always be enough variety to guarantee survival.

With more complex animals, the story is different. To be sure, the same natural forces that cause mutations in one-celled animals affect the cells of a larger animal. However, because larger animals are not able to reproduce quickly, they cannot depend upon the size of their population to generate enough variety to meet the demands of natural selection. Another mechanism is needed.

As I explained earlier, one-celled animals use a relatively simple system to create DNA for a new cell: they simply make a copy of the old DNA. Larger animals use a different system, one in which two different strands of DNA are combined into one. Here is how the system works.

Two different animals, called PARENTS, each donate a single copy of their DNA. During the reproductive process, these two strands of DNA are combined and spliced in a way that an entirely new strand is created. Some of the DNA is taken from one parent, some is taken from the other parent, and all the extra is thrown away.

The brand new strand of DNA — which is different from the DNA of either parent — is then used as the blueprint of the new animal (that is, the CHILD). Because each child's DNA is significantly different from its parents, enough variety is created to support natural selection.

The process by which two strands of parental DNA are combined into a completely new strand of DNA is called SEXUAL REPRODUCTION. The simpler system, used by one-celled animals, in which a single strand of DNA is merely copied, is called ASEXUAL REPRODUCTION.

Why We Need Relationships

Complex animals have a lot of advantages over one-celled animals. They have more control over their environment and, generally, have much richer life experiences. For example, very few amoebas get to vacation in the Bahamas or buy clothes at Victoria's Secret. However, these advantages come at a cost.

First, as we have seen, complex animals must use sexual reproduction instead of the much-simpler asexual reproduction. Second, complex animals take a long time to grow and mature, and during that time, they require a great deal of outside help.

For example, when a one-cell animal splits into two, each new cell is already fully mature and ready to survive on its own. A human being, on the other hand, must live within its mother's womb for 40 weeks before it can even be born. Moreover, after the birth, it takes years before a young human being is able to survive on its own.

The question arises, then, since baby humans need to be nurtured for an extended period of time, who should provide this service? Evolution has supplied the answer. Since human beings must use sexual reproduction, and each new child requires two parents to act as DNA donors, why not use one or both parents to take care of the baby after it is born?

Indeed, this is the case for all mammals. With the ones that develop quickly, such as cats, the babies are taken care of by a single parent (the mother). In such cases, because the children develop quickly, it is not a big deal that the other parent (the father) is not around to help with the babies. A kitten, for example, will start to crawl when it is only a week old and, by three weeks, it is walking like a pro. By eight weeks, the kitten will be weaned from its mother and ready to live on its own.

Human beings, of course, are a lot more complex than cats and, as a result, they develop much more slowly. For example, it takes a full year for a human baby to learn how to walk, and many more years until it is ready to survive on its own. As such, human babies, unlike cats and other mammals, need more than one parent to take care of them.

Although this sounds like a good system, it is not as straightforward as it seems. For one thing, after conception, the baby won't come along for 40 weeks. During that time, there is nothing for the father to do, so why should he bother to stick around? However, if the father doesn't stay with the mother, what will happen when the baby is born?

The mother, of course, will be there, but nurturing a baby is a full-time job; so who is going to gather the food, find shelter, and protect the children against predators? Clearly, if a human baby needs to survive, it needs the help of more than one adult.

The solution is to make sure that a strong emotional bond exists between the mother and the father. In this way, the father will want to stay with the mother long enough to help take care of the baby. Similarly, once the baby is born, it is important that there be strong bonds between the parents and the child in order to ensure that the family will stay intact until the child is old enough to survive on its own.

For this reason, evolution has provided human beings with the drive to form three very strong emotional bonds: with a mate, with our parents, and with our children. This is why we have (and need) relationships: it is the only way Nature can guarantee that a life form as complex as a baby human being will be able to survive long enough to take care of itself.

Why We Need Friends and Family

So far, I have explained why we have a biological need to form three types of relationships: with a mate, with our parents, and with our children. These relationships create the strong emotional bonds necessary to keep the family intact long enough to care for the children.

But there is more. Although it is crucial that babies have parents, there is also a significant advantage in having more than two adults living together. When there are more people to share the work, it is easier to gather food, find shelter, and protect the children from predators. For this reason, human beings — like many other mammals — are born with an instinct to live in groups in which the members of the group help one another survive.

For this reason, we are all born with a biological need to form emotional bonds with other people. These bonds are not as strong as the ones between mates, or between parents and children, but they are important. In primitive cultures, the need for such bonding manifests itself in the form of extended families and tribes. In more modern cultures, this same need is the one that causes us to form friendships.

Thus, there are two conditions we must meet if we are to be happy. First, we must be able to sustain very strong relationships with a mate and with our children (at least while they are young). Second, we must maintain less strong, but significant, relationships with a group of friends.

At the beginning of the chapter, I put forth the idea that it is impossible to find real happiness unless we live according to our nature. As such, we will never be completely content if we cannot form the relationships we need to satisfy our inborn emotional needs.

Although it is possible to live without a mate, without strong bonds to our children, and without friends, it doesn't mean we should do so. To thrive as human beings, we need these relationships — not because they are good or desirable for some cosmic reason — but because we have evolved in such a way that these needs are part of our biology.

Consider this analogy. When pilots first learn how to fly in a fog, they are taught to depend upon their instruments and not their senses. This is because human beings were not designed to fly and, under certain conditions, our senses can be fooled. At times,

"When we use the Net, we expose ourselves to a great many social forces. In such situations, our emotions and our gut feelings can lead us astray."

what a pilot thinks is real may not be real at all and, when you are flying in a fog, such mistakes can be deadly.

Similarly, when we use the Net, we expose ourselves to a great many social forces (and temptations) that our minds were just not designed to handle. In such situations, our emotions and our gut feelings can lead us astray.

(Such pitfalls are not confined to the Net. Be truthful now. How many times have you deluded yourself into believing that you absolutely must have something-or-other in order to be happy, only to find that, later, you didn't really need it at all?)

In this chapter, we are going to deal with the important social problems you and your family will encounter on the Net. As we discuss these issues, I have a goal. I want you to learn that, when you are looking for answers to difficult social questions, you must set aside your momentary feelings. Instead, slow down, take a deep breath, and ask yourself, "Which course of action will be of the most benefit to the relationships I have with my mate, my children and my friends?"

What Really Happens When You Talk on the Net

In Chapter 8, we discussed a biological urge that we all have, the need to communicate with other people. At the time, I explained why communication over the Internet is not as satisfying as talking to someone in person. Let's have a quick recap.

It took a long time (hundreds of thousands of years) for modern man to evolve from his ancestors. During that time, there was no such thing as communication at a distance. There were no telephones or telegraphs; no postal mail, no email, no chat rooms, and no instant messaging. If two people wanted to communicate, they had to do so in person. For this reason, our communication skills evolved to work in a physical, face-to-face environment. Without this environment, our brains have trouble processing information, and we make assumptions without realizing what is happening.

When you talk with someone in person, you notice a lot more than just his words. You hear the nuances of his voice, such as the tone, the volume and the rhythm. You also see his body language and his gestures. You might touch the other person and he might touch you. These cues create a great deal of context that is missing when you talk on the Internet. On the Net, all you have are the words you see on your screen.

Because of the environment in which we evolved, our minds are not capable of making adequate judgments about people unless we are able to interact with them in person. This is not to say that, one day, there might not be robots that are designed to have meaningful relationships over the Net. The point is that human beings are not designed that way, and the Net is never going to be able to satisfy our biological need to connect to other people. There is just too much missing.

There are many different ways you can talk to someone on the Net: chat rooms, instant messaging, IRC, email, discussion forums, Usenet groups, muds, and so on. You can even use voice (if you have a microphone) and video (if you have a webcam). However, no matter how you do it, talking over the Internet will never be a real face-to-face conversation. For this reason, you must remember that, when you talk on the Net, a lot of the context you need will be missing, and your mind will make up the missing details automatically. That is normal. This is how human minds work.

When you talk to a stranger in a chat room, for example, your subconscious mind is constantly analyzing the conversation, looking for nuances and patterns that might allow it to create a context that has meaning to you. However, because there is no physical context, as soon as your mind notices a pattern, you will unconsciously begin to make assumptions.

For instance, if, in some way, the stranger in a chat room were to remind you of your best friend in college, you would, unconsciously begin to think of that stranger as having your friend's characteristics. Similarly, if you are having a pleasant (or enticing!) online conversation with a stranger of the opposite sex, you will imagine that person as being attractive, even though you have no idea what he or she really looks like.

All of this happens unconsciously, which is normal. However, if you are going to keep yourself out of trouble, you need to be aware of what is going on.

What trouble might you get into talking to people on the Net? The biggest single problem caused by talking on the Net is *hurt feelings caused by unrealistic expectations*. When you talk with someone online, it is far too easy to become too intimate, too quickly. Jumping in too fast and too deeply on the Net is not just a romantic problem. It happens a great deal in many different situations, especially in online support groups.

Why? There are two reasons.

First, as we have discussed, when you talk on the Net, your unconscious mind creates an artificial context that makes you feel comfortable far sooner than you really should.

Second, on the Net, you are safely anonymous, which makes you feel far more secure than you would be in person. As a result, you find yourself feeling comfortable with strangers on the Net a lot faster than you do in person.

This is especially true when you are looking for a romantic relationship. Even though your feelings may seem as if they are real, your interpretation of what is happening is skewed. Chatting online promotes intimacy, and it is easy to find yourself becoming personal far too quickly. Indeed, it is common for people to suddenly find themselves in the middle of an online romantic relationship they had no intention of starting.

If this happens to you, force yourself to become aware of what you are really doing. Stop, take a deep breath, and tell yourself that you are not really opening your heart to the eternal soul mate with whom you are fated to find eternal bliss. You are sitting in front of a computer, typing messages to someone you don't know.

The Nature of Friendship

As we discussed earlier in the chapter, human beings have an innate biological need to have a mate and to make friends. Because these needs are so important, you will find that many people on the Net are looking for companionship and for love. If you are tempted to do so yourself, please be careful. The Net creates the illusion of closeness to other people, but it is only an illusion.

To understand this better, let's take a moment to consider exactly what has to happen in order for you to make a friend. First, you must meet someone. Then, you and the other person must share thoughts, feelings and experiences. Normally, this happens when you spend time with the person, talking and participating in a variety of activities: watching TV, eating, exercising, going to a movie, telling jokes, shopping, giving someone a backrub, and so on.

Eventually, you come to enjoy the other person's company and you feel affection for him or her. However, this is not enough to make that person a friend. Before someone can become your friend — a real friend — he or she must know you for an extended period of time and must demonstrate loyalty toward you. In this sense, if you stop to think about it, you will realize that most of the people in your life do not qualify as real friends.

And what about romance? What has to happen before you are able to form an enduring and committed romantic relationship with another person?

Again, you must start by meeting the person. Then, over a period of time, the two of you must share thoughts, feelings and experiences, just as you do when you are getting to know a friend. However, for a romantic relationship, there must be more. You and the other person must take time to discover each other's values, goals and morals. You must also allow yourself to be influenced by the other person, in order to see if the two of you are able to bring out the best in one another. Finally, you must be physically attracted to the other person, and (if you are so inclined) you must find out whether or not you are sexually compatible.

Normally, these requirements are satisfied in two ways. First, you watch how the other person behaves over an extended period of time in a variety of situations. In particular, you notice how he or she interacts with other people, including your friends and family.

Second, you spend time together on dates. This gives you a chance to share experiences and to begin to influence one another.

(By the way, here is the official definition of a date: A DATE is a social occasion during which two romantic, or potentially romantic, people share entertainment, food and affection.)

As you can see, the steps you must go through in order to forge a real friendship or a romantic relationship are only possible in person. For this reason, the Net is *not* a good place to make friends or to choose a mate.

This is not to say that you won't meet people on the Net who you want to be your friends. If you talk to a lot of strangers, you are bound to meet people you like and who like you. Indeed, you may even find someone special with whom you want to have a romantic relationship. However, if you want to be real friends — or real lovers — you must spend time together in person and let the friendship or romance develop in the normal manner.

On the Net, where there is no physical presence, friendship is an illusion. Moreover, the lack of real interaction makes you feel less threatened by strangers and, unless you are careful, you will find yourself opening up to people a lot more quickly than you would in person. In such situations, you may feel that someone you don't really know all that well is a good friend, or even a lover. When this happens, come back to this book and reread the following:

What you are feeling is an artifact. It is caused by (1) your inborn need to connect to other people, and (2) the tendency of your mind to fill in the blanks when you try to communicate at a distance.

Trust me. Talking to someone on the Net is not enough to create a friendship, even if you talk for hours and hours, night after night. When you talk on the Net, all you really have are the words you see on your screen. The only way to create an enduring, committed relationship with someone — friendship or romance — is for the two of you to spend a great deal of time together in person.

You may think that you have friends online, but you don't. What you have are acquaintances, and the difference is enormous.

A Modern-Day True Love Story

There was something missing from Barbara's life. She was in her early 40s and more or less satisfied, but she sometimes felt a nagging feeling of discontent that was difficult to put into words. Barbara did have her hobbies, though, and one of them was watching and discussing Woody Allen movies. Although she had a nice group of friends, she didn't know anyone who appreciated Allen's films as much as she did and, at times, she felt a bit lonely.

On the Net, however, it was different. Barbara found Web sites devoted to Woody Allen's work, and she loved to spend time visiting them.

One day, she discovered that one of the Web sites had a discussion forum and, without a second thought, she joined the group. Finally, Barbara had found people who liked her favorite films as much as she did, and she found herself spending more and more time online, talking to her new friends.

She especially enjoyed talking to Charles, one of the regulars. Although Barbara lived in the U.S. and Charles lived in Europe, they hit it off immediately. Charles shared Barbara's passion for films, and he seemed to have a lot of the same tastes and opinions. As Barbara explained to one of her friends, "Charles is really something special. It's amazing how we like the same things, how he seems to know exactly what I am thinking. I do have a lot of friends, but with Charles everything is different. We think so much alike that we can communicate really well without even trying."

As the weeks passed and Barbara spent more and more time chatting, her new friends — especially Charles — became more and more important to her life. Although Barbara and her Internet friends talked a lot, it was only over the Net and she hoped that, one day, they would all be able to meet in person.

Finally, she got her chance.

Woody Allen (who is an accomplished clarinet player) had just announced that he was planning a European concert tour with a jazz band. This was big news among Barbara's friends. Wouldn't it be great if they could all go to see Allen's concert together? It was expensive for Barbara to travel to Europe, but her friends had decided to meet in the country where Charles lived so, as a birthday present to herself, she decided to go.

It was Barbara's first trip to Europe and she had a wonderful time. Not only was she able to meet the people with whom she had spent so much time online, but she got to meet Charles in person, which was even better than she had expected. She felt such a strong connection with him, that she stayed for an extra night after the rest of the group had gone home. When it came time to leave, Barbara had to force herself to get on the plane. "Maybe it's better that I go home now," she told herself. "I need to find out if my feelings for Charles are real."

So, she went home and found, to her delight, that her feelings were real: she missed Charles enormously. Finally, she had found someone who understood her and could bring real meaning to her life. For the first time in her life, Barbara felt complete.

There were some challenges, of course. There always are. For one thing, Charles was 20 years younger than Barbara. Fortunately, the Net was able to help. Barbara found a support group for "age gap relationships". She spent hours talking to people in similar situations, where there was a significant age difference between the two partners, and she read wonderfully romantic stories in which everything worked out perfectly and the two people lived happily ever after. This, she knew, was exactly what was going to happen with her and Charles.

However, if Barbara and Charles were to live happily ever after, there was another obstacle to overcome: they lived in different countries. After a lot of talking and soul searching, they decided that Charles would leave Europe and immigrate to the United States. But that meant that the two of them had to navigate the U.S. immigration regulations.

Once again, the Net came to the rescue. By searching on the Web, Barbara was able to find another support group, one for people who needed help with immigration to the United States. Barbara found out that the best way for Charles to move to the U.S. was for him to apply for a fiancé visa. That suited her just fine. By now, Barbara knew that Charles was her soul mate, and the thought of spending the rest of her life with him made her giddy.

How did it all end? Less than a year from the time they met on the Net, Barbara and Charles were married and living together, and Barbara was happier than she had been in years. She had met her soul mate and, finally, her life was complete.

By now, you probably have a warm spot in your heart for Barbara. If you are like me, you enjoy romantic stories, and you feel that it is wonderful when two people are able to find one another, overcome the obstacles that stand in their way, and live happily ever.

There's only one problem. Eleven months earlier, when Barbara had met Charles on the Net, she was married, living with her husband of 21 years and their 11-year-old daughter.

Couples and the Net

Isn't it interesting how the story of Barbara and Charles sounds so different when you find out that Barbara was married and had a child? Just imagine you are reading the story again, but this time, leave out the last paragraph.

Clearly, how you interpret the story has a lot to do with the circumstances of the people involved. If Barbara were single, the story would be a wonderfully romantic example of how the Internet can help lonely people reach out into a cold, impersonal world and find someone to love. However, because Barbara was married (which was the case in real life), the story is a sad one, showing what happens to a family when one of the spouses takes the energy that might have revitalized a marriage and uses it, instead, to pursue an unhealthy fantasy.

So how do we make sense out of all of this?

One of the reasons we have such a problem with understanding relationships in our society is because the popular culture does not distinguish between infatuation and real love. Love stories — in books, in magazines, on TV, and in the movies — focus primarily on falling in love, not on the process of sustaining love. It's fun to watch a movie in which a couple ends up together, all ready to live happily ever after, but what happens next? How *do* you live happily ever after?

Thoughtful people know that a successful marriage requires a lot of effort. From time to time, every marriage goes through rough spots, and when this happens to you, the mature thing to do is to communicate with your spouse and work things out. It may not be easy, and it may not be fun, but you should do it anyway.

Unfortunately, too many people get in the habit of using the Net as an escape, especially after a few years of marriage, when the infatuation and novelty have worn off. In such cases, it is common for one of the partners to spend more and more time at the computer, wrapped up in his or her own world. Eventually, this behavior will cause a serious problem, because it takes energy away from the relationship.

This is the case even if the person is using the Net to do something that is basically wholesome, such as buying and selling old books or playing games. However, when one partner uses the Net to get involved with another person, the situation becomes devastating. Sometimes, it happens when a husband or wife deliberately looks for emotional companionship. Often, it happens unexpectedly, as with Barbara and Charles, when innocent chatting gets out of hand.

In both cases, what usually happens is that the magic in a marriage is chased away by the daily grind of life: working, paying the bills, taking care of the kids, cleaning the house, shopping for food, cooking the meals, taking out the garbage, and on and on. For many people, life is so demanding that there is no longer much time for romance and sex, and it gets more and more difficult to conjure up the feelings of mutual attraction that created the relationship in the first place. The husband and wife take one another for granted and, all too often, begin to get on each other's nerves. Once this happens, each partner will begin to feel that the other one is not "meeting my needs".

In a way, this is normal, and it is one of the responsibilities of marriage to work through such feelings, to learn how to build a partnership that can survive the pressures of living together and managing a household. Unfortunately, if, in such situations, one of the partners is tempted to stray, the Internet can make things a lot worse.

When a frustrated lonely person starts to chat on the Net, it is certain that the person will have no trouble at all finding people who seem to be more sympathetic and understanding than his or her spouse. There are several reasons for this.

First, as we have discussed, talking on the Net is a lot different from talking in person. When you talk on the Internet, your mind fills in the missing details automatically. As a result, it is common to misinterpret the meaning of online relationships, especially when they become intimate or romantic.

In other words, if you are married and you think you have met your soul mate online, chances are it is an illusion. People who chat online have no real responsibility towards one another. Unlike your spouse, your online friend does not live with you, and she doesn't share the day-to-day frustrations of work, bills, children, cleaning, shopping and cooking. Moreover, your Internet friend did not take a sacred vow to share your life for better or for worse. If she doesn't feel like chatting, she won't, so when she does choose to chat, chances are she will be in a good mood.

When you are married, you must live together and share responsibilities, day after day, even when you don't feel like it. Since you can't ignore your spouse every time one of you is in a bad mood, you will find that, unlike your experiences with your online friends, you will have to talk to your partner when you don't feel like it.

Of course, sometimes trouble at home is real, and the discontent you feel can be more than you want to bear. However, before you jump to conclusions — such as "my wife doesn't understand me", or "my husband doesn't care about my needs" — it is important that you understand the source of your discontent.

One major source of discontent is that we criticize most in others what we dislike about ourselves. This happens because of what is called PROJECTION. When we feel guilty or anxious about something, we will often, without thinking, project our own attitudes and feelings onto another person. For example, Rachel feels guilty about having sexual thoughts about her boss, so she becomes jealous of her husband and nags him about the way in which he interacts with other women. Brad worries a lot about money so, when his wife forgets to balance the checkbook, he gets angry at her and accuses her of being irresponsible.

It is important to remember that the intermittent difficulties and frustrations that attend married life are normal and, for this reason, it is normal to feel temptation from time to time. There is nothing wrong with this. After all, without temptation to put us to the test, commitment is just an idea.

However, just because we are tempted does not mean that we should act upon our feelings. Earlier in the chapter, I explained that it is part of our nature to need a strong emotional connection to a mate. Thus, before you engage in a questionable activity, take the time to ask yourself, "Will my action serve to help or to hinder the relationship I have with my mate?"

If you want to be happy, you must, in the long run, stay focused on your priorities, and not allow yourself to be driven by transient emotions and passions. This is especially important when you use the Internet because, as we have discussed, what you think is happening online is not as real as it seems.

One of the more interesting examples I know of is a young lady in California who fell in love with a wonderful man she met in a chat room. It was only after she made arrangements to travel to New York to meet her beau, that she discovered that the person she had spent so many hours talking to online was really another woman.

8 Signs That Your Spouse is Having an Online Affair

Intimate relationships are *very* common on the Net, and they pose a big problem to many marriages. How can you tell if your spouse is having an online affair? Here are the warning signs to look for if you suspect that your husband or wife might be leading a secret life on the Net.

1. Time. Your spouse spends more and more time on the Net, even to the exclusion of other activities that he (or she) used to enjoy.

2. Need for privacy. Your spouse hides what he is doing. For example, when he is using the computer and you walk into the room, he quickly does something to the machine to switch away from what he is doing. When you try to see what is happening, he gets angry at you and complains about a lack of privacy.

3. Secret identities. Your spouse has email addresses or online screen names that he is keeping secret. When you question him about it, he makes up some excuse, but he won't let you see the mail or watch his conversations.

4. Denial. When you question your spouse about his Internet activities, he denies that he is doing anything wrong in a way that makes you suspicious.

5. Dishonesty. Your spouse lies about what he is doing online. When you catch him in a lie, he tells you one false story after another.

6. Addiction. You notice that your spouse develops a strong need to spend a lot of time online. For example, whenever he comes home, the first thing he does is rush to the computer to check his mail. He gets upset when you suggest that he turn off the computer.

7. Emotional withdrawal. Your spouse stops talking to you about personal matters. He becomes less and less interested in shared intimacy, including sex.

8. Rationalization. Your spouse admits to some online intimacy, but explains that it is okay because (a) it is not physical, or (b) they are only friends, or (c) it is important for him to be able to share his feelings with another person.

What should you do if you suspect that your spouse is misbehaving on the Net, but you can't prove it? If you aren't able to talk to him about the problem, you may want to track his activities to see exactly what is going on.

One obvious move is to check out your spouse's computer. Examine his email, his personal files, his downloaded files (look for pictures), the cache, the cookies folder, and the browser history. (See Chapters 3 and 4 for the details.)

You can also try entrapment. For example, if you know what chat rooms your spouse likes to visit, you can get a friend to engage him in conversation and see just how far he will go. This is easy if your spouse uses AOL. Have a friend add your spouse's screen name to her buddy list. Your friend will be able to see when your spouse is online. She can then "locate" him and join the same chat room. (Of course, your spouse may have a secret screen name you don't know about, and he may be chatting in private.)

Finally, you can use a type of program, referred to as SNOOPWARE, that will allow you to monitor all the activity that takes place on your spouse's computer: email, instant messaging, chatting, Web activity, and so on. Here are some resources to help you find such software. (Note, some of these programs cost money.)

```
http://www.iopus.com/starr.htm
http://www.softdd.com/pcspy/
http://www.softec-e.com/shareware/ws/
http://www.spectorsoft.com/
http://www.spytech-web.com/
http://www.winwhatwhere.com/
```

Internet Resources: Software to help you snoop

What to Do If Your Spouse is Having an Online Affair

If your spouse is having an Internet affair, there is something drastically wrong with your relationship. Obviously, you don't know your husband or wife as well as you think you did. These types of problems can take a long time to resolve, and it can't be done by arguing or by pretending nothing is wrong.

It is important that you and your spouse make an effort to develop better communication. This will allow you to explore the reasons why your spouse turned away from you in the first place. For example, it is common for a spouse to turn to the Net in order to fulfill a need that is not being satisfied within the marriage.

Usually, this means nothing more than looking for the company of a friendly, easy-going companion. In some cases, however, the situation may be more sinister, if a spouse is interested in a particular sexual perversion or fetish. There is a lot of support for such activities on the Net, including Web sites, chat rooms, discussion forums and personal ads.

So, what do you do? You have two problems to solve. First, you need to convince your spouse that something is wrong. This may be more difficult than it sounds, because there is a good chance that your spouse is addicted, not only to the infatuation of an extramarital relationship, but to the stimulation of a large amount of Internet activity. If so, he may have no idea how much time he really spends online, and he will be oblivious to the fact that he is ignoring other members of the family.

Second, you need to work with your spouse to improve your relationship. Again, this can be especially difficult where the Net is involved, because your spouse will be fooled into thinking that the feelings he shares with his Internet friends are genuine and important. He may even be convinced that he has found his soul mate, the one person for whom he has been searching his entire life.

For many people, it is difficult to trade a rich fantasy life for the day-to-day routine of family responsibilities. For example, on the Net, a man may be a smooth-talking stud, and a woman may feel like a seductive temptress. If you ask your spouse to give up his Internet identity, you are asking him to forgo a big chunk of his life. He may not want to do so, and even if he does, it will be difficult. For this reason, it would probably help the two of you to go to a marriage counselor. If you do, here are three hints to help you.

First, go *together*. Couples who go to marriage counseling together have the best chance of success. If you go to a marital counselor by yourself, your spouse is not going to know what is going on. As a result, you will become frustrated and discouraged when he or she does not respond to your efforts to change the marriage. Indeed, among troubled marriages, the ultimate divorce rate is *higher* when one spouse goes to marital therapy alone than when the couple receives no counseling at all.

Second, realize that solving Internet-related problems requires special expertise. When you choose a counselor, look for one who has experience with such problems and who understands the technology. Such a counselor will be able to keep your spouse from misrepresenting what he is doing.

Third, look for a counselor who emphasizes the idea that couples should work to stay together. Avoid counselors who think that each person should be concerned with his or her own personal fulfillment.

Net Sex and Pornography

I don't have to tell you that sex is an important part of life. We live in a highly sexualized society, in which erotic images are used to sell just about everything that can be sold. There are several reasons for this.

First, sexual instincts are of vital importance to human beings. Our survival depends on our ability to reproduce, and the primary role of sexual desire is to make us want to engage in the sexual activity necessary to conceive children. As a matter of fact, the only reason you and I are here today is because a long line of people, stretching back thousands of years, felt this type of sexual desire and acted upon it.

Because sexual desire is such a powerful force, most cultures keep it under wraps. Although this allows a society to rechannel excess sexual drive into more productive areas of life, it also serves to make sexual images highly effective when it comes to stimulating thinking about what is, after all, a mostly forbidden activity.

This is especially true for men, who are easily aroused by visual stimulation, which is why you can use an image of a beautiful young woman to help sell virtually any type of consumer product, from toothpaste to beer. It is this forbidden aspect of sex — the idea that we must keep the details out of public discourse — that serves to make sex the center of so many controversial issues. This is particularly true in the United States and Canada, which are especially prudish countries (compared, for example, to much of Europe and Latin America).

One of the most controversial issues is the role that the Internet plays in sex-related activities. I have already mentioned two such aspects: that the Net affords many people the opportunity to meet and form romantic liaisons, and that the Net supports a wide variety of sexual fetishes and deviant behavior. In this section, I'd like to discuss two pastimes that we might characterize as more "hands on" experiences, net sex and pornography.

NET SEX is an interactive activity in which two people type erotic messages back and forth, usually accompanied by masturbation. Net sex is also referred to as CYBER SEX, and, in this sense, the word CYBER is often used as a verb. For example, "Cynthia had not been in the chat room more than five minutes before three different men asked her if she wanted to cyber."

The goal of net sex is to achieve a state of arousal followed by physical resolution. To do so, two people share their intimate feelings and fantasies — usually by typing, but sometimes with a webcam and a microphone — while gratifying themselves at the same time.

In many ways, net sex is like phone sex. The biggest differences are:

• Net sex is readily available for free, with no long distance charges.

• Net sex is usually carried out by people who have never met one another in person.

• Net sex requires significantly more physical dexterity.

PORNOGRAPHY is the depiction of sexually explicit ideas with pictures or writing. Although there is a lot of disagreement about the importance of pornography as a moral issue, there is no doubt whatsoever that the pornography business is thriving on the Internet.

Pornography is, by far, the largest and most successful business on the Net, in fact, the only one that is virtually recession-proof. Unlike most online consumer services, pornography Web sites sell a product that many people are more than willing to pay for. As such, online pornography businesses do not have to depend on selling advertising in order to make a profit.

There is a huge variety of pornography on the Net, representing every normal and abnormal sexual proclivity known to mankind. Much of it is available for free. However, if you are willing to pay, you can buy yourself access to all the convenience, variety and quality you desire, courtesy of the modern-day "adult entertainment" industry (the same people and companies who bring you all those charming videos and magazines).

The main point I want to make here is that the human mind and body were designed to have sex in person, not at a distance. Although activities such as net sex and pornography might bring you some short-term satisfaction, they cannot, in the long run, make you happy.

One might argue that for some people, such pastimes are harmless diversions that hurt no one. However, by their very nature, these activities titillate without offering real satisfaction, a characteristic that can cause a great deal of trouble for human beings. As a result, for many people, both net sex and online pornography foster serious addiction problems, with the concomitant collateral damage to their relationships and marriages.

Perhaps even more common is the problem that, if you engage in such activities over a long period of time, you are likely to develop a pattern of isolation and desensitization that will significantly interfere with your ability to form and sustain healthy relationships.

In principle, it is not necessarily bad to share an erotic experience with another person or, within reason, to stimulate yourself artificially. However, the Internet is a high-capacity information system that, by its nature, provides too much stimulation, too quickly, and it does so in a form that is not good for people.

To be brutally practical, if you are already in a relationship, using the Net for erotic activities is likely to come between you and your partner. If you are alone, the habit of finding solace on the Net will likely change you in a way that will make it *more* difficult to find a real-life relationship that will satisfy your long-term needs. As such, net sex and online pornography, as attractive as they might seem at times, are two activities that are best avoided.

If you think that you may be having a problem in this area, my advice is to err on the side of caution, and take a few moments to decide whether or not you need to make some changes in your life. Here are some resources that can help you:

```
http://www.onlinesexaddict.com/
http://www.pureintimacy.org/
http://www.sexaa.org/
```

Internet Resources: Help with online sex addiction

Children and the Net

Children are tricky. One day they're smiling up at you with big blue eyes, perfect in every way, wrapping a tiny doll-like hand around your finger as they gurgle and laugh with the delight of just being alive. The next moment, they're talking to you in a voice that drips with barely disguised condescension, "Fine. I won't get my tongue pierced. That's just great. Now I can be the first person in the history of the school to graduate without ever going on a date."

Somewhere in between these two events, you need to decide how and when to introduce your kids to the Net.

Young children go through a great deal of neurological development and, at various times, their minds need different types of stimulation. For this reason, children naturally reach out into the world, not only to look for new experiences, but to enjoy familiar sensations over and over. So, don't worry about when to introduce your children to computers. They will watch you use the computer and, when the time comes, they will naturally want to try it for themselves.

The same goes for the Net. Children who grow up with the Internet don't feel that there is a big difference between running a program on their own computer and doing something on the Net. Using the Net is just part of the experience of using a computer.

Still, as we have discussed throughout the chapter, the Internet is a completely artificial environment, one that will give all of us trouble if we aren't careful. The best plan with children is to watch what they do and see how it goes. Every child is different, even within the same family. One child may sit quietly playing an Internet game for a long period of time. Another child might zip around the Web, looking for all sorts of new things. A third child might love to visit chat rooms and talk to strangers. Each of these children will require a different type of supervision.

Some children are good at following rules and will never have a problem, so you can let them do whatever they want (within reason). Other kids are more adventurous and will need more supervision to keep them out of trouble.

No matter how well behaved a child may be, he or she will need some guidance in using the Net. Children have limited life experience, and they often don't have the context in which to make proper judgments. Here are some guidelines to help you make a plan that works for your family.

1. Put all the computers in a common area.

You can avoid a lot of problems by keeping the family computers in the living room or family room. Although your children may complain, especially as they get older, letting them use the Internet for hours on end behind closed bedroom doors is tempting fate.

When you keep the computers out in the open, it makes it more likely that your kids will avoid behaving in a way they know is wrong. It also allows you to glance unobtrusively at the computer each time you walk by, just to check up on what is happening.

2. Set rules and stick to them.

As soon as your children begin to use the Net, you can teach them how to avoid trouble. Here are some rules you can tell the kids:

• *Personal information:* Do not give out any personal information about you or your family. This includes your name, email address, postal address, phone number or the name of your school. You may not give out this type of information to a person, and you may not type it into a form on a Web site.

• *Chatting:* Do not use your real name. If someone in a chat room starts to act strangely, call over a parent and ask for help. Never arrange to meet anyone in person. If someone starts to bother you, stop talking to him immediately. (Most kids know to do this without being told, so don't worry too much.)

• *Safety:* Never accept files, pictures, email or Web addresses from strangers. Never send a picture to a stranger. Never give out your password, even to a friend.

• *Using the Web:* You are not allowed to use the Web to look at certain types of information or pictures. For example, you are not allowed to look at sites that are meant for adults. (This is a good place to be specific.)

• *Downloading:* Do not download programs of any type, including games or screensavers, without permission. (The idea here is to protect your computer as well as your children.)

3. Don't allow too much privacy.

Make sure your kids know that you have the right — and you will use it — to check up on what they are doing. This means that, from time to time, you may watch them use the computer, even if they are instant messaging to their very best friend. Your kids should know that you may read their email, look at their Favorites (Bookmarks) list, and check out their browser history. (For instruction on how to do this, see Chapters 3 and 4.)

As your children get older, you can explain that, the more responsible they are, the more freedom they will get. However, as long as they are living with you, they will never get the absolute freedom to do whatever they want behind closed doors.

If you think you have reason to worry about what your children are doing on the Net, you can use one of the Snoopware programs I mentioned earlier in the chapter. This will allow you to keep track of your kids' activities.

If you decide to get such a program, I suggest that you use it proactively. Let your children know that they are being monitored and that, if necessary, you can check up on what they have been doing. The idea is to avoid problems, not to find them. (This is what companies do when they monitor their employees' Internet usage.)

4. Watch for warning signs that your child might be having a problem.

How do you know if your child is spending too much time using the computer or the Internet? Think about what you would like to see as your children grow. You want them to:

- Develop socially.
- Do well in school.
- Maintain a variety of interests.
- Get exercise.

As long as your children are progressing normally in these areas, they are probably okay. The time to start worrying is when a child is doing something that crowds out the important activities in his or her life. The warning signs are:

- Stops playing with friends.
- School work slips (stops doing assignments, grades begin to fall, and so on).
- Loses interest in hobbies and other activities.
- Stops exercising.

You should also be on the lookout for unusual personality changes for no apparent reason, for example, if your child becomes sullen, irritable, lethargic or secretive for an extended period of time. In general, this is how people act when they are frustrated because they have important needs that are not being met. (It is also how they act when they are using drugs.)

If one of your children is having a problem, the goal is to help him bring his life back into balance. In some cases, you'll only need to talk to him. ("I'd like to remind you of the rules for using the computer.") In other situations, you may have to take definite action, such as restricting the amount of time your child is allowed to use the computer. Remember, when all else fails, you can always pull the plug.

If it becomes necessary, there are tools you can use to control your children's use of the Internet. For example, AOL has what are called "Parental Controls" that allow you to restrict how your children use AOL.

There are also a number of programs that can control what Web sites your children are allowed to visit. These tools are known by a number of different names: FILTERING SOFTWARE, parental control software, content filters, or (depending on your point of view) censorware. Basically, they work in one of two ways.

Some programs use a BLACKLIST of forbidden Web sites. In this case, the job of the filtering software is to make sure that your child is unable to access any of the sites on the blacklist. Other programs use a list of approved sites called a WHITELIST. In this case, your children are allowed to visit only these Web sites that are on the list.

If you decide to use one of these programs, don't depend on it too much. A smart kid will find a way to get around any type of restriction. Overall, the best plan is to watch what your children do on the Net and help them understand the rules that you set. To help you, here are some resources:

```
http://www.familyguidebook.com/
http://www.getnetwise.org/
http://www.ou.edu/oupd/kidsafe/warn_kid.htm
http://www.safesurfin.com/
http://www.smartparent.com/
```

Internet Resources: Helping kids use the Net safely

One last suggestion. I'd like to recommend my book *Harley Hahn's Internet Yellow Pages* (published by Osborne McGraw-Hill). You'll find a lot of information, fun and resources. In particular, I have included many resources specifically for parents, families, young children and teenagers, so you can spend time using the Net *with* your kids.

One of my main goals throughout this book has been to help you understand the basic principles behind the Internet and how we use it, both as a society and as individuals. As such, I have steered you away from the unfounded fears that hinder so many people and, instead, helped you understand what is really happening in the world, on and off the Net, so you can make the choices that are best for you and your family.

You will notice that, in this section, I have stayed clear of the scare stories about children who are seduced, exploited or corrupted on the Net. From time to time, such things happen, but they are rare, so don't worry. True, as your children use the Net over the years, various unpleasant things are bound to happen, but this is also the case in school, on the playground, or at summer camp.

Children do not need us to make every moment of their lives simple and trouble-free. What they do need from us is the wisdom to know when and when not to interfere in their activities, encouragement to explore and discover, and the security that comes from knowing that their parents, who love them more than anyone else in the world, are watching them carefully (even if it is from the next room).

Appendix

Abbreviations Used While Talking on the Net

There are many abbreviations used while talking on the Net. Some of these are to save typing time; others are used to express feelings and actions. Chapter 8 contains a detailed discussion of how such abbreviations are used and why they are important.

The following list shows the most common abbreviations used while talking on the Net. You will also see them used in email and discussion groups.

Note to parents and teachers: You will notice that a few of the words in this list are profanity. I have included them for two reasons. First, people really do talk like this on the Net, so don't get excited; second, I want you to know what your kids mean when they use these abbreviations.

:)	smiley
: -)	smiley
: -O	surprised smiley
: -P	disgusted smiley (with tongue sticking out)
: -P	excited smiley (with tongue sticking out)
; -)	winking smiley
<G>	grin (same as a smiley)
<GRIN>	grin (same as a smiley)
A/S/L	what is your age, sex and location?
ADDY	address
AFAIK	as far as I know
AFK	away from keyboard
BBL	be back later

BF	boyfriend
BFD	big fuckin' deal
BG	big grin
BRB	be right back
BTW	by the way
CU	see you
CUL	see you later
CUL8R	see you later
CYA	see ya (good-bye)
F2F	face to face (in person)
FAQ	frequently asked question list
FOFLMAO	falling on the floor laughing my ass off
FRP	fantasy role playing
FUBAR	fucked up beyond all recognition
FWIW	for what it's worth
FYI	for your information
GAL	get a life
GD&R	grinning, ducking and running
GF	girlfriend
GG	good game (if playing an online game)
HB	hurry back
HTH	I hope this helps
IANAL	I am not a lawyer
IC	I see
IC	in character (while role playing)

ICWUM	I see what you mean
IM	instant message (he sent me an IM)
IMHO	in my humble opinion
IMNSHO	in my not so humble opinion
IMO	in my opinion
IMs	instant messages
IOW	in other words
IRL	in real life
J/K	just kidding
L8R	(see you) later
LDR	long distance relationship
LMAO	laughing my ass off
LMK	let me know
LOL	laughing out loud
MOTAS	member of the appropriate sex
MOTOS	member of the opposite sex
MOTSS	member of the same sex
NM	nevermind
NP	no problem
Ob-	(as a prefix) obligatory
Objoke	obligatory joke
OIC	oh, I see
OMG	oh, my God!
OOC	out of character (while role playing)
OS	operating system

OTOH	on the other hand
PAW	parents are watching
PDA	public display of affection
PM	private message
POV	point of view
PUTER	computer
RL	real life
ROFL	rolling on the floor laughing
ROTF	rolling on the floor laughing
ROTFL	rolling on the floor laughing
ROTFLMAO	rolling on the floor laughing my ass off
RPG	role playing game
RTFM	read the fuckin' manual (before asking a question)
SO	significant other
THX	thanks
TTFN	ta-ta for now (good-bye)
TTYL	talk to you later
TTYS	talk to you soon
TY	thank you
TYVM	thank you very much
WTF	who the fuck?/what the fuck?/why the fuck?
WU?	what's up?
WUF?	where are you from?

Index

E

early computers, cost of, 192
economic interdependence, history of money, 350–351
economic stability
control of money supply, 356–359
creating money, 360–362
factors in, 379–380
economies of scale, Internet companies, 398
economy. *See* money
ego, 184
Eisenstadt v. Baird (1972), right to privacy, 137
electronic commerce
advantages of, 384–386
buying from Web sites, 386–388
customer service problems, 397–399
effect on economy, 385–386
evaluating online vendors, 403–405
examples of, 383–384
fraud, 396–399
medical fraud, 401–402
online auctions. *See* online auctions
privacy protection, 388–389
safety of, 392–394
search engines, 410–411
shipping and handling charges, 405–408
shopping bots, 408–410
stolen credit card numbers, 394–395
tips for protecting yourself, 399–403
Electronic Privacy Information Center (EPIC), 165
Eliza and Renaldo story, 321–327
elusiveness of power, 148
email
avoiding mistakes, 226–232
client/server operational overview, 81–82
folders, 89
privacy of, 88–90
Web-based mail, 83–85
Web-based mail, privacy of, 85–88
what not to send, 231
email addresses. *See* addresses (mail)
email clients, 81

email hoaxes
examples of, 223–226
identifying, 219–223
email messages. *See* messages (mail)
email programs, security settings, 312–314
email viruses
avoiding, 286–289
security versus convenience, 290–291
spread of, 283–284
triggering automatically, 312
emotional needs
human nature, 435–437
importance of family relationships, 442–444
importance of friendship, 444–446
encryption on secure servers, 393–394
entrapment, verifying online affairs, 458
environmental needs, reason for desire for privacy, 123
EPIC (Electronic Privacy Information Center), 165
eradicating viruses, 300–301
escrow services, 427–428
etiquette, what not to send via email, 231
European Convention on Human Rights and Fundamental Freedoms (1953), 179–180
evaluating
online vendors, 403–405
sellers, 425–427
evolution, 437–439
defined, 437
importance of family relationships, 442–444
importance of friendship, 444–446
role of DNA, 439–440
Excel. *See* Microsoft Excel
executing programs, 252
Existential Worm, 267
expectation of privacy, 23–25
extensions (files)
defined, 69
deleting from master table, 317–318
list of, 70
opening files, 285
safe from viruses, 287
unsafe from viruses, 287–288
viewing registered file types, 286
Exxon, identifying mail hoaxes, 222

F

faith in monetary system, 371
fake information, supplying at Web
  sites, 390–392
family relationships, importance of,
  442–444
FBI (Federal Bureau of Investigation)
  Carnivore (Internet monitoring
    device), 6–7
  statement on Carnivore, 7–9
fear, financial decisions driven by, 416
Fed. *See* Federal Reserve
Federal Bureau of Investigation. *See*
  FBI (Federal Bureau of
  Investigation)
federal funds rate, 367
Federal Reserve
  banking regulations, 360–362
  bond market, 362–365
  changing reserve rate, 366
  control of money supply, 358–359
  defined, 358
  effect on interest rates, 367
  loaned reserve deposits, 366–367
  phone number for, 365
fight or flight response, 125–126
"Fighting Computer Viruses"
  (*Scientific American* article),
  255–256
file attachments. *See* attachments
file servers, 65
file storage. *See* data storage
files
  case sensitivity, 72
  defined, 69
  deleting, 74–75
  moving/copying, 75
  naming, 69
  opening, 284–286
  organization of, 69–72
filtering software, 467
financial services. *See* online personal
  financial services
firewalls
  defined, 318
  lack of need for, 321
  protecting networks with, 318–321
Fitzgerald, F. Scott, xvii
floppies, 64
floppy disks
  defined, 64
  spread of viruses, 280–281
flushing the cache, 77–78
  defined, 58

FOAF (friend of a friend), 224–225
folders
  case sensitivity, 72
  defined, 70
  deleting, 74–75
  organization of files, 69–72
folders (mail), 89
forbidden aspect of sexual desire, 460–
  461
Forbidden Planet (movie), 187
formatting disks, 67, 107
forwarding email messages
  example, 214–216
  polite tips for, 209–211
  warning against, 205–209
France, paper money in, 343–344
Franklin, Benjamin, history of paper
  money, 344–345
fraud
  electronic commerce, 396–399
  medical fraud, 401–402
  protecting against auction fraud,
    425–429
free email addresses. *See* disposable
  email addresses
Freud, Sigmund, 183–185
friendship. *See also* relationships
  example of Internet relationship,
    451–453
  importance of, 444–446
  nature of, 448–450
frontier, effect on American psyche,
  143–145
fungible, 334

G

Gallienus (emperor of Rome), 341
gambling, invention of dice, 338
Gates, Bill, lawsuit against Microsoft,
  151–153
GDP (Gross Domestic Product), 377–
  379
Gemmellaro, Faye, xxi
George III (king of England), history
  of paper money, 345
Germany, history of money, 348–349
glass houses, 192
global economics, 350–351
gold standard
  defined, 352
  end in U.S., 351–354
gold, as money, 336–337
Golden Age, xii
Golden Age of Computing, 194–198

Golden Age of the Internet, xiii
government
   example of Internet monitoring, 9–11
   representing individuals' right to privacy, 142
   use of SSNs (Social Security Numbers), 173
gray market, 400
Great Depression, 355
   defined, 351
Greece, history of money, 339
greed, financial decisions driven by, 416
Griswold v. Connecticut (1965), right to privacy, 137
Gross Domestic Product (GDP), 377–379
Group of Thirteen (IBM), 199
Guerrieri, Patti, xxi
"Guidelines for the Regulation of Computerized Personal Data Files," U.N. resolution, 159–160
guilt, motivation for privacy, 124
GUIs, history of, 265
Gutenberg, Johann, history of paper money, 343

H

hackers
   defined, 318–321
   obtaining credit card numbers, 394–395
hacking, 318–321
Hahn, Harley, personal note from, i–iii
hard disks, 64
hardware, data storage, 64–66
Harley Hahn's Internet Advisor, 411
Harley Hahn's Internet Yellow Pages, 280, 411, 468
header lines (email messages), 211
headers (email messages)
   defined, 211
   overview of, 211–212
Hearn, Lydia, xviii
help information, online auctions, 429
Hemingway, Ernest, xvii
Heydt-Long, Alexis, xxi
Highland, Harold (history of macro viruses), 294
history list in browsers, 54–55
   clearing, 61–62
   defined, 54

history of computing
   mainframes, 192–194
   PCs, 198–199
   terminals, 194–198
history of GUIs, 265
history of the Internet, 3
history of money
   American Revolution, 344–346
   commodity-based systems, 334–337
   economic interdependence, 350–351
   end of gold standard in U.S., 351–354
   Germany, 348–349
   Greece, 339
   inflation, 346–350
   invention of coins, 337–338
   paper money, 342–346
   Roman Empire, 339–341
   Russian Revolution, 347–348
   Spain, 341–342
history of SSNs (Social Security Numbers), 173–175
history of viruses, 263–263
   macro viruses, 294–295
   worms, 264–269
Hitler, Adolf, history of money, 349
hoaxes
   examples of, 223–226
   identifying, 219–223
   virus hoaxes, 224, 259–261
   Web sites for, 226
home pages, 53
hope through money, 374
Hotmail, avoiding spam on, 236
HTML, in email messages, 312–314
HTML files, avoiding viruses, 288
HTTP (Hypertext Transport Protocol), 52
http (in URLs), 51
human nature
   emotional needs, 435–437
   importance of family relationships, 442–444
   importance of friendship, 444–446
   nature of friendship, 448–450
human rights agreements, right to privacy in, 133–136
Hupp, Jon, history of viruses, 265
hyperinflation, 347
Hypertext Transport Protocol (HTTP), 52
hypertext, 52

I

Iarkowski, Lisa, xxi
IBM
    capitalization, 149
    history of PCs, 198–199
    mainframes, 192–194
IBM 5100 and 5110
    (microcomputers), 198
icons, 76
ID numbers
    correlation of data with, 168–172
    national ID numbers, 172–173
    SSNs (Social Security Numbers),
        172–175
id, 184
IFCC (Internet Fraud Complaint
    Center), 396
    auction fraud, 425
ignorance, effect on market forces,
    115–116
illegal activities, desire for privacy in,
    122
immediate sale price (online auctions),
    423–424
impersonation on workplace
    computers, 40–41
increment (online auctions), 424
individual interests versus
    organizational interests, 148–
    151, 175–178
individual wealth versus corporate
    wealth, 148–149
individuals' right to privacy versus
    organizational interests, 141–
    142
inflation
    defined, 341
    history of money, 346–350
informational privacy, 118–119
interest rates, Federal Reserve effect
    on, 367
International Covenant on Economic,
    Social and Cultural Rights
    (1976), right to privacy, 135
Internet
    backbone, 17
    as communication medium,
        advantages/disadvantages, 201–
        205
    connecting to, 16–17
    defined, 3
    effect on emotional needs. *See*
        emotional needs
    effect on money supply, 374–379

    effect on prices, 386
    effect on privacy, 116–117
    electronic commerce. *See*
        electronic commerce
    expectation of privacy, 23–25
    history of, 3
    lack of authority over, 17–19
    lack of prejudices, 203–204
    market forces on, 115–116
    nature of, 19–22
    need for regulation, 153–155, 182–
        187
    as the Net, 4–5
    reasons for misinformation, 216–
        219
    supervising children's usage of,
        463–468
    terminology, 51–53
    transition period, 115–116
Internet Explorer
    defined, 82
    linkage with Windows Explorer,
        72–73
    safe environment for HTML email
        setup, 313
    security settings, 309–311
Internet Fraud Complaint Center
    (IFCC), 396
    auction fraud, 425
Internet monitoring
    example of, 9–11
    statement by Len Babin, 12–14
Internet monitoring devices
    Carnivore, 6–7
    Carnivore, FBI statement on, 7–9
    on workplace computers, 43–47
Internet Relay Chat (IRC), 243
Internet Service Provider. *See* ISP
    (Internet Service Provider)
Internet stocks, 375–376
Internet worm, 270–274
    benefits from, 274–275
interview with Bruce Slane, New
    Zealand privacy commissioner,
    178–182
intrusion, motivation for privacy, 124
invention of coins, 337–338
investigations on computers
    methods of, 36–38
    network backups used for, 39–40
investment services
    as online personal financial service,
        412
    warning about, 413–414
IRC (Internet Relay Chat), 243

national ID numbers, 172–173
National Security Agency (NSA),
    example of Internet
    monitoring, 9–11
natural objects, as money, 335
natural selection, 437–439
    defined, 437
    reproduction, 440–442
    role of DNA, 439–440
nature of Internet, 19–22
nerds, 292
Nero (emperor of Rome), 340
Net
    defined, 5
    Internet as, 4–5
net sex
    compared to phone sex, 461
    defined, 461
Netscape
    defined, 82
    security settings, 311–312
Network Access Points (NAPs), 17
network backups, use for
    investigations, 39–40
Network Service Providers (NSPs), 17
networked computers, probing, 321
networks
    protecting with firewalls, 318–321
    reasons for, 199–201
never@amazon.com email address,
    164–165
Nicholas II (Tsar of Russia), history of
    money, 347
Nixon, Richard, end of gold standard
    in U.S., 354
Norton, Rob, xxi
Notepad (text editor), cleaning up
    email messages, 209–210
NSA (National Security Agency),
    example of Internet
    monitoring, 9–11
NSPs (Network Service Providers), 17

O

OAS (Organization of American
    States), right to privacy, 136
observational privacy, 118–119
online affairs
    danger of, 453–456
    marriage counseling for, 458–460
    signs of, 456–458
online auctions
    description of, 419–421
    items available at, 420–421

payment methods, 420
    protecting against fraud, 425–429
    terminology, 422–424
    tips for using, 429–431
online payment services, 417–419
    defined, 417
online personal financial services
    tips about using, 413–416
    types of, 411–413
online rating services, 404–405
online sex. See net sex; pornography
online sex addiction, 463
online vendors, evaluating, 403–405
online, 5
OPEC (Organization of Petroleum
    Exporting Countries),
    identifying mail hoaxes, 222
Opel, John (IBM executive), 198–199
opening files, 284–286
operators (computer), 192
organism, Internet as, 4–5
Organization of American States
    (OAS), right to privacy, 136
organization
    of files, 69–72
    of mail messages, 89–90
Organization of Petroleum Exporting
    Countries (OPEC), identifying
    mail hoaxes, 222
organizational interests
    versus individual interests, 148–
        151, 175–178
    versus individuals' right to privacy,
        141–142
organizations, anthropomorphizing,
    151–155
Orwell, George, 1984, 5–6, 46
Outlook
    email viruses, 286
    security settings, 314
    triggering viruses automatically,
        312
Outlook Express
    email viruses, 286
    security settings, 313–314
    triggering viruses automatically,
        312

P

packets, 15
pages. See home pages; Web pages
paper money
    advantages and disadvantages, 347
    in American Revolution, 344–346

paper money *(cont.)*
  Chinese emperors, 342
  France, 343–344
  history of money, 342–346
  Sweden, 343
parental control software, 467
parents, 442
"Password Security: A Case History"
  (Communications of the ACM),
  271
passwords, AutoComplete (in
  browsers), 60
pathnames, 71
paths, 71
payment methods, online auctions,
  420
payment services, as online personal
  financial service, 413, 417–419
PCs
  history of computing, 198–199
  isolation of users, 199–201
Peeker Worm, 268
Pepper, Jeff, xviii
Perkins, Maxwell, xvii
Perl (scripting language), 308–309
permanently cleaning out files, 106–
  109
personal activities, avoiding at work,
  33–35, 41–43
personal computers. *See* PCs
personal email, at workplace, 228–229
personal financial services. *See* online
  personal financial services
personal firewalls
  defined, 318
  lack of need for, 321
personal information
  corporate privacy policies, 160–166
  extracting with Profile Assistant,
  103
  U.N. resolution, 159–160
Pet Sounds (Brian Wilson), xi–xii
phone numbers
  Federal Reserve, 365
  unlisted, 182
phone sex, compared to net sex, 461
pictures in cache, 56–58
pirated software, 282
police. *See* law enforcement
Polo, Marco, history of paper money,
  342
POP servers, 82
pornography, 461–463
Post, Tom, xx

power
  elusiveness of, 148
  through money, 372–374
preferences, setting in Windows
  Explorer, 76–77
prejudices, lack on Internet, 203–204
prices
  electronic commerce tips, 399–400
  Internet effect on, 386
privacy
  assumptions about privacy in
  workplace, 31–33
  avoiding problems at workplace,
  33–35, 41–43
  Big Brother, 5–6
  biological need for, 129–130
  children's Internet usage, 465–466
  of computer data (U.N.
  resolution), 159–160
  effect of Internet on, 116–117
  electronic commerce, 388–389
  example of lack of, 102–104
  expectation of, 23–25
  human desire for, 122–123
  Internet monitoring. *See* Internet
  monitoring; Internet
  monitoring devices
  lack of vocabulary about, 120–121
  of mail, 88–90
  maintaining in talk facilities, 240–
  243
  motivations for desiring, 124–126
  protecting email addresses, 232–
  235, 237–240
  protecting with TweakUI, 110–111
  and social status, 126–128
  SSA (Social Security
  Administration), concerns of,
  173–174
  supplying fake information at Web
  sites, 390–392
  types of, 117–119
  versus business interests, 96–97
  versus secrecy, 179
  of Web-based mail, 85–88
privacy, right to, 133
  in constitutions and human rights
  agreements, 133–136
  European Convention on Human
  Rights and Fundamental
  Freedoms (1953), 179–180
  individuals versus organizations,
  141–142
  reasons for American views on,
  143–145

scanning faces at Superbowl, 140
Scott McNealy (CEO of Sun
Microsystems) comments on,
138–139
Supreme Court rulings, 136–138
Privacy Act (New Zealand), 179
Privacy Act (U.S.), 174
privacy commissioners, interview with
Bruce Slane (New Zealand
privacy commissioner), 178–
182
privacy policies, 160–166, 388–389
Amazon.com example, 163–166
defined, 161
Schwab example, 161–163, 166
views on, 167–168
privacy software, Web sites for, 112
probing networked computers, 321
processors, 253
Profile Assistant, 103
profit margin, 95
programmers, 252
programming viruses, challenge of,
251–253
programs
application programs, 292
defined, 251
running, 252
system programs, 292
uninstalling, 108
projection, 455–456
protecting
addresses (mail), 232–235, 237–
240
networks with firewalls, 318–321
protocols, TCP/IP, 14–15
proxy bidding (online auctions), 424
psychological conditioning, reason for
desire for privacy, 122–123
punch cards, 193
puzzle, 275–276
solution to, 302
Python (scripting language), 308–309

Q–R

Radhuber, Nick, xxi
Radio toolbar (Internet Explorer), 60–
61
Rawlings, Marjorie Kinnan, xvii
RCMP (Royal Canadian Mounted
Police), statement by Len
Babin, 12–14

recession
defined, 355
war as solution to, 356
Recycle Bin, 74
Redd, Michael, xxi
referrer fields, 102
regedit (registry editor), 110
registered file types
deleting, 317–318
viewing, 286
registering at Web sites
defined, 87, 387
privacy protection, 388
supplying fake information, 390–
392
registry, 109–110
regulation of Internet, need for, 153–
155, 182–187
relationships. See also friendship
danger of online affairs, 453–456
defined, 437
example of Internet relationship,
451–453
importance of family relationships,
442–444
marriage counseling for online
affairs, 458–460
signs of online affairs, 456–458
Renaldo and Eliza story, 321–327
reproduction, 440–442
reserve price (online auctions), 423
reserve rate
changing, 366
defined, 360
retail market, invention of, 338
return policy, electronic commerce
tips, 401
right to privacy, 133
in constitutions and human rights
agreements, 133–136
European Convention on Human
Rights and Fundamental
Freedoms (1953), 179–180
individuals versus organizations,
141–142
reasons for American views on,
143–145
scanning faces at Superbowl, 140
Scott McNealy (CEO of Sun
Microsystems) comments on,
138–139
Supreme Court rulings, 136–138
right-clicking in Windows Explorer, 75
Roe v. Wade (1973), right to privacy,
137–138

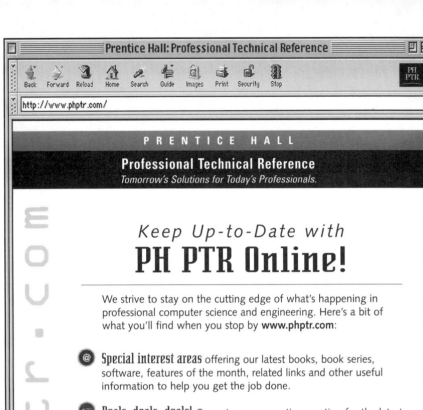